SO-BZS-064

Flagstaff Public Library
Arizona Collection

A Courtroom of Her Own

A Courtroom of Her Own

The Life and Work of
Judge Mary Anne Richey

by
Barbara Ann Atwood

CAROLINA ACADEMIC PRESS

Durham, North Carolina

Flagstaff Public Library
Flagstaff, Arizona

Copyright © 1998 by Barbara Ann Atwood

Library of Congress Cataloging-in-Publication Data

Atwood, Barbara Ann, 1947–
    A courtroom of her own : the life and work of judge Mary Anne
Richey / Barbara Ann Atwood.
        p.   cm.
    Includes bibliographical references.
    ISBN 0-89089-654-2
    1. Richey, Mary Anne, d. 1983. 2. Women judges—United States—
Biography.   I. Title.
KF373.R485A88   1998
347.73'014'092--dc21
[B]   96-39329
                                                        CIP

CAROLINA ACADEMIC PRESS
700 Kent Street
Durham, North Carolina 27701
Phone (919) 489-7486
Fax (919) 493-5886

Flagstaff Public Library
Flagstaff, Arizona

529a

To my son Jacob

So long as we live, they too shall live,
for they are now a part of us, as we remember them.

Rabbi Jack Riemer

Contents

Preface

An obituary published shortly after Judge Mary Anne Richey's death in 1983 described her in the following terms: "She was a woman of 'firsts' who opened opportunities for others of her gender. In the early 40's, women were not traditionally pilots. She became one. Women were not traditionally lawyers. She became one. Nor were they judges—an office she gained, and filled, with typical Richey vigor and insight.... Judge Richey was a unique combination of intellect, spirit, strength and ambition."[1] As a feminist and lawyer, I chose to write this biography to explore Mary Anne Richey's pioneering role in the legal profession and to collect and preserve her story—from her roots in Indiana to the federal bench in Arizona.

In the last decade, women's studies scholars have begun to write about women's biography as a separate genre of feminist literature.[2] Two themes of feminist biography are the inevitable subjectivity of one person's interpretation of another's life, and the centrality of gender in interpreting *women's* lives. The subjectivity of this biographical work is intense, because I worked for Mary Anne Richey as her first law clerk after she was appointed to the United States District Court, and our friendship continued after our professional association ended. I have drawn liberally from my interactions with her, and the process of researching and writing has extended that interaction past her death. I remain fascinated by the ways in which Mary Anne Richey defied cultural norms for her gender without antagonizing either men or women. A central focus of this project has been the tension between the social construct of gender and Mary Anne's successful redefinition of that construct for her own life.

In this biography I have tried to portray the complexity, exuberance, and sheer power of Mary Anne's personality. Additionally, I have suggested ways in which her ambitions, sympathies, and "hard edges" may have been influenced by the forces of her childhood and young adulthood. As a close-up look at a woman who balanced, often uneasily, the divergent demands of being a wife, a mother, and a pathbreaker in law,

---

1. "In Memoriam—Hon. Mary Anne Richey," The Writ, December 1983, at 2.

2. *See generally* CAROL ASCHER, LOUISE DESALVO, SARA RUDDICK, BETWEEN WOMEN (1984); SUSAN GROAG BELL, MARILYN YALOM, REVEALING LIVES (1990); SHERNA BERGER GLUCK & DAPHNE PATAI, WOMEN'S WORDS—THE FEMINIST PRACTICE OF ORAL HISTORY (1991).

this book is intended to advance our understanding not only of "early" women lawyers and judges,[3] but also of women professionals generally. Finally, the pages that follow offer an interpretation of her judicial philosophy and suggest ways in which her life informed her decisionmaking. Since her life was influenced by the constraints of her gender, her struggles in the face of those constraints necessarily shaped the judge that she became.

In the text, I have chosen to call Mary Anne Richey by the name "Mary Anne" for several reasons. "Mary Anne" is the term of address she preferred. To call her by a married name or a paternal surname would be inappropriate and confusing, since she was born a "Reimann," adopted her first husband's name of "Showers," later reassumed her family name of "Reimann," and finally in her second marriage took the name of "Richey." My use of "Mary Anne" is intended to capture both her warmth and natural informality as well as her female identity separate from her role as daughter and wife.

In re-creating Mary Anne's life, I received the help of countless people. Apart from my own memories, my sources have included public and private documents from her lawyering and judging days, newspaper accounts, and many personal interviews. I owe an immense debt to members of Mary Anne's family: her husband Bill Richey, her daughter Annie Richey, and her niece Ann Bruner. Each of these individuals shared memories with me, supplied me with valuable photographs and memorabilia, and gave me much needed encouragement. I also thank Judge William D. Browning for facilitating my research at the United States District Court in Tucson, Arizona. The people who agreed to be interviewed for this project are too numerous to list, but their generosity of time and energy is greatly appreciated. I am indebted to a group of talented student research assistants who helped in all phases of the project: Megan Austin, Piroschka Glinsky, Matt Erickson, Dave Caylor, Suzanne Crawford, Sidney Ricks, Derek Pfaff, Stellisa Scott, and Jane Westby. I deeply appreciate the generous support of the Arizona Humanities Council through a Study Grant in 1992, and the summer faculty research grants from the

---

3. Recent additions to that genre of literature includes CONSTANCE BACKHOUSE, PETTICOATS AND PREJUDICE (1990); DOROTHY M. BROWN, MABEL WALKER WILLEBRANDT—A STUDY OF POWER, LOYALTY, AND LAW (1984); JANE FRIEDMAN, AMERICA'S FIRST WOMAN LAWYER (1993); KAREN BERGER MORELLO, THE INVISIBLE BAR (1986); JEANETTE E. TUVE, FIRST LADY OF THE LAW (1984); Barbara Babcock, *Clara S. Foltz, First Woman*, 30 ARIZ. L. REV. 673 (1988); Connie Bruck, *The First Woman Everything*, 4 AM. LAW 32 (1982); Sylvia Law, *Crystal Eastman: Organizer for Women's Rights, Peace, and Civil Liberties in the 1910's*, 28 VAL. U.L. REV. 1305 (1994).

University of Arizona College of Law under the deanship of Tom Sullivan from 1993 through 1995. I am grateful to my colleagues, Kay Kavanaugh and Jane Korn, for reading the manuscript and offering their insightful comments, to Toni Massaro for her encouraging advice throughout the project, and to David Wexler for introducing me to the dedicated people at Carolina Academic Press. The support staff at the University of Arizona College of Law provided careful and good-humored work in transcribing interviews and producing the manuscript. In particular, I am grateful for the assistance of Barbara Clelland, Kay Clark, Norma Kelly, Rebecca Scheibley, and Angela Badilla. Finally, I thank my husband Peter Eisner and my son Aaron for cheering me on when I needed a boost, for helping me step back when I needed a rest, and for reminding me always of what is important.

Introduction

In examining the life and work of Mary Anne Richey, I have used as my compass the central question of how her experiences shaped and informed her judicial identity. Since she was a trial court judge for nineteen of her sixty-six years, she was defined by that role, and it was through her judicial work that she made her most significant professional contributions. The story of her life is also the story of her progression toward the role of judge and her personal evolution within that role.

Mary Anne's life experiences cannot be understood without consideration of gender—the social construct deriving from her biological sex that affected her opportunities, her perceptions, and her self-image. The seamless influence of gender in a person's life is inarguable, but the task of defining the impact of gender for an individual or for groups has proved formidable. The literature on gender is already immense, and new books appear almost daily.[1] As women have moved into positions of power in the professions in recent decades,[2] observers have wondered whether

---

1. Any "complete" listing of gender literature would be voluminous. The following is a representative sample that reveals the cross-disciplinary nature of feminist research. *See* SANDRA LIPSITZ BEM, THE LENSES OF GENDER (1993)(psychological inquiry into the interplay of gender polarization, androcentrism, and biological essentialism); NANCY J. CHODOROW, FEMINISM AND PSYCHOANALYTIC THEORY (1989)(feminist critique of psychoanalytic theory); BARBARA J. HARRIS, BEYOND HER SPHERE (1978)(historical exploration of women in western culture who attained professional status against tradition); CYNTHIA EAGLE RUSSETT, SEXUAL SCIENCE (1989)(reconstruction of early scientific literature on sex differences); DEBORAH RHODE, JUSTICE AND GENDER: SEX DISCRIMINATION AND THE LAW (1989)(legal and historical analysis of sex discrimination in western law); MARTHA ALBERTSON FINEMAN, THE ILLUSION OF EQUALITY (1991)(feminist critique of divorce reform in the United States).

2. Women now comprise about 20 percent of the total lawyers in the United States, *see* BARBARA A. CURRAN & CLARA N. CARSON, AMERICAN BAR FOUND., THE LAWYER STATISTICAL REPORT: THE U.S. LEGAL PROFESSION IN THE 1990's 3–4 (1994), as compared to less than 3 percent in 1950. *See* CYNTHIA FUCHS EPSTEIN, WOMEN IN LAW 4 (2d ed. 1993). In 1981, Epstein reported that women judges constituted 5.4 percent of the federal judiciary and about 5 percent of the judges in state appellate and trial courts. *See id.* at 242. In contrast, as of 1993, women constituted about 11 percent of the total number of federal judges and 10 percent of all state supreme court judges. *See* MARY BECKER, CYNTHIA GRANT BOWMAN, & MORRISON TORREY, FEMINIST JURISPRUDENCE: TAKING WOMEN SERIOUSLY 893–94 (1994).

women will have different leadership or professional styles from their male counterparts.[3] Central to the subject of this book, a question that fuels many current debates in legal academic circles is whether, and to what extent, women judges bring a "difference" to the bench.[4] This Introduction provides an overview of existing theories and empirical scholarship on gender and judging and also explores my own answer to the question of how gender influences a person's judicial identity.

The subject of gender and judging encompasses some obvious and perplexing questions. Are there unique worldviews, moral values, life experiences, or interpersonal skills that women bring to the bench? Will women judges noticeably influence the legal processes of dispute resolution? Will they make a difference in the development of substantive law? On a more mundane level, do woman judges face unique issues in performing their jobs? Do the combined responsibilities of career and home that most professional women shoulder significantly distinguish the professional lives of women judges from those of their male counterparts?

In my view, any approach to the topic of gender and judging should eschew monolithic or categorical views about women as judges. The rich differences among women render suspect most predictive claims about uniquely "female" or "feminine" traits, values, or perspectives. Such claims ignore the critical variables of race, economic class, age, sexual orientation, and lifestyle, among others; they are difficult to test empirically; and the studies that have been done do not seem to support such assertions. The notion that women judges will change the law in predefined ways, or that they will bring a particular style of dispute resolution to the bench, is incompatible with the "feminist insight." As Martha Minow has observed, feminist critiques of legal, political, and economic institutions have often challenged the "unstated assumptions....that presuppose the universality of a particular reference point or standpoint." Feminists theorizing about women, Minow reminds us, must acknowledge the diversity among women's experience and formulate theories that do not obscure "this multiplicity by representing a particular view as the view of all."[5] Minow is just one of many feminists who have cautioned against "essen-

---

3. See, e.g., ROSABETH M. KANTER, MEN AND WOMEN OF THE CORPORATION (1977); CATALYST, FEMALE MANAGEMENT STYLES: MYTH AND REALITY (1986); Judy Rosener, *Ways Women Lead*, HARV. BUS. REV. (Nov. Dec. 1990), 119–125.

4. See generally Michael E. Solimine & Susan E. Wheatley, *Rethinking Feminist Judging*, 70 IND. L.J. 891 (1995); Sharon E. Rush, *Feminist Judging: An Introductory Essay*, 2 S. CAL. REV. L. & WOMEN'S STUD. 609 (1993).

5. Minow, *Feminist Reason: Getting It and Losing It*, 38 J. LEGAL EDUC. 47, 50 (1988).

tialist" views of women,[6] but a form of essentialism has clearly influenced the thinking about gender and judging.

Some scholars have built on the work of Carol Gilligan, whose book *In a Different Voice* posits an alternative model of moral development.[7] In her book, Gilligan challenges traditional theories of moral development, which she describes as embodying an "ethic of rights" and a progression away from dependence toward autonomy and achievement.[8] She views the existing theories as having neglected or subordinated women as subjects of psychological studies. Her own empirical studies, which included male and female children and young adults, revealed a competing model of moral development that she labels the "ethic of care." Gilligan's model is associated more with female moral development than with male moral development and exists in contrast to a model of rights, or justice. Her empirical study indicates that while both her male and female subjects employed both models, the majority of women focused on an ethic of care, and the majority of men relied primarily on an ethic of rights.

Because Gilligan's work suggests that differences in moral thinking exist between men and women, some theorists have posited that women, and therefore women judges, are generally more caring and compassionate than men; that they are more committed to compromise and cooperation; and that they are more interested in preserving relationships than parceling out rights.[9] Some theorists have argued that women are more interested in mediative techniques of conflict resolution than in the adver-

---

6. In recent years, much attention has been devoted to the danger of generalizing or "essentializing" about the feminine experience. *See, e.g.,* PATRICIA WILLIAMS, THE ALCHEMY OF RACE AND RIGHTS (1991); Angela Harris, *Race and Essentialism in Feminist Legal Theory*, 42 STAN. L. REV. 581 (1990); Mari J. Matsuda, *When the First Quail Calls: Multiple Consciousness as Jurisprudential Method*, 11 WOMEN'S RTS. L. REP. 7 (1989); AUDRE LORDE, *Age, Race, Class, and Sex: Women Redefining Difference*, in SISTER OUTSIDER (1984).

7. CAROL GILLIGAN, IN A DIFFERENT VOICE: PSYCHOLOGICAL THEORY AND WOMEN'S DEVELOPMENT (1982).

8. Gilligan focused in particular on Lawrence Kohlberg's six-stage model of moral development that associated progression in moral thinking with increasingly abstract levels of reasoning.

9. *See generally* KATHARINE T. BARTLETT, GENDER AND LAW—THEORY, DOCTRINE, AND COMMENTARY 736–40 (1993); WENDY KAMINER, A FEARFUL FREEDOM: WOMEN'S FLIGHT FROM EQUALITY 6 (1990). Judith Resnik has suggested that Gilligan's work and other feminist theories could be useful in rethinking western ideals for judges and in questioning the norms of disconnection and impartiality. Resnik, *On the Bias: Feminist Reconsiderations of the Aspirations for Our Judges*, 61 S. CAL. L. REV. 1877 (1988). *See also* Kenneth Karst, *Woman's Constitution*, 1984 DUKE L.J. 447.

sary combat of the courtroom.[10] Others have suggested that women as decisionmakers are more communitarian and less abstract and rights-oriented than men.[11]

One commentator has gone so far as to argue that communitarianism and contextualism appear in the Supreme Court decisions of Justice Sandra Day O'Connor.[12] Relying on Gilligan, Suzanna Sherry takes the traits associated with the ethic of care and the ethic of rights and abstracts them into generalized descriptions of female and male worldviews. Sherry asserts that women have a connected, contextual and responsibility-oriented perspective, whereas men have an autonomous, abstract, and rights-oriented perspective. Sherry links these contrasting worldviews with two contrasting paradigms of political theory: classical republicanism and modern liberalism. She argues that civic republicanism, with its Aristotelian emphasis on a "community of virtue," is feminine, and that liberalism, with its focus on individualism, is masculine.

Operating from the premise that a uniquely feminine worldview endorses communitarianism, Sherry goes on to locate civic republicanism in Justice O'Connor's reported opinions. In particular, she identifies a number of opinions in which O'Connor arguably upheld rights that protect individuals against exclusion from communities.[13] Sherry also finds a contextual approach in O'Connor's decisionmaking and a tendency to reject rigid rules. From her assessment of O'Connor's writings, Sherry concludes that

---

10. Carrie Menkel-Meadow, *Excluded Voices: New Voices in the Legal Profession Making New Voices in the Law*, U. MIAMI L. REV. 29 (1987); Menkel-Meadow, *Portia in a Different Voice: Speculations on a Woman's Lawyering Process*, 1 BERKELEY WOMEN'S L.J. 39 (1985).

11. *See* Suzanna Sherry, *The Gender of Judges*, 4 LAW & INEQUALITY 159, 163–69 (1986); Robin West, *Jurisprudence and Gender*, 55 U. CHI. L. REV. 1 (1988)(arguing that a different worldview exists for women because of women's unique biological lives); Leslie Bender, *From Gender Difference to Feminist Solidarity: Using Carol Gilligan and an Ethic of Care in Law*, 15 VT. L. REV. 1 (1990)(advocating an increased emphasis in law on an ethic of care, culturally associated with women).

12. Suzanna Sherry, *Civic Virtue and the Feminine Voice in Constitutional Adjudication*, 72 VA. L. REV. 543 (1986). Another writer has suggested that O'Connor writes with a distinctively feminine outlook. *See* Frank Michelman, *The Supreme Court 1985 Term—Foreword: Traces of Self-Government*, 100 HARV. L. REV. 4, 17 n. 68, 32–36 (1986).

13. Sherry focuses on employment discrimination and establishment clause cases in advancing this argument. She notes that O'Connor diverged from her political ally William Rehnquist in notable cases in those areas, voting more often with the party claiming discrimination or a violation of the establishment clause. Sherry explains the divergence as a function of the feminine worldview of communitarianism.

the Justice's jurisprudence showed a "uniquely feminine perspective."[14] Not surprisingly, O'Connor has distanced herself from the suggestion that she speaks with a uniquely feminine voice through her opinions.[15]

Numerous scholars have challenged "different voice" theorists such as Sherry on ideological grounds. The late Mary Jo Frug, among others, articulated a solid critique of Sherry's application of Gilligan's theories.[16] Frug pointed out that Sherry's uncritical and selective reading of O'Connor's opinions, and her particular use of Gilligan's work, idealized the domestic role traditionally assumed by white middle-class women and endorsed a gender stereotype that neglected the experience of non-white, non-middle-class women, among others. Uncomfortable with the implications of a "uniquely feminine" worldview, Frug warned against romanticizing self-sacrifice.[17]

Similarly, Catherine MacKinnon suggests that the purportedly-female virtues of compassion, interconnectedness, and selflessness are, in reality, responses to a brutally discriminatory society, and that celebration of those qualities would amount to a celebration of patriarchy. According to MacKinnon, the differences in moral reasoning identified by Gilligan are qualities that "male supremacy has attributed to women for its own use." In MacKinnon's view, "[w]hen difference means dominance as it does with gender, for women to affirm differences is to affirm the qualities and characteristics of powerlessness."[18] Thus, MacKinnon refuses to charac-

---

14. Sherry, *supra* note 12, at 592. In a recent study, Sue Davis reexamined the data compiled by Sherry and extended it forward in time. Davis, after comparing the votes of Supreme Court justices in the same substantive categories selected by Sherry through the 1991 Term, concluded that the findings did not support the assertion that O'Connor's decision making was explainable in terms of gender characteristics. *See* Sue Davis, *The Voice of Sandra Day O'Connor*, 77 JUDICATURE 134, 139 (1993).

15. Sandra Day O'Connor, *Portia's Progress*, 66 N.Y.U.L. REV. 1546, 1553 (1991).

16. *See* MARY JO FRUG, POSTMODERN LEGAL FEMINISM 30–49 (1992).

17. *Id.* at 47–49. Professor Frug saw other dangers inherent in Sherry's "conservative reading" of Gilligan, including the risk that a woman judge might be screened from responsibility for her legal positions because of her gender, and that the reading ignores alternatives postures of women of different races, different socio-economic levels, different sexual orientations, and different ages. *Id.*

18. CATHERINE A. MACKINNON, TOWARD A FEMINIST THEORY OF THE STATE 51 (1989). MacKinnon elaborated further on this point:

"Women are said to value care. Perhaps women value care because men have valued women according to the care they give. Women are said to think in relational terms. Perhaps women think in relational terms because women's social existence is defined in relation to men." *Id.*

terize cultural differences between men and women as innate. Similarly unpersuaded by some theorists' use of Gilligan's work, Cynthia Fuchs Epstein has noted the dangers inherent in assigning unique traits to women. In reflecting on what women as a group might bring to the legal profession, Epstein refuses to consign women lawyers to the role of social reformers. "No one group," she admonishes, "ought to be burdened with the expectation of unilateral altruism."[19]

Empirical researchers from the social sciences have devoted considerable energy to determining whether significant differences exist between male and female judges in terms of decisionmaking, and the results are far from definitive. The work in this area has often focused on criminal sentencing because of the ease with which sentencing behavior can be quantified; when researchers venture beyond the criminal area, they tend to rely on superficial categories to create data. In any event, in both the criminal and non-criminal fields, the results are ambiguous[20] and seem to suggest that most female judges do not decide cases in a distinctively feminist or feminine manner.[21] In one study, researchers examined the voting behavior of federal appellate court judges in employment discrimination cases, cases involving criminal procedural rights, and obscenity cases.[22] The

---

19. EPSTEIN, *supra* note 2, at 385.

20. Overall, the older studies are contradictory, but many show little difference between male and female judges. In a study of 30,000 felony cases, for example, the investigators found few significant differences in conviction rates of male and female judges, but they did discern a slight tendency of male judges to give lesser sentences to female defendants. Gruhl, Spohn & Welch, *Women as Policymakers: The Case of Trial Judges*, 25 AM. J. POL. SCI. 308 (1981). In analyzing the behavior of federal district court judges, another investigation revealed no significant differences in cases involving criminal procedure and women's policy issues, but for personal liberties and minority policy issues, the differences between male and female judges were significant: male judges were 1.5 times more likely than female judges to support the "liberal" position, and females were more likely than males to defer to positions taken by the government. Walker & Barrow, *The Diversification of the Federal Bench: Policy and Process Ramifications*, 47 J. POLITICS 596 (1985). Other studies have not yielded definitive results. *See* Kritzer & Uhlman, *Sisterhood in the Courtroom: Sex of Judges and Defendant in Criminal Case Dispositions*, 14 SOC. SCI. J. 77 (1977)(study revealed no difference between male and female judges); Gottschall, *Carter's judicial appointments: the influence of affirmative action and merit selection on voting on the U.S. court of appeals*, 67 JUDICATURE 165 (1983)(study showed that women were slightly more inclined than men to side with plaintiffs in voting on race and sex discrimination cases, but more inclined to side with government in criminal cases).

21. *See* Solimine & Wheatley, *supra* note 4, at 897–905.

22. Sue Davis, Susan Haire, & Donald R. Songer, *Voting Behavior and Gender on the U.S. Courts of Appeals*, 77 JUDICATURE 129 (1993).

votes of all judges on United States courts of appeals in the identified categories were analyzed over a ten year period.[23] When the researchers controlled for political party, they found statistically significant gender differences only in employment discrimination cases among Democratic judges. In those cases, the few women judges in the sample were more likely than their male counterparts to support the employment discrimination claimant.[24]

The authors' interpretation of their own data is that the analysis provides only limited support for the proposition that women judges will bring a unique perspective to the bench,[25] and they acknowledge the difficulty of explaining voting patterns based on a particular gendered worldview. They note, for example, that the purported female concern for "connection and community" did not seem to surface in predictable ways across the case categories.[26] Moreover, they question whether the judges' votes might have reflected their different life experiences rather than an innate difference in moral reasoning.[27] The authors also speculate that even if a "different voice" could be attributed to women, those differences may be neutralized by the socialization of the legal profession itself, both because American law is thoroughly grounded in a political theory of liberal individualism and because the few women who have attained the level of success necessary for appointment to the federal bench may have learned to emulate the (male) leaders of the profession.[28]

A study undertaken by political scientists David Allen and Diane Wall focused on state supreme court justices and attempted to categorize the voting patterns of women justices according to four categories of role ori-

---

23. More than 63 percent of the votes cast by women judges supported the plaintiffs' claim of discrimination, whereas 46 percent of the male judges supported the plaintiff. In the criminal procedure area, 18 percent of the women, as compared to 11 percent of the men voted in favor of the criminal defendant's position. *Id.* at 132.

24. *Id.*

25. *Id.* at 132.

26. *Id.* at 132–33.

27. *Id.*

28. *Id.* at 133. The stark disparity in the pool of women federal appellate court judges as compared to the male pool additionally undermines the validity of any assertions of categorical difference. The study was based on the votes of 9 female and 122 male judges in obscenity cases, 15 females and 237 males in search and seizure cases, and 16 females and 188 males in employment discrimination cases. *Id.* at 131. Finding a similar ambiguity of result, one of the authors conducted a recent study of opinions of judges on the United States Court of Appeals for the Ninth Circuit. She observed that while women judges sometimes spoke in a different voice, men judges did as well. Sue Davis, *Do Women Judges Speak in 'A Different Voice?' Carol Gilligan, Feminist Legal Theory and the Ninth Circuit*, 8 Wis. Women's L.J. 143, 171 (1992–93).

entation.[29] The categories they devised were "outsiders," who disregard institutional traditions and exhibit extreme voting behavior; "tokens," who conform to the dominant majority to obtain legitimacy in the majority's eyes and who gravitate toward a centrist position on their court; "representatives," who view themselves as representing women on the court and who try to incorporate a woman's viewpoint in legal matters directly impacting on women; and "different voice" adherents, who reflect fundamental differences from their male counterparts and who dissent separately more often than others on the court.[30] The study analyzed the voting behavior of twenty-four female justices in three areas—criminal rights, economic liberties, and women's issues—and categorized votes as liberal or conservative (generally determined by whether the justice voted to uphold the claim of the plaintiff).

Their analyses of justices' votes revealed, intriguingly, that women jurists view themselves as anything but "tokens," as defined by the authors. The data showed that women justices voted more often than their male counterparts to affirmatively support women's rights in so-called "women's issues cases," and that women's votes did not follow a centrist pattern in criminal rights or economic liberties cases but instead tended to occupy *extreme* positions at either end of the political spectrum. Finally, the data showed that women justices were more likely than men to join minority positions and to write sole dissents. The authors conclude that women supreme court justices act as representatives when confronted with issues of immediate concern to women, that women occupy positions at the extreme liberal or conservatives ends (with differences more pronounced among Democrats), and that they tend to engage in both extreme and isolated dissenting behavior in criminal and economic cases.[31]

The Allen & Wall study has the virtue of looking beyond mere gender to the central question of how the woman judge sees herself *vis a vis* the institution. The willingness of females justices to dissent and to take extreme positions on their courts, moreover, is consistent with established psychological understandings about female leaders—that women who are early entrants to a political institution have extremely high scores on intelligence, dominance, adventurousness, unconventionality, and radicalism.[32]

---

29. David W. Allen & Diane E. Wall, *Role Orientations and Women State Supreme Court Justices*, 77 JUDICATURE 156 (1993).

30. *Id.* at 158–59.

31. *Id.* at 161–65.

32. *See* Werner & Backtold, *Personality Characteristics and Women in American Politics*, in JAQUETTE, WOMEN IN POLITICS 83 (1983).

The study avoids the pitfall of attempting to isolate relational themes in a justice's decision making. The authors' empirical work, freed from its labels, indicates that women jurists are more willing than their brethren to take positions in opposition to the majority, that they are more willing to dissent separately, and that political party affiliation heavily influences voting behavior.

On the other hand, the Allen & Wall study necessarily simplifies judicial rulings in order to create analyzable data. The authors, for example, identified the "liberal" and therefore "pro-woman" position in cases involving rights of adoptive children as a vote for the "best interest of child." The complex and conflicting policies at stake in adoption cases hardly lend themselves to such simple categorizations. Similarly, the authors categorized as "liberal" a vote for the "individual" rather than "business" in contract disputes. Again, the categorization ignores the substantive or procedural issue before the court.

Empirical comparisons of male and female judicial behavior, and categorical conclusions stemming from the studies, are especially problematic in that judicial decision-making is bound by the facts and relevant law in a particular case and the skill of counsel in marshalling those facts into a tenable legal argument. Ascribing a judge's vote to a particular worldview, or role orientation, would seem to drastically oversimplify the act of adjudicating. At the appellate level, moreover, where much of the empirical work has been done, a judge's response to arguments of counsel will be informed by the posture of the case on appeal, the lucidity of the record, the standard of review, and the vigor of the trial judge in 'protecting' his or her ruling.

Other theorists have suggested that behavioral and perceptional differences between men and women may have particular significance for trial court judges. They posit that women may be more culturally skilled at listening and picking up on nuances of personality and context than men.[33] Building on the supposition that women, by virtue of their own life experiences, are more sensitive than men to women's realities, such as the details of domestic labor, some have argued that women as fact-finders perform a unique role.[34]

Because theories about perceptional differences are highly dependent on individualized reactions to context, little empirical support for such

---

33. *See* Gretchen H. Schoff, *Women, Justice, and Judgment*, 4 LAW & INEQUALITY 137, 139–40 (1986).

34. *See* Carol Weisbrod, *Images of the Woman Juror*, 9 HARV. WOMEN'S L.J. 59 (1986).

theories exists. Moreover, the existing body of empirical literature on the analogous question of gender differences among jurors is inconclusive. Contrary to popular wisdom,[35] most empirical studies have found that gender is not a good predictor of a juror's vote,[36] and the studies that do suggest the existence of gender differences in juror behavior or voting are often contradictory. While some work has indicated that women jurors are more lenient in their attitudes toward criminal defendants, for example, others have suggested the opposite.[37] The absence of definitive conclusions from the empirical work in the jury area is illuminating. If categorical perceptional differences between male and female jurors remain ambiguous, the likelihood of establishing such differences between male and female trial judges would seem even more problematic. The judge's responses to a case will be filtered through her years of training, institutional experience, and function. Thus, the very professionalization of the judge might diminish the predictability of her gender's influence.

---

35. Commercial guides for lawyers in juror selection frequently engage in stereotype about the predispositions of males or females in particular cases. Some of these manuals, for example, advise that women are less likely to feel sympathy for an attractive woman, less likely to feel sympathy for personal injury plaintiffs since they have endured the rigors of childbirth, and less likely to reach a prompt decision. *See, e.g.*, FRED LANE, GOLDSTEIN TRIAL TECHNIQUE Secs. 9.45–9.47 (1984); 3 MELVIN M. BELLI, MODERN TRIALS Secs. 50.59, 51.68 (1986).

36. *See* VALERIE P. HANS & NEIL VIDMAR, JUDGING THE JURY 76 (1986); REID HASTIE, STEVEN D. PENROD & NANCY PENNINGTON, INSIDE THE JURY 140 (1983).

37. Empirical work has included post hoc analyses of jury verdicts, mock jury studies, and surveys of potential jurors about publicized cases. Many studies have suggested that women are more likely to be lenient toward the accused, *see, e.g.*, Mills & Bohannon, *Juror Characteristics: To What Extent Are They Related to Juror Verdicts?*, 64 JUDICATURE 23, 24 (1980); Schulman, *Recipe for a Jury*, 6 PSYCHOLOGY TODAY 41 (1973). Mock jury studies, according to one researcher, have provided no consistent evidence that males and females differ with regard to sympathy for the defendant. Nemeth, *From the 60's to the 70's: Women in Jury Deliberations*, 39 SOCIOMETRY 293, 295 (1976). Moreover, one study, based on interviews with potential jurors about criminal cases widely publicized in the community, showed that women were more likely than men to prejudge a defendant's guilt. *See* Edmond Costantini, Michael Mallery, and Diane M. Yapundich, 122 JUDICATURE 121 (1983). Other studies suggest that even if women are more likely to prejudge a case, they are also more likely to change their minds during deliberations and to defer to male jurors. *See* Beckman and Aronson, *Selection of Jury Foreman as a Measure of the Social Status of Women*, 43 PSYCHOLOGY REP. 475 (1978); Strodtbeck & Mann, *Sex Role Differentiation in Jury Deliberations*, 19 SOCIOMETRY 3 (1956). Finally, at least one study has suggested that women jurors are more likely to reach a verdict of guilty in rape cases. *See* Hastie, Penrod, & Pennington, *supra* note 36, at 140–41.

An individual woman judge cannot be expected to embody at any given time what a theorist has decided are female traits, or to carry out a "feminist" agenda. Such theories disregard the dynamic nature of judicial philosophy and personal role orientations. As more women join the judiciary, the significance of gender will change. A woman judge's response to her role may vary according to whether she is the only woman in her professional milieu, one of several, or one of a majority. In Mary Anne Richey's case, for example, she was one of only two women trial court judges in the state of Arizona during most of her state court tenure. Throughout her tenure as United States District Judge, she was the only woman federal trial court judge in the District of Arizona. The personal meaning of her gender in such a context would necessarily contrast with that of a woman jurist who had numerous female colleagues.

Nevertheless, the undeniable contrasts between most women's lives and the lives of most men still suggest that women judges bring a different perspective to the bench. Gender shapes experience and one's gender identity may evolve with experience. The inextricable link between gender and experience will inevitably influence a judge's work, but generally not in predictable, categorical ways. Instead, the influence is highly individualized and fluid. Women judges as a group and over time will influence the law by "completing the picture." The empirical conclusions of the many task forces studying gender bias in the courts across the United States suggest that the overwhelming predominance of men as adjudicators has disadvantaged women as participants in the court systems, whether as lawyers, litigants, witnesses, or court employees.[38] Thus, as the number of women judges increase, we can expect an incremental decrease in overt gender bias, but we cannot expect every woman judge to embody a particular judicial philosophy or worldview. Mona Harrington, in her contemporary study of women in the legal profession, warns that we do not know what women have in common beyond cultural oppression, that we cannot know what women's potential is until it is released, and that "the effort to predefine that potential is itself oppressive."[39] The growing

---

38. After many state court task forces on gender bias were in operation, the Ninth Circuit became the first federal circuit to create such a task force. *See Report of the Ninth Circuit Gender Bias Task Force*, 45 STAN. L. REV. 2143 (1993)(Special Section).

39. *See* MONA S. HARRINGTON, WOMEN LAWYERS: REWRITING THE RULES 249 (1994). The position that women judges will profoundly yet unpredictably impact the law parallels the views of some post-modern theorists. Drucilla Cornell, for example, who draws heavily on the work of psychoanalyst Jacques Lacan, the philosopher Jacques Derrida, and the political theorist Michel Foucault, argues that language is an all-important cultural construct, and that we cannot know what language would be like if it were

presence of women at trial and appellate court levels will inevitably, profoundly, yet unpredictably, impact the discourse within the courthouse, among courts, and between courts and other institutions.

Since the inception of the legal realism movement, the subjectivity of judging has been widely recognized,[40] and women judges have acknowledged the influence of their subjective experience on their judging, including the experience of being a woman. Judge Patricia Wald of the United States Court of Appeals for the District of Columbia has commented, "A woman's experience does add something special to the interpretation of events, which is a crucial element of judging. This need not be seen as a discrete woman's voice which changes the outcome of cases, but rather as an additional lens through which arguments, rationales and justifications are filtered to create an accurate image of reality."[41] She points out the fallacy of assuming that all judges can reason alike, "given their different backgrounds, experiences, perceptions, and former involvements, all of which are part of the intellectual capital they bring to the bench. The cumulative knowledge, experience, and internal bents that are in us are bound to influence our notions of how a case should be decided."[42]

Arguing that subjective experience *should* influence judging, New York Court of Appeals Chief Judge Judith Kaye has written: "[On the Court of Appeals] I have come to appreciate how as a court of law, deciding only issues of law, within a government of law, we can and do and must also bring the full measure of every human capacity to bear in resolving the cases before us.... [T]he danger is not that judges will bring the full measure of their experience, their moral core, their every human capacity to bear in the difficult process of resolving the cases before them. It seems to me that a far greater danger exists if they do not."[43] Focusing on the contribution of female experience, Justice Christine Durham of the Utah Supreme Court observes, "[Women judges] bring an individual and collec-

---

removed from its patriarchal moorings, only that it would be different. *See* CORNELL, BEYOND ACCOMMODATION: ETHICAL FEMINISM, DECONSTRUCTION, AND THE LAW (1991).

40. *See* CHARLES WYZANSKI, WHEREAS—A JUDGE'S PREMISES 9 (1965)("From the day he takes his seat [the trial judge] is aware that while he has more personal discretion that the books reveal, he is hemmed in by impersonal usages, canons, and legitimate expectations.")(essay first published in 1952). *See generally* ROBERT E. KEETON, JUDGING 20–23 (1990).

41. Hon. Patricia M. Wald, *Some Real-Life Observations About Judging*, 26 IND. L. REV. 173, 183 (1992).

42. Patricia M. Wald, *Thoughts on Decisionmaking*, 87 W. VA. L. REV. 1, 12 (1984).

43. Judith S. Kaye, *The Human Dimension in Appellate Judging: A Brief Reflection on a Timeless Concern*, 73 CORN. L. REV. 1004, 1006–1015 (1988).

tive perspective to [their] work that cannot be achieved in a system which reflects the experience of only a part of the people whose lives it affects."[44]

Some jurists have argued that the ultimate goal of the judicial system—the dispensing of justice—is more likely to be attained if the decision-makers represent a fuller picture of humanity. Judge Ilana Rovner, who sits on the United States Court of Appeals for the Seventh Circuit and was formerly a United States District Judge, has remarked: "[L]ife experience is the one profoundly different ingredient in women judges, the one that enables them to understand more freely the life experiences that women encounter in our society.... The body of law must be the work of many minds in dialogue. Diversity of experiences is necessary not only to inspire confidence in the judicial system or make it comfortable to its diverse constituency—public perception aside, diversity of experience on the bench is necessary, period."[45]

Referring to another kind of diversity on the bench, Cardozo wrote that "[t]he eccentricities of judges balance one another.... one is a formalist, another a latitudinarian, one is timorous of change, another dissatisfied with the present; out of the attrition of diverse minds there is beaten something which has a constancy and uniformity and average value greater than its component elements."[46] Similarly, the increased presence of women on the bench at all levels will produce a system of justice that promises a richness and multiplicity of viewpoint that cannot be attained in their absence.[47]

Examination of the lives and work of individual women judges may be more illuminating ultimately than either the data-driven empirical study or

---

44. Christine Durham, "President's Column," NAWJ NEWS AND ANNOUNCEMENTS vol. 8, no. 1 (1987) at 1. Justice Shirley Abrahamson of the Wisconsin Supreme Court has offered a similar perception: "'What does my being a woman specially bring to the bench?' It brings me and my special background. All my life experiences—including being a woman—affect me and influence me." Hon. Shirley S. Abrahamson, *The Woman Has Robes: Four Questions*, 14 GOLDEN GATE L. REV. 489, 492–94 (1984)(remarks given October 5, 1980, at the Second Annual Meeting of the National Association of Women Judges).

45. Remarks of Judge Ilana Rovner, at Symposium on Gender Bias in the Law, University of Chicago Law School, December 2, 1994 ("Will Women Judges Make a Difference?").

46. BENJAMIN N. CARDOZO, THE NATURE OF THE JUDICIAL PROCESS 177 (1921).

47. In describing the influence of women on juries, Justice William O. Douglas wrote, "[T]he two sexes are not fungible; a community made up exclusively of one is different from a community composed of both; the subtle interplay of influence one on the other is among the imponderables. To insulate the courtroom from either may not in a given case make an iota of difference. Yet a flavor, a distinct quality is lost if either sex is excluded." Ballard v. United States, 329 U.S. 187, 193–94 (1946).

the grand theory about the female as jurist. Feminist scholars have recognized the power of narrative, especially in resisting generalizations about women's experiences.[48] Through biography as narrative, we learn about particular women, and the resulting knowledge helps us understand "woman" as subject. This book traces the life of one woman judge—her struggles, her defeats, and her victories. The book explores how Mary Anne's life experiences were informed by her gender and how her experiences, in turn, influenced her demeanor, her values, and her decisionmaking on the bench. My hope is that this work and other similar projects can enrich our understanding of the complex women beneath the robes.

---

48. As Kathryn Abrams has observed, narratives reveal the particularity and complexity of experience and can serve as a "vehicle for exploring women's struggles, as well as documenting their all-too-frequent defeats." Abrams, *Ideology and Women's Choices*, 24 GA. L. REV. 761, 795–99 (1990). *See also* Abrams, *Hearing the Call of Stories*, 79 CAL. L. REV. 971 (1991); Patricia J. Williams, *On Being the Object of Property*, SIGNS: JOURNAL OF WOMEN IN CULTURE AND SOCIETY, vol. 14, no. 1 (1988); Anne C. Dailey, *Feminism's Return to Liberalism*, 102 YALE L. J. 1265, 1274–1277 (1993)(book review); Richard Delgado, *Storytelling for Oppositionists and Others: A Plea for Narrative*, 40 J. LEGAL EDUC. 1 (1989).

A Courtroom of Her Own

Part One
1917–1946

CHAPTER ONE

An Indiana Girlhood

On a hot morning in July of 1976, Mary Anne Richey, then fifty-eight years old, pulled into the parking lot of the United States Courthouse in Tucson, Arizona. After twelve years as a trial judge in the Arizona state court system, she had become the only woman to be appointed by President Gerald Ford to the federal bench, and only the eighth woman in the history of the United States to join an Article III court. She parked her car and paused to admire with satisfaction her new place of work. Suddenly, a security guard approached her and brusquely announced, "Lady, you can't park here. You're gonna have to leave. These spaces are reserved for federal judges." Mary Anne slowly got out of the car, raised herself up to her considerable height, looked the man in the eyes, and said "Well, what the hell do you think I am?"[1]

Who was this woman, with her piercing gaze and plain talk? Why did she come to assume the role of a pathbreaker? How did she surmount sexist stereotypes to get to the doorstep of the federal courthouse in the summer of 1976? And how did her unique personal history ultimately shape her judicial identity? Mary Anne's story, pieced together in the pages that follow, suggests answers to these questions and reflects, in a broad sense, the story of American women in the twentieth century. Her opportunities, ambitions, achievements, and failures were inevitably informed by the changing cultural milieu in which she lived. From her birth in 1917 to her death in 1983, Mary Anne brought an individualized and often defiant response to the messages of her times.

* * *

Although Mary Anne often spoke of Arizona as "God's country," her emotional ties to the places and people of Indiana remained vibrant throughout her life. Shelbyville, Indiana, county seat of Shelby County in central Indiana, was Mary Anne's home for her first thirty years. Located on the Big Blue River, Shelbyville sits in the midst of rolling farmlands interspersed with thick forests and picturesque streams. The Flatrock River and Sugar Creek are within a few miles of the town. Today, when driving

---

1. Interview with Hon. Lawrence Ollason, United States Bankruptcy Judge, Tucson, Arizona (Feb. 27, 1996). Judge Ollason was a witness to the exchange.

into Shelbyville from Interstate 74, one senses that the town has changed little over time. The Public Square still forms a central hub surrounded by small businesses. The newspaper office where Mary Anne worked as a young woman is located near the square. A few blocks away is the First Presbyterian Church, where Mary Anne's mother was a longtime leader. The church, with its tall spire and high stained-glass windows, looks much as it did at the turn of the century. Multi-story Victorian houses line the streets in neighborhoods near the square, and tall dogwood and maple trees shade the sidewalks. Only at the outskirts of the town does one see the shopping centers and fast-food chains that have become the hallmark of the late twentieth century.

Located in the midst of fertile cornfields, Shelbyville has attracted moderate industry over the years, including the grain elevator business, in which Mary Anne's maternal grandfather was an early leader; furniture manufacturing, which had its zenith in the prosperous late 1920s; and the manufacturing of small business machines, which was the source of great family wealth for Mary Anne's first husband.[2] Shelby County was incorporated in 1850, and the population was recorded then as 1,407 whites and seven "coloreds."[3] Census data show that 9,700 people lived in Shelbyville in 1920, and by 1990 the number had risen to just 12,000.[4] The population has remained overwhelmingly white[5] and Protestant. During Mary Anne's childhood, the small Black community in Shelbyville lived in segregated neighborhoods and had to send their children to a racially segregated elementary school.[6]

Mary Anne was the child of Emma Nading Reimann and Harry Wallace Reimann, a socially prominent couple in Shelbyville. Her mother Emma was a descendant of respected pioneering families in Indiana.

---

2. For a detailed description of the business life of Shelbyville during the early 20th century, see MARIAN MCFADDEN, BIOGRAPHY OF A TOWN—SHELBYVILLE, INDIANA 1822–1962, at 281–303 (1968).

3. EDWARD H. CHADWICK, CHADWICK'S HISTORY OF SHELBY COUNTY, INDIANA 282 (1909).

4. UNITED STATES BUREAU OF THE CENSUS, FOURTEENTH CENSUS OF THE UNITED STATES TAKEN IN THE YEAR 1920, VOL. III, General Report and Analytical Tables, Table II: Composition and Characteristics of the Population for Places of 2,500 to 10,000, at 302 (1923).

5. According to the census data, only about 300 of the Shelbyville residents in 1920 were black. See id.

6. The Shelbyville School Board proudly announced its plans for a new school, the Booker T. Washington School for "colored children," in 1931. See THE SHELBY DEMOCRAT, Sept. 29, 1931.

Mary Anne's grandmother and namesake, Mary (Compton) Nading (1859–1930), was the daughter of a successful farmer, and the "Compton" name is still known in the Indiana agricultural community.[7] According to family members, Mary Nading was a physically striking woman, "beautiful and regal," who carried on a tradition of strong women in the Nading family.[8]

Mary Anne's grandfather, William Nading (1853–1926), founded a grain elevator business in southern Indiana. Regarded as a leading citizen, he was an astute businessman, known as shrewd but honest. Although he began his career in Flatrock, Indiana, Nading later settled in Shelbyville, probably for market reasons, and in 1904 founded the Nading Mill and Grain Company. He handled corn and wheat primarily and had the most extensive business of the county's grain dealers.[9] When he died in 1926, the newspaper reported, "All of Shelby county mourned the passing of the prominent business man, whose reputation for honesty and fairness in business had been one of the outstanding features in his successful career."[10]

Emma, the oldest of the Nadings' four daughters, was born on May 28, 1883. She and her three sisters, Lillian, Mildred, and Kate, grew up in the privileged upperclass of Shelbyville. Their three-story Victorian home, with handcrafted turrets, intricate ornamental woodwork, and curved balconies front and back, rose majestically on a tree-lined street of Shelbyville. The Nading family employed live-in maids who performed all the domestic chores, including cooking, cleaning, laundry, and much of the daily childcare.

At maturity, Emma was a dark-haired, brown-eyed woman whose slight physical presence belied her strength of character. She was soft-spoken, gentle, and unpretentious in manner. She had an appealing face with pale skin and strong features; her wide mouth was often serious. Her attire, at least for photographs, was frequently a long white cotton dress.

In contrast to the Nading heritage through her mother, Mary Anne's paternal ancestors were not members of an elite social class. Her father, Harry Wallace Reimann, was born in Shelbyville on February 17, 1882, the only son of Charles J. Reimann (1857–1915) and Anna (Schweitzer) Reimann (1864–1939), both of German descent. Little is known about

---

7. Mary Compton was the daughter of David and Sarah (Snepp) Compton. David Compton is identified in an early history as "one of the best known citizens of Shelby County." CHADWICK, *supra* note 3, at 784.

8. Interview with Mary Louise (DePrez) Harris, Indianapolis, Indiana (Oct. 12, 1992).

9. CHADWICK, *supra* note 3, at 961.

10. THE SHELBY DEMOCRAT, April 26, 1926.

Reimann's father except that he was a baker at some point in his adult life.[11] The family moved to Crawfordsville, Indiana, when Wallace was a child, and their means of livelihood in that town is unknown. Anna, seven years younger than her husband, was a stern woman with a thick German accent. She lived twenty-four years past her husband's death, residing during her later years with Wallace and Emma and their children.[12] The modest circumstances of the Charles Reimann family may have had much to do with Wallace Reimann's fierce ambition and competitive drive that later characterized his adult life.

Wallace Reimann attended school in Crawfordsville, and enrolled in Purdue University in 1899, most likely on an athletic scholarship, to study mechanical engineering. Although his grades were excellent, student records show that he left Purdue in 1902, without earning a degree.[13] Later in his life, news articles would inaccurately report, presumably with his acquiescence, that he graduated from Purdue with a degree in accounting.[14] Reimann's failure to complete a university degree was information that he apparently hid even from his family. Perhaps his false claim to a degree from Purdue generated, in some turn of psychology, the stern moralism and self-righteousness that his children would come to fear.

As an adult, Wallace was a tall man with light brown hair, a high forehead, and a strong square jaw. His grandchildren remembered him as always wearing a cashmere camel jacket and holding a cigar.[15] In photographs he was generally serious; with the addition of gold-rimmed glasses as he approached middle age, he was quite distinguished in appearance. Wallace Reimann had various occupations, including a brief interlude as an accountant, two decades as a businessman with the Nading Mill and Grain Company, a year as a state purchasing agent for a Republican administration in Indiana, and a final decade and a half as a salesman with Republic Coal and Coke. Reimann did not achieve eminence in any of these occupations. Indeed, under his helm, the Nading Mill and Grain Company suffered a drastic financial decline and ultimately failed. Nevertheless, he maintained the appearance of a comfortable lifestyle for most of his life and remained active in community affairs and civic clubs

11. THE SHELBY DEMOCRAT, January 26, 1907 (describing Emma Nading's engagement party and identifying Charles Reimann of Crawfordsville as "formerly a baker of this city.")

12. Interview with Ann (Reimann) Bruner, Shelbyville, Indiana (Oct. 14, 1992).

13. Academic Record of Harry Wallace Reimann, Office of the Registrar, Purdue University, provided by letter to author, July 7, 1993.

14. See, e.g., H.W. Reimann Dies at 77, THE SHELBYVILLE NEWS, April 3, 1959.

15. Bruner Interview, supra note 12.

until his retirement. As a staunch Republican, he resented the New Deal policies of the Roosevelt years, despite the fact that he suffered financial disaster during the Great Depression.

The characteristic for which Wallace Reimann was best known was not his business record or his public service but his lifelong passion for athletics. Crawfordsville, the town of his youth, was the birthplace of Indiana basketball, and Reimann reportedly played the game there for the first time at age eleven in 1893.[16] As a sophomore at Purdue, he played forward on the first official Purdue "Boilermaker" basketball team in 1900 and also served as team captain. Under his leadership, the Purdue team enjoyed back-to-back winning seasons. One history of Boilermaker sports dubs him "the father of Purdue basketball,"[17] a characterization that rivals sainthood in the sports lore of Indiana.

Following his departure from Purdue, sports continued to dominate Reimann's life. He coached at the Wabash Preparatory School for two years. He then went into Big Ten officiating and served as a prominent basketball official in the Midwest until 1919. After his officiating days had ended, he faithfully attended Purdue basketball games.[18] He was an avid and emotional fan and did not hold back from vociferously criticizing the officials when a call seemed unfair. Indeed, his enthusiasm and raw emotion for Purdue basketball reached such intensity that he was formally ejected from games on more than one occasion.[19] Moreover, Reimann remained close with the coaching staff at Purdue throughout most of his life and assisted athletically-talented young men in obtaining scholarships to Purdue University. He apparently had little interest in helping the non-athlete; one young man, a high school valedictorian and family friend, sought Reimann's assistance for a purely academic scholarship. Reimann summarily refused the request.[20]

Emma Nading and Wallace Reimann married in 1907, in a grand Shelbyville wedding, and, by all accounts, they were very much in love.[21] The

---

16. *Honor City Man Posthumously*, THE SHELBYVILLE NEWS, March 18, 1971.

17. ALAN R. KARPICK, BOILERMAKER BASKETBALL—GREAT PURDUE TEAMS AND PLAYERS 5 (1989).

18. Reimann's only grandson recalled that his grandfather always kept ten salt and pepper shakers within reach on the dining room table so that "he could instantly go over basketball plays at the table." Interview with William Reimann, Jr., Shelbyville, Indiana (Oct. 10, 1992).

19. Bruner Interview, *supra* note 12.

20. Interview with Mary Louise Van Winkle, Shelbyville, Indiana (Oct. 8, 1992).

21. Emma, who was twenty-four at the time of her marriage, had an imaginative and romantic approach to her wedding. In January of 1907, six months before the wedding date, she staged an elaborate luncheon party to announce her engagement to the tall and

elegance of the celebration reflected Emma's position of considerable economic advantage. The June wedding between Emma and Wallace was, according to local news accounts, a "brilliant affair" attended by "[t]he elite of Shelbyville."[22] Along with their accolades for the ceremony and the bride's attire, the news reports subtly revealed that the socially prominent Emma Nading had stepped down in her choice of husband. The articles mentioned in glowing terms the high prominence of the Nading family, but references to the Reimann social status, or even to Charles Reimann's means of livelihood, were notably absent.[23] The Nading family was indisputably superior to the Reimann family in social standing and economic class, and Wallace Reimann must have been determined to show the world that he was worthy of his genteel bride.

At the outset of their marriage, Emma and Wallace Reimann resided in Indianapolis where Wallace worked for the Typographical Union as an accountant. The couple moved to Shelbyville two years later and Reimann commenced his long and ill-fated association with the Nading Mill and Grain Company. He began as a bookkeeper-accountant and eventually, through a career track made smooth by his status as son-in-law, assumed leadership of the company.

The consensus among those who knew Emma and Wallace Reimann is that, notwithstanding Wallace's gregarious social style and fierce athletic competitiveness, Emma possessed greater strength of character. In her quiet, gracious manner, Emma was viewed as the force in the family. She was widely admired in Shelbyville, and acquaintances recall her apparent selflessness, religious spirituality, and inspirational devotion to helping others. Not surprisingly, Emma's influence on her only daughter would be profound, and Emma's early death would be a personal loss of such magnitude for Mary Anne that its memory could evoke tears forty years after the fact.

Emma and Wallace Reimann had two sons before the birth of Mary Anne. William Nading Reimann was born on June 7, 1912, and Charles John Reimann on February 6, 1915.[24] The boys, both physically attractive

handsome Wallace Reimann. Newspaper accounts described the affair as a "long and entertaining afternoon" attended by "50 handsomely gowned ladies." THE SHELBY DEMOCRAT, January 26, 1907.

22. THE SHELBY DEMOCRAT, June 3, 1907.

23. As one article summarized, "Miss Nading is the eldest daughter of Mr. and Mrs. William Nading. Her father is a prominent businessman at the head of the Nading Mill and Grain Company of Shelby County. Mr. Reimann is a son of Mr. and Mrs. Charles Reimann of Crawfordsville. His parents were formerly residents of Shelbyville. He is now employed in an Indianapolis printing establishment." THE SHELBY DEMOCRAT, June 3, 1907.

24. When William was born, the local newspaper, perhaps in recognition of the athletic worldview of Wallace Reimann, heralded the event as the arrival of "a new ballplayer." THE SHELBY DEMOCRAT, June 7, 1912.

children, were very different in character. Bill throughout his life was perceived as an altruistic, and gentle person who was much like his mother Emma. His actions as an adult would be consistent with such an image; he became a much-admired civic leader in Shelbyville and devoted extraordinary time and energy to fundraising for charitable causes. Chuck, on the other hand, was perceived as gregarious, ambitious, and, at times, "arrogant."[25] Throughout his short life, he was a charismatic and popular young man. Intelligent and movie-star handsome, the blond-haired Chuck would become the "golden boy" of Shelbyville, a young man who seemed, as a teenager and young adult, to have the world in his hands. His influence on Mary Anne would be dramatic, and the raw shock of his early death, like the death of her mother, would reverberate within Mary Anne's world for years.

When Bill and little Chuck were five and two years old, respectively, Emma Reimann became pregnant again. In the fall of 1917, the residents of Shelbyville, like the inhabitants of other small towns across the United States, continued to focus on their daily routines and to engage in the intimate age-old dramas of human society—commemorations of marriage, birth, death, and the seasons. The leaves of the dogwood, maple, and elm were brilliant in the forested hills surrounding Shelbyville as the town citizenry celebrated a newly-instituted Harvest Festival.[26] Mary Anne was born October 24, 1917, at the peak of the autumn colors, and her parents were delighted with their new child. In that era, their aspirations for their only daughter probably reflected prevailing cultural attitudes. Emma and Wallace most likely expected Mary Anne to follow in her mother's footsteps as a homemaker, a vocation increasingly exalted by the popular media and even by women's colleges.[27] If she were to seek employment as an adult, census data from 1920 revealed that Mary Anne's opportunities would lie in the fields of teaching, nursing, and library science, and not in the learned professions.[28]

Although Mary Anne was born into the idyllic life of the Reimann family, her arrival came against the backdrop of international upheaval and domestic social unrest. In 1917, the United States, after steadfastly

---

25. Telephone Interview with Martha (Mull) Gutting (Jan. 10, 1993).

26. *City in Gala Dress and Festival Crowd is Here*, THE SHELBY DEMOCRAT, October 25, 1917.

27. *See* BARBARA J. HARRIS, BEYOND HER SPHERE—WOMEN AND THE PROFESSIONS IN AMERICAN HISTORY 134–35 (1978).

28. UNITED STATES BUREAU OF THE CENSUS, FOURTEENTH CENSUS OF THE UNITED STATES TAKEN IN THE YEAR 1920, vol. 4, Occupations 34, 42 (1923).

holding on to neutrality for several years, formally joined the Great War in Europe, declaring war against Germany in April and against Austria-Hungary in December.[29] In the United States, life proceeded in the shadow of the war. War bonds were sold at an ever increasing rate. Congress passed, among other war-related statutes, the Espionage Act,[30] the Trading with the Enemy Act,[31] and the Selective Draft Act,[32] conscripting young men from small towns across the nation. Rationing of goods because of war-related shortages was common. Sugar became scarce, and in Shelbyville in late 1917, only one dollar's worth could be sold to one customer; "meatless" and "wheatless" days soon followed, and later "heatless" Mondays were declared for commercial establishments.[33]

In the fiercely patriotic state of Indiana, hostility to immigrants increased, and new immigration from European countries came to a virtual standstill during and after World War I. That hostility was particularly evident in attitudes toward German immigrants. In Indiana, as elsewhere, legislation was passed prohibiting German language instruction in public schools, and pressure mounted to stop publication of German language newspapers, to cease performances of German music, and to change German street names.[34] Presumably, Wallace Reimann felt the sting of anti-German sentiment during that period, but no record remains of his experience.

On the other hand, Mary Anne arrived at a propitious time for women's rights. In 1917, as suffragists nationwide were heading toward victory,[35] a measure allowing Indiana's women to vote in presidential elections was passed. Although it was later held to be unconstitutional in a court challenge,[36] it was an early recognition of the equal civil status of women. In 1921, a year after the ratification of the nineteenth amendment

---

29. President Woodrow Wilson had been reelected in 1916 as the "president who kept us out of war," but two weeks after the inauguration, three U.S. ships were torpedoed by German submarines, and Wilson's cabinet advised him to seek a declaration of war from Congress. Wilson did just that, announcing that "the world must be made safe for democracy." *See* WILLIAM MILLER, A NEW HISTORY OF THE UNITED STATES 377–82 (1958).

30. Act of June 15, 1917, ch. 30, 40 Stat. 217.

31. Act of Oct. 6, 1917, ch. 106, secs. 1–31, 40 Stat. 411.

32. Act of Oct. 6, 1917, ch. 105, sec. 3, 40 Stat. 410.

33. McFADDEN, *supra* note 2, at 284.

34. *See* JAMES H. MADISON, THE INDIANA WAY 16 (1986); *A Brief History of Indiana* 38–39 (Indiana Historical Bureau 1966)(monograph).

35. *See generally* AILEEN S. KRADITOR, THE IDEAS OF THE WOMAN SUFFRAGE MOVEMENT, 1890–1920, at 6 (1965).

36. *See* Vivian Sue Shields & Suzanne Melanie Buchko, *Antoinette Dakin Leach: A Woman Before The Bar*, 28 VALPARAISO L. REV. 1189, 1200 (1994)(describing unreported decision).

to the United States Constitution, Hoosier voters ratified an amendment to the state constitution granting women the vote.[37] Interestingly, almost twenty-five years before Mary Anne's birth, the Indiana Supreme Court issued an opinion holding that women could be admitted to the practice of law in the state. In 1893, in *In re Leach*,[38] the court rejected the view that the functions of womanhood belonged to "the domestic sphere," noting that such fictions were disappearing and "few, if any, of them exist in Indiana."[39] Although the court may have been overly optimistic in its observation that few barriers existed to women's equality, Mary Anne was able to move well beyond the domestic sphere in her own life.

The Reimanns' pleasure at Mary Anne's birth was tempered as news of Shelbyville's first casualties in the War began to arrive in early 1918.[40] Toward the end of that year, however, celebrations were in order. On November 11, 1918, when Mary Anne was just over a year old, the town was awakened by the striking of an anvil at the public square. The crash and clamor marked the victorious end of the Great War in Europe, and a day of wild rejoicing ensued in Shelbyville. In the decade ahead, Shelbyville enjoyed a period of prosperity: construction increased, new businesses came to the town, old businesses expanded, and service clubs, such as Kiwanis and Rotary, were established. Shelbyville, like much of the nation, celebrated the end of the war and looked forward to what promised to be an unending path of economic well-being.[41]

Mary Anne's early childhood was joyful, active, and relatively privileged. The family enjoyed a comfortable, but not opulent, lifestyle. Their circle of friends included the family of Charles Major, the noted author whose books about growing up in the Midwest in the nineteenth century are widely known. Both Emma and Wallace were civic and church leaders and were well-known throughout the community of Shelbyville. Wallace Reimann belonged to the full array of civic clubs and was an officer of the First Presbyterian Church where Emma conducted a Sunday school class for many years. Wallace served, moreover, as president of the Shelby County School Board for three years in the late 1920s, stepping down from that position when Mary Anne was eleven years old. His tenure was praised in the local newspaper as "a splendid record of efficiency and good business judgment in handling school affairs."[42]

---

37. James H. Madison, Indiana Through Tradition and Change 36 (1982); The Indiana Way, *supra* note 34, at 224.

38. In re Leach, 134 Ind. 665 (1893).

39. 134 Ind. at 667–68.

40. McFadden, *supra* note 2, at 286.

41. *Id.* at 287–91.

42. The Shelby Democrat, August 15, 1929.

Although Emma and Wallace Reimann were prominent in Shelbyville society, they were not wealthy. As with many families of that era, the 1920s marked the high point of economic prosperity for the Reimanns and of notable civic involvement for Wallace Reimann. Wallace's retirement from the Shelbyville school board came just two months before the stock market crash of October 1929. His management of the Nading family grain business progressed moderately well until the 1930s, when Mary Anne was in high school. Even when the business was healthy, however, the family did not have the trappings of the very rich. Instead of a hired cook, for example, Wallace's mother prepared most of the meals for the family, and Mary Anne and her brothers frequently wore clothes that Emma Reimann had sewn by hand.[43]

On the other hand, the Reimann children often played with their wealthier cousins, members of the DePrez family. Emma's sister, Lillian Nading, had married Herbert DePrez, the scion of a leading Indiana family. The DePrez name is associated with several business establishments in Shelbyville, including an ice plant and a hotel, and John DePrez, Sr., was the longtime publisher of the main Shelbyville newspaper. Through the family connection with the DePrez clan, Mary Anne and her brothers were able to enjoy the benefits of the DePrez's affluent lifestyle. On weekends, Mary Anne and her cousin Mary Louise DePrez often rode the DePrez horses to the Blue River Country Club for breakfast.[44]

During Mary Anne's earliest years, the Reimanns resided in a large two-story wood-sided house directly behind the ornate Nading home in Shelbyville. The backyards of the two houses adjoined, and a shared garden trellis connected the properties. The Reimann children roamed freely between both houses, playing often with the cousins from the Nading side of the family.[45] In 1930, before Mary Anne reached high school age, her family, including the elderly Anna Reimann, moved into the grander Nading home. The Reimanns remained in the stately Nading residence for the next seven years, until Emma's death in 1937. With its high ceilings, spacious hallways, and numerous rooms, the house was an elegant setting for Mary Anne's teenage years. A grand piano occupied the entry hall, and the sounds of Emma's playing would often fill the house.[46] The Reimanns, however, remained a family of relatively modest means.

Emma Reimann was devoted to all of her children, but her last-born child and only daughter engendered a special affection and bond. Al-

---

43. Harris Interview, *supra* note 8.

44. *Id.*

45. *Id.*

46. Telephone Interview with Merrylin (Greenlee) Crosby (April 25, 1993); Letter to Author from Ann (Reimann) Bruner, March 30, 1993.

though Mary Anne ultimately chose a path radically different from that of her mother, Emma Reimann's influence on her was undeniable. Emma provided her children with a nurturing and peaceful family environment. When Wallace Reimann experienced the vicissitudes of an erratic business career, Emma functioned as the stabilizer. As the core of the family unit, she was gentle in disposition, hardworking, religiously devout, and committed to her role as a moral educator of her children.

Emma's style of parenting was one of individual encouragement and the teaching of a firm morality through example. She had high ideals and wanted her children to aim for excellence. She repeatedly told Mary Anne, for example, that her grades in school would reflect on the family name and that she must therefore always try to excel.[47] One of Mary Anne's childhood friends recalled that Emma was a patient listener and a reliable source of good advice. "But she never demanded a particular action. She always ended her advice with the admonition, 'Now you must do what you think is right.'"[48] Emma's gentle side had its limits, and when Mary Anne misbehaved, her mother was quick with appropriate punishment. Once, when Mary Anne was in her teens, she and a friend dumped garbage on a neighbor's front porch as a Halloween prank. When Emma learned of the incident, she forced Mary Anne to scrub the porch clean on her hands and knees.[49] Through such assiduous parenting, Emma may have helped Mary Anne form her personal code of honor—a set of principles that seemed to include, by the time Mary Anne was in high school, a strong notion of fairness, a requirement of honest dealing with others, and an abiding sympathy for the underdog.

Family and friends remember Mary Anne as a "tomboy" almost from the beginning. She was the disheveled and uninhibited pal of her big brothers Bill and Chuck. Throughout her youth in Shelbyville she was known by the nickname of "Peter," often shortened to simply "Pete." She did not abandon the nickname, which may have originated with her performance of Peter in an elementary school production of "Peter Pan," until she moved to Arizona at the age of thirty.[50] Mary Anne's tomboyishness was in part the little girl's effort to keep up with her beloved older brothers. Perhaps due to their proximity in age, Mary Anne and Chuck were emotionally closer than were Mary Anne and her older brother Bill. Chuck took a keen interest in his kid sister and urged her to be tough, to

47. Interview with Annie Richey, Tucson, Arizona (Aug. 2, 1992).

48. Crosby Interview, *supra* note 46.

49. Margaret Hatmaker, "Memories of Emma Reimann," Brochure for Fiftieth Anniversary Celebration of Emma Reimann Class, May 14, 1976.

50. Annie Richey Interview, *supra* note 47.

always try her best, to never be a whiner.[51] Together Chuck and Mary Anne planned "to fly to the moon," she recalled in a newspaper interview years later.[52] "We always knew we'd really get there someday," she said.

The two brothers taught Mary Anne to throw and catch a baseball, to swing a bat, and to sink a basket from twenty feet. They rolled her down a hillside in a wooden barrel and used her as a tackling dummy when football was in season. Hunting quail and wild turkey in the lush country-side surrounding Shelbyville, the brothers helped Mary Anne acquire a sure and steady aim with a rifle. Likewise, perched on the banks of the Big Blue River, the three children would try their luck at the bass and catfish hiding within the dark green waters.

In these early outings, Mary Anne developed an enduring ease in the company of males and an affinity for activities normally associated with the "stronger sex." As an adult she would frequently find herself the only woman on a hunting trip, the only woman on a deep-sea fishing excur-sion, or the only woman in a horse corral. Moreover, her love of the coun-try and her physical and psychological ease in the out-of-doors were surely the product, in part, of a childhood spent in an enticing natural en-vironment marked by dramatic seasonal changes. The children of Shel-byville enjoyed not only the security of a small town, where crime was rare, but also the lure of nearby rivers and streams, covered bridges, forests, hiking trails, and open fields. In the wooded areas and on the prairies, deer, muskrat, rabbits, squirrels, raccoons, and other wildlife were plentiful. Residents of Shelbyville, young and old, often took to the hills to relax, and Mary Anne would find renewal in the country through-out her life.

As a child and young woman, Mary Anne was daring, even reckless, and always willing to take a risk. In the 1920s and 1930s, aviation was a glamorous and still dangerous form of transportation. In that era, the Shelbyville newspapers routinely carried articles describing in glowing phrases the perilous flights of women and men aviators.[53] In May 1927, when Mary Anne was ten years old, Shelbyville along with the rest of the world waited for news of a young handsome aviator flying alone across the Atlantic. The town immediately adopted Charles Lindbergh as its hero when he landed safely in Paris.[54] A few years later, when Mary Anne

---

51. Crosby Interview, *supra* note 46.

52. *Judge Takes To Her Mount When Balked At The Bench*, TUCSON DAILY CITIZEN, January 24, 1969.

53. *See, e.g.*, THE SHELBY DEMOCRAT, July 18, 1929 (French aviatrix in endurance test); THE SHELBY DEMOCRAT, Sept. 5, 1929 (Los Angeles flappers competing for women's endurance record).

54. McFADDEN, *supra* note 2, at 303.

was in junior high, a young barnstormer came into Shelbyville. He offered to take Mary Anne and her friend John Page up in the plane. The two agreed, and they buzzed the town square in what must have been a hair-raising ride. For both Mary Anne and John, the experience marked their first encounter with aviation, and each would go on to become a pilot.[55]

When the Reimann brothers obtained their first automobile, an old Dodge affectionately dubbed "Esmeralda," Mary Anne again exhibited her exuberant curiosity. Defying warnings from her father and brothers, Mary Anne, then about fourteen years of age, climbed behind the wheel of Esmeralda. She gave the car gas and sped off to circle the block. When her family finally realized that Mary Anne did not know how to apply the brakes on the vehicle, it was too late. She brought the car to a stop only by plowing into a hedge lining the street.[56] On another occasion, Mary Anne accepted a dare and descended a newly-installed water slide at the town swimming pool on her feet. Unfortunately, the stunt ended with a trip to the town hospital after she struck her head on the bottom of the shallow pool.[57]

Mary Anne's impetuosity was combined with a tolerance for embarrassment and an ability to laugh at herself. At the close of her senior year in high school, for example, Mary Anne's class celebrated with its traditional end-of-the-year picnic at the river in Flatrock, Indiana. A classmate recalled that Mary Anne, wearing a borrowed bathing suit that was too large, was one of the few girls to jump off a high tower into the river. The force of her entry pulled the bathing suit from her body, at which point several boys in the class promptly retrieved the suit and held it from Mary Anne's reach on shore. Mary Anne remained in the water amid much laughter until the bathing suit was finally tossed back to her. She reportedly endured the episode with good humor and only slight chagrin.[58]

During Mary Anne's early years, a social movement was underway in the United States that had a particularly pernicious influence in Indiana. The Ku Klux Klan first surfaced in Indiana in 1920 in Evansville, and by 1923 it was visible in most of the cities and towns of the state. Between 1922 and 1925, Indiana was the epicenter of the national Klan movement; it was the state that produced the Klan's largest membership, the Klan's greatest political victories, and the Klan's most influential leaders

55. Interview with John Page, Shelbyville, Indiana (Oct. 13, 1992).

56. Interview with William K. Richey, Nutrioso, Arizona (July 15–16, 1992).

57. Page Interview, *supra* note 55.

58. *Id.*

59. LEONARD J. MOORE, CITIZEN KLANSMEN—THE KU KLUX KLAN IN INDIANA, 1921–1928, at 6–7 (1991). The Klan gained control of the state Republican party in 1924. Klansman David Curtis Stephenson, one of the most prominent leaders, boasted

outside of Atlanta.[59] Flaming crosses appeared in Shelby County in the spring of 1923, and in April a cross was burned on the town square. Large rallies were held in several towns, including Shelbyville, in which white-robed, hooded paraders marched through the streets.[60] In July, a "monster" torchlight procession wound through the streets before a crowd of silent spectators, a crowd that possibly included the five-year-old Mary Anne. That same year, the Klan was rumored to have set a fire that destroyed the St. Vincent de Paul Church, a Catholic Church in Shelby County.[61]

The Hoosier Klan members embraced an agenda of "100% Americanization," based on their narrow philosophy of patriotism and Protestantism. In that context, the Klan in Indiana defined its enemies as Catholics, Blacks, and Jews, probably in that order.[62] In the elections of 1924, Klan-endorsed candidates, including Republican gubernatorial candidate Ed Jackson, won surprising victories throughout the state.[63] Although the Klan had an undeniably powerful impact on politics at the state level, by mid-1925 the Klan movement had lost much of its momentum.[64] In 1929, the *New York Times* Indiana correspondent noted that the "Klan is virtually dead as a political element...."[65] In Shelbyville, according to at least one account, the Klan "only presented a short flurry of excitement."[66]

Speculations about the impact of Klan activity and anti-German hostility on the Reimann family are problematic. While there is no evidence of Wallace Reimann's having been the victim of discrimination, it is unlikely that he, as a German American, totally escaped the anti-foreigner mindset of that era. Perhaps his determination to become a civic leader in his com-

---

that he was "the law" in Indiana. *Id*. Scandal plagued the Klan, however, and D.C. Stephenson eventually found himself in prison serving a life sentence for murder. *See* INDIANA THROUGH TRADITION AND CHANGE, *supra* note 37, at 68. Moore's book advances the thesis that the Klan's success in Indiana was not the result of a strong nativist movement but rather was a populist organization. As such, according to Moore, the Indiana Klan's antagonists were the political and business elite.

60. INDIANA THROUGH TRADITION AND CHANGE, *supra* note 37, at 44. Apparently, after a "monster torchlight procession" in Shelbyville in July 1923, the Klan did not surface again in that town and was not visibly active in local politics.

61. MOORE, *supra* note 59, at 25; Interview with Norman Thurston, Tucson, Arizona (Feb. 1, 1993).

62. INDIANA THROUGH TRADITION AND CHANGE, *supra* note 37, at 48–49.

63. *Id.* at 44–74; MOORE, *supra* note 59, at 152.

64. MOORE, *supra* note 59, at 184.

65. THE NEW YORK TIMES, December 8, 1929, cited in INDIANA THROUGH TRADITION AND CHANGE, *supra* note 37, at 74.

66. MCFADDEN, *supra* note 2, at 292.

munity, a well-known figure within the First Presbyterian Church, and a respected Republican was in part an effort to compensate for his vulnerable pedigree. Evidence exists, on the other hand, that Wallace was a stalwart segregationist. Plans for the building of a new segregated elementary school for black children were developed when he headed the Shelbyville school board. Moreover, he staunchly opposed the enrollment of black athletes at Purdue University. His opposition persisted even after Purdue's rival, the University of Indiana, integrated its basketball team.[67] Reimann's antipathy to blacks, if it existed, may have been the reaction of a man who himself had borne the brunt of social ostracism.

Thus, Mary Anne was exposed as a young girl to the sordid face of racism through the public activities of the Ku Klux Klan, the apparent views of her father, and the segregation of the society in which she lived. Nevertheless, she developed an egalitarianism as an adult, an outlook that may have reflected antipathy to the racist milieu of her youth but was surely influenced by her own experience in overcoming cultural barriers to gender equality. Whatever its roots, her eventual egalitarianism seemed less a conscious ideological choice than the product of her personal history. Although she never became a champion of social reform, she seemed to embrace racial equality on an individual level as an adult and made efforts to communicate that message to her own daughter.[68] In one of the many ironies of Mary Anne's life, fifty years after her father's stewardship of Shelbyville's racially segregated school system she would preside over a racial desegregation lawsuit in federal court involving the largest school district in Arizona. As will be seen, in that role she displayed a commitment—albeit one tempered by pragmatism and judicial restraint—to the constitutional mandate of *Brown v. Board of Education*.[69]

Bigotry aside, Reimann's lasting legacy to his daughter was an unrelenting competitive drive, independence of spirit, and determination to succeed. Under the fierce pressure from Wallace and the more subdued encouragement from Emma, the Reimann children were very high-achieving. Mary Anne's brother Chuck was a straight-A student during his years at Shelbyville High School, and Bill received recognition for academic achievement in high school as well.[70] Mary Anne's public school record was similarly distinguished. In sixth grade at John Major Elementary School (1928–29), her grades were high, and a standardized test at that

---

67. Interview with William Showers, Shelbyville, Indiana (Oct. 10, 1992).

68. Annie Richey Interview, *supra* note 47.

69. 347 U.S. 483 (1954).

70. *Reimann Was Star Athlete*, THE SHELBYVILLE NEWS, March 9, 1942. The awards to Bill and to Chuck recognized their outstanding academic performances in high school as well as their athletic accomplishments.

time estimated her I.Q. to have been 134. In her two years of junior high at Shelbyville's only junior high school, she was matriculated into the highest of three academic tracks.[71] At Shelbyville High School, Mary Anne again excelled, graduating magna cum laude and ranking 16th in her high school class out of 104 students. It is doubtful, however, that she thought of herself as an academic star. Classmates believed she had to work hard for the grades she earned,[72] and her closest friends in high school, Merrylin Greenlee and Martha Mull, were gifted young women who graduated first and third in the class, respectively. Mary Anne apparently moved in a circle of young people who were academically motivated and whose families expected scholastic success.

Perhaps more important than academic success, Wallace Reimann expected that his children would excel in athletics, and Mary Anne and her brothers did not disappoint him. Bill and Chuck participated in organized competitive sports throughout their youth and managed to garner significant public recognition. In high school, they became star athletes, a status taken quite seriously within the small towns of rural Indiana, and each brother received prestigious awards at graduation for their athletic prowess. At the United States Naval Academy at Annapolis, where Chuck ultimately attended college, he became a football hero among the cadets.[73]

Athletics likewise played an essential role in the development of Mary Anne's self-image and undoubtedly contributed to her capacity for self-determination and her emotional strength as an adult. Studies now suggest that young women who are proficient athletes are more likely to have a sense of psychological well-being and a positive physical self-image than the female non-athlete.[74] The athletic woman may be more inclined to

---

71. Academic Records of Mary Anne Reimann, City Public Schools, Shelbyville, Indiana; Gutting Interview, *supra* note 25.

72. A different standardized test was given to Mary Anne in her freshman year of high school. On that examination, her I.Q. was recorded as 113, considerably lower than the earlier score. While I.Q. testings are viewed as less reliable than once believed, the second lower score may be more reflective of her innate intellectual abilities than the first score. Academic Records of Mary Anne Reimann, City Public Schools, Shelbyville, Indiana.

73. THE SHELBYVILLE NEWS, September 29, 1969; UNITED STATES NAVAL ACADEMY 1938 STUDENT YEARBOOK at 426–33. Indeed, Charles Reimann's peers would acknowledge his legendary determination in the 1938 yearbook. "By his work in football and his triumphant struggle against academics, Chuck has displayed large quantities of that competitive spirit so necessary to success in this cold, cold world." *Id.* at 160.

74. *See* Susan L. Morse, *Women and Sports*, CQ RESEARCHER 195–215 (March 6, 1992); Eldon E. Snyder & Joseph E. Kivlin, *Women Athletes and Aspects of Psychological Well-Being and Body Image*, THE RESEARCH QUARTERLY, vol. 46, no. 2, at 191–99 (1975); Anita Myers & Hilary Lips, *Participation in Competitive Amateur Sports as a Function of Psychological Androgyny*, SEX ROLES, vol. 4, at 571–88 (1978).

view her body as a tool, for example, than as an object of ornamentation and less inclined to fret over her body's failure to fit cultural standards of beauty. Studies exploring women's perceptions of their own girlhoods also indicate that women who self-identified as "tomboys" were more likely as adults to have achieved success in the business world than women who did not so characterize themselves.[75]

In the era of Mary Anne's youth, however, when no federal law mandated equal opportunity in athletic programs for males and females,[76] Mary Anne's opportunities for formal competitive play were limited.[77] The family lore suggests that, given the chance, she could have been an athlete superior even to her brothers. Her strength, agility, and competitiveness were well-known among her peers. She was tall, reaching a height of almost five feet seven inches at maturity, large-boned, and strong, and she seemed comfortable in her physical self. She was elected president of the high school's relatively new Girls' Athletic Association in her senior year in high school and continued her interest in athletics through her years at Purdue University. As her close friend Martha Mull recalled, "Pete always outclassed the rest of us in whatever sport we tried. She was just a natural, and very, very competitive."[78]

Mary Anne played "alley ball" with her brothers and friends, using a basketball hoop suspended near the side of the house. Touch football and field hockey became favorites as she grew older. She learned to play tennis from the minister of the First Presbyterian Church. A friend remembered that Mary Anne was an intense competitor in tennis, never letting a high

---

75. *See* Joanna Bunker Rohrbaugh, *Femininity on the Line*, PSYCHOLOGY TODAY 30, 42 (Aug. 1979)(reporting study by Leanne Schriber in which 80 percent of surveyed "accomplished" women identified as tomboys as children, and that majority of "most highly placed women in American business" had been tomboys and had participated in whatever organized sports were available); WOMEN AND ACHIEVEMENT 410–11 (Martha T.S. Mednick, Sandra S. Tangri, Lois W. Hoffman, eds. 1975)(reporting that married women professionals often described themselves as aggressive and independent "tomboys" as young girls).

76. Title IX of the Education Amendments of 1972 explicitly prohibits sex discrimination in educational programs and activities receiving federal financial assistance. *See* Pub. L. No. 92–318, Title IX, Sec. 901(a)(3), 86 Stat. 373 (June 23, 1972), codified at 20 U.S.C. Sec. 1681 et seq. It has been construed to require equal opportunity, albeit in a "separate but equal" manner, for males and females in school-sponsored athletics.

77. The common solace for female athletes in high school was membership in the Girls' Athletic Association. Through the "GAA," girls could organize their own team-play and sports activities. Mary Anne was president of the GAA at Shelbyville High School during her senior year. 1935 SHELBYVILLE HIGH SCHOOL YEARBOOK ("The Squib").

78. Harris Interview, *supra* note 8.

lob get past her, and that she did not hesitate to throw herself on the clay to reach a ball. "She was always dirty after a game," he recalled, "because she was on the ground more than not. There was hardly anyone in town who could beat her."[79] Accustomed to swimming in the many swimming holes along Big Blue River, Mary Anne was at home in the water. After Porter Pool, the community swimming pool, opened in Shelbyville in 1932, Mary Anne became an avid and disciplined swimmer. She and a friend began a daily routine of lap-swimming, a practice she would continue throughout her life.[80]

Mary Anne was, by nature, gregarious and seemed to always have a great many friends. Like her handsome older brother Chuck, who had been president of both his junior and senior classes at Shelbyville High, Mary Anne was a popular student. Following in Chuck's footsteps, she was elected vice-president of her senior class. The high school yearbook noted that a girl had been elected to office "in spite of the boys' dark ideas concerning women in politics."[81] Perhaps because of her mother's influence, Mary Anne displayed a sensitivity to the feelings of others during her youth and seemed to posses a natural capacity for empathy. When a young woman classmate was ostracized because of a reputation for sexual promiscuity, for example, Mary Anne defended her among her peers and sought to include her in social outings. She stood up for a young man who, because of an impoverished and unstable family background, had suffered social rejection.[82] As she matured, Mary Anne displayed increasing willingness to depart from convention, and she seemed to sense as a young woman that community approval was evanescent.

Much of the socializing among young people in Shelbyville was done in group outings. A favorite pastime in the heat of August was the "Chautauqua," an educational and entertainment festival patterned after the out-of-doors assemblies that originated in the Chautauqua Lake region of western New York. The Chautauqua came every summer to the fairgrounds outside of Shelbyville in the early 1900s, featuring nationally-known performers and treating the crowds to opera, chamber music, dance, and even scientific and political lectures. Mary Anne attended several Chautauquas with her cousins,[83] and it was perhaps through the Chautauqua that she was first exposed to opera and developed her life-long love of that musical form.

Although Mary Anne enjoyed the conviviality and lively dynamics of

79. Thurston Interview, *supra* note 61.

80. *Id.*

81. 1935 SHELBYVILLE HIGH SCHOOL YEARBOOK ("The Squib").

82. Crosby Interview, *supra* note 46.

83. Harris Interview, *supra* note 8.

such activities, by the time she graduated from high school, she had settled on one young man among the local set as her regular companion. William Showers, who would eventually become her first husband, was a soft-spoken youth with deepset, almost brooding eyes. He was the youngest son of Joseph Ralph Showers, a wealthy, cigar-toting, physically-imposing man who had founded Indiana Cash Drawers, a successful manufacturing company that remains productive today.[84]

Bill Showers and Mary Anne had very different personalities and were a puzzling couple from the start. Unlike his domineering father or the outgoing Mary Anne, Bill was reticent, deliberate in manner, and had more of an interest in music than in sports. Their trumpet playing may have catalyzed their relationship since they sat side-by-side in the high school band. They became a known couple in the Shelbyville milieu, and Bill was memorialized as "Pete's beau," in the high school yearbook.[85] Nevertheless, their acknowledged relationship was insufficient to tie the headstrong Mary Anne to Shelbyville after graduation.

The idyllic family life and comfortable social position enjoyed by the Reimann family had a dark side. Were it not for the gentle intermediation of Emma, Wallace's pressure on his children to excel would surely have taken a toll on the psychological health of Bill, Chuck, and Mary Anne. As it was, family expectations must have been intense in order to propel Chuck into earning flawless grades throughout high school, performing as a star on the football field and on the basketball court, and winning election as president of his class two years in a row.

That same family atmosphere pushed Mary Anne toward similar high achievement to the extent it was available to girls. Aside from the emotional tension associated with a young person bent on perfection, the cultural milieu was problematic for females. While high-achieving boys of that generation could hope for success in a particular career and could rely on familial assistance and direction toward that goal, girls of Mary Anne's socioeconomic class were expected to become wives and mothers, securing their adult identities through their husbands. The scholastic accomplishments of Mary Anne and her friends during high school did not lead to serious career counseling. Instead, the girls, even those with outstanding high school grades, faced a future in which their inchoate talents might never emerge beyond the domestic sphere. Although only slightly

---

84. As a young man, the senior Showers had conceived of the idea of connecting an adding machine to a cash drawer; the idea took hold, and a successful business was born. Showers Interview, *supra* note 67.

85. 1935 SHELBYVILLE HIGH SCHOOL YEARBOOK ("The Squib").

fewer women attended college in that era than men, the overall numbers were small,[86] and women were often guided toward female-dominated occupations or toward homemaking. Mary Anne's high school friends Merrylin Greenlee and Martha Mull headed off to Smith College and the University of Indiana, respectively, after graduation, but they did not often talk about career plans or ambitions for the future.[87]

The Depression, moreover, took its toll on the aspirations of Shelbyville's young people, just as it did throughout the nation. Although the stock market collapse of October 29, 1929, may not have had immediate repercussions in Shelbyville, by 1931 the town's Community Chest funds were depleted and by 1932, the list of properties—most of them farms— put up for sale because of nonpayment of taxes was the longest the county had ever known. Budgets for the public schools, the library, and government services declined drastically, and by 1933 several local banks had closed. A disastrous fall in the price of farm produce and of land occurred.[88] The Depression may have had a particularly unfortunate impact on the young women of that era. Studies suggest that the scarcity of work during the Depression led to hostility towards working women, especially married women. Women's tentative status in the professional occupations slipped during the 1930s, and working wives encountered widespread discrimination.[89] A 1936 Gallup Poll showed that 82 percent of Americans thought that wives whose husbands were employed should not have a job.[90] One scholar has concluded that "[b]y the time the employment of married women burgeoned during and after World War II, a positive ideology encouraging personal and occupational progress and equality had vanished—a casualty of the Depression decade."[91] To Mary Anne and her female friends, the message of the times was that serious career goals were incompatible with the more lofty calling of marriage and motherhood.

In addition, the economic collapse in the industries of the Midwest did not occur without human suffering. The Nading Grain and Mill Com-

---

86. *See* STEVEN D. MCLAUGHLIN, BARBARA D. MELBER, JOHN O.G. BILLY, DENISE M. ZIMMERLE, LINDA D. WINGES, & TERRY R. JOHNSON, THE CHANGING LIVES OF AMERICAN WOMEN 32–42 (1988)(reporting that over half the women aged 25–34 had not graduated from high school in 1940, and that while approximately 10 percent of women of that age group had attended some college, only about 6 percent were college graduates).

87. Crosby Interview, *supra* note 46; Gutting Interview, *supra* note 25.

88. *See* MCFADDEN, *supra* note 2, at 303–309.

89. *See generally* LOIS SCHARF, TO WORK AND TO WED—FEMALE EMPLOYMENT, FEMINISM, AND THE GREAT DEPRESSION (1980).

90. *Id.* at 23.

91. *Id.* at 65.

pany suffered the fate of many of the farming-dependent businesses. In 1932, after several years of steady decline, the company's earnings fell sharply. Wallace Reimann's management of the company may not have been at fault; rather, as farm prices skidded downward, the services of the company were no longer needed. One afternoon, during the period in which the company's profits were spiraling downward, Wallace Reimann fell from one of the Nading grain elevators outside of Shelbyville. He lay undiscovered for several hours and suffered serious and debilitating injuries in the fall. The people of Shelbyville widely speculated that Wallace had thrown himself from the elevator in an attempted suicide so that his family could benefit from life insurance proceeds. The speculation was never corroborated; no clear evidence existed that the fall was not accidental. Nevertheless, the mere rumors themselves deeply embarrassed the Reimann family. After the injury, Herbert DePrez, Emma's brother-in-law, took over the Nading company and attempted to resuscitate the failing business. He was unsuccessful, and the company closed down all operations in the mid-1930s.[92]

After the fall, Wallace Reimann's business fortunes were uneven at best. He recuperated at home—his wife's family home—for several months under Emma Reimann's care. The failure in managing his wife's family business, and his rumored act of desperation amidst the business failure, shadowed him for the remainder of his life. In 1933, during the final year of Governor Harry Leslie's administration, Wallace obtained a job as a state purchasing agent. That short-lived position ended with the close of the Republican governor's term. Wallace later found employment as a traveling salesman with the Republic Coal and Coke Company, headquartered in Chicago, and stayed with that firm until retirement in 1952.[93] Throughout this period, Wallace remained a stalwart Republican and a consistent critic of Roosevelt's New Deal programs.

Mary Anne's brother Bill responded in character to his father's misfortune. Bill had enrolled in Purdue University after graduation from high school. When Wallace was injured in the fall, Bill dropped out of college and returned home to Shelbyville to help his family. He moved back in with Emma, Wallace, and Mary Anne, as well as the aging Anna Reimann, Wallace's mother, and found what work he could in the Depression-struck town.

For Mary Anne, who was just entering adolescence, the public and private struggles of her family must have been painful, indeed. As with other

---

92. Harris Interview, *supra* note 8; Thurston Interview, *supra* note 61; Interview with Martha Bowers, Shelbyville, Indiana (Oct. 12, 1992); Bruner Interview, *supra* note 12; Showers Interview, *supra* note 67.

93. *H. W. Reimann Dies at 77*, THE SHELBYVILLE NEWS, April 3, 1959; Bruner Interview, *supra* note 12; Thurston Interview, *supra* note 61.

families living through the Depression, she necessarily became accustomed to budgetary strains, to the myriad ways in which the lack of money limits opportunities. Perhaps the bitter experience of her father's business failure helped Mary Anne develop a self-sufficiency that would become a key personal value for her as an adult. In addition, the example of Emma Reimann during the Depression years remained with her as an inspiration. Through her own resourcefulness, Mary Anne's mother was able to secure certain advantages for her children. Even when Wallace was still managing the Nading Grain and Mill Company, Emma did what she could to bring in extra money for the family. An accomplished seamstress, she designed and made children's clothing and sold the clothing privately to individuals and to stores in Shelbyville. After Wallace's fall, Emma secured a formal job working at a furniture company on the Public Square. The image of Emma Nading working at retail sales must have been startling to the old guard of Shelbyville.[94]

Through Emma, Mary Anne's brother Chuck secured an appointment to the United States Naval Academy. The governor of Indiana from 1933 to 1937 was Paul V. McNutt, a Democrat. The Reimanns, as staunch Republicans, ordinarily would have had little hope of securing a gubernatorial appointment to Annapolis for one of their sons. But McNutt's secretary of patronage was Pleasant Greenlee, Merrylin Greenlee's father. Greenlee, a longtime resident of Shelbyville and important figure in Indiana politics in the 1930s, was fond of the Reimanns, especially Mary Anne and Emma. He arranged for the appointment across party lines as a favor to his friends. As a result, Chuck was able to withdraw from Purdue University and enroll in the Naval Academy at a time of economic exigency within the family.[95]

In her indefatigable way, Emma also used her ingenuity to enable Mary Anne to attend an exclusive girls' camp in Vermont that was the summer camp of choice for the daughters of affluent Shelbyville families. The normal tuition was well beyond the Reimann family budget, but Emma Reimann struck a deal with the camp through which she was able to enroll Mary Anne either free of charge or at a greatly reduced rate in exchange for recruiting local girls to attend the camp.[96] The camp's director

94. Bruner Interview, *supra* note 12.

95. In order to gain admission to the Naval Academy, Charles Reimann needed not only the recommendation of a high-ranking state government official but also a passing score on the Academy's stringent entrance examination. Chuck studied for the exam through a course at the Cochran-Bryan Preparatory School at Annapolis and actually enrolled in the Academy in June of 1934. C. *Reimann Succeeds in U.S. Academy Test*, SHELBYVILLE DEMOCRAT, May 1934.

96. Crosby Interview, *supra* note 46; Harris Interview, *supra* note 8.

was an unmarried woman of uniquely strong character who taught the campers to think positively about their own abilities and to pursue their goals with fierce determination. Her message to the campers was, simply, "You can do anything if you think you can."[97]

The camp's emphasis on discipline and inner-competition, in a setting of great natural beauty, suited Mary Anne well,[98] and the unique joy of strenuous physical exercise in the out-of-doors remained with her all of her life. In her later years, she would pursue that same joy regularly, and she would work hard to enable underprivileged girls in Arizona to experience an out-of-doors camp. The director's message of self-reliance, optimism, and determination resonated with particular force in Mary Anne's mind. As the child of Emma and Wallace Reimann, Mary Anne already had an exuberantly competitive spirit. From young adulthood forward, she seemed to welcome challenge and to seek out adventure. When faced with alternative paths, she frequently would choose the more difficult but more promising route, and complacency was never to be her guiding principle.

Thus, Mary Anne as a maturing young woman possessed an athletic, daring, and robust nature, a character starkly in conflict with cultural messages of the time regarding ideals of womanhood. Although Emma Reimann may have met the contemporary definition of ideal woman,[99] Mary Anne rejected it from the beginning and continued to reject it throughout her life. Her interests were not in the domestic realm, and she did not expend energy on self-beautification. Instead, she savored high-risk adventure and competition. She had an adolescent's joy for life and an ambition, albeit unguided, to do something different from the path chosen by her mother.

---

97. Harris Interview, *supra* note 8.

98. *Id.*

99. According to one essay, woman is "a homemaker, a picture of health, refinement, and the modern spirit in corsetry, and belongs to a first family, reflects quiet elegance, appreciates the truly smart, can afford only the best, is a critical buyer, and always well-gowned to her finger tips." *The American Woman According to Advertisers*, LIFE MAGAZINE (March 10, 1927) at 15. *See also* LIFE MAGAZINE (July 7, 1927) at 7, and (Nov. 17, 1927) at 13 (pictures showing leisurely women at the soda shop or a friend's elegant home indulging themselves with treats and tea).

Chapter Two

The World Beyond

When Mary Anne graduated from Shelbyville High School in 1935, she was a young woman of great potential but little direction or career-related ambition. Although she mentioned to her family that she might want to study journalism at the University of Indiana, Wallace Reimann extinguished that flicker of interest immediately. Unwilling to countenance his daughter's attendance at the arch rival of Purdue University, he announced to Mary Anne, "I will help you go anywhere but Indiana."[1]

In truth, the Reimann family had little means to send Mary Anne to college in 1935. Nevertheless, in a turn of luck that would be typical of Mary Anne's adulthood, the seventeen-year-old girl created an alternative for herself, apparently aware that exposure to the world beyond the shaded sidewalks of Shelbyville could only benefit her. Acting very much in character, Mary Anne aggressively pursued an unusual opportunity, the seeds of which began with a man named Robert Markley. Markley had been a close friend of the Reimann family ever since his outstanding performance as a high school athlete in Shelbyville. Like several other promising young sportsmen, Markley attracted the attention of Wallace Reimann. Always eager to recruit promising candidates for his beloved Purdue athletic program, Reimann had helped secure a scholarship for Markley to attend Purdue University where he earned a degree in engineering in 1919. After graduation, Markely found employment with Standard Oil and was promptly dispatched to Karachi, India, where he served for thirty years and ultimately rose to the position of manager of Standard Oil's operations in the region.

When Mary Anne was a young girl, Robert Markley and his wife Ruth were in the United States on one of their triennial "leaves" from Karachi. During a visit to the Reimann residence, Markley told Mary Anne, then not yet in her teens, that he would take her to India once she graduated from high school. The remark, although perhaps uttered casually and without serious intent, remained with Mary Anne.

The Markleys again passed through Shelbyville in the summer of 1935, coincidentally the year of Mary Anne's graduation from high school. The tenacious teenager reminded Robert of his promise of a few years past. According to Markley's wife, Ruth, Mary Anne announced in her forth-

---

1. Telephone Interview with Martha (Mull) Gutting (Jan. 25, 1993).

right style, "OK, Bob and Ruth, I have graduated from high school. Now I am ready to go to India." The young girl's insistence was something of a surprise to the Markleys, who had not anticipated returning to India with Mary Anne in tow. Ruth Markley's parents were appalled that their daughter, then in her thirties and childless, might assume responsibility for the Reimann girl in the mysterious and politically tumultuous Far East. Despite the protests of Ruth's family, the Markleys ultimately agreed to take Mary Anne with them on their return to Karachi. The expectation was that Mary Anne would remain with them until their next regularly-scheduled visit to the United States, sometime in 1937 or 1938.[2] Although the Reimanns paid some of Mary Anne's expenses, the Markleys willingness to assume significant financial responsibility for Mary Anne was most likely a function of Robert Markley's sense of indebtedness to Wallace Reimann. Whatever the nature of Mary Anne's relationship with her high school beau, Bill Showers, it apparently did not eclipse the lure of the Far East.

When Mary Anne announced to her friends that she was heading to India for two to three years, the members of her Shelbyville circle were astounded. "We were all getting ready for college," explained Martha Mull. "Then Pete comes along and tells us she's going to India! We were amazed. No one from Shelbyville had ever done such a thing."[3] The Indian sojourn, in fact, allowed Mary Anne to avoid, temporarily, the question of her future, and the trip became an interim substitute either for college or for employment.

The Markleys and Mary Anne left for India in late summer of 1935. The trip, primarily by ship, lasted about six weeks. To the teenager from Shelbyville, the luxurious life of the Markleys must have been awe-inspiring. From New York, the trio sailed to England and then, to Mary Anne's delight, flew across the English Channel to France. On a brief stop-over in Monte Carlo, the Markleys put dark glasses on the under-age Mary Anne and escorted her into the lavish casino at the resort where the gambling tables sprawled beneath ornate chandeliers. In Marseille, the night before the Markleys and Mary Anne were to set sail for Bombay, the young Hoosier over-indulged on fine French chocolates at the close of a multi-course meal at the hotel. Mary Anne became ill during the night; still feeling miserable the next day, she boarded the ocean liner with difficulty and did not remain on deck for the departure. Instead, she spent the first twenty-four hours of her long journey to Bombay in her cabin. She recov-

---

2. Telephone Interview with Ruth Markley (Sept. 12, 1992).

3. Gutting Interview, *supra* note 1.

ered quickly, however, and enjoyed the amenities of the luxurious ship during the voyage to Bombay.[4]

Pulling into the debris-strewn waters of the Bay of Bombay, Mary Anne saw the Gateway to India a short distance from the shoreline. The arch, bearing an inscription commemorating "the landing in India of their imperial majesties George V and Queen Mary on the second of December MCMXI," welcomed the voyagers into the colonial world of wealthy and privileged Brits and Americans, Indian servants, religious factions, and poverty. Once in Bombay, the threesome changed to a smaller ship and traveled the remaining five hundred miles of coastal waters to Karachi.

India in 1935 was in the midst of turbulent change. Bitter rivalry between the Hindus, comprising about 65 percent of India's population at the time, and the Muslims was reaching a crescendo as the country moved inexorably toward independence. Hinduism and Islam were each more than a religion; each was a way of life, and those ways were in fundamental opposition. The Hindus caste system, prohibited today by Indian law, dictated one's occupation, the circle within which one might marry or socialize, and the foods that might be eaten. At the bottom of the caste system were the Untouchables, the menials of India who performed degrading work and whose lives were segregated from the rest of the population. In contrast, Islam was essentially monotheistic and based on a belief in the equality of humankind. In the years preceding independence, as the struggle for political power intensified, hostility between these two religious worlds was often violent.[5]

Under the gifted leadership of Mahatma Gandhi, the nationalist movement finally persuaded Britain to take concrete steps toward releasing India from its colonial grip. After a decade of pressure from the Congress party, dominated in the 1930s by Gandhi's tactics of civil disobedience, the British had reached a consensus of sorts that Britain and India should work, slowly and conservatively, toward Indian independence.[6] In 1935, the British Parliament passed the Government of India Act as the first clear step toward that goal. The Act, which created a new Indian constitution, offered the provinces a degree of local autonomy they had not enjoyed in the past. Under the Act, provincial ministries were to be created that would be responsible to the electors, and the franchise, based on ownership of property, was expanded to include thirty million voters, one sixth of the adult population. It also provided that each governor form his

---

4. Markley Interview, *supra* note 2.

5. T. Walter Wallbank, A Short History of India and Pakistan 38 (1958).

6. Larry Collins & Dominique LaPierre, Freedom at Midnight 52-65 (1975); Percival Spear, A History of India, Vol. 2, at 206-14 (1956).

cabinet from members of the majority party in the provincial legislature and, significantly, that all cabinet members were to be Indians. Nevertheless, the viceroy and the governors, British appointees, kept their veto power over all legislation.[7]

When Mary Anne and her hosts settled into their privileged life in Karachi in 1935, the rumblings of independence were thus beginning to sound. The Muslim-dominated Karachi was still part of India at that time, and tensions between Muslims and Hindus were rising, since Muslims feared that independence would result in the establishment of a Hindu-favoring government.[8] It was not until 1947 that the Muslim territory was finally partitioned and the nation of Pakistan was created simultaneously with the independence of India.

Nevertheless, the life of the Americans in Karachi proceeded in luxury, relatively isolated from the political unrest and the religious rivalry. The Markleys lived in a large home on the outskirts of Karachi and socialized almost exclusively with other Americans or British citizens. Their main contact with Indians came through their monitoring of the many servants that worked in the Markley household. Their lives revolved around the ubiquitous British club, the "Gymkhana" or sports club, and the pastimes that the British brought to India: tennis, golf, field hockey, cricket, squash, hunting, riding, and bridge. According to one account, golf was introduced in Calcutta three decades before it reached New York, and the world's highest course was laid out in the Himalayas at 11,000 feet.[9] Mary Anne enjoyed the nine-hole course, accessible only by horseback, at least once on a sidetrip to Kashmir.[10]

Ruth Markley recalled that a typical day would begin with wake-up tea served at bedside by a servant. After breakfast, the car would call for her husband to go to work, and Mary Anne and Ruth would be free for the day to go swimming in an inlet of the Arabian Sea, to shop at the native bazaar, and to engage in some form of sports. Because of the heat, rigorous physical activity was limited to early morning or late afternoon. After lunch, the servants were off duty until the four o'clock tea. Dinner,

---

7. SPEAR, *supra* note 6, at 208; COLLINS & LAPIERRE, *supra* note 6, at 70.

8. Gandhi resisted until the last minute the partition of the country into Hindu and Muslim nations, but the Muslim leader who emerged in the 1930s, Muhammad Ali Jinnah, stirred the masses with a power almost equal to that of Gandhi. *See* SPEAR, *supra* note 6, at 230–43.

9. COLLINS & LAPIERRE, *supra* note 6 at 19.

10. *Smugglers Don't Faze Mary Anne Reimann*, THE ARIZONA DAILY STAR, February 9, 1958.

a formal meal for which one "dressed," would be served around nine at night. Although the Markleys ate curry about once a week, their cooks were British-trained and consequently the meals were primarily British cuisine.[11]

The sports that Mary Anne seemed to particularly enjoy included field hockey, squash, crew rowing, golf and riding. She tried her luck at trout fishing and even joined a few alligator hunts. She and the Markleys attended Arabian horse races frequently, and Mary Anne bought an Arabian horse called "Folly" from the British Army. She later recalled, "I thought I was getting a real bargain but later discovered the British sold him because they couldn't handle him. Folly handled me quite often. I was thrown several times."[12]

During Mary Anne's stay in India, she indisputably enjoyed the good life and confided to Ruth Markley that she especially appreciated not having to clean a bathtub.[13] As an unmarried, young, vivacious, and robustly attractive American girl (the first single American woman to live in Karachi, according to Ruth Markley) Mary Anne was the center of much attention and her social calendar was always full. The Americans and British routinely carried engagement books with them to make plans for an upcoming dinner party, a dance, a horse race, or a paper chase outing. Mary Anne's host, Bob Markley, reportedly remarked that he never saw her enter a club without a trail of Army officers behind her, engagement book in hand. Years later Mary Anne related that she had received her first flying instructions in India, most likely from an obliging member of the British Indian Army. One determined officer was so smitten with Mary Anne that he followed her back to Indiana when she returned to the United States and proposed marriage.[14]

Mary Anne made frequent side trips while in India, sometimes alone, and the modes of transportation were generally unreliable and short on comfort. Train, motor car, and horse and buggy were the means of land travel, and trips to points of interest within India would frequently take the traveler through temperatures in excess of 100 degrees. According to Mary Anne's correspondence to her parents, the train journeys were singularly unpleasant; dusty, hot, crowded, and always delayed. On one such trip, she wrote that "[t]he only way we managed to live was to buy a tub

---

11. Markley Interview, *supra* note 2.

12. *Smugglers Don't Faze Mary Anne Reimann*, THE ARIZONA DAILY STAR, February 9, 1958.

13. Markley Interview, *supra* note 2.

14. *Id.*

and fill it full of ice. Then we would play the fan on it and cool off a bit and too get some moisture in the room."[15]

Through organized group outings, Mary Anne saw many of India's landmarks and cultural attractions, and through solitary walks she explored the countryside and poor urban neighborhoods. According to her host, she "was not afraid of anything," and she seemed to relish exploring new places and meeting new people.[16] Mary Anne wrote her parents about the picturesque sight of native women in the fields carrying jars on their heads, their full skirts of bright colors and heavy Indian silver jewelry shimmering in the sun. She was impressed with the lavish marble palaces in Delhi and the visibly extravagant lives of the former kings, but she announced in letters home, and to friends years later, that it was in Agra in northern India that she saw what to her was the most beautiful sight of all.

The Taj Mahal, built in the seventeenth century by the Indian ruler Sha Jahan in memory of his favorite wife, is a monument of white marble resting on a platform of red sandstone, its distinctive central dome rising more than one hundred feet above ground. When Mary Anne visited the Taj Mahal, she was especially struck by the beauty of the surrounding gardens and long reflecting pool. She told friends in Shelbyville after the trip that the sheer loveliness and serenity of the monument made her think of her mother and it may have been there that she had a premonition about her mother's death. In a more spirited response to the monument, she reportedly returned to the gardens in the moonlight and swam in the reflecting pool on a dare.[17] Years later, she would point out on photographs the exact spot where she plunged into the water, bareskinned and exuberant.

A favorite side trip was to beautiful Kashmir. Kashmir, covering an area of about 85,000 square miles in the northwest of the Indian subcontinent, was at that time a princely state ruled by a Hindu maharajah; since partition, the picturesque region has been the object of an ongoing political and often bloody dispute between India and Pakistan. Nevertheless, with its stunning snow-capped peaks of the Himalayan Mountains, its green valleys, and a multitude of streams and lakes, Kashmir has long been a vacation mecca. Mary Anne "camped" with friends during May of 1936 in the Kashmir region and also spent several weeks during the summer of 1936 in a houseboat on Kashmir's Dal Lake in Srinagar. The camping experience involved tent-living in the mountains, but the ever-present Indian servants performed all menial tasks for the campers, and British formality required that the campers dress for dinner. The days were filled with hiking, riding,

---

15. Letter from Mary Anne to Emma and Wallace Reimann, April 16, 1936.

16. Markley Interview, *supra* note 2.

17. Interview with William K. Richey, Nutrioso, Arizona (July 16–17, 1992); Telephone Interviews with Richey (Sept. 20, 27, 1992, Sept 21, 1994).

trout fishing, golf, and the card game of bridge. Mary Anne would have preferred something different: "The camp we have is really grand—too grand in fact. I'd like to ruff it a bit more than we do but then, they always bring their servants out in camp. So we do practically nothing but lead the nice and easy life in the great outdoors."[18]

Mary Anne's letters from India reveal an emerging political awareness and social conscience, brought out most acutely by the stark poverty she observed. Although she clearly relished the luxurious life she was experiencing, she was also troubled by the misery in which the Indian masses lived. Her letters reveal the young woman's struggle to make sense of it all. Some passages clearly show her discomfort as a wealthy white person among the destitute Indians; in others, she applied her eighteen-year-old's logic and compassion to the abject poverty and political strife she was witnessing. In describing the conditions of the people of Kashmir, she wrote,

> The only thing that mars the beauty of this beautiful place is the terrible poverty of the people. Oh it's really awful. They have nothing. This part of India is not owned by the British. It has an emperor, and this big fat lumox taxes his people so that they have nothing. The filthy clothes they live in, they are just rags, sewn together.... They have children all the time and believe it or not they have three baths in a lifetime, one when born, one when married, and one after they die. They never wash. The little girls mat or braid their hair some way and it's never combed or washed until they are married. They beg and beg. Today I wandered around through the country and came across several of these families. I tried to talk with them a bit. However, they are scared of white people for they see so few. The little kids heads were just covered with sores, and they didn't even have enough clothes to cover their bodies. That's the state of millions and millions of these people. It's really pathetic and it will take hundreds of years to change it. They farm in the most primitive methods. The old wooden plow draw by oxen. Really about all these poor devils are are beasts of burden. They don't live, they exist, but they know nothing else and in their way I'm sure they have their happiness, thrills and sorrows just as we do. Although it's horrible, it's interesting to study them.... We come up here to camp, rough it a bit (though we sure don't much), yet we have comforts these people never heard or dreamed of. A funny world, isn't it. Oh there are so many whys one can ask. I guess we just mustn't or we wouldn't know where we were.[19]

Commenting on the British efforts to restrict the powers of the Indian royalty and to muffle religious dissonance, she wrote, presciently, "Some-

18. Letter from Mary Anne to Emma and Wallace Reimann, May 11, 1936.
19. Letter from Mary Anne to Emma and Wallace Reimann, May 11, 1936.

times when you think about it you think that its cruel for the British to step in and not let these people live as they want and have their courts and such. However, they would be fighting among themselves so much and the British do stop that to a certain extent. I sure think that Gandhi is going to have a hard time to get the people united. Their religions are too different and these people simply live their life by their religion. It will take several hundred years."[20]

Never one to enjoy pomposity, Mary Anne was critical of Karachi's new governor, appointed under the Government of India Act for the Sind province, but her criticism was naively expressed:

> They have a new governor here now....I personally think that he is going to be a menace to the community. My gosh if his car is going to drive down a road they line the thing with policemen. If he enters a place every body is supposed to stand up....It think its a lot of baloney. I can't see why he is any better than any one else. My American coming out in me. They do all of this for show and nothing else. If they have any kind of a party at government house which they are bound to do you have to go in [formal clothes] so gosh knows what I will appear in. Guess I'll have to stay home. Which I wouldn't mind for I should think the whole affair would be very stiff and formal which I don't like.[21]

Clearly, Mary Anne was not content to simply enjoy, without reflection, her privileged status in British India. She wandered among the native people and was profoundly affected by the deprivation she observed. The young woman from the tree-lined streets of Shelbyville seemed to be as awed by the searing poverty of the Indian people as by the towering beauty of the Himalayas and the grandeur of the Taj Mahal. She formed astute perceptions of the religious rivalry that plagues India even today, and she readily condemned the excesses of the native Indian royalty. Her assessments of the plight of the Indian people were characteristically pragmatic and down-to-earth. Moreover, although she was comfortable with persons of great wealth and prestige, she did not seem to envy their social or economic status. Visiting British India as she did, the guest of an American corporate executive in the waning years of Britain's colonialism, Mary Anne had a remarkable ability to see past the manicured golf courses and cricket fields to the other India, and she was profoundly moved by what she saw. Years later, as a federal trial court judge in Tucson, Arizona, she occasionally presided over naturalization ceremonies and would always give a heartfelt welcome to the new citizens, sometimes including people from India and Pakistan. Her memories of India's

---

20. Letter from Mary Anne to Emma and Wallace Reimann, April 16, 1936.
21. *Id.*

breathtaking scenery and equally breathtaking poverty would return with force during those ceremonies.

Mary Anne's emotional bond with her home, and particularly her mother, was a constant theme of her correspondence from India. The closing paragraph of one letter makes the point: "I love you oh so much. More than I could ever say in words. I miss you. I'll be happy oh so happy to be home again. It's all been wonderful, but it's quite true there's no place like home. I'm yours always. Peter." [22]

Similarly, Mary Anne's letters from this time period reveal an intense concern about the money that her trip was costing her parents. Her trip's financial impact on her family worried her, and her excursions throughout India apparently increased the ultimate cost substantially. Camping in Kashmir, for example, was expensive. "I'm afraid it's going to cost more than I had hoped or planned for and that worries me to know [sic] end. It wouldn't have to cost much to camp out like this but they have done it so grandly. I can't say anything about it because I rather stuck my nose in at the last minute. These people don't have any money worries, I'm afraid.... Oh, mother and daddy, I do want you to know that I appreciate all your [sic] doing for me. I realize all the hardships you're going through for my sake. I do feel such a pig, really, it worries me no end. I don't feel I deserve all this somehow. Someway I'll repay you—how exactly I don't know, but I will." [23]

As it happened, Mary Anne's planned three years in India were cut short. Her mother Emma, who suffered from high blood pressure, had been ill for some time, and letters from home reported on Emma's continuing health problems. Mary Anne later recounted that while she was in India she had a premonition that her mother was near death and decided to return to the United States as soon as possible. Ruth Markley, unaware of the premonition, remembered that Mary Anne agreed to accompany her back to the United States when Ruth discovered that she needed to return for medical reasons of her own. Despite the medical problem, Ruth was not in discomfort, and she and Mary Anne decided to make the most of the return trip. In order to see different parts of the world, they chose to return by way of the Far East.

In late summer of 1936, Ruth and Mary Anne traveled by ship to Bombay. There they boarded an Italian oceanliner, the "Victoria," and in luxurious accommodations they traveled to Japan. Ruth recalls that they spent several days in different Japanese ports, including Kobe and Yokohama, and also made short train excursions into the interior. After a

---

22. Letter from Mary Anne to Emma and Wallace Reimann, May 11, 1936.
23. Letter from Mary Anne to Emma and Wallace Reimann, May 11, 1936.

smooth trip across the Pacific to San Francisco, the pair traveled by train to the Midwest. Ruth's destination was Chicago, Illinois, where she was scheduled for surgery, and Mary Anne's destination was Shelbyville. Although the two said goodbye in Chicago, Mary Anne remained in close contact with Ruth Markley, who in later life settled in California.[24]

When Mary Anne, then eighteen, returned to Shelbyville in the fall of 1936, Emma Reimann's health was on a path of steady deterioration. Emma's vibrant energy and ready laugh were gone, and her countless volunteer activities had been severely curtailed; she was fatigued and plagued by circulatory problems. At that time, Mary Anne's brother Bill, his new wife Marjorie Angel, and their infant daughter Ann had moved temporarily to Buffalo, New York, where Bill worked as a salesman for the Indiana-based Kennedy Car Liner Company. Immediately before their move, the young family had lived for a short while with Emma and Wallace in the Nading home. Emma was fond of Marjorie and doted on her little granddaughter; when the trio left for New York, Emma missed them deeply. Her younger son Chuck, by then a midshipman, sent frequent letters home from Annapolis, but visits were rare. Although Emma must have taken great pride in Chuck's accomplishments, she felt very alone in her suffering before Mary Anne's arrival.

Mary Anne, relieved that she had returned in time to help her mother, moved back into the Nading home. For the succeeding few months, Mary Anne remained in Shelbyville, working part-time at a local bookstore and providing companionship to her ailing mother. The transition from the lavish lifestyle in Karachi to the somber scene in Shelbyville must have been difficult for Mary Anne, and correspondence from Emma during that period reveals concern for Mary Anne's future. In a letter to her son Bill, Emma noted that Mary Anne had been working at a bookstore and that she was seeking other employment. Reflecting the attitudes of that era, Emma wrote, "Pete went to ask [a local business] about a job. I think she could have had one if she knew short-hand. She was turned down about four times for that reason. I think she will have to learn it." In the same letter, Emma explained that her failing health had forced her to give up her work, the making of children's clothes, and she added, with some resignation, "I don't think Pete warms up to it much. She may though."[25] Thus, the mother believed her headstrong daughter should learn short-hand to enhance her employability, and she recognized that Mary Anne

---

24. Markley Interview, *supra* note 2.

25. Letter from Emma Reimann to Bill Reimann, January 1937. The letter, though undated, can be reliably placed within January 1937 because of its reference to the famous flood on the Ohio River. *See* JAMES H. MADISON, INDIANA THROUGH TRADITION AND CHANGE 326 (1982).

was not inclined to find fulfillment in the creation of fine children's clothes or other traditional female occupations.

A few weeks after that correspondence, on February 26, 1937, in the early morning, Emma died. Her obituary recorded that for eight months Emma had suffered from debilitating high blood pressure, followed by uremic poisoning. She was fifty-three years old, and Mary Anne was just nineteen. The obituary sheds light on Emma's legacy in the community:

> The death of Mrs. Reimann removes one of the best loved and most active women in the civic affairs of Shelbyville. She was always interested in anything pertaining to the good of her community. Active in church, social and club affairs, her time and advice was always at the command of those who needed her. She has left an indelible impress on the life of the entire community."[26]

In accordance with the tradition of the time, the Reimanns hosted a visitation for family and friends at their home immediately following Emma's death. The group of women who called themselves "The Emma Reimann Sunday School Class" visited the Reimann home on the evening of Emma's death, when "she lay a corpse." One account of that visitation reveals Mary Anne's sense of obligation to her mother's memory. "While we were there the night before the funeral, Mary Anne stood at the foot of her bed and said her mother had left her with such high hopes and high ideals for her. She said it was such a big place for her to fill."[27] Later, when Emma's body was removed from the Reimann home, Mary Anne became hysterical and had to be physically restrained from interfering with the grim task of the pall bearers, all the while shouting, "Don't take my mother away."[28] At the funeral, Mary Anne was again open with her grief. "I'll never forget Mary Anne at her mother's funeral," one person in attendance recalled years later. "She knelt on the ground and sobbed so hard and then said, "I've lost my best friend."[29]

The image of the distraught girl, raging against an event over which she had no control, is suggestive of a facet of Mary Anne's psychological drive. Her mother's loss, combined five years later with the death of her brother Chuck, seemed to leave her with an abiding need to control events, circumstances, and people of importance to her. Her most bitter disappointments in life would be variations on the central theme of loss of

26. *Beloved Woman Succumbs Today*, SHELBYVILLE DEMOCRAT, February 26, 1937.

27. *Biography of Emma Reimann*, by Cecille Schoelch, written for Fiftieth Anniversary Celebration of Emma Reimann Class, May 14, 1976.

28. Interview with Martha Bowers, Shelbyville, Indiana (Oct. 10, 1992).

29. *Memories of Emma Reimann*, by Margaret Hatmaker, written for Fiftieth Anniversary of Emma Reimann Sunday School Class, May 14, 1976.

control. Conversely, her grandest successes would be instances in which she was in command, ostensibly shaping outcomes—sitting astride a 1,000-pound horse, holding the throttle in the cockpit of a military plane, or pounding the gavel in the courtroom.

Mary Anne's sense of loss from her mother's death remained just beneath the surface throughout her life. In 1976, on the fiftieth anniversary celebration of a Sunday school class that Emma Reimann had founded, Mary Anne sent a letter to the surviving members of the class. She wrote: "It is hard for me to believe that Mother was younger than I am when she died. At that age she had given more of herself to her family and friends than one who lives a complete life. I have been fortunate to accomplish several things that have received Public Recognition. Truthfully, these accomplishments are infinitesimal to the every day accomplishments of Mother in her love of people and life. Her many acts of help and kindness were never known other than by the individuals who were directly affected. I am sure that everyone of you who knew her can remember her words of encouragement which made an unpleasant task or situation easier. Too one cannot forget her delightful sense of humor.... Certainly your honoring her after 50 years is an indication of your dedication and the strength of Mother's character."[30]

The letter, written while Mary Anne was awaiting the confirmation hearing before the Senate Judiciary Committee on her nomination to the United States District Court, reveals the great admiration she had for her mother. The selflessness for which Emma Reimann was famous, as well as Emma's sense of humor and enthusiasm for life, apparently inspired Mary Anne. In her letter, Mary Anne characteristically diminished her own accomplishments when juxtaposed with the altruism of her mother. In reality, Emma's gentle example may have tempered the ambition and competitiveness that seemed to come so naturally to Mary Anne.

Following her mother's death, Mary Anne remained at home to help her father attend to the myriad mundane and painful details that arise when a life ends. Emma, who died without a will, had accumulated few assets in her estate. Probate documents showed that her estate, consisting primarily of a hospital savings bond, was worth only about $600 after expenses, and that amount was to be divided between Wallace Reimann and the three children. By the time of Emma's death, the once-successful Nading Mill and Grain Company had ceased operations, and her estate contained no shares of stock in the family company that her father had founded.[31]

---

30. Letter of June 6, 1976, from Mary Anne Richey to Emma Reimann Sunday School Class.

The task of disposing of Emma's personal property fell primarily upon Mary Anne's shoulders, and she held an estate sale at the Nading home that drew a large crowd. Mary Anne tended to safeguard items that had an emotional value to her, and to dispose of things, even things of significant monetary worth, that carried no such emotional weight. She sold her mother's piano, for example, and, according to at least one account, used the money on flying lessons.[32] On the other hand, she kept for almost forty years the worn black notebooks that contained her mother's music sheets. Never having developed a knowledge of, or longing for, household luxury items, Mary Anne faced some difficulty in deciding which items should remain in the family and which should be sold or given away. She almost gave away a set of fine china, for instance, but called her friend Martha Mull at the last minute to get a second opinion. Martha said in no uncertain terms, "You can't get rid of that. It's Poge!" Although the name meant nothing to Mary Anne, she acquiesced and kept the dishes.[33]

Mary Anne, aware that she faced a bleak future without further education, once again pondered her delayed college career. Wallace Reimann had moved out of the Nading home shortly after Emma's death but remained in Shelbyville for the rest of his working years. He continued in the employ of Republic Coal and Coke Company, earning a modest salary and commissions as a salesman. Continuing to reside with her father during those months, Mary Anne harbored resentment toward Wallace for having squandered, as she saw it, the family funds on contributions to the athletic program at Purdue University. Nevertheless, yielding to an offer from Wallace to help finance her attendance at Purdue, Mary Anne decided to enroll as a freshman in September of 1937. She paid for tuition and expenses through contributions from her father and her own earnings at a part-time job at the campus bookstore.[34]

Purdue University, located in West Lafayette northwest of Indianapolis, is a land-grant institution founded in 1869. The 1930s campus, replete with dignified, ivy-covered stone and brick buildings and tree-lined walkways, extended over 150 acres. Although Purdue had admitted women since 1875, the student population was still predominately male. Of the 6,800 students enrolled in Mary Anne's era, about one-fifth were women. Purdue's curricular emphasis was in the sciences—it offered no liberal arts degree—and engineering was the focus. The eight colleges at Purdue were

---

31. Information about Emma Reimann's estate is taken from the Final Report of Inventory, *In re Estate of Emma B. Nading Reimann, Deceased* (Shelby County Circuit Court).

32. Richey Interviews, *supra* note 17.

33. Gutting Interview, *supra* note 1.

34. Interview with William Showers, Shelbyville, Indiana (Oct. 10, 1992).

Civil, Mechanical, Electrical, and Chemical Engineering, Agriculture, Science, Pharmacy, and Home Economics. [35] According to the 1939 Purdue yearbook, "As the School of Engineering is primarily a men's school and the School of Home Economics is primarily a women's school, the School of Science might be called the 'melting pot' of Purdue, for there are an equal number of women and men enrolled."[36]

Predictably, Mary Anne chose Science as her major when she entered Purdue, perhaps in part because of her abiding love for animals. As an adult, she occasionally remarked that she had at one time wanted to become a veterinarian. Mary Anne's two-year hiatus from school, combined with the strain of losing her mother, clearly took its toll on her intellectual focus. Her entrance scores on a standardized math test placed her in the twelfth percentile, and she scored only at the fiftieth percentile on a standardized English test.[37] Nevertheless, through characteristic self-discipline, she managed to earn high grades in what was known as a demanding curriculum. In her two years at the school, she earned "high honor" in government, history, and physical education, and her lowest grades—"Passed, with bare minimum objectives"—were in mathematics and German.[38]

In her freshman year, Mary Anne pledged Kappa Kappa Gamma, and for two years threw herself into her school work, sports, and sorority activities, probably in that order. Her sorority sisters regarded her as extroverted, fun-loving, pragmatic, unpretentious, and possessed of a keen sense of humor. "She didn't put on any airs whatsoever. And, she had no use for those who did," one remarked.[39] She was remembered as strong-minded: "She seemed more 'formed' than many of us at that time. She knew what she liked and didn't like, and her tastes were sophisticated."[40] From all appearances, Mary Anne was happy at Kappa Kappa Gamma and at Purdue.

During her second year at Purdue, Mary Anne resided in the Kappa house, an attractive three-story stone building on the main campus. The lifestyle of the Kappa house may have been constraining for her, since she had only recently been wandering with relative freedom in the distant Himalayas. The rules of the house, enforced by the everpresent house-

---

35. 1939 PURDUE UNIVERSITY YEARBOOK 53–54 ("Debris").
36. 1939 PURDUE UNIVERSITY YEARBOOK 142 ("Debris).
37. Academic Records of Mary Anne Reimann, Purdue University, provided by Office of the Registrar, July 7, 1993.
38. Id.
39. Telephone Interview with Manette Hollingsworth Speas (May 15, 1993).
40. Telephone Interview with Mary Jane Carr Catlin (May 17, 1993)

mother, included curfews of eleven o'clock weekdays and one o'clock on weekends. The sorority members were expected to dress for lunch and dinner, with a somewhat more formal dinner every Friday night; if a girl were not suitably dressed, the housemother would see that she be served separately in the kitchen. Kappa sponsored two formal dances each year, one in the fall and one in the spring, at which floor-length gowns were de rigour.[41] Given Mary Anne's discomfort in the aristocratic lifestyle in India, the decorum and protocol of the sorority life at Purdue could not have appealed to her. Moreover, she was older by two years than the other members of her pledge class, a fact which few of them knew.[42] The age difference may have contributed to Mary Anne's unease, a sense of not quite belonging.

The major outlet for Mary Anne at Purdue was, characteristically, athletics. She joined the Women's Athletic Association, a group organized in 1922 for the quaintly-described purposes of "[a]ffording every Purdue girl the opportunity to keep herself physically fit and furnishing hearty and wholesome recreation."[43] The Triton Club, a swimming club begun only one year before Mary Anne entered Purdue, accepted her into membership after she performed the necessary tests for initiation. Finally, she joined the Riding Club, an organization formed in the fall of 1937, and through it was able to pursue her love of horses.[44] In the spring of her second year, she participated in the "Gymkhana," a riding show that included exhibition riding, drilling, and games on horseback. The name "Gymkhana" echoed the name of the sports clubs, so familiar to Mary Anne, that the British had brought to colonial India.[45]

Although Mary Anne did not seriously pursue flying while at Purdue, the adventure and glamour of aviation was well-known on campus. In 1935, Amelia Earhart joined the staff of Purdue as Consultant on Careers for Women and promulgated her creed that "women should step into their rightful place in the world." In the spring of 1937, just before Mary Anne enrolled in the university, the forty-year-old Earhart planned her last flight, an attempt to circle the globe and test her "Flying Laboratory." Mary Anne learned later that Earhart and her navigator Fred Noonan had communicated with Bob and Ruth Markley in India in the course of that last mission and that the Markleys, presciently, had been concerned about Earhart's safety.[46] Earhart's flight lost all radio contact near How-

---

41. *Id.*
42. Telephone Interview with Caryl Hamman (Oct. 23, 1992).
43. 1939 PURDUE UNIVERSITY YEARBOOK 267 ("Debris).
44. *Id.* at 267, 269, 317.
45. Hamman Interview, *supra* note 42.

land Island in the central Pacific Ocean, on July 2, 1937.[47] Amelia
Earhart's presumed death tragically cut short her life but enhanced the
legend that already surrounded her name. Even though Earhart was not
physically present at Purdue when Mary Anne arrived, the vivid memory
of her courage and her proud achievements for women remained palpable
at the school. The 1938 yearbook carried a moving tribute to the "gallant
lady whose sole motivating purpose in life centered about furthering
womanhood's accomplishments."[48]

The lopsided ratio of men to women on the Purdue campus meant that
few female students were without male escorts if they desired one. According to sorority sisters, Mary Anne dated frequently but did not reveal
special attachments to anyone. Bill Showers, then a student at Purdue's
archrival, Indiana University, came to date Mary Anne occasionally, and
his appearances may have become more frequent during Mary Anne's second year. Although Mary Anne and Bill shared relatively few interests,
they did both enjoy horse-racing. In the spring of 1939, Mary Anne and
Bill traveled with another couple to Churchill Downs for the Kentucky
Derby. Mary Anne and a companion drove down from West Fayetteville
to Bloomington to pick up Bill, and then on to Louisville, Kentucky. They
had to drive all night to reach Louisville, and then, lacking enough money
for general admission tickets, they surreptitiously climbed under various
fences to get into the stands. Although their "bribes" to several young
boys guarding the fences almost equalled the cost of four admissions,
their sense of adventure was exquisite.[49]

Mary Anne's willfulness and occasionally headstrong determination
were known to her close friends, if not to her sorority sisters. One friend
recalled an evening when she returned from Indianapolis to Shelbyville
with Mary Anne. Mary Anne was driving the family car on Highway 421,
the old route between Indianapolis and Shelbyville. Unexpectedly, a thick
fog descended on the dark highway. "The fog was so dense," the friend
remembered, "that you couldn't see five feet in front of the headlights. I
was absolutely petrified." Mary Anne drove, however, as if there were no
fog, seemingly without fear. Maintaining what seemed to be a reckless
speed, Mary Anne unflinchingly navigated the car through the black mist.
When the friend exclaimed at the time, "Pete, we're lucky we are alive,"
Mary Anne replied, "Oh, there isn't anything to worry about. There's no
point in pulling off and getting hit by someone. It's best to just keep moving."[50] Speeding through the fogged-in night, Mary Anne seemed to enjoy

---

46. Markley Interview, *supra* note 2.

47. SUSAN WARE, STILL MISSING 220–221 (1993).

48. 1938 PURDUE UNIVERSITY YEARBOOK 321 ("Debris).

49. Showers Interview, *supra* note 34.

the challenge of the elements notwithstanding the potential danger to herself and her passenger. The experience revealed aspects of Mary Anne's character that were often in tension and would surface in other contexts in her later life: calm nerves and cold logic in the face of danger, on the one hand, and, on the other, a propensity for risk-taking, for confronting the unknown for the sheer pleasure of it.

In spite of Mary Anne's outward signs of contentment, a close friend from that era believed she was frequently depressed. Rufina Sexton, her roommate in the 1938–39 academic year, recalled, "She wasn't frivolous, but she didn't know what direction she wanted to take. . . . Really, the only careers open to women then were teaching and nursing. She never mentioned law."[51] Lacking in focus, Mary Anne also constantly worried about money.

In April 1939, during Mary Anne's second year at Purdue, Wallace Reimann married a longtime family friend, Bess Jones, a widow and successful businesswoman. Wallace, following a pattern established with Emma, moved into the Jones residence after the marriage. Later that spring, the couple drove up to West Fayetteville to take Mary Anne to dinner. Although Mary Anne did not dislike Bess personally, she resented the marriage and was not pleased about the visit. She "begged" her roommate Rufina to go with them, and angrily protested her familial obligation to treat her father and his new wife with civility. Rufina finally did agree to accompany Mary Anne. Rufina's perception was that Mary Anne felt neither affection nor much respect toward her father. Rufina surmised that Mary Anne's unhappiness regarding her father's marriage and her emotional discomfort in the new residence of Wallace and Bess Reimann propelled the headstrong young woman toward a marriage of her own.[52]

In the summer of 1939, as the grim reality of a new war in Europe seemed more imminent with each passing day, Bill Showers asked Mary Anne to marry him. Mary Anne, at that point, had no true home. Her connections with the Kappa Kappa Gamma house were ephemeral, at best. Although she became close friends with a few of the Kappa members, for the most part her sorority sisters knew her only superficially. In any event, because of money problems, Mary Anne's father was unlikely to be able to continue supporting his daughter at Purdue University. Mary Anne's brothers, moreover, were engrossed in their own lives. Bill had returned to Shelbyville with his wife Marge and growing young family, and was hard at work in the KCL Corporation. Chuck, having graduated from the Naval Academy in 1938, was serving on the U.S.S. Hughes in

---

50. Telephone Interview with Natalie Banowitz (Oct. 13, 1992).
51. Telephone Interview with Rufina Sexton Burton (Feb. 11, 1993).
52. *Id.*

the Atlantic fleet. If Mary Anne's brothers offered no feasible refuge for her, she vehemently resisted the alternative of living indefinitely in Shelbyville with Wallace Reimann and his new wife.

Surely exacerbating her sense of disconnection, Mary Anne's closest friends from high school, Merrylin Greenlee and Martha Mull, had graduated in May 1939 from Smith College and Indiana University, respectively. They each found work, albeit work for which they were overqualified. Mary Anne, with only two years of college, had less marketability and little ambition. No counselor urged her to stay in school to pursue training for a particular career. Under the circumstances, an offer of marriage from young Bill Showers seemed to provide Mary Anne with what she lacked: a home where she belonged, a sense of direction, and financial security.

CHAPTER THREE

Tragedy and Triumph

Bill Showers had completed three and one-half years at Indiana University by the summer of 1939. In the wake of the Depression, however, he decided to forego graduation and join his two brothers and father in Shelbyville to help manage the family company, Indiana Cash Drawers. Mary Anne, feeling the press of a money shortage as well, chose likewise to withdraw from Purdue and return to Shelbyville to marry Showers. A sorority sister recalled that Mary Anne did not tell the sorority of her plans in advance. "We were all surprised when we realized Pete was not coming back in the fall and that she was getting married. We didn't know that she was two years older than the rest of us. She was a little different, I guess, and chose a different path."[1]

Although Mary Anne had known Bill Showers for many years and had dated him in high school, their plans to marry apparently did not formalize until the summer of 1939. Mary Anne decided to marry Showers rather impulsively, as her close friends saw it, and they worried about their beloved Pete. Martha Mull and Merrylin Greenlee believed Mary Anne's decision to marry was ill-considered. In their view, Bill and Mary Anne, sharing few interests and possessing very different personal styles, were fundamentally incompatible. Although the young women did not discuss those concerns explicitly at the time, both Martha and Merrylin perceived that Mary Anne was not truly happy about her impending marriage.[2] According to sorority sister Rufina Sexton, "Pete married Bill because he wanted her to, and everybody expected her to, and there was no place else that she felt she could or wanted to go."[3] As it happened, the friends' misgivings were well-founded.

The wedding took place on September 7, 1939, during a time of ominous international upheaval. Martha Mull recalled that she, Merrylin Greenlee, and Mary Anne were sitting in Shelbyville on September 3, 1939, just days before the wedding, when a news flash came over the radio announcing that Hitler had invaded Poland and that Britain and France had declared war on Germany. The young women listened quietly

---

1. Telephone Interview with Caryl Hamman (Dec. 23, 1992).
2. Telephone Interview with Martha (Mull) Gutting (Jan. 25, 1993); Telephone Interview with Merrylin (Greenlee) Crosby (April 25, 1993).
3. Telephone Interview with Rufina Sexton Burton (Feb. 11, 1993).

to the broadcasts, sombered by the knowledge that war had returned to Europe. The three friends, however, talked little of the war after that day.[4]

Mary Anne's wedding ceremony was a lavish celebration, replete with bridesmaids and strolling musicians, and the details of the event were recounted by the local press. Revealing the high stature of the Showers family, if not the Reimanns, the newspaper declared in a headline, "Prominent Couple Married in Impressive Ceremony."[5] Mary Anne and Bill left for a honeymoon in the Smokey Mountains of Tennessee after the event.[6]

Mary Anne's marriage to Bill Showers lasted ten years, but during much of that period, the couple lived apart. In the first four years, however, they lived under the same roof and enjoyed the good life, enjoying the many privileges available to the wealthy Showers sons. In that post-Prohibition, post-Depression era, Indiana and the rest of the country, fueled by wartime production, enjoyed a sense of economic well-being. Mary Anne and her new husband maintained a busy social life; they moved among the country club set in Shelbyville and treated their wide circle of friends to gay parties at which alcohol flowed freely. The Showers family owned several country cottages outside of Shelbyville, located among wooded hills and flowing creeks, and they were the site of many weekend retreats. Although Bill had little interest in riding, Mary Anne often rode the horses belonging to the Showers family, to the delight of the elder Showers. Bill did enjoy attending horse races, however, and the couple drove to Churchill Downs for several Kentucky Derbys. Indeed, in 1941, they were so taken with the Triple-Crown win of a horse named "Whirlaway" that they gave a favorite cocker spaniel puppy the same name. Mary Anne and Bill frequently vacationed in Florida for weeks at a time. They also visited Cuba, enjoying the balmy and gracious resorts of that pre-revolutionary Caribbean island.[7]

Through the Showers family, Mary Anne became acquainted with the successful business-machine magnate R.C. Allen, and she came to be close friends with Marge Allen, R.C. Allen's wife. Mary Anne and Bill made annual sojourns to the Allen's summer estate on Lake Michigan, enjoying excursions on the Allen's yacht and often attending the famous yacht races between Chicago and Mackinac Island, held each July. Marge Allen would remain within Mary Anne's intimate circle of friends well beyond the termination of her marriage to Showers and would have a direct role in Mary Anne's future life in Arizona. Other friends from that period were lawyer Wilbur Pell, a Shelbyville native, and his wife Mary Lane Chase. Like Mary

---

4. Gutting Interview, *supra* note 2.

5. SHELBYVILLE DEMOCRAT, September 8, 1939.

6. Interview with William Showers, Shelbyville, Indiana (Oct. 10, 1992).

7. *Id.*

Anne, Pell would eventually join the federal judiciary; in 1970, the Harvard law graduate was appointed to the United States Court of Appeals for the Seventh Circuit by President Richard Nixon. Mary Anne also remained close to her high school friends, Martha Mull and Merrylin Greenlee, and appeared in their weddings, held, respectively, in 1940 and 1941.[8] To their many acquaintances, Mary Anne and Bill were an attractive and dynamic couple who moved in the higher echelons of Shelbyville society.

Mary Anne's ostensibly idyllic married life, however, was tinged with unhappiness. The highly intelligent and energetic young woman worked only sporadically during that period and must have sensed that she was capable of greater accomplishment than what was immediately available to her as a married woman who lacked a college degree. For a time she worked for the Public Service Corporation in Shelbyville demonstrating stoves, a task that her friend Martha Mull found comically ironic in light of Pete's distinct disinterest in things domestic.[9] She also worked as a reporter for the Shelbyville Republican, covering court trials for several months. She later recounted that the experience as a reporter first sparked her interest in the law.[10] She did not take any steps, however, toward establishing a career, in law or otherwise.

Mary Anne's behavior, for a brief while, was consistent with the cultural norm. In that post-Depression era, before the United States joined World War II, only about fifteen percent of married women in the nation were gainfully employed,[11] and vocal opposition in the country had formed against working wives, mainly for fear that the working wife would take jobs from men and that her absence from the home would disrupt family stability.[12] A section of the federal Economy Act of 1932 had stipulated that whenever reductions in force took place in the executive branch, married persons were to be the first discharged if their spouse was also a government employee, and the legislative history revealed that the target of the provision was the working wife.[13] Although the measure

---

8. Gutting Interview, *supra* note 2.

9. *Id.*

10. *Judge Richey, ex-city woman, eyes high court*, THE SHELBYVILLE NEWS, June 25, 1976.

11. LOIS SCHARF, TO WORK AND TO WED — FEMALE EMPLOYMENT, FEMINISM, AND THE GREAT DEPRESSION 150 (1980).

12. *Id.* at 143–47; BARBARA J. HARRIS, BEYOND HER SPHERE — WOMEN AND THE PROFESSIONS IN AMERICAN HISTORY 142 (1978).

13. *See* Section 213 of the Economy Act of 1932, 47 Stat. 382, ch. 314, June 30, 1932. The debates in Congress revealed that proponents of the measure desired to curtail the employment of married women. *See* 75 CONG. REC. 9062, 9514–20 (1932), described in SCHARF, *supra* note 11, at 47–48.

was repealed in 1937,[14] the attitudes underlying it persisted. Similarly, a few states passed legislation restricting the employment of married women, and whole cities went on crusades to fire them.[15] Interestingly, when married women did work, they tended to justify their employment on the basis of economic necessity rather than personal satisfaction. A *Ladies Home Journal* editorial from 1941 echoed that sentiment: in defending the existing numbers of working wives, the story proclaimed that "no selfish desire for a career prompts [them] to work, simply the pressure of financial need."[16]

Clearly, Mary Anne's primary identity as wife of the wealthy Showers, while compatible with prevailing social attitudes, became less and less satisfying as time went on. She did not easily assume the domestic responsibilities of a housewife. After she grew impatient with her husband's habit of leaving his dirty clothes on the floor, for example, she simply threw the things into the garbage.[17] Also, Bill's domineering family demanded greater accommodation from Mary Anne than the independent young woman was accustomed to giving. When Rufina Sexton visited Mary Anne and Bill once in 1942, she found, to her dismay, that the normally robust Mary Anne was flat on her back in bed with a respiratory ailment, diagnosed at the time as tuberculosis. According to Rufina, the extended Showers family constantly filled the small home where Bill and Mary Anne lived and seemed to be smothering Mary Anne with their ministrations.[18] In addition, Ralph Showers and his sons were heavy drinkers, and Mary Anne's friends began to see the effects in Bill of the excesses so common to that post-Prohibition era.[19]

As a constant dark storm beyond the scenes of Mary Anne's day-to-day life, World War II rumbled forward in Europe. The draft was reinstituted and registration began in October 1940, and the National Guard was mobilized. Shortages on various items began to appear in the Shelbyville stores. Although most people expected that the United States would eventually be drawn into the conflict, the Japanese attack on Pearl Harbor sent shock waves through the nation. Bill Showers and Mary Anne heard the news along with the rest of the country, on a Sunday afternoon, December 7, 1941. They could not have known then that the war would directly touch their lives in irrevocable ways.

---

14. *See* 81 CONG. REC. 6925–28 (1937), described in SCHARF, *supra* note 11, at 50.
15. HARRIS, *supra* note 12, at 142.
16. *Should Wives Work?* LADIES HOME JOURNAL 58 (January 1941).
17. Telephone Interview with Kerry Bjorn (Feb. 13, 1996).
18. Burton Interview *supra* note 3.
19. Interview with Norman Thurston, Tucson, Arizona (Feb. 1, 1993).

Immediately, the Shelbyville community swung into wartime activities, including blood drives, collections for relief efforts, and war bond promotions. Goods shortages were dramatic. In early 1942, a quota was placed on tire purchases; new cars became unobtainable; and sugar purchases were limited immediately. The rationing list grew to include such things as gasoline, rubber footwear, fuel oil, coffee, canned goods, and meat. Because of the proximity of nearby Camp Atterbury, Shelbyville citizens became accustomed to the sight of soldiers. Eventually, Italian prisoners of war held at Atterbury would be put to work on local farms.[20]

Three months after the bombing at Pearl Harbor and the entry of the United States into World War II, the grim reports of wartime casualties contained news of a personal tragedy for Mary Anne, her family, and the people of Shelbyville—the death of her brother, Charles Reimann, Jr. The dashing Chuck had graduated from the United States Naval Academy in 1938 and, after three years of service on surface vessels, had gone into naval air training at Pensacola, Florida. While in Florida, he had married a young bride in a handsome, full-regalia military wedding. After earning his wings, Chuck was assigned to a patrol squadron in the Pacific. On March 8, 1942, at Tongue Point, Oregon, Reimann, then twenty-seven years old and married less than a year, was killed when his amphibious aircraft, a Catalina bomber, crashed in an attempted nighttime take-off. Apparently, the huge craft, under Reimann's command, had collided with logs submerged in the roiling Columbia River at the point of lift-off and had pitched into the waters. Seven other enlisted men died in the same crash. Only the navigator, who was thrown clear, survived.[21]

The news of Chuck's death arrived in Shelbyville the next morning, a Sunday. Mary Anne was attending services at the First Presbyterian Church at the time, and Bill Showers, who was not a church-goer, was at home when the call came. He went immediately to the church to inform Mary Anne. "She knew something was very wrong when I pulled her out of the services," he recalled. "It was a very hard message to deliver. Chuck was so admired."[22] Mary Anne was shocked and profoundly saddened at the news, and for a while she, her father, and her brother Bill were united in their grief.

Chuck's body was not recovered for over a week. In the interim, simultaneous "Lost-at-Sea" funeral services were held at the Tongue Point

---

20. Marian McFadden, Biography of a Town—Shelbyville, Indiana 1822–1962, at 312–14 (1968).

21. *Charles Reimann is Fifth Victim of World War II*, Shelbyville Democrat, March 9, 1942; *Reimann's Body Found in Oregon*, Shelbyville Democrat, March 18, 1942.

22. Showers Interview, *supra* note 6.

Naval Air Station and at the Reimann family home in Shelbyville. No eulogy or sermon was given; rather, the brief ceremony was built around a few poems that Chuck had especially liked during his high school and naval academy days.[23] His widow and her parents were in attendance. Ten days later his body was found near Astoria, Oregon, a few miles from the Tongue Point Naval Air Station.[24]

Chuck Reimann's death was the fifth fatality of World War II for Shelby County, and his loss had an impact not only on the Reimann family but on the entire community. News articles announcing his death described in glowing terms his athletic and academic accomplishments in high school and at the naval academy. A letter published in the local newspaper praised him as a man of "rare courage," a "sportsman of the highest plane" who thrived on competition.[25] Coming only five years after Emma Reimann's death, the loss of her beloved older brother left a void in Mary Anne's life. Although Chuck had departed Shelbyville almost nine years earlier, his frequent letters had kept the Reimann family very much apprised of his life as a midshipman and then as a Navy pilot. Only gradually did Mary Anne grasp the realization that Chuck, the handsome football hero, the straight-A student, the heroic Navy flier, the gentle older brother, her would-be copilot on their trip to the moon, was truly gone. Mary Pell, whose own brother had died some years earlier, was a source of empathy and emotional support, and the two engaged in long conversations about life and death and loss.[26]

When Bill Showers and Mary Anne were still reeling from Chuck Reimann's death, Bill received his inevitable draft notice and chose to join the United States Navy. In 1943, after his initial training, Mary Anne and Bill moved to Chicago, Illinois, where Bill was assigned to the Great Lakes Naval Station. Although he expected the Navy to eventually send him overseas, the war ended before that need arose, and his full military service consequently took place within the United States. During his brief military career, Bill traveled to various bases around the country to teach typing and other office skills. Although he served honorably in the capacity the Navy directed, his modest record contrasted sharply with the legendary heroism of Charles Reimann.

---

23. *Chuck's Favorite Poems Are Read As Family Holds Memorial Rites for Pilot,* SHELBYVILLE DEMOCRAT, March 15, 1942.

24. *Reimann's Body Found in Oregon,* SHELBYVILLE DEMOCRAT, March 18, 1992.

25. *Fellow-Athlete Pens Words of Praise for Character of Lieut. Charles J. Reimann,* SHELBYVILLE DEMOCRAT, March 19, 1942.

26. Telephone Interview with Hon. Wilbur F. Pell, Jr., Judge, United States Court of Appeals, and Mary Lane Pell (April 8, 1993).

With the entry of the United States into World War II and the concomitant departure of so many of the nation's men, women became vital to the nation's economic health. As women were actively recruited by industry and encouraged by government to regard jobs as patriotic obligations, previously existing gender barriers seemed to disappear overnight. The number of women in the labor force increased dramatically as women, married and single, went to work in record numbers in factories, ordnance plants, and government offices. As a result of the war, six and one-half million more women were employed, and the proportion of adult women in the labor force increased from 27.4 percent in 1940 to 35 percent in 1944.[27] The percentage of working married women rose from 15 percent in 1940 to over 24 percent by 1945.[28] In the spirit of the new egalitarianism, some states dropped bans against women jurors, and women's baseball teams began to play in the minor leagues.

Initially, Mary Anne worked part-time at sundry jobs while living in Chicago. Showers recalled that Mary Anne was employed at a brokerage house, while another friend remembered her working in a munitions factory. Mary Anne, however, never recorded her Chicago employment in any of her biographical materials, and it is clear that the work experience, whatever its nature, did not figure prominently in her memories. Mary Anne's time in Chicago derives importance not from her work but from her decision to make some personal contribution toward the war effort in memory of her brother Chuck. As it happened, her contribution was characteristically daring and a surprise to her friends. In the winter of 1943, Mary Anne decided to join the Women Airforce Service Pilots (WASP), a civilian program affiliated with the United States Army Airforce. To Mary Anne, the WASP offered grand adventure, the means for her to make a concrete contribution to the war effort, and a respite from a constraining marriage. That adventure appealed to the young woman from Shelbyville who loved to fly planes, and thus, at the age of twenty-six, Mary Anne began the application process. Just prior to Mary Anne's entry into the WASP, Rufina Sexton visited her in Chicago, and she was struck by how well and happy she appeared. "She looked gorgeous," Rufina said, "and was so very excited about the WASP. She wore a black coat with a mink collar, and it was open at the neck. I thought, "what is she doing, in the dead of winter in Chicago with her neck exposed and she just had T.B.!"

* * *

27. UNITED STATES BUREAU OF THE CENSUS, HISTORICAL STATISTICS OF THE UNITED STATES, COLONIAL TIMES TO 1970, pt. 1 (1975).

28. SCHARF, *supra* note 11, at 159.

The WASP evolved, in large part, from the efforts of the indomitable Jacqueline Cochran, one of the United States' most famous and aggressive women pilots. In 1937 Cochran won the women's division of the Bendix Air Race, broke Howard Hughes's transcontinental speed record, and was awarded the Harmon International trophy as the outstanding woman aviator in the world, presented to her by First Lady Eleanor Roosevelt.[29] Two years later, shortly after the Nazi invasion of Poland, Cochran wrote to Eleanor Roosevelt, proposing that women pilots could release men pilots for combat duty should the need arise, by "flying ambulance planes, courier planes...and transport planes."[30] She garnered the First Lady's endorsement of her vision of a women's air corps, under her command, that would handle almost any noncombat flying task and would free up men for duty overseas.[31]

Cochran pursued her goal tenaciously. After convincing Henry Arnold, the Commanding General of the U.S. Army Air Force, that the use of women pilots was essential to alleviate the shortage of male pilots, she was designated by the Army Airforce as director of training for women pilots. In a sometimes strained collaboration with another woman pilot named Nancy Love, Cochran began training women for a civilian ferrying squadron, under Love's direction, that was engaged in war-related piloting tasks within the United States.[32]

Cochran's group, originally dubbed the Women's Flying Training Detachment (WFTD), began in November of 1942, operating out of a private airfield near Houston, owned by Howard Hughes. The trainees in "43-W-1," the numerical symbol for the first graduating class of 1943, underwent a rigorous screening process that included a regular Army Air Force physical, a personal interview, and a family background check. From the beginning, Cochran was reluctant to require an absolute minimum number of certified flying hours; instead, individuals were selected

---

29. MARIANNE VERGES, ON SILVER WINGS—THE WOMEN AIRFORCE SERVICE PILOTS OF WORLD WAR II (1991), at 11.

30. BYRD HOWELL GRANGER, ON FINAL APPROACH—THE WOMEN AIRFORCE SERVICE PILOTS OF W.W.II (1991), at 1.

31. VERGES, *supra* note 29, at 14.

32. In September of 1942, while Cochran was in England, Secretary of War Henry Stimson announced the formation of the Women's Auxiliary Ferrying Squadron, a civilian unit, with Nancy Love as director. Cochran, angry that she had been left out of the negotiations leading to the establishment of the ferrying squadron, flew back to the United States immediately and complained in person to General Arnold. Within a few days, she was designated by the Army Airforce as director of the Women's Flying Training Detachment. For details of the feud between Cochran and Love, see VERGES, *supra* note 29 at 29–43; GRANGER, *supra* note 30, at 25–43.

"based upon their own qualifications." Cochran's ultimate goal was to prove that any healthy, stable young American woman could learn to fly the army way as well as her brothers.[33] That initial class was paid $150 per month and had to arrange for their own room and board in nearby Houston. As successive classes entered in the succeeding months, an esprit-de-corps developed among the trainees, and the members of 43-W-1 enjoyed their status as "upperclassmen."

By the spring of 1943, the Army Air Force decided to expand the women's program. Wanting 750 pilots by the end of that year and 1,000 pilots by the end of 1944, the military moved the training facility from Houston to Avenger Field in Sweetwater, a small west-Texas town. As the need for women pilots increased and as the graduates of Cochran's training program demonstrated their expertise in numerous heavy aircraft, the merger of the WFTD with Nancy Love's ferrying squadron seemed inevitable, despite continuing friction between Cochran and Love. Finally, in August of 1943, the two programs were officially merged under the name of the Women Airforce Service Pilots, with Cochran designated as director.[34]

During its year and a half of existence, the WASP attracted great interest. Over 25,000 women applied to the WASP, about 1,830 were accepted, and of that number only 1,074 trainees actually earned their wings.[35] All but two of the 18 WASP classes trained at Avenger Field in Sweetwater. Once the WASP was officially established, there were regularly four to five classes at Avenger at a time, with as many as six hundred women in various stages of training. The people of Sweetwater became accustomed to the constant drone of airplane engines: advanced trainees received instruction not only in daylight hours but in night flying as well. The women endured their rugged and dangerous "boot camp" with the proud knowledge that they were literally making history.[36]

At that time, other opportunities for women in the military were opening, but with very different characteristics. Congress in 1942 created the Women's Army Auxiliary Corps, changed the following year to the Women's Army Corps (WAC), and the Women Accepted for Volunteer Emergency Service (WAVES), both composed exclusively of volunteers. The WAC enabled more than 100,000 women to serve in noncombat roles in the United States and in every major overseas theater, and the 86,000 women in the WAVES were sent to naval bases across the country to work as air traffic controllers, mechanics, and at a variety of desk jobs.

---

33. VERGES, *supra* note 29, at 66–67.

34. VERGES, *supra* note 29, at 102–03.

35. Ann Darr, *The Women Who Flew—but Kept Silent*, THE NEW YORK TIMES MAGAZINE, at 70 (May 7, 1995). The author, Darr, was a member of the class of 44-W-3.

36. *See* VERGES, *supra* note 29, at 31–43.

Unlike the civilian WASP that Mary Anne joined, members of the WAC and WAVES were entitled to insurance and health care and to the benefits of the newly-created G.I. Bill.[37] Moreover, unlike the members of the WASP, the women volunteers in the WAC and the WAVES did not seem to provoke the ire of public critics.

From the beginning, public reaction to the use of women pilots in the WASP was mixed. Within the military, Cochran's program met with resistance from men who resented the presence of women in the formerly all-male domain. Veteran military pilots questioned whether women were capable of handling large aircraft or of enduring long flights. A common fear was that the women pilots would hurt men's chances of flying for the military.[38] Hostility from G.I.'s became a fact of life for many WASP trainees, ranging from the open rudeness of some male flight instructors to dangerous episodes of sabotage.[39] The ambivalence of the higher echelon military leaders toward the program would ultimately spell its defeat and contributed to Congress's failure to bestow veteran status on former WASPs for over three decades.

Eager to offset criticism of her pilots, Cochran mandated that the WASP trainees and graduates present a feminine public image. She imposed a code of conduct encompassing all aspects of their lives, and the general command was to act as a "lady" at all times. For their regulation attire, she chose a suit in Santiago-blue wool, adorned with silver wings, and a beret.[40] The public remained fascinated with the young female pilots, and Hollywood obligingly produced a romanticized film on the first women pilots, "Ladies Courageous." Walt Disney, in turn, created a winged female gremlin as the WASP emblem; "Fifinella," as it was called, was on the front gate of Avenger Field in Sweetwater to welcome arriving rookies.[41] On the other hand, the glamorized image of the WASP did not reflect the true nature of the women pilots' work, and the public did not seem to respect the pilots' competence or the dangers which the women were facing. One magazine article decried "Jackie Cochran's glamour girls" and jeeringly suggested, "How about some of these 35-hour female wonders swapping their flying togs for nurses' uniforms? But that would

37. *See generally* Diane Sherwood, *Women in the Military,* GOVERNMENT EXECUTIVE MAGAZINE (July 31, 1989), reprinted in 135 CONG. REC. E2753-01, 101st Cong., 1st Sess. (July 31, 1989).

38. GRANGER, *supra* note 30, at 331–36.

39. *See* Darr, *supra* note 35, at 70–71, describing the discovery of sugar in the gas tank of a plane scheduled for a WASP flight, and the discovery of a severed rudder cable in a WASP-piloted plane.

40. VERGES, *supra* note 29, at 134.

41. *Id.* at 49 (photograph).

be down right rub-and-scrub work—no glamour there."[42] Thus, the WASP, like its founder, was controversial and often maligned.

On April 18, 1944, Mary Anne joined the WASP as a trainee in class 44-W-9 at Avenger Field, the second to last class to graduate. Mary Anne's desire to join the WASP was intense and she was determined to get accepted. When she scored poorly on a written exam that tested each applicant's knowledge of aircraft design, she purportedly sent a telegram to Jacqueline Cochran that angrily asked, "Are your recruiting mechanics or pilots?"[43] Ironically, the challenging tone of Mary Anne's telegram may have appealed to Cochran's combative nature; despite Mary Anne's test scores, she was accepted into training. Virginia Potthoff Trumbull, a classmate in the WASP who became a lifelong friend, recalled another demonstration of Mary Anne's tenacity. By the spring of 1944, the WASP had lowered its flying-hours standard such that rookies were required to have only thirty-five hours of certified flying time to gain admission to the program. "Mary Anne had not even flown that much, but she wanted to get in so badly that she padded her logbook," Trumbull recalled. "On her first training flight, the instructor discovered that Pete lacked the necessary hours, but they kept her in anyway, almost as a test case. After all, Cochran wanted to prove that women could learn from the ground up, just like men."[44] Mary Anne's deception was not unique. Trumbull herself had joined the WASP earlier but had been hospitalized due to an eye infection. In order to get reinstated as a WASP trainee, she faked a passing score on the regulation eye exam.[45]

The new trainees, who were paid $150 per month and had to buy their own flying gear out of that meager sum, faced a grueling program of instruction. The failure, or "wash-out," rate was high: of the 132 women who arrived as members of 44-W-9, only fifty-five graduated seven months later.[46] Trainees lived in barracks located at Avenger Field, with six cots to a bay, sharing a bathroom with a dozen or so trainees.

The Army Air Force devised a rigorous training schedule, replete with calisthenics, that mirrored the training for G.I.'s. Awakened by the sound of Reveille at dawn, the WASP trainees divided their days between the field, the classroom, and the cockpit, and they marched in formation to every class and every meal. In ground school they studied aircraft mainte-

---

42. *See* Darr, *supra* note 35, at 71.
43. Interview with William K. Richey, Nutrioso, Arizona (July 16–17, 1992).
44. Telephone Interview with Virginia Pothoff Trumbull (Aug. 29, 1992).
45. Trumbull Interview, *supra* note 44. *See also* GRANGER, *supra* note 30, at 443.
46. GRANGER, *supra* note 30, at A-88/D (Appendix—WAFS and WASP Class Lists).

nance, instrument flying, LINK instruction, and other flying techniques. In the air they often trained in the Stearman PT-17, an open-cockpit biplane with a 220-horsepower engine, but the WASP flew aircraft ranging from the small primary trainers up to the B-29 Super Fortress. Indeed, one WASP's recollection is that the first B-29 flight by WASP's was to show men who balked at flying the enormous craft that this was a plane "even women could fly."[47]

In the windy cockpits, the trainees underwent check rides in which an instructor would observe their flying ability. Normally, a trainee needed six to eight hours of dual instruction in the Stearman before the first solo flight. Once an instructor decided that a student was ready, the student began long hours of intense solo practice to perfect loops, spins, and chandelles in preparation for the check flight.[48] Because of the high wash-out rate, the check rides were white-knuckle flights for the nervous trainees. Eventually, the women received the same primary-through-advanced flight training as male Army Air Force cadets, with the exception of aerobatics and formation flying. The course included 400 hours of ground school and 210 hours of flight instruction.[49]

The WASP training was Mary Anne's first exposure to the southwest and contributed to her affinity for the desert. She may have decided then that she would someday return to the singular beauty of the wild open land and the enormity of the desert night sky. At the same time, she became accustomed to the blinding hot winds that swept across the west Texas plains and made take-offs and landings difficult. In particularly high wind conditions, trainees would line up on both sides of the runway and, as each plane came in, would grab the wings to steady it and prevent a roll.[50] Like the other WASPs, she became familiar with desert animals, especially rattlesnakes and tarantulas.

Conditions were often quite grim. In the windy cockpits, trainees flying at 6,000 feet or higher would get very cold. Eventually, as winter approached, the Army Air Force issued fleece-lined jackets to keep the women somewhat warmer. Apart from their flying instruction, trainees engaged in an arduous regimen of physical exercise, marching, and endurance tests. "At one point, we had to run through poisonous gas," remembered Trumbull, "just so we would be familiar with it."[51] Calisthenics were part of the daily regimen. One WASP recalled, "We trained by run-

---

47. Darr, *supra* note 35, at 70.
48. Verges, *supra* note 29, at 161.
49. *Id.* at 110.
50. *See* Darr, *supra* note 35, at 70.
51. Trumbull Interview, *supra* note 44.

ning as fast as we could and throwing ourselves on to the ground, learning to land on our backs instead of breaking the fall with hand or foot and risk breaking an arm or leg. Later we jumped from a high platform, or swung down on a pulley apparatus, all in preparation for an accident."[52]

Mary Anne became known as "Groundloop Pete" during her WASP training. Groundlooping, or spinning a plane on the ground, was an embarrassing piloting error but also a common problem with the Stearman because of its narrow wheel base. After three recorded incidents of groundlooping, Mary Anne was facing a probable wash-out in the WASP. Fortunately, her flight instructor discovered that Mary Anne had sprained her ankle sometime earlier and was physically unable to control the plane's rudder with her foot. Since her problem was physical and temporary, rather than the result of inadequate skill, she was kept in the program.[53] The nickname of "Groundloop Pete" followed her, however, even after she regained her ability to control the planes.

The WASP training program and the work carried on by WASP graduates were inherently dangerous. In addition to ferrying military planes, WASP graduates towed gunnery targets for cadets in training and tested trainers before they were released for use by the Army Air Corp. On occasion, a test flight by a WASP would end in tragedy, yielding definitive evidence after the fact that the equipment was defective.[54] Mary Anne had her own encounter with defective equipment when she was practicing forced landings in an AT-6, an advanced trainer plane. During aerial maneuvers, her engine started "cutting out and getting very hot. I called the tower and was instructed to cut off the engine and come back to land." The field had been cleared and emergency equipment was waiting in case she crashed. She landed safely and, undaunted, jumped into another plane to complete her exercise. "As I was taking off, the quadrant, with throttle, prop pitch, and mixture control, fell off the plane into my hand. I had to hold and maneuver the controls, get airborne and call the tower to let them know I had an emergency situation and determine whether to crash land ahead or try to go around." Again the field was cleared and emergency equipment readied, but Mary Anne managed to land without injury. "They wanted me to take up another plane, but I told them two emergency situations in one day was enough!"[55]

On a cross-country training flight from Sweetwater to Enid, Oklahoma,

52. *See* Darr, *supra* note 35, at 70.

53. Trumbull Interview, *supra* note 44.

54. For examples of WASP deaths related to test flights, see GRANGER, *supra* note 30 at 398, 425.

55. Florence Graves, *WASPS: A Case of Discrimination*, TUCSON MAGAZINE 64 (May 1977)(quoting Mary Anne Richey).

Mary Anne experienced another misadventure with the AT-6 which likewise drew on her qualities of calm logic in the face of danger as well as her spirit for fun. According to regulations, before take-off she noted her flight plan and visual landmarks on her knee pad and also plotted the flight on a map. After departing, the summer heat became intense. Mary Anne opened her canopy to allow air to circulate, and her map immediately flew out. At that point, all she had to direct her flight were the notes on her knee pad and her compass, a malfunctioning compass, as it happened. After flying for several hours with Enid no where in sight, she decided to land on an abandoned airstrip that she had spotted from the air.

As she taxied toward a hangar, a group of men emerged and were astonished to find a woman pilot grinning at them. They helped her radio her commanding officer to report the incident, and all agreed that she should spend the night before flying back to Sweetwater. Mary Anne's hosts treated her to a spaghetti dinner at a local restaurant, and the group later engaged in a long poker game. Mary Anne reportedly went to bed that night several dollars richer. When her commanding officer arrived the next morning to escort Mary Anne back to Avenger Field, he was furious at her for getting lost. She explained to him that her compass was the problem. "I don't believe you," he responded, "Let me fly your plane and you fly mine." When the two finally arrived back at Sweetwater, he apologized to her. During the flight, he had discovered that her compass was, in fact, defective.[56]

The risks associated with the WASP program were starkly demonstrated during Mary Anne's relatively brief tenure. In April of 1944, three members of the WASP died on active duty, and two trainees were killed in a midair collision near Avenger Field. The accident taking the lives of the trainees occurred just two days before Mary Anne's initial appointment. Moreover, two members of Mary Anne's own 44-W-9 class were killed within months of their starting day. In one incident, in June of 1944, Gleanna Roberts was doing low altitude work near Avenger Field. Making a steep downwind turn, her PT-17 stalled. She was too low to recover, and the plane crashed. The death sent a chill throughout the training program, but members of 44-W-9, including Mary Anne, felt the shock most acutely. In October of that same year, Marjorie Davis, also a trainee in 44-W-9, attempted a landing in an AT-6 in Mississippi as part of her cross country flight test. Her plane snagged on wires at the last minute, flipped, and crashed. In all, thirty-eight women died in the WASP program, either as trainees or as graduates.[57] Unlike the death of a serviceman, the death

---

56. Trumbull Interview, *supra* note 44.
57. GRANGER, *supra* note 30, at 363, 426.

of a WASP generated no death benefits, no military escort, and no flags to drape her coffin. For the families of the young women who perished, and their friends and classmates in the WASP, there were no military honors to assuage the grief.

Despite the strenuous and risk-laden training, spirits were generally high at Avenger Field. Trainees were expected to be on base every night unless they were using their solitary weekend pass. After twelve noon on Saturday and all day Sunday, however, they were permitted to sleep, do their wash, write letters, or go into Sweetwater for a few hours. The town people were accustomed to seeing groups of young women in the cafes, soda fountains, and movie theaters. Mary Anne was regarded as an outgoing, mischief-loving woman whose pranks were legendary. In a characteristically exuberant display of high spirits, she reportedly rode a horse into the lobby of the Blue Bonnet Hotel, Sweetwater's finest place of accommodation, on a dare.[58] On the other hand, Mary Anne's mood quickly could become somber when she spoke of her brother Chuck.

As a married woman, Mary Anne was entitled to more frequent leaves than the single women, but over the long months of WASP training, spousal visits were few and far between. Mary Anne used one weekend pass to see Bill Showers in Chicago during training, and Showers, in turn, visited her once in Sweetwater.[59] The marriage, ill-fated from the beginning according to Mary Anne's friends, was weakened by the long separation.

News of the war raging in Europe and in the Pacific dominated conversations at Avenger Field. Periodically, a trainee would be called in to headquarters to receive the grim news that a spouse, father, or brother had been killed in the war. During Mary Anne's training, however, the news from the warfront was increasingly optimistic. The monumental achievement of the Allied troops on D-Day on June 6, 1944, held the attention of the world. Before the day was over, 70,000 Americans landed on the Normandy coast. Despite tremendous losses, the Allies clung to the beachheads and pushed the German line back. Similarly, just two weeks later, when the Battle of the Philippine Sea resulted in victory for the Allies, there was much rejoicing in Sweetwater, Texas. And in late August, after four years of German occupation, the Allies entered and "liberated" the city of Paris. Again, the world celebrated.

Ironically, as the successes of the Allies mounted, the pressing need for women pilots decreased, and the future of the WASP program dimmed. On June 22, 1944, President Roosevelt signed into law the Servicemen's Readjustment Act, which came to be known as the "G.I. Bill of Rights." The Act

---

58. Telephone Interview with William K. Richey (Sept. 20, 1992); Trumbull Interview, *supra* note 44.

59. Showers Interview, *supra* note 6; Trumbull Interview, *supra* note 44.

was designed to help the ten million returning veterans adjust to peacetime. It offered guaranteed loans to buy a home, farm or business; unemployment insurance and job placement services; and up to four years of federal aid for education. The revolutionary social legislation, strongly championed by Roosevelt, did not provide any benefits whatsoever to the civilian WASP.

During the active phase of the WASP program, a volatile battle ensued in Congress and in the media over the question of militarization. House Bill 4219 was introduced in Congress in 1944 "to provide for the appointment of female pilots and aviation cadets in the Air Forces of the Army."[60] Jacqueline Cochran had long championed the goal of militarization, arguing that her young women were performing the same (noncombat) piloting tasks at the same risks as the members of the Army Air Force and deserved the same compensation and benefits. Supporters in Congress similarly urged passage of the bill and added the promise of military discipline in hopes of attracting votes. "The sole purpose of this bill is simply this," urged Representative Costello, "to take these women who are now with the Army Air Forces in a civilian capacity and convert them into a military capacity.... This should be done, because these women at present are denied hospitalization; they are denied insurance benefits, and things of that kind to which, as military personnel, they should be entitled, and because of the work they are doing, they should be receiving at this time. Likewise, these women then would be subject to military discipline."[61] Ultimately, President Roosevelt, Secretary of War Stimson, and General Arnold all supported the WASP bill.

Notwithstanding the support of the administration, public opposition to the bill was heavy. Unemployed male pilots and veterans groups were vociferous, and several prominent newspapers ridiculed the idea of granting military status to members of the WASP. According to critics in the media, the WASP program had been an expensive, dangerous, and failed experiment.[62] They denigrated the flying skills of members of the WASP and pointed to the low qualifications for entry into the program.[63] On June 21, 1944, the day before the G.I. Bill of Rights was signed into law, the proposal to make the women pilots a part of the Army Air Force was defeated by nineteen votes.[64]

---

60. 1944 CONGRESSIONAL RECORD-HOUSE 6398, 78th Cong., 2nd Sess. (June 21, 1944).

61. *Id.* at. 6404 (Remarks of Representative Costello).

62. VERGES, *supra* note 29 at 193–96.

63. 1944 CONGRESSIONAL RECORD-HOUSE 6408, 78th Cong., 2nd Sess. (June 21, 1944)(Remarks of Representative White).

64. 1944 CONGRESSIONAL RECORD-HOUSE 6416, 78th Cong., 2nd Sess. (June 21, 1944)(Vote on H.R. 4219). The final debate in the House of Representatives on H.R. 4219 is reproduced at *id.* at 6398–6416.

The defeat of the WASP's militarization in Congress demoralized the women at Avenger Field. Their sisters in uniform—the Women's Army Corps and the Women Accepted for Voluntary Emergency Service—had been organized during World War II and had been granted full military status. The rejection of such status for the women pilots, who were performing far riskier assignments than members of the WAC or the WAVES, was a slap in the face. Some concluded that the WASPs, by their surprising competence in the male domain of military piloting, simply pushed the boundaries of sex roles too far.[65]

The final disheartening news arrived late in Mary Anne's training. In October of 1944, letters went out to all WASP trainees and graduates stating, in confirmation of rampant rumors, that the program would be deactivated as of December 20, 1944. At the same time, the Army Air Force made clear that Cochran's continuing efforts to achieve military status for the WASP were doomed. There would be no militarization of the program. The graduation dates of the final two classes, 44-W-9 and 44-W-10, were advanced so that all successful trainees could receive their wings before the deactivation.

With the formal announcement of the deactivation, the mood at Avenger Field in Sweetwater was grim and angry. "There was a deathly silence at Avenger Field the night the news came in," according to Virginia Trumbull. "For those of us in 44-9, it meant we would have only a month of actual service after graduation."[66] The women trainees felt betrayed, and some blamed the egotism of Jacqueline Cochran. The WASP graduates felt equally abandoned. "It was just, 'So long, girls.' It was a terrible letdown," one WASP member recalled. "We were hoping we would be taken into the Army. But with the men returning from combat, they didn't need women pilots."[67]

Mary Anne's class lost two weeks of training and graduated on November 6 instead of November 20.[68] The speaker, Assistant Chief of Staff, Col. E.W. Suarez, of the Training Command, congratulated the class members on their flying skills, and he voiced regret that the sight of WASPs flying the large P-40s had aroused so much male resentment.[69]

Upon graduation, Mary Anne received her prized wings,[70] an increase in pay from $150 per month to a $250 monthly allotment, and orders to re-

---

65. GRANGER, *supra* note 30, at 469–72.

66. Trumbull Interview, *supra* note 44.

67. Joe Salkowski, *In the line of fire*, THE ARIZONA DAILY STAR, July 2, 1995 (quoting Allaire Bennett, a former WASP).

68. GRANGER, *supra* note 30, at 419–20.

69. GRANGER, *supra* note 30, at 443.

70. The WASP wings, officially awarded to graduates of 44-W-1 through 44-W-10, were pilots wings with a diamond-shaped silver shield in the center, symbolizing the shield

port to the Army Air Force base at Shaw Army Air Base in Sumter, South Carolina.[71] More than a dozen WASPs served at Shaw Field, but Mary Anne was the only member of her class to be assigned there. Their duties included "engineering testing," ferrying of aircraft, target towing, instrument instructing, and administrative work.[72] According to Trumbull, the benign-sounding "engineering testing" was the task that clearly placed WASPs in the role of guinea pigs. When a plane was damaged, it would be sent in for repairs at one of the many engineering departments at Army bases around the country. After Army mechanics repaired the craft, a WASP pilot would take the plane up for a test flight before it was re-certified as safe for military use. Trumbull remembered more than one occasion during which the allegedly-repaired plane proved to be defective.[73]

At Shaw Field, Mary Anne devoted herself primarily to ferrying trainers and to towing gunnery targets.[74] Target towing, in particular, appealed to Mary Anne since it required sophisticated flying skills and steady nerves. As a target tower, she pulled a large canvas sleeve through the air by means of a long cable attached to her aircraft. Ground soldiers in aerial-gunner training would then attack the billowing fabric with guns of varying types and calibers. The gunners were given automatic machine guns with clips of live ammunition that had been dipped in colored wax to identify their strikes, red for nose gunner, blue for tail gunner, green and yellow for side gunners.[75] Target pilots flew at higher altitudes for larger artillery and then swooped down lower for small arms. At intervals, the training officers on the ground would radio for the planes to dive. Towing was extremely dangerous not only because of the unreliable aim of the greenhorn cadets on the ground but also because of the poor condition of many of the aircraft. The planes were often worn-out survivors of months in combat.[76]

Although Mary Anne had worked hard to earn her wings and found the work at Shaw Field exciting, her service in the Women Airforce Service Pilots came to an end on December 9, 1944, with her resignation. Her personnel papers reveal that she resigned "due to the deactivation of

---

carried by the goddess of war, Athena. Graphical illustrations can be found in GRANGER, *supra* note 30, at A-69/C.

71. United States Military Personnel Record, Notification of Personnel Action for Mary Anne Showers, December 9, 1944.

72. GRANGER, *supra* note 30, at A-61/B.

73. Trumbull Interview, *supra* note 44.

74. Don Carson, *Judge Richey, Pal Recall War Days*, THE ARIZONA DAILY STAR, June 19, 1966.

75. Darr, *supra* note 35, at 70.

76. VERGES, *supra* note 29, at 128–29.

the WASP Program in the very near future."[77] Mary Anne's decision to re-sign before the termination of the program was a refusal to be a passive victim of the WASP's deactivation and perhaps reflected her increasing de-sire to control her own life.

Following her resignation, Mary Anne showed no signs of wanting to return immediately to her domestic role as Mrs. William Showers. In-stead, she followed a course that attracted many former WASPs. She en-gaged in contract flying, carrying surplus military planes, including dan-gerously damaged aircraft, to private purchasers. She and a close friend and classmate from 44-W-9, Deanne Ferguson, spent several months fly-ing up and down the East Coast in such work. That private occupation, like the WASP experience itself, was strenuous, risky, and poorly compen-sated. Once Mary Anne flew an open cockpit plane from Virginia to Con-necticut during a snow storm.[78]

World War II dragged on for another nine months after the deactivation of the WASP program. The day after Mary Anne's graduation from WASP training, Franklin D. Roosevelt defeated Thomas Dewey and was elected for the fourth time to the presidency of the United States. In February of 1945, Roosevelt, Churchill, and Stalin met at Yalta to discuss the prob-lems of the postwar world, but Roosevelt was not to witness the fruition of his diplomatic efforts. He died April 12, 1945; one month later, Ger-many submitted its unconditional surrender to the Allied forces. In Au-gust, President Truman, in the most controversial decision of his public life, approved the dropping of the atomic bomb on Hiroshima and Na-gasaki, Japan. The bombs were dropped from B-29's, huge aircraft some-times flown by WASPs. One week after the devastation of the Japanese cities, Japan decreed its surrender to the Allies and transmitted the docu-ment through neutral embassies. Finally, on September 2, 1945, General MacArthur and Admiral Nimitz received the formal surrender of Japan aboard the battleship *Missouri* in Tokyo Bay, and the most brutal war in history came to an end.

Despite the efforts of its critics, the deactivated WASP did not die. Many of the 1,074 graduates maintained contact over the years, continu-ing their spirit of camaraderie and proud accomplishment, reminiscing about their days at Avenger Field and other military bases around the country, and persisting in the effort to achieve retroactive military status. Mary Anne attended several of the WASP reunions and was a staunch supporter of the efforts toward militarization.

---

77. United States Military Records, *supra* note 71.

78. Don Carson, *Judge Richey, Pal Recall War Days*, THE ARIZONA DAILY STAR, June 19, 1966.

In 1976, the same year that women first officially joined the United States Air Force as military pilots, legislation was again introduced in Congress to retroactively grant the WASP full military status and make the women pilots eligible for veterans' benefits. Senator Barry Goldwater, a former World War II Ferry Division pilot, sponsored the legislation. Unfortunately, veterans groups surfaced once again in opposition; although the WASP amendment passed the Senate, the House Veterans Affairs Committee killed the proposal.[79] The following year, proponents of militarization were better prepared and marshalled widespread support for the WASP bill when it was reintroduced as an amendment to the G.I. Bill Improvement Act of 1977. On November 3, 1977, the House passed the WASP amendment, and the Senate approved the legislation the following evening. President Jimmy Carter signed the bill into law on Thanksgiving Day, November 23, 1977.[80] As a result, each woman pilot with sufficient service received, retroactively, an honorable discharge as well as the World War II Victory medal. Although Mary Anne was alive and jubilant for the enactment of the WASP militarization law, her Victory medal did not arrive until May of 1984, six months after her death.

Mary Anne was fiercely proud of her membership in the WASP and maintained strong bonds with several of her classmates throughout her life. She and the other graduates had succeeded in completing a grueling training program and had proven to themselves that they could fly as well as men. They had performed bravely under the most dangerous conditions, and some of them had lost their lives to the cause. Their accomplishment embued them with a sense of power and possibility. Conversely, the hostile reactions to the WASP inside and outside the military had exposed the women to raw sexism. They came away with first-hand knowledge of discrimination and harassment, and that knowledge itself surely influenced their choices in the future. For Mary Anne, the WASP experience was an invaluable part of her personal history that would inform her decisionmaking as a judge years later.

---

79. GRANGER, *supra* note 30, at 232–36.
80. Public Law 95-202, 91 Stat. 1449 (Title IV) (November 23, 1977).

Part Two

1946–1964

CHAPTER FOUR

Coming Into God's Country

With the end of World War II in 1945, Mary Anne faced a society that was ambivalent about the future role of women in the labor force. The popular media began to promulgate the message that women should now repair to the homefront to embrace their roles as wives and mothers.[1] As social historian Myra Dinnerstein has reported, postwar America was concerned that traditional gender relationships had been endangered during the war and continued to be at risk. Women's new-found independence aroused fears that customary sex roles might be changed forever. The result was a strident "postwar ideology that prescribed a limited domestic position for women."[2] By early 1945, the New York Times was already referring to "the rise and fall of women in wartime industry."[3] A Wall Street Journal article from the same period began, "Women workers on the West Coast have nearly completed their wartime cycle from the kitchen to war jobs and back to the kitchen again."[4] Across the United States, employers severed women from employment at much higher rates than men through such measures as male-only job classifications.[5] State governments renewed their interest in "protective" legislation that restricted hours and other conditions of employment for women.[6]

---

1. See Fara Warner, *Imperfect Picture*, WALL STREET JOURNAL, April 24, 1995 (describing the efforts by advertisers to move women back into the home, including sending the message that a working mother was bad for children).

2. MYRA DINNERSTEIN, WOMEN BETWEEN TWO WORLDS: MIDLIFE REFLECTIONS ON WORK AND FAMILY 2–3 (1992).

3. THE NEW YORK TIMES, February 10, 1945.

4. *West Coast Bosses Cheer As Women War Workers Quit Jobs to Go Home*, THE WALL STREET JOURNAL, January 22, 1945.

5. See Sheila Tobias & Lisa Anderson, *What Really Happened to Rosie the Riveter? Demobilization and the Female Labor Force, 1944–47*, in WOMEN'S AMERICA 354–73 (LINDA K. KERBER & JANE DeHART MATHEWS, EDS. 1982). Based on union surveys and historical data about female job seekers in the postwar period, Tobias and Anderson concluded that most women who were in the labor force during the war years wanted to continue working in the postwar period and resisted the efforts to remove them from the labor force. *See also* PHILIP FONER, WOMEN AND THE AMERICAN LABOR MOVEMENT 388–89 (1980). Foner reports that in various industries, the percentage of total layoffs that were female workers ranged from 85 to 98 percent.

6. *See, e.g,* Goesaert v. Cleary, 335 U.S. 464 (1948)(upholding a Michigan law that barred women from serving as bartenders except where they were the wives and daughters of male tavern owners).

Many labor leaders likewise believed that unless women returned home so that the veterans could find work, the Great Depression would return.[7] As a result, women in the United States were laid off or voluntarily quit in the immediate postwar period in huge numbers.[8] Between September 1945 and November 1946, 2.25 million women voluntarily left jobs and 1 million were laid off.[9]

Nevertheless, women's economic and psychological need to remain in the workforce proved too deeply ingrained for the social forces dictating otherwise. Scholars have now shown that most women did not return to a life of domesticity willingly in the postwar period.[10] By 1947, women reentering the job market began to make up for the immediate post-war losses, and by the mid-1950's the labor force participation rate of women was as high as it had been during the war.[11] Against this turbulent post-war backdrop, Mary Anne found herself at a turning point in her own life.

Following the war and his honorable discharge from the United States Navy, Bill Showers rejoined his brothers and father at the family-owned Indiana Cash Drawers in Shelbyville. Knowing that she did not want to make a career of contract-flying, Mary Anne, then twenty-seven years old, returned to Indiana and to a marriage that had been more of a formality than a reality for several years. The reunion, however, was to be short-lived. Shortly after her return to Shelbyville, Mary Anne began to consider divorce. In the immediate postwar period, the United States for a variety of reasons experienced a sharp increase in divorces, with 1946 showing the highest national divorce rate recorded as of that time.[12] The separation of spouses occasioned by the war, the stress of daily life under

---

7. STEVEN D. MCLAUGHLIN, BARBARA D. MELBER, JOHN O.G. BILLY, DENISE M. ZIMMERLE, LINDA D. WINGES, TERRY R. JOHNSON, THE CHANGING LIVES OF AMERICAN WOMEN 24–25 (1988)(hereinafter CHANGING LIVES).

8. BARBARA J. HARRIS, BEYOND HER SPHERE 154–55 (1978)(reporting that in some industries, 50 to 100 percent of women workers were fired).

9. HARRIS, *supra* note 8, at 155.

10. Social historians have vividly described the resistance with which women met the reconversion of the post-war period. *See* Tobias & Anderson, *supra* note 5; AMY KESSELMAN, FLEETING OPPORTUNITIES—WOMEN SHIPYARD WORKERS IN PORTLAND AND VANCOUVER DURING WORLD WAR II AND RECONVERSION (1990).

11. CHANGING LIVES, *supra* note 7, at 24.

12. Almost 630,000 divorces were decreed in 1946, translating into a rate of one divorce for every 55 existing marriages, or between 4 and 5 divorces for every 1,000 persons (as compared to 2 divorces per 1,000 persons in 1940). Interestingly, the divorce rate sharply declined after 1946 and did not surpass the 4/1,000 mark again until the 1970s. *See generally* RODRICK PHILLIPS, UNTYING THE KNOT 210–13 (1991); HERBERT JACOBS, SILENT REVOLUTION—THE TRANSFORMATION OF DIVORCE LAW IN THE UNITED STATES 27 (1988).

wartime conditions, and, perhaps, a postwar desire in the population to bury the past, may all have contributed to the sharp jump in divorce.[13] In addition, the war years had provided to many women their first taste of economic independence and may have allowed them to consider life outside the confines of marriage.

Mary Anne's own experience paralleled that of many women and her contemplation of divorce was in tune with the times. After the incomparable challenge and raw excitement of her months in the WASP and as a contract pilot, she was unwilling to commit herself to the role of homemaker, and she bristled under the constant attentions of the Showers family. Her participation in the WASP had instilled in her the sense that she could succeed in competition with men and that she was capable of having a career on equal terms with men. Although her options remained unclear, Mary Anne knew she must have independence. Moreover, her vision of independence seemed to require that she physically distance herself from Shelbyville. Her relations with her father were cordial but strained, and she had never felt a sense of belonging in the house he shared with his second wife Bess. Her brother Bill was engrossed in his young family, his work, and his expanding civic responsibilities. Although the town of Shelbyville had provided an idyllic childhood setting for Mary Anne, it offered little to keep the strong-willed adventurer within its borders.

Sometime in 1946, Mary Anne visited New York City alone, perhaps to contemplate her future away from the physical and emotional constraints of Shelbyville. She ran into a sorority sister on Madison Avenue, a woman she had not seen for seven years, and told her on the spot that she was considering divorce.[14] Similarly, she discussed the possibility of divorce with friends Wilbur and Mary Pell. Indeed, a sense of integrity compelled her to explain to Pell, an attorney, that, even though she wanted a divorce from Bill Showers, she would feel uncomfortable having Pell represent her in the divorce action because of his mutual friendship with both Mary Anne and Bill.[15]

Despite Mary Anne's contemplation of divorce, she and Bill Showers traveled to Tucson, Arizona, in late 1946 to give Bill a chance "to try to make it on [his] own" and for the couple to "try a new life" together away from Shelbyville.[16] The idea of moving to Tucson may have originated with Mary Anne, who had enjoyed the stark expanses of the western desert as a

---

13. See PHILLIPS, *supra* note 12, at 187–90.

14. Telephone Interview with Manette Hollingsworth Speas (May 15, 1993).

15. Telephone Interview with Honorable Wilbur F. Pell, Jr., Judge, United States Court of Appeals (April 8, 1993).

16. Interview with William Showers, Shelbyville, Indiana (Oct. 10, 1992).

WASP trainee. Also, Marge Allen, by then estranged from her husband R.C. Allen, lived part-time in Tucson. Marge had seen Mary Anne frequently over the years because of the Allens' business and social connections with the Showers family and had developed a deep maternal affection for her. Thus, Marge's presence in Tucson was an additional draw.

The city that Mary Anne and Bill encountered was in a postwar growth period. Before World War II, Tucson had been a sleepy town of about 35,000, but the war years brought an increase in population and an infusion of economic life, in large part because of the Davis-Monthan Air Force Base. Davis-Monthan, designated a U.S. Army Air Corps base in 1940, was one of the major heavy bombardment operational training bases for the Second Air Force throughout the war. Troops assigned to the base were a familiar sight on the Tucson streets and a boon to Tucson businesses. After the war and a short-lived economic slump, the economy regained its strength as returning veterans came to Tucson by the thousands, funded by the G.I. Bill of Rights. By 1950, Tucson's population had expanded to more than 45,000 in the city limits and to 118,000 in the metropolitan area.[17]

In spite of the economic momentum within the city, Mary Anne and Bill did not fare well. For several months, Showers sold adding machines to businesses in the Tucson area with Mary Anne helping out as she could, but the work was slow. Those months were not a happy period for the couple, who were struggling for financial independence amidst a deteriorating marriage. Showers remained in Tucson for less than a year and then moved to Long Beach, California, to pursue the same sales work there. Eventually, he returned to the safe harbor of Shelbyville and his family's business.[18] Showers' departure signaled the end of the marriage, although the formal divorce did not come for another two years. Mary Anne may have viewed her decision to stay in Tucson as temporary, but over time she would develop a lasting affinity for the West and would spend the next thirty-five years in "God's country."

Characteristically, Mary Anne had a benefactor to help her find her way. Marge Allen, wanting to assist her beloved Pete, suggested that she try managing a guest ranch outside of Tucson owned by Marge's friend, Bill Veeck. Veeck was a flamboyant sports promoter whose career included ownership of the Milwaukee Brewers, the St. Louis Browns, the Cleveland Indians, and the Chicago White Sox. He was well-known for his creative attempts to increase public attendance at baseball games, and he conceived of the idea of the exploding score board. As his Tucson at-

---

17. Colette M. Bancroft, *The future came*, THE ARIZONA DAILY STAR, September 3, 1995; United States Bureau of the Census, 1950 Census of Pop., Vol. II, at 3–5(Table 2).

18. Showers Interview, *supra* note 16.

torney Hal Warnock remarked, "Veeck was a personality in the true sense of the word. He was smart, lightning-quick, daring, and with an impish sense of humor."[19] Veeck purchased the guest ranch near Tucson, known as the "Lazy Vee," after selling the Milwaukee Brewers in 1946. The Lazy Vee was a rugged but exclusive ranch, located in the rolling foothills of the Rincon Mountains, southeast of Tucson. As with many of Arizona's guest ranches, the clientele consisted largely of wealthy easterners. Veeck wrote that "[w]e had some delightful people out there, people I still bump into now and then. I could have enjoyed them all tremendously if they had not been paying me, as it were, to be charming to them."[20]

Veeck's exuberance for life matched that of Mary Anne, and she began managing the ranch in 1947 after Veeck grew restless being away from baseball. Pleased to have a job now that she was separated from Showers, she remained in that position, supervising all guest services as well as general maintenance at the ranch, from September 1947 until the fall of 1948.[21] Horseback riding was the focal point of ranch activities, and the Lazy Vee had a diverse group of Western horses. Riders had a choice of flat desert range or mountain trails, and Mary Anne frequently accompanied the guests on their rides. Her gregarious nature, her enjoyment of the out-of-doors, her love of animals, and her particular interest in horses suited her well for the demands of the Lazy Vee. At the ranch she enjoyed for the first time the seasonal beauty of the high desert, the smell of creosote after a summer rain, the springtime brilliance of the barrel cactus and saguaro in bloom, and the snowcapped peaks of the surrounding mountains in the winter—the Rincons to the east, the Catalina Mountains to the north, and the Santa Rita Mountains to the south. She found a certain peace on the evening rides, and she enjoyed sitting under the eucalyptus trees that flanked the ranch house, gazing out at the ravines and red cliffs leading up to the majestic Rincons.

While at the Lazy Vee, Mary Anne worked more closely with horses than ever before, and acquired a keen knowledge of horse care, training, and breeding. At some point she acquired a poster that depicted the history of the thoroughbred; the poster adorned a wall of her living space for years.[22] Her social milieu revolved around ranch activities and horse racing. She frequently saw Marge Allen, who owned several thoroughbreds

19. *Attorney represented Arizona in two sports*, THE ARIZONA DAILY STAR, December 25, 1994. Other sources on Veeck include his autobiography, with ED LINN, VEECK—AS IN WRECK (1962).

20. VEECK, *supra* note 19, at 82.

21. Biographical Form Letter to Dean John D. Lyons, Jr., Sept. 10, 1948, Student File for Mary Anne Reimann, University of Arizona College of Law.

22. Interview with Hon. Richard M. Roylston and Hon. Robert O. Roylston, Judges, Pima County Superior Court, Tucson, Arizona (Aug. 19, 1992).

and was a horse-racing enthusiast, and even vacationed with her in Wyoming once. Mary Anne also became close friends with a woman named Jerry Kelso, who shared her passion for horses. Kelso, who was smart, ambitious, and independent, went on to found the nation's first woman-owned life insurance company.[23]

Despite its recreational benefits, the manager's position at the Lazy Vee was arduous and low paying. The physical demands of the job were significant, but the real challenge lay in satisfying the whims of an affluent clientele. Although Mary Anne had always had an ability to get along with people of diverse socio-economic classes, she found the job to be "damn hard work." When the cook at the ranch abruptly left during peak season, Mary Anne had to be in the kitchen three times daily to prepare meals for the guests. She told herself at that point that there had to be an easier way to make a living.[24]

Mary Anne's decision to divorce Bill Showers remained firm, but her immediate plans were uncertain. At thirty years of age, she must have felt some trepidation in facing the future as an unmarried woman. Jerry Kelso, who had become a fiercely loyal friend to Mary Anne, propitiously suggested a change of career after enduring Mary Anne's complaints about her work at the Lazy Vee for several months. Kelso brought to the ranch a catalogue of course offerings from the University of Arizona and pointed out to Mary Anne the listings for the College of Law. Since none of Mary Anne's relatives had studied or practiced law, she had no sense of destiny about the legal profession. Her work as a fledgling courthouse reporter for the Shelbyville Republican had sparked an early interest in courtroom drama, but she had not seriously considered law as a potential career path until her divorce seemed imminent. The divorce experience itself may have added to her motivation to attend law school. She once remarked in private conversation that her lack of knowledge of the legal rules governing divorce jurisdiction left her with a sense of powerlessness and that she was determined not to be in such an impotent position again in her life.[25]

According to her responses to a student survey, she first considered studying law "at a time [when] I realized I would be obliged to earn my living."[26] On the same survey, Mary Anne answered the question, "What caused you to turn to the law?" in the following way: "Was always very interested. Means of earning living." Revealing some ambivalence about

---

23. Telephone Interview with Lois Dusenberry (Jan. 11, 1993).

24. Interview with William K. Richey, Nutrioso, Arizona (July 16-17, 1992).

25. Dusenberry Interview, *supra* note 23.

26. Student File for Mary Anne Reimann, University of Arizona College of Law.

her articulated motivations, she also wrote, but then crossed out, "Felt it offered a course that women...." Perhaps she had second thoughts about calling attention to her gender or perhaps she was uncertain about the opportunities available to women in the legal profession; some belated inhibition clearly led her to delete the reference to the legal profession's particular promise for women. In any event, Mary Anne's decision to apply to law school seemed to result from a coalescence of factors, including most immediately her dissatisfaction with the job at the Lazy Vee and the pressing need to find a means of support. That she chose a male-dominated and highly-competitive profession was consistent with her evolving self-image.

In the year Mary Anne matriculated at the University of Arizona College of Law, a few of the nation's law schools, including Harvard, still barred women from admission, but most had eliminated the formal gender barriers. Nevertheless, women's presence in legal education remained almost negligible until the 1970's. In 1948, only three percent of the entering law students in the United States were women,[27] and in that same year, women comprised only 1.8 percent of the practicing lawyers in the United States.[28] The statistics reveal the persistence of cultural attitudes about the proper and separate domains of women and men, reflected in the infamous decision in *Bradwell v. Illinois*,[29] upholding Illinois' exclusion of women from the practice of law. In contrast to the patriotic encouragement of women's entry into men's fields during World War II, the postwar culture urged women to reclaim their domesticity, to go back into the home, and to free up jobs for men. Although the Arizona Territory had admitted its first woman to the practice of law before the turn of the century,[30] many lawyers and judges across the United States were still convinced that the difference between the sexes disqualified women from the practice of law, as well as from other occupations.[31]

Mary Anne, however, was not dissuaded from pursuing a "male" pro-

---

27. AMERICAN BAR FOUNDATION, WOMEN LAWYERS: SUPPLEMENTARY DATA TO THE 1971 LAWYERS STATISTICAL REPORT (1973) at 13. According to the ABA data, 746 women were first-year law students at a law school in the United States in 1948, or 3.12 percent of the total number of entering law students.

28. CYNTHIA FUCHS EPSTEIN, WOMEN IN LAW 4 (2d ed. 1993). The figure for practicing lawyers is derived from Martindale-Hubbell listings, and a somewhat higher figure (3.5 percent) appears in census data. *Id.*

29. 83 U.S. (16 Wall.) 130 (1873).

30. *See* Jacquelyn Gayle Kasper, *Arizona's First Woman Lawyer: Sarah Herring Sorin*, ARIZONA ATTORNEY 49 (January 1996).

31. *See* Michael H. Cardozo, *Women Not in the Law Schools, 1950 to 1963*, 42 J. LEGAL EDUCATION 594, 595 (1993)(describing virtual absence of women from legal education and the practice of law before the mid-1960s).

fession. Her rough-and-tumble years as the Shelbyville tomboy had blurred her perception of sex roles at an early and formative time, and her adventures in the Far East, her hazardous missions in the WASP, and her recent command at the ranch had all convinced her that she could succeed in a "man's world." Also, as she stated in an interview years later, she simply "wanted to enter something with a definite future."[32] Thus, she applied to the University of Arizona College of Law in the summer of 1948, at the age of thirty. Simultaneously casting off the girlhood moniker of "Pete" and the married name of "Showers," Mary Anne began the new chapter in her life under the name of "Mary Anne Reimann."

The application process at the University of Arizona Law College in 1948 was very different from today's highly competitive system. In order to accommodate the large numbers of returning veterans from World War II, the school maintained an open-door policy for Arizona residents, admitting many students but graduating few. During the immediate postwar period when applications were high, only about fifty percent of the entering students successfully completed law school. To ride out the temporary flood of students, three full semesters were offered each year, and enrollment was limited to legal residents of Arizona for the five years beginning in 1946.[33] In 1948, applicants to the law school did not have to possess an undergraduate degree, and they did not have to take an entrance examination.[34] In order to pursue a Bachelors of Law (LL.B.), applicants had to have completed only 62 1/2 units of acceptable undergraduate study, maintaining at least a C average. Ironically, if Mary Anne had delayed just one year before applying to law school, she would not have qualified, since the college increased its admissions requirements for the class entering in 1949. In 1948, however, Mary Anne's total of 70 and 2/3 undergraduate units at Purdue University satisfied the admission standards. Dean John D. Lyons, Jr., the white-haired former judge who had taken over as dean in 1947 when James Byron McCormick resigned the deanship to assume the presidency of the University, always showed a special interest in Mary Anne. He wrote on September 9, 1948, that "Mrs. Reimann has the necessary amount and quality of pre-legal work..." In the characteristically sexist language of the times, the registrar's form for Mary Anne certified that "[t]his man apparently meets

32. Rosemary Gallon, *History of Arizona Women Lawyers and Judges*, (1971)(unpublished manuscript)(Arizona Historical Society Museum).

33. John D. Lyons, *The First Fifty Years of the College of Law*, 7 ARIZ. L. REV. 173, 177 (1966).

34. *College of Law Announcement 1947/48—1948/49*, UNIVERSITY OF ARIZONA RECORD, at 6–7 (April 1947); THE UNIVERSITY OF ARIZONA COLLEGE OF LAW 1915–1986, at 9 (1987)(monograph).

minimum requirements for admission to first year law."[35] She was admitted to the law school as an Arizona resident in September 1948.[36]

Mary Anne discovered on the first day of the fall semester that she was the only woman in her class of one hundred thirteen students, then the largest class in the history of the law school.[37] She was surrounded by young men, most of them military veterans, eager to get on with their lives. As the students filed into the Law College, then housed in a three-story red brick and limestone building originally built for the University's Library, Mary Anne felt conspicuous. In an interview ten years later, Mary Anne described her emotions: "[W]hen I saw that the entire University of Arizona law college student body consisted of men, I nearly quit. It scared me."[38] Indeed, women students were such a rarity that the school had not yet designated a women's restroom in the classroom area. Instead, female students were advised to use the restroom that had been provided for the secretary of the dean.[39]

Twenty-five women, in fact, had graduated previously from the College of Law since its first graduating class of 1918, and several of those graduates were steadfast supporters of incoming women law students. Lorna Lockwood was the second woman to graduate from the University of Arizona law school and the first to receive a Juris Doctor degree, then available to graduates holding an undergraduate degree. By the time Mary Anne entered law school, Lockwood had already served in the Arizona legislature and practiced with a private firm for several years. In 1951 she would be elected to the Maricopa County Superior Court, making her the first woman superior court judge in Arizona, and would be elected Chief Justice of the Arizona Supreme Court in 1965, becoming the first woman chief justice of any state high court in the nation.[40] In 1948, however, Lockwood was serving as assistant attorney general in Phoenix, and she made frequent trips to Tucson to meet with the women law students and welcome them into the Kappa Beta Pi Legal Sorority. Also, a few women were in the law school's upper classes when Mary Anne matriculated, and

---

35. Check Sheet—College of Law, August 25, 1948, Certificate of Eligibility for Admission to the College of Law, Student File for Mary Anne Reimann, University of Arizona College of Law.

36. Mary Anne's status as a resident under the University's admissisons standards apparently proved useful to her in later establishing residency for the purposes of obtaining a divorce in the local Arizona court. Richey Interview, *supra* note 24.

37. In 1948, due to large enrollments of returning veterans, 113 students were meeting in a classroom designed for forty-two. *Id.* at 8.

38. *Smugglers Don't Faze Mary Anne Reimann*, ARIZONA DAILY STAR, Feb. 9, 1958.

39. Interview with Jo Ann Diamos, Tucson, Arizona (Sept. 22, 1992).

40. ARIZONA SUPREME COURT, THE SUPERIOR COURT IN ARIZONA 1912-1984 at 29 (1985).

they provided encouragement by example. By coincidence, a former WASP trainee, Virginia Hash, was in the class ahead of Mary Anne. Mary Anne had met Hash before in Sweetwater, Texas, where Hash had been in the last WASP class, 44-W-10, graduating just days before the WASP's deactivation. She had worked as a private pilot after the war and then enrolled at the College of Law. Just as Mary Anne had encouraged Hash at Avenger Field in Texas, Hash in turn was able to encourage Mary Anne as an entering law student in Tucson.[41]

At the time of her entry into law school, Mary Anne lived at the Lazy Vee Ranch and gave its post office box as her permanent address. Shortly after the beginning of that first semester, however, she quit her job at the Lazy Vee and moved with Jerry Kelso to a one-bedroom apartment at the Old Adobe Stables owned by Marge Allen. The stables, located on River Road, boarded horses for local owners, including several race horses, and also operated a riding school. In exchange for watching the racing stables, arranging for studding, and occasionally accompanying Allen's horses on racing trips, Mary Anne received the apartment rent-free as well as a small monetary stipend. The stipend was essential, since, unlike many of her classmates, she was not a beneficiary of the G.I. Bill.

During the first semester, Mary Anne was known as something of a "mystery woman" among the other law students. As the students packed into the crowded lecture halls, Mary Anne's female presence attracted attention and she became uncharacteristically reserved. Most students sat in wooden pew-like benches, two to a bench, but a few single chairs were available along the sides of the lecture hall. At the beginning Mary Anne chose to occupy one of the single chairs.[42] She seldom chatted with her peers outside of class, and she did not spend her free time at the school. Instead, she would leave the school midday as soon as classes were over, often in a chauffeured station wagon. Her classmates were intrigued. Robert Roylston, who, with his twin brother Richard, became close friends with Mary Anne, recalled, "At first nobody knew what or who she was. We tried to figure out why she was in law school and where she lived and we heard she lived on a guest ranch. Of course, she wasn't going to give us any information unless we asked the right questions."[43]

Mary Anne's somewhat aloof demeanor during that first semester was probably the result of several factors. She and the other students were well aware of the discouraging odds that they would ever graduate. The attrition rate was known to be especially dramatic after the first semester's

41. *Interview with Virginia Hash*, March 9, 1987, Evo DeConcini Oral History Project: Arizona Legal History (Arizona Historical Society 1988).

42. Robert Roylston Interview, *supra* note 22.

43. *Id.*

much-feared final exams. Thus, the students during the first semester lived in a perpetual state of trepidation. "We were all very anxious," explained one classmate, who achieved academic distinction in law school despite his fears. "We were scared that we would flunk out. Everyone was generally floored by the whole system. You didn't know what to expect, and your future rode on one exam at the end of the course."[44]

In addition to her acute awareness of the failure rate, Mary Anne, as the only woman in a class of one hundred thirteen people, had her own unique pressure. Her failure would be noticed and might be viewed by some as evidence that women were not equipped to study law. Mary Anne, of course, had known a similar pressure during her training for the WASP, where each trainee felt that a botched landing or sloppy aerial maneuver would be held against women pilots generally. Mary Anne's response to the pressure of being the only woman in her law school class was stalwart: she studied assiduously in between the demands of her job at the Lazy Vee ranch and later at the Old Adobe Stables.

During that first semester, Mary Anne was under yet another kind of pressure—she was in the process of divorcing Bill Showers. She filed a complaint for divorce in October of 1948 and was granted the divorce in November. In that era of fault-based divorce, the complaining party had to allege and prove one of several statutory grounds for dissolving the marriage.[45] Mary Anne's complaint alleged the following misconduct against Showers:

---

44. Interview with Hon. Earl H. Carroll, United States District Judge, Tucson, Arizona (Feb. 19, 1993).

45. ARIZONA CODE OF 1939, Sec. 27-802, provided that divorce could be granted in any of the following cases:

(1) When adultery has been committed by either party;

(2) When one of the parties was physically incompetent at the time of marriage and has so continued to the time of commencement of the action:

(3) When one of the parties has been convicted of a felony, not on the testimony of the other party, and sentenced therefor to imprisonment;...

(4) When either party has wilfully deserted the other for the term of one [1] year next preceding the commencement of the action, or for habitual intemperance of either party;

(5) Where the husband or wife is guilty of excesses, cruel treatment or outrages toward the other, whether by the use of personal violence or other means;

(6) When the husband has neglected for the period of one [1] year to provide his wife with the common necessaries of life, having the ability to provide the same, or has failed to do so by reason of his idleness, profligacy or dissipation;

(7) When prior to the marriage either party shall have been convicted of a felony or infamous crime, in any state or country, without the knowledge of the

"(a) Excesses, cruel treatment and outrages toward the plaintiff such as to cause the plaintiff great mental suffering;

(b) Has been guilty of habitual intemperance;

(c) Has neglected for the period of one year last past to provide the plaintiff with the common necessaries of life, having the ability to provide same."[46]

The complaint, framed in the accusatory language of the then-existing divorce code, may appear more hostile in retrospect than Mary Anne felt at the time. The fault-based divorce laws required a showing of misconduct, and "cruel treatment" and "neglect" were standard allegations in divorce complaints. The additional and unnecessary allegation of "habitual intemperance" suggests that Showers's drinking had become a factor leading to the demise of the marriage. Although Showers denied all allegations of misconduct, he did not appear to actively contest the grounds for divorce. To the contrary, the divorce was granted without adversary hearings, and Showers and Mary Anne entered into a property settlement agreement to resolve the economic consequences of the dissolution.

The agreement divided the couple's household possessions and unenumerated "stocks and bonds," and awarded their automobile to Showers. Beyond her personal possessions, her share of mutually-held property, and $100 in attorneys fees, Mary Anne took nothing in the divorce. She waived all rights to alimony (a claim then available only to women).[47] She had not looked to Showers for support for at least a year, and her relinquishment of any alimony claim was in character. She had accepted the burdens of independence along with its advantages, and she apparently did not wish to prolong her ties, economic or otherwise, to her wealthy first husband. As she finalized the divorce from Showers, Mary Anne's focus was not on the past but on the future.

The administration of the College of Law prescribed the courses for the first and second years of law school and then gave the students a range of elective courses for the third year. Mary Anne's courseload was reduced

---

other party of such fact at the time of such marriage;

(8) In favor of the husband when the wife at the time of the marriage was pregnant by a man other than the husband, and without the husband's knowledge at the time of such marriage;

(9) When for any reason the husband and wife have not lived or cohabited together as husband and wife for a period of five [5] years or more.

46. Complaint for Divorce in the case of Mary Anne Showers v. William Showers, No. 30926 (Pima County Sup. Ct. Oct. 16, 1948).

47. *Id.* Property Settlement Agreement.

from the norm by one class each semester in her first year, presumably to enable her to take advantage of a policy allowing such reductions so that the student could pursue "gainful occupations."[48] Mary Anne's need to work must have served as a constant reminder to her of the government's failure to extend military status to the WASP. Nevertheless, she seemed to throw herself into the academic studies and her tasks at the Lazy Vee and the Old Adobe with gusto and without bitterness. Through her modest earnings at the ranch and the stables, she was able to support herself and pay the $55 in tuition and fees owing to the Law College each semester.

In the postwar climate in legal education, law faculties were responding to the skepticism of Legal Realism and the perceived need to carefully distinguish the American legal and political system from the totalitarian States that had been defeated in the war.[49] In that atmosphere, many academics emphasized the values of process and institutional restraint as a substitute for the discredited view that disputes of substantive law could be resolved by reference to certain, fixed, immutable principles. Morton Horwitz has observed that "[t]he single dominant theme in post-war American academic legal thought is the effort to find a 'morality of process' independent of results."[50] According to Horwitz, "the legal process school sought to absorb and temper the insights of Legal Realism after the triumph of the New Deal. Its most important concession to Realism was in its recognition that doctrinal formalism was incapable of eliminating discretion in the law. The task was instead to harness and channel that discretion through institutional arrangements."[51] Scholarly publications from the Arizona faculty in that era revealed an emphasis on doctrinal problems and procedural reforms.[52] Thus, Mary Anne received her legal education at a time when many legal scholars exalted strict adher-

---

48. *College of Law Announcement 1947/48—1948/49.* UNIVERSITY OF ARIZONA RECORD, at 10 (April 1947).

49. The identifiable beginnings of Legal Realism are often associated with the publications of Carl Llewellyn and Jerome Frank. *See* Karl Llewelyn, *A Realistic Jurisprudence—The Next Step*, 30 COLUM. L. REV. 431 (1930); *Jerome Frank, Law and the Modern Mind* (1930). *See generally* MORTON J. HORWITZ, THE TRANSFORMATION OF AMERICAN LAW 1870–1960 (1992); Singer, *Legal Realism Now*, 76 CALIF. L. REV. 465 (1988)(reviewing L. KALMAN, LEGAL REALISM AT YALE, 1927–1960 (1986)).

50. HORWITZ, *supra* note 49 at 253.

51. *Id.* at 254.

52. *See, e.g.,* Claude H. Brown, *The Hearsay Rule in Arizona*, 1 ARIZ. L. REV. 1(1959); Claude H. Brown, *Removal Procedure Under the Revised Judicial Code*, 19 U. CINN. L. REV. 171 (1950); Floyd E. Thomas, *Book Review*, 35 IOWA L. REV. 156 (1949)(reviewing A.S. CUTLER, SUCCESSFUL TRIAL TACTICS (1949)); Jack J. Rappeport, *The Husband's Management of Community Real Property*, 1 ARIZ. L. REV. 13 (1959).

ence to institutional roles. To them, the concept of judicial restraint was essential in a democratic system.[53] This philosophy was undoubtedly reflected in the mid-century teachings at the University of Arizona and necessarily influenced Mary Anne's own interpretation of the proper role for the state and federal judiciary.

Revealing an emphasis on common law subjects, Mary Anne's first-year curriculum included Contracts, Common Law Pleading, Criminal Law, Personal Property, Rights in Land, Agency, and Equity. For each course the students laboriously made their way through thick casebooks, briefing the cases and trying to distinguish the important from the trivial in the sea of words. She became accustomed to the socratic teaching method—the pedagogic technique in which the professor, through a series of elliptical questions, attempted to lead students to an enlightened understanding of their readings. The threat of public humiliation for the student was intensified in Mary Anne's era by the tradition that students stand, alone and vulnerable, to respond to the instructor's questions.

Some members of the all-male faculty had notorious reputations. Professor Claude H. Brown, a prolific scholar who taught Code Pleading and Evidence, was legendary in his capacity to instill terror in the students. "He would explore the limit of your knowledge," recalled Charles Ares, who graduated the year after Mary Anne and would eventually assume the deanship of the College of Law. "I remember starting out and he asked me a question and I answered it. He asked me another and I answered that, and the next day he asked me another question. It went on like that for three or four days, and finally he asked me a question I couldn't answer. I said, 'Mr. Brown, I'm sorry but I don't know.' That was the last question that he asked me. He had demonstrated the limit of my knowledge."[54] Brown's tough style could reduce the most confident of students to a mass of nerves. "I remember guys who had seen combat in World War II," another student commented, "but when they left Claude Brown's evidence class, the muscles in their faces would be twitching. His effect was that powerful."[55]

At the opposite end of the spectrum was Professor Chester H. Smith, a popular character whose lecturing style put students at ease. His property and legal ethics classes were favorites among the student body. Smith capitalized on his popularity by offering a bar review course after law school

---

53. Two of the most influential commentators were Judge Learned Hand and Professor Herbert Wechsler. *See* LEARNED HAND, THE BILL OF RIGHTS (1958); Herbert Wechsler, *Toward Neutral Principles of Constitutional Law*, 73 HARV. L. REV. 1 (1959).

54. Interview with Charles E. Ares, Tucson, Arizona (Aug. 20, 1992).

55. Carroll Interview, *supra* note 44.

in which students assembled in his back yard for his friendly lectures.[56] William S. Barnes, professor of criminal law and constitutional law, was less popular. His lecturing style left many students unmoved, and he did not project a sense of vision about his subjects. One former student expressed dismay that Barnes did not even hint that certain transformative changes in equal protection theory were imminent in the *Brown v. Board of Education* litigation.[57]

In one of the few remembered acknowledgements of Mary Anne's gender during law school, Professor Barnes reportedly asked Mary Anne in criminal law if she would like to leave the classroom during the discussion of a rape case. Mary Anne declined.[58] Another recollection of the "rape question" is different. According to that version, Barnes did not welcome the presence of women in the law school and made a point of calling on Mary Anne to recite whenever the readings touched on a sexual theme.[59] Thus, when the topic of rape came up in criminal law, all the students knew that Barnes would put Mary Anne on the spot. As predicted, Barnes asked Mary Anne how much penetration was necessary for the commission of the crime of rape. Without faltering, Mary Anne responded, "The slightest penetration."[60] According to classmates, Mary Anne did not appear to be troubled by the attention or the veiled hostility underlying Barnes' questions. Some twenty years later, she would revisit the definition of rape from the perspective of a trial court judge.

At the end of the first semester, the students sat through multi-hour final examinations in each of their courses, and the anxiety during that period was palpable. Mary Anne studied primarily alone and was intent on getting through the battery of tests. Having been out of an academic setting for almost ten years, however, the requisite close analysis of case law and memorization of doctrinal elements were difficult for her, especially in Dean Lyons' Contracts class. When she completed the first semester exams, she was convinced that she had failed. So strong was her sense of defeat that she came close to dropping out of law school. In January, at the beginning of the second semester, Mary Anne did not register for classes, and her absence from the class roster was noticeable. After some concerted searching, Dean Lyons learned that she was in Phoenix visiting

---

56. Robert Roylston Interview, *supra* note 22.

57. Carroll Interview, *supra* note 44. *Brown v. Board of Education,* 347 U.S. 483 (1954), was first argued before the United States Supreme Court in 1952 and was in litigation while Judge Carroll and Mary Anne were in law school.

58. Interview with James F. McNulty, Jr., Tucson, Arizona (July 16, 1992).

59. Interview with William Kimble, Tucson, Arizona (Sept. 29, 1995).

60. Interview with Daniel J. Sammons, Tucson, Arizona (Oct. 19, 1992); Kimble Interview, *supra* note 59.

friends. He telephoned her and asked her why she had not registered in law school for the second semester. She explained to him, with pragmatic logic, that she believed she had done poorly on her exams and that she did not think it worthwhile to register. "I'm not going to put up my tuition money and have to fight to get it back," she reportedly informed him. Just as patiently, he replied, "Miss Reimann, if I were you I would get back down here and sign up for the next semester."[61]

Without the encouragement from Dean Lyons, Mary Anne might have ended her legal career then and there. Instead, she returned to the school as Dean Lyons had urged. Although her grades the first semester were unexceptional (she earned the equivalent of a "C" in every course but Contracts, in which she received the equivalent of a "D"), she had at least proven her ability to do passing work. For the duration of law school she continued to study for long solitary hours in her apartment at the stables. Although the academic work never came easily to Mary Anne, she did not receive a grade lower than a "C" for the remainder of law school. In her second year, she completed all the required courses (Equity, Titles, Wills, Legal Bibliography, Private Corporations, Legal Profession, Code Pleading, and Trusts), and also made up the Torts course that she had omitted from her first year. In her third year, she took the required courses of Evidence and Constitutional Law, and found the Constitutional Law course especially challenging.[62] To meet the minimum requirement of 80 units for graduation, Mary Anne also enrolled in an assortment of electives, including Domestic Relations, Tax, Water Rights, and a variety of commercial law and trial practice courses. Some of her highest grades were in litigation-oriented courses, such as Practice Court, Trial Procedure, and Torts. Her final grade point average placed her at about the fiftieth percentile mark within her graduating class.[63]

After the first semester of law school, Mary Anne loosened up in her relations with her classmates. She became close friends with the Roylston brothers, whose twinly antics kept their peers laughing. The Roylstons, identical twins who had moved to Arizona from Tennessee, were large, rose-complexioned, affable men, and Mary Anne appreciated their irrepressible, homespun wit. The twins not only shared a wooden bench in the lecture halls, they also shared a single notebook on which they jointly created a single set of lecture notes. Robert explained, "One of us would be writing something at the top of the page, and the other one would pick

61. Richey Interview, *supra* note 24.

62. *Id.*

63. Mary Anne's transcript from the College of Law shows that she was ranked 37th in her graduating class of seventy-six students. Student File, Mary Anne Reimann, University of Arizona College of Law.

up another point in the lecture and put it in at the bottom of the page. We never had to say anything to each other." Similarly, if one twin were called on in class, he would start the answer, but the other might finish the response if the first one faltered.[64]

Mary Anne and the Roylstons forged a bond of friendship during law school that would last throughout her life. They frequently pooled their money at the end of the week and would meet for beer and a game of poker. Occasionally, Mary Anne and her roommate Jerry Kelso would entertain the Roylstons for dinner at the stables apartment. Although Mary Anne preferred to study alone, she and the Roylstons and several other friends gathered one memorable evening at the end of their second year in law school to study for the final exam in Dean Lyons' Legal Profession course. Mary Anne, of course, was the only woman among a group of several men. Because the exam was the last of the semester and the class was only a one-unit course, the group felt a distinct absence of pressure. They bought some beer and met at the modest residence belonging to one of the members. According to Robert Roylston, they drank a little beer, told a few stories, talked about ethics, and then drank a little more beer. Although they stayed up for most of the night, the attention to ethics diminished as the evening progressed. The next morning, the group trudged into the examination room and performed poorly. Roylston recollected that everyone in the study group except Mary Anne received either a "D" or an "F" in the course. She earned a "C."[65]

As time went on, Mary Anne felt increasingly at ease within the male camaraderie of the law school, and the students ostensibly accepted her as "one of their own." Classmates found that she could drink, swear, play cards, golf, fly planes, and talk sports with the best of them. They did not view her as a "woman" or "different," and her lack of stereotypical femininity eased her entry into the male world. She was physically imposing— tall, large-boned, and muscular. Her demeanor was direct and forceful, and her gaze steady. Her clothes were tailored and understated, and she always wore "sensible shoes."[66] The low-heeled shoes portrayed an unfeminine practicality, a world view that valued physical ease and stability above contemporary aesthetics.[67] Her loud, robust laughter, often triggered by self-mockery, contributed to her popularity.

---

64. Robert Roylston Interview, *supra* note 22.

65. *Id.*

66. Interview with W. Edward Morgan, Tucson, Arizona (Sept. 9, 1992).

67. Susan Brownmiller's passage on "sensible shoes" seems to capture Mary Anne's viewpoint:

> "Sensible shoes" announce an unfeminine sensibility, a value system that
> places physical comfort above the critical mission of creating a sex differ-

As much as she was a part of the male world, however, she was not in-vited into the two legal fraternities on campus, Phi Delta Phi and Phi Alpha Delta. According to one classmate, "We did not even consider inviting her to join. I don't recall anyone even thinking 'maybe it would be nice to include Mary Anne.'"[68] If such exclusions offended Mary Anne, she did not express her feelings to others. Similarly, she did not criticize the male-only membership rules of several prestigious Tucson clubs in later years. Although she rankled at discriminatory laws that excluded women from particular walks of life, she apparently saw private associa-tions (however important they might be for professional contacts) as free of a moral obligation to open their memberships to all individuals.

At the same time, Mary Anne valued her friendships with women lawyers and she remained supportive of new women law students. She be-came the twenty-fourth member of Kappa Beta Pi, the legal sorority at the Law College, in March of 1949 and she went on to assume its presidency in 1951. According to Jo Ann Diamos, who graduated from the Law Col-lege in 1953, Mary Anne helped welcome the incoming women law stu-dents by regularly attending Kappa Beta Pi social functions. Diamos saw the basic purpose of Kappa Beta Pi as one of "networking"—to help new women lawyers establish contacts and get into the field. As such, the orga-nization was an acknowledgement that women, vastly outnumbered in the legal profession, could benefit from mutual support. At the same time, the sorority gatherings provided a safe environment in which the women could "let down their hair." At the meetings, Mary Anne, as the sole third-year woman, along with a few extroverted women graduates, would engage in antics to make the new students laugh, such as less-than-flatter-ing imitations of professors or male students.[69]

During her second year in law school, Mary Anne began to establish a friendship with William K. Richey, a man five years her junior who would ultimately become her second husband. Richey, whose father Tom Richey had been a well-known lawyer in Arizona since before statehood and one-time president of the Arizona State Bar Association, had come to the Col-

---

ence where one does not exist in nature. Sensible shoes betray a lack of concern for the aesthetic and sexual feelings of men, or a stubborn unwillingness to compromise graciously in their direction. Sensible shoes aren't fun. They hold no promise of exotic mysteries, they neither hint at incapacitation or whisper of ineffectual weaponry. Sensible shoes aren't sexy.... They are crisply efficient, providing a firm, stable anchor, a bal-anced posture, a sturdy base from which to turn on the heel and quickly move on.

BROWNMILLER, FEMININITY 186–87 (1984).

68. Carroll Interview, *supra* note 44.

69. Diamos Interview, *supra* note 39.

lege of Law after serving in the South Pacific in the United States Marine Corps in World War II. He was a man of contrasts—an expert boxer, on the one hand, who in 1941 held the Arizona State Light Heavyweight Amateur Championship and had attended Michigan State University on a boxing scholarship, and an artist, on the other hand, whose western bronze sculptures are graceful works of beauty. Richey's passion for sculpture was perhaps linked to his artistically gifted mother, Marie Grandpre, who was a light opera singer of some fame at the turn of the century.[70]

Richey entered the Law College in 1947 but dropped out for financial reasons and traveled to the territory of Alaska to find work. He remained in Alaska, where he was engaged in rugged blasting work for the construction of new roads, until the fall of 1949. A horse-racing enthusiast, Richey had noticed Mary Anne at the Rillito Race Track in Tucson several times before law school but did not get to know her until he returned from his labors in Alaska. The two had their first date on New Year's night, January 1, 1950, and soon became an acknowledged couple in Tucson. During the remainder of law school, Mary Anne often helped Bill study. Bill did not enjoy academic work, and, in his words, he would not have made it through law school without Mary Anne.[71] As it was, Bill did not graduate until 1952, one year after Mary Anne's graduation. Over the course of their long courtship, the two discovered mutual joy in such pastimes as horseback riding in the washes and arroyos surrounding Tucson, hunting and fishing in the forested White Mountains of central Arizona, and attending sporting events at the University of Arizona. Characteristically, Mary Anne was at ease when she would find herself to be the only woman in a group of male hunters, heading for the back country to bring down a deer. With her 20-gauge shotgun in tow and Bill by her side, she was as comfortable on those excursions as she had been years earlier on the many outings with her brothers in the hills of Indiana.

In May of 1951, Mary Anne graduated from the College of Law. Of the 113 students who entered in 1948, only seventy-six remained in the graduating class. Mary Anne's immense pleasure at graduating was diminished slightly when she attended a luncheon held by the local bar association in honor of the graduates. On the luncheon programs, the association had printed each graduate's name, home state, and birth date. Mary Anne was chagrined to realize that the luncheon programs revealed her age, a bit of personal information she had not publicized during law school. By then quite at ease with being the only woman in the graduating class, she was less comfortable with being known, at age thirty-three, as one of the oldest

---

70. Richey Interview, *supra* note 24.
71. *Id.*

graduates in the class. She complained to her friends that she "had kept her age a secret for three years and with one fell swoop, the whole world knows it."[72]

Chester Smith's backyard bar review course began in early June. Through Smith's lectures, often presented in the sweltering summer evenings, and additional independent studying, the applicants prepared themselves for the grueling two-day bar examination at the end of July. Mary Anne passed the Arizona State Bar exam on her first attempt, the only woman among the forty-five successful applicants that July. Her presence among the candidates was sufficiently noteworthy for the local daily newspaper to announce her success in the headline, "Tucson Woman Is Bar Member."[73]

Many of the graduates, perhaps feeling the bond that often connects the survivors of an ordeal, remained close friends throughout their professional lives. Moreover, many members of the class went on to excel in their professional lives, including four who were appointed to the federal district court bench: Earl Carroll, Valdemar Cordova, Alfredo Marquez, and Mary Anne. Those who achieved prominence helped others find success through a network of friendship. Mary Anne, the pioneer whose gender was "hardly noticeable"[74] to many of her colleagues, was firmly situated within that network, and her connections among her graduating class would serve her well in the future.

---

72. Robert Roylston Interview, *supra* note 22.

73. THE ARIZONA DAILY STAR, October 7, 1951.

74. Interview with Hon. Alfredo C. Marquez, United States District Judge, Tucson, Arizona (Jan. 26, 1993).

CHAPTER FIVE

The Early Years of Lawyering

When Mary Anne Reimann graduated from law school in 1951, the local market for law graduates was limited. Nationwide, the majority of graduates in that era entered the legal profession as solo practitioners, a demographic fact which did not change until the early 1960s.[1] In Arizona, moreover, large law firms had not yet arrived, and the most recent graduates of Arizona's only law school often were forced to pursue the next logical alternative: they opened up their own offices, hung out the proverbial shingle, and hoped for the best.[2]

The market for women lawyers was even less promising. Women at that time comprised slightly less than three percent of all practicing lawyers in the nation.[3] In Arizona, only thirty women were listed in the membership directory of the Arizona State Bar the year of Mary Anne's graduation, out of a total of approximately 920 members.[4] In the private law firm world, women applicants of sterling credentials fell victim to blatant sexism in hiring, sometimes justified on the basis of the perceived need to cater to the biases of the clientele. In the 1950s, women were virtually invisible in the leading private firms across the country.[5] As a result, the few women who possessed law degrees in that era turned disproportionately to government agencies where there was less resistance to their gender.[6] Cynthia Fuchs Epstein has posited that women historically have had greater success in finding employment with the government than in

---

1. *See* RICHARD L. ABEL, AMERICAN LAWYERS 300 (1989)(Table).

2. Mary Anne's law school friends Richard and Robert Roylston and Norval Jasper, for example, opened up small downtown law offices in an old adobe building near the Pima County Courthouse. At the beginning, they spent much of their time playing cards in a back room, stopping only when the rare client would walk in the front door. Interviews with Hon. Richard N. Roylston and Hon. Robert O. Roylston, former Judges, Pima County Superior Court, Tucson, Arizona (Aug, 19, 1992); Interviews with Hon. Robert O. Roylston, Tucson, Arizona (Aug. 24, 1992, Oct. 5, 1992).

3. *See* CYNTHIA FUCHS EPSTEIN, WOMEN IN LAW 4 (2d ed. 1993)(Tables 1.1, 1.2). According to Epstein, estimates of the percentage of women in the legal profession in 1950 and 1951 have ranged from 2.5 percent to 4.1 percent, depending on the source.

4. STATE BAR OF ARIZONA, 1951 MEMBERSHIP DIRECTORY.

5. *See* EPSTEIN, *supra* note 3, at 175–80, 194–95; KAREN BERGER MORELLO, THE INVISIBLE BAR 194–217 (1986).

6. *See* EPSTEIN, *supra* note 3, at 97 (reporting that in 1950, about 28 percent of women lawyers worked for government, as compared to 14 percent of male lawyers).

the private sector because government provides a "haven of universalism" and has more readily disavowed discriminatory attitudes.[7]

The experience of another Arizona woman attorney is illustrative of what women faced upon graduation. Sandra Day O'Connor, who grew up on the sprawling acreage of the "Lazy B" Ranch in southeastern Arizona, achieved academic distinction during her law school career at Stanford, graduating in 1953. Nevertheless, as she put it, "after graduating near the top of my class at Stanford Law School, [I] was unable to obtain a position at any national law firm, except as a legal secretary."[8] O'Connor took a job instead as deputy county attorney with the San Mateo County Attorney's Office in southern California. Her subsequent career moves included public service in all three branches of government in Arizona, culminating in her appointment by President Ronald Reagan in 1981 to the United States Supreme Court.[9] Reflecting an attitude common to early women achievers, O'Connor was not bitter about her initial lack of job prospects. In an interview in 1971, she explained that "[w]hile women traditionally have not been encouraged in our society to compete with men, this is changing." She opined, moreover, that women had not yet contributed greatly to the law but that in the future women could be expected to make an "equal" contribution. Interestingly, her remarks did not suggest that she perceived of herself as having been the object of discrimination in her professional life.[10]

Although Mary Anne's later assessment was that "women were handicapped in the legal profession because the big law firms would not accept them,"[11] she was one of the few women to find a position in a private firm upon graduation. After being admitted to the State Bar of Arizona, Mary Anne accepted a job offer from the well-regarded Tucson law firm of Scruggs, Butterfield & Rucker. Partner Edward W. Scruggs, an influential Republican leader, had a distinguished career, serving as Clerk of the United States District Court from 1936 to 1947 and then leaving the court to establish his own law firm. In addition to his law practice,

---

7. *Id.* at 112–13 (quoting Robert K. Merton, in part).

8. Justice Sandra Day O'Connor, *Portia's Progress*, 66 N.Y.U. L. REV. 1546, 1549 (1991).

9. O'Connor served as an assistant attorney general in Arizona from 1965 through 1969, when she was appointed to the Arizona state senate to fill a vacancy. She subsequently was elected to two full terms. In 1974, she won election to the Maricopa County Superior Court, and in 1979, she was appointed to the Arizona Court of Appeals. THE SUPREME COURT JUSTICES 339 (MELVIN I. UROFSKY, ED. 1994).

10. Rosemary Gallon, *History of Arizona Women Lawyers and Judges*, 28–29 (1971)(Unpublished manuscript on file with the Arizona Historical Society).

11. *Id.*

Scruggs held the position of United States Attorney for the District of Arizona, then considered a part-time government job. Under the administration of President Dwight Eisenhower, however, the Justice Department in 1953 declared all U.S. Attorney positions to be full-time appointments and prohibited outside employment. With that change, Scruggs, whose law practice was too lucrative to sacrifice for public service, resigned as U.S. Attorney and devoted himself full-time to the law firm.[12]

Scruggs liked Mary Anne's demeanor and her apparent willingness to work on any legal task. He ultimately offered her the position of "clerk/associate" at $50 per week.[13] Mary Anne's employment at the firm was unusual for two reasons: she was a woman, and she was at that time a registered Democrat. Those "shortcomings," however, were overcome by her winsome personal manner, her solid record at the College of Law, and several strong recommendations by acquaintances. Her politically-active classmate Norval Jasper, for instance, who was president of the Young Republicans in Arizona, strongly encouraged Scruggs to hire Mary Anne,[14] and Bill Richey, through his contacts in Republican politics, also helped Mary Anne's prospects.

Although Mary Anne's tenure at the law firm lasted only a few months, she seemed to feel immediately comfortable within the male-dominated world of private law practice. She was temperamentally equipped to deal coolly with unwarranted settlement demands from opposing counsel and to drive hard bargains for her clients. Her disarming honesty and direct speech earned her a reputation as a trustworthy adversary. "You always knew where you stood with Mary Anne," commented one lawyer who had tried cases against her. "She was an honorable opponent."[15]

While most of the work at Scruggs, Butterfield & Rucker was in general civil litigation, Mary Anne received a few criminal appointments that served as her introduction to the trial courtroom. Her first appearance in a courtroom was in defense of "Alice Miller, former operator of Pima County houses of prostitution."[16] Mary Anne was appointed to represent the indigent Miller in Pima County Superior Court on a charge of crimi-

---

12. Scruggs remained active in Republican politics and in 1964 was appointed by Governor Paul J. Fannin to the Arizona Supreme Court for one year, to complete the term of Justice Renz Jennings who resigned to run for the United States Senate. *See* 96 Arizona Reports V ("Supreme Court Justices"). Scruggs' appointment expired January 4, 1965. Ernest McFarland was elected to fill the Jennings spot, effective as of the same date.

13. Interview with William K. Richey, Nutrioso, Arizona (July 16–17, 1992); Telephone Interviews with Richey (Sept. 20, 1992, Sept. 27, 1992, and Sept. 21, 1994).

14. Interview with Norval W. Jasper, Tucson, Arizona (Aug. 27, 1992).

15. Interview with W. Edward Morgan, Tucson, Arizona (Sept. 9, 1992).

16. *Mary Anne Reimann To Aid County*, TUCSON DAILY CITIZEN, January 1, 1952.

nal contempt of court.[17] Miller was accused of failing to respond to a subpoena to appear as a witness in an unrelated criminal trial. Although Mary Anne lost the case and Miller was sentenced to ninety days at the Pima County Jail, the client apparently developed a liking for her young counsel and complimented her on her courtroom performance. With a twinkle in her eye, the brothel owner assured Mary Anne that if she ever found herself out of work, there would always be a place for Mary Anne in one of the houses.[18] That anecdote would surface in some of Mary Anne's stump speeches when she ran for a judgeship ten years later, much to the delight of her audiences.

Mary Anne's competitive nature surfaced in litigation, and her normally calm demeanor sometimes gave way to raw anger when she sensed that she had been defeated by ruse or subterfuge. On occasion that anger led her to make heated accusations. For example, she once represented a male defendant in a criminal action prosecuted by her friend Norval Jasper, then working as deputy county attorney. During the course of the prosecution, Mary Anne apparently developed the belief that Jasper had been less than forthcoming in his pretrial disclosures of evidence. When the jury returned with a verdict of guilty, Mary Anne leaned over to Jasper and angrily whispered, "You son of a bitch, you took advantage of me." Her words wounded Jasper, who recalled, "I had such admiration for Mary Anne. I would rather have had God accuse me of doing something underhanded."[19] That impulsive burst of anger from Mary Anne, always surprising to the targeted person, seemed to flare in circumstances that threatened her sense of control. As she matured professionally, her desire to influence or control events, outcomes, or people seemed to grow as well.

Mary Anne's intermittent forays into the courtroom while at Scruggs, Butterfield & Rucker were a seductive first taste of trial lawyering. Sensing that she could be a successful trial attorney, she decided to seek out a position where she could get more frequent trial experience. That oppor-

---

17. Alice Miller was a material witness in criminal actions against two government officials and was therefore held on a bond of $5,000 imposed by the Justice Court of Pima County. *See* State of Arizona v. Guiney, No. A-7566 (Pima County Sup. Ct. 1951)(Order Holding Material Witness). In exchange for her cooperation, the Pima County Attorney ultimately petitioned for a grant of immunity regarding offenses to which she testified. *See* State of Arizona v. Alice Miller, No. A-800 (Pima County Sup. Ct. 1951)(Petition for Grant of Immunity to State's Witness). Mary Anne's representation came after the request for immunity and apparently was triggered by Miller's failure to further cooperate with the County Attorney's Office.

18. Richey Interviews, *supra* note 13.

19. Jasper Interview, *supra* note 14.

tunity came sooner than she had expected. On January 1, 1952, Mary Anne was hired by Pima County Attorney Robert Morrison to join his staff of deputy county attorneys in Tucson. Mary Anne's move into public service was heralded in the local press, with one paper's headline proclaiming, "Woman Deputy Atty Is Hired."[20]

Although the hiring was notable because of Mary Anne's gender—she was the first woman deputy county attorney in Pima County—County Attorney Morrison's contemporaneous statements reveal the influence of stereotypical assumptions about women. In one newspaper account, Morrison described Mary Anne's unique value to the government agency: "Miss Reimann will handle adoptions, non-support complaints and other cases arising from domestic problems 'which a woman lawyer is particularly fitted to handle'.... [According to Morrison] many women coming into the county attorney's office hesitate to tell their troubles to a man."[21] Thus, although Mary Anne would soon move beyond the stereotypical array of women's concerns, her entry into the prosecutor's office was viewed as particularly beneficial because of her gender. Morrison's statements about the suitability of his new hire for "female" work were consistent with assumptions prevalent at the time about the narrow range of work appropriate for women lawyers.[22]

Mary Anne's colleagues in the Pima County Attorney's Office were a distinguished group and included some of the finest trial lawyers in the state. Like Mary Anne, a number of her colleagues went on to positions of prominence. Morris Udall, who graduated from the University of Arizona College of Law in 1949, was elected Pima County Attorney the same year Mary Anne joined the office. After a surprising defeat in a bid for a superior court judgeship in 1956, he established a thriving private practice. In 1961 he was elected to the U.S. House of Representatives and thus began his thirty-year career in Congress. Alfredo Marquez, Mary Anne's classmate in law school, enjoyed a successful private law practice in Tucson before his appointment in 1979 to the United States District Court by President Jimmy Carter. Charles Ares, a 1952 graduate of the College of Law, practiced with Udall & Udall after his service with the County Attorney's Office and then joined the law faculty at New York University in 1961. He returned to Tucson to serve as Dean of the University of Ari-

---

20. *Woman Deputy Atty. is Hired*, THE ARIZONA DAILY STAR, January 1, 1952.

21. *Mary Anne Reimann To Aid County*, TUCSON DAILY CITIZEN, January 1, 1952.

22. A government publication in 1958 reflected a similar set of biases. A Labor Department announcement advised women lawyers to pursue a narrow range of work, including real estate, juvenile law, domestic relations, patent, and probate. *See* VERNA ELIZABETH GRIFFIN, EMPLOYMENT OPPORTUNITIES FOR WOMEN IN LEGAL WORK (U.S. Gov't Printing Office 1958), cited in EPSTEIN, *supra* note 3, at 81.

zona College of Law from 1966 to 1973 and remained with the College as a member of the faculty. Raul Castro, a native of Mexico, graduated from the University of Arizona College of Law in 1949. He was elected Pima County Attorney in 1956, defeating his Republican opponent Bill Richey by several thousand votes. He was elected to the Pima County Superior Court in 1958 and remained on the bench until 1964, when President Lyndon B. Johnson appointed him ambassador to San Salvador, a presidential action that indirectly benefitted Mary Anne, since she would be appointed by Governor Paul J. Fannin to fill Castro's vacancy on the Superior Court. Castro's later career included two more ambassadorships in Latin America and election to the office of governor of Arizona in 1974.[23] Thus, Mary Anne joined an unusually talented and ambitious group of men; with her aura of self-confidence, her forceful physical presence, and her bravado, she held her own among them.

At the County Attorney's Office, Mary Anne initially concentrated on "domestic relations matters"—as predicted by the local press. She prosecuted parents who were delinquent in their child support payments and finalized adoption petitions on behalf of petitioning adoptive parents. She disliked the support work but enjoyed the adoption petitions, since the outcome in the latter context was almost always positive for everyone concerned. Unlike the grim and often frustrating business of pursuing recalcitrant fathers on support obligations, in adoptions a victory meant a successful placement of an infant with an exuberantly appreciative couple.[24]

In her criminal work, she began by trying misdemeanors in the Pima County Justice Court, but rapidly worked her way up to felony prosecutions in the Pima County Superior Court, including first-degree murder, rape, assault, kidnapping, burglary and larceny, and arson. Under the tutelage of her mentors, she honed the unique skills of the trial lawyer. Morris Udall was a master at summations, the closing argument before a jury. According to Charles Ares, "[Udall] had an uncanny knack for putting himself inside jurors' heads and understanding what would appeal to their common sense. Once he had done that and taken to his feet with his yellow pad in hand, his command of the courtroom was awe inspiring. One lawyer who had witnessed the performance said he had just watched Morris Udall tuck twelve jurors under his arm and march them

23. In 1968, Castro was appointed ambassador to Bolivia, one of the more important diplomatic positions in South America. He was elected Governor of Arizona in 1974, and in 1977 was appointed ambassador to Argentina by President Jimmy Carter. He has since returned to Arizona where he still engages in private practice. *Raul H. Castro*, ARIZONA BAR FOUNDATION ORAL HISTORY PROJECT: ARIZONA LEGAL HISTORY (June 7, July 10, 1991).

24. Richey Interviews, *supra* note 13.

purposefully to the jury room. Some defense lawyers even went so far as to waive final argument just to deny him the final word."[25] Although Mary Anne did not possess Udall's legendary gift for homespun oratory, she learned from him the value of marshalling the bits and pieces of evidence in a case into a coherent whole, and his casual and forthright style with jurors came naturally to Mary Anne. In addressing a jury, she was plain-spoken. "She seemed to know what juries would understand, what they would be interested in," a colleague remembered. "She had her eyes on the facts and she brought them out."[26]

Another Udall practice in the County Attorney's Office was to make available to criminal defense counsel the entire prosecutorial file. Although the rules of criminal procedure at that time did not require such disclosures, Udall believed in an open-file policy as a matter of fairness. Mary Anne and the other deputies followed his example, and she would continue that practice when she moved to the United States Attorney's Office.

In the early 1950s, before the Warren Court's expansion of constitutional protections for persons charged with crime, coercion of confessions from criminal defendants was an unfortunate reality. In Pima County, the physical location of the county jail invited such action by prosecutors. The Pima County Jail was housed in the same building as the Pima County Attorney's Office, removed by only one flight of stairs. Alfredo Marquez recalled, "As soon as you were assigned a case, you knew the guy was right above you and you could get a statement from him. I used to get a little upset with the deputies who would go up and get a confession. You knew the guy was up there, and he didn't have a lawyer."[27] Mary Anne, to Marquez's memory, was not inclined to take advantage of the jail detainees in that manner.

In her two years in the County Attorney's Office, Mary Anne got the trial experience she had been wanting. With Morris Udall at the helm, the deputies enjoyed a fair amount of independence. Not a zealous administrator, Udall was busy with his own caseload for the county, and at the same time he continued to practice privately with his brother Stuart. Mary Anne and the other deputies were in the courtroom on a daily basis, and she quickly established her competence to act as lead trial counsel. Her first felony trial was a first-degree murder case in which she was second chair to Raul Castro. Castro recalled that the defendant was an inmate of the Pima County Jail who had murdered a fellow inmate with a metal

---

25. Charles E. Ares, *Morris K. Udall, Arizona Lawyer*, THE UNIVERSITY OF ARIZONA LAW RECORD, Vol. 13, No. 1, at 7 (Fall 1991).

26. Interview with Charles E. Ares, Tucson, Arizona (Aug. 20, 1992).

27. Interview with Hon. Alfredo C. Marquez, United States District Judge, Tucson, Arizona (Jan. 26, 1993).

fork. Castro and Mary Anne succeeded in obtaining a conviction, and Castro was impressed with Mary Anne's competence and willingness to put in long hours for trial preparation. He found that although the jurors were surprised to see a woman prosecutor in the courtroom, they forgot about her gender once she began examining witnesses. She was clear-headed under pressure, she was aggressive when necessary, and she was not easily intimidated.[28]

During her tenure at the office, Mary Anne tried approximately sixty cases, serving as sole counsel in four-fifths of the cases. About one-third of her total caseload was civil, cases in which she represented Pima County in commercial disputes and in defending tort claims. Of all the cases she tried, more than two-thirds were to a jury.[29] As deputy county attorney, she established a reputation as a promising trial lawyer—well-prepared, blunt and forceful in her arguments, and unintimidated by the grisly facts or surly characters common to many criminal cases. She was known to be meticulous in her evidentiary proof, and she excelled at cross-examination. Her style was not fireworks and flamboyance; rather, she would build the case through careful questioning of witnesses. And, she would sometimes show anger at witnesses who "turned" on the stand.

Charles Ares recalled that in his first jury trial, he second-chaired Mary Anne. The case was a criminal action involving first-degree burglary charges against a defendant named "Bunky" Bossert.[30] In preparing for the case, Mary Anne had spoken with a young female witness whose testimony was material to the government's proof. On the stand, under Mary Anne's questioning, the witness began to change her story from the version she had previously given. Mary Anne requested a recess, called the witness into the corridor outside the courtroom, and asked Ares to wait for her down the hall. Ares recalled seeing Mary Anne, her muscular frame leaning against the wall, fiercely warning the witness to tell the truth. Ares thought he heard a caveat along the following lines: "You little bitch, if you don't tell the truth, I'll haul you in for perjury." The young woman revised her testimony immediately after the recess.[31]

In spite of Mary Anne's rigorous schedule at the County Attorney's Office, she characteristically made time for recreation. She managed to play tennis and golf regularly, ride horses frequently, hunt occasionally, and maintain her relationship with Bill Richey. As they had recognized during

---

28. Telephone Interview with Raul H. Castro (July 28, 1993).

29. Mary Anne Richey Biographical Data Questionnaire, completed March 3, 1976, for Nomination for Appointment to United States District Court.

30. *See* State of Arizona v. Albert M. Bossert, No. A-9064 (Pima County Sup. Ct. 1954).

31. Ares Interview, *supra* note 26.

law school, Richey and Mary Anne were profoundly compatible. Her fierce competitiveness seemed to meld well with his more complacent attitude toward life. Moreover, throughout their relationship, his solid self-image allowed him to be comfortable in the shadow of her professional career. Perhaps Richey's artistic creativity and talent, always impressive to Mary Anne, provided a necessary dimension in which he alone excelled. Also, they shared a passion for the outdoors, for hunting and fishing, for animals, and for the craggy mountains of the western states.

During the two years that Mary Anne spent with the County Attorney's Office, Richey served as the elected representative from District 19 in the Arizona House. A Republican, he had been elected in 1952, the same year he graduated from the College of Law. Issues before the Twenty-first Legislature included matters of great public interest, such as school finance reform, revision of the state's income tax laws, and water law reform.[32] Among the House bills that actually achieved enactment during Richey's tenure were several pieces of significant legislation, including bills regulating the health and safety of railroad employment, the sale of state lands, school finance, and a bill imposing modest limits on the possession and sale of firearms. The legislative session saw its share of less momentous measures as well, such as a bill establishing the name of Hoover Dam, and a bill establishing the Palo Verde as the state tree of Arizona.[33]

Richey, however, did not play a prominent role in securing the passage of any particular legislation and did not enjoy his term as representative. He recalls leaving the legislature with a sense of disgust for state politics. Richey saw the legislators as devoted primarily to enhancing their own positions and increasing their chances of reelection, and he disliked the

---

32. *See* 1953 Session Laws of Arizona, 21st Legislature, 1st Regular Session; 1954 Session Laws of Arizona, 21st Legislature, 2nd Regular Session. Governor Howard Pyle opened the First Regular Session by introducing the major issues facing the representatives. He proposed a complete revision and modernization of the state income tax law, and he urged attention to public finance and taxation, with special consideration to the impact on school districts. He also suggested activating an Arizona Boundary Commission to work with a parallel commission in California to establish a true boundary between the two states. Finally, the Governor expressed his concern about the unsettled legal position on water ownership and Arizona's continually receding underground water table. In opening the Second Regular Session, Governor Pyle addressed the issue of public school financing, the need for greater attention to public health, and the establishment of a tourist and industrial development commission to improve the economic life of Arizona. *Id.*

33. Also enacted during Richey's tenure were bills creating the Department of Finance, the Department of Public Schools, and the Arizona Commission of Indian Affairs. *See* 1953 & 1954 Session Laws of Arizona, *supra* note 32.

time-consuming politicking that seemed to be an inevitable part of legislative work. A pragmatic, down-to-earth, unpretentious man, Richey remarked, "I didn't like the way they did business up there. I like to get things done."[34] In order to "get things done," Richey did not run for re-election but, instead, entered fulltime private practice after his two years of service in Phoenix.

Mary Anne and Bill were inseparable during their lengthy "courtship," and she made frequent visits to Phoenix when Bill was there on legislative business. On one memorable visit, she flew up to Phoenix with Ed Scruggs in Scruggs' private plane to watch Richey when the House was in session. On flying toward the landing field with Scruggs, Mary Anne saw that the aircraft was coming in at a bad angle. As she recounted to Bill Richey later, she shouted to Scruggs that the plane's nose was too low, and a few second later Scruggs did indeed drive the plane's nose into the ground, damaging the propeller and jostling the passengers considerably in the cockpit. Shaken but unhurt, Mary Anne proceeded to the statehouse where she watched Richey from the balcony, and informed him only at lunch that she and Scruggs had crashed their plane. Together they laughed about the narrow escape, but Bill silently marveled at Mary Anne's cavalier attitude toward the event.[35]

Although Richey's term in the House of Representatives did not advance his career significantly, his association with one fellow legislator did help Mary Anne. Jack Hays served one term in the House alongside Richey. After working as state chairman of the Eisenhower for President Committee, Hays was appointed by Eisenhower to the position of U.S. Attorney for the District of Arizona when Ed Scruggs resigned.[36] Hays, a leading Republican in the state, would ultimately be appointed to the Arizona Supreme Court by Governor Paul Fannin. After Hays received the appointment from Eisenhower, Richey suggested that he consider Mary Anne for an opening in the U.S. Attorney's Office in Tucson.[37] Hays, who already was an admirer of Mary Anne's, took the suggestion seriously. At the time, Mary Anne's close friend and classmate from law school, Robert Roylston, was Assistant U.S. Attorney in the Tucson office, having been hired under Scruggs. Roylston was exuberantly in favor of Mary Anne's hire and let his wishes be known. Moreover, Scruggs himself, the departing U.S. Attorney, supported Mary Anne.

---

34. Richey Interviews, *supra* note 13.

35. *Id.*

36. ARIZONA SUPREME COURT, THE SUPERIOR COURT IN ARIZONA 1912–1984, at 13 (1985).

37. Richey Interviews, *supra* note 13.

Thus, with direct assistance and constant support from Bill Richey and others, Mary Anne continued on an upward career climb. In the late fall of 1953, after slightly less than two years at the Pima County Attorney's Office, she accepted an offer of employment with the U.S. Attorney's Office as Assistant U.S. Attorney. In deference to the political party affiliation of the Eisenhower administration, Mary Anne changed her party registration from Democrat to Republican several months before her appointment.[38]

That switch in party alliance is telling. Independent in her thinking, she was not a person who identified strongly with a categorical set of political beliefs. Indeed, her original registration as a Democrat when she arrived in Tucson resulted from friends' advice that the Democratic primary was the only election that mattered in the state or the county, since Democrats were so dominant at the polls. At that time, registered Democrats outnumbered Republicans by a ratio of more than four to one in the state as a whole.[39] Her registration as a Democrat at that point was the result of her desire to have some input into local politics rather than a commitment to the platform of Harry Truman or agreement with the Democratic administration. Her career ambitions, on the other hand, were strongly held, and she readily made the party change from Democrat to Republican in 1953 to make herself more acceptable to her new employer. Moreover, the Republican Party was enjoying a surge of popularity nationally. Eisenhower's election in 1952 marked the first time Republicans had succeeded in electing a

---

38. *Mary Anne Reiman (sic) Named Assistant U.S. Dist. Attorney*, THE ARIZONA DAILY STAR, December 1, 1953. Voter registration records show that Mary Anne registered as a Democrat for the primary election of September 1952, and that she had changed her affiliation to Republican by the time of the primary elections in March of 1954. *See* 1952 DEMOCRATIC PRIMARY ELECTION SIGNATURE ROSTER, 1954 REPUBLICAN PRIMARY ELECTION SIGNATURE ROSTER, Pima County Registrar of Voters.

39. According to reports in July of 1948 based on registration figures for an upcoming primary election, registered Democrats in Pima County totaled almost 27,000 as compared to only 7,000 Republicans. *Peak Primary Vote Forecast*, TUCSON DAILY CITIZEN, July 20, 1948. Registration for the general election in November 1950 showed a similar imbalance of 39,709 Democrats to 11,687 Republicans. *Total Registration of Voters for General Election, November 7, 1950*, Office of the Secretary of State. At that time, registration for the state as a whole showed Democrats leading Republicans by more than four to one (about 225,000 Democrats as compared to 50,191 Republicans). *Id.* Interestingly, Maricopa County, dominated by the heavily-populated Phoenix metropolitan area, was also majoritarian Democratic until 1970, when Republicans overtook Democrats by a slight margin. *Primary Election Registration, September 8, 1970*, Issued by Rose Mofford, Secretary of State. The Republican advantage in Maricopa County has increased significantly in the last two and a half decades and has tilted the overall state figures toward a Republican Party majority.

president in twenty years. Eisenhower and his running mate, Richard Nixon, then known best for his role in the prosecution of Alger Hiss, had garnered an overwhelming majority of electoral college votes in the 1952 election, and Republicans had likewise gained control of both Houses of Congress. The changing political climate may have left Mary Anne with a desire to clothe herself with a more promising political identity.

As with her appointment to the Pima County Attorney's Office, the federal appointment was heralded in the local press. One news account noted that "[r]ecords at the federal building fail to show a woman in [the position of Assistant United States Attorney] since statehood."[40] "So far as is known in the U.S. attorney's office here," reported another, "Miss Reimann will be the first woman to hold the position of an assistant in Arizona."[41] Thus, as would be typical of her entire career in law, she assumed professional roles that had previously been the province of men. The seeming ease with which she adapted to those roles derived in part from her lifelong refusal to be cabined by gender stereotype.

40. *Miss Reimann In U.S. Job?* TUCSON DAILY CITIZEN, November 30, 1953.
41. *Mary Anne Reimann Named Assistant U.S. Dist. Attorney,* THE ARIZONA DAILY STAR, Dec. 1, 1953.

CHAPTER SIX

"Trying Cases Like a Man"

Mary Anne began work as a federal prosecutor against the backdrop of a changing legal landscape. On June 19, 1953, Ethel and Julius Rosenberg were executed for violation of the federal Espionage Act—the first civilians in the United States to suffer capital punishment for such a crime. The Rosenberg prosecution had been condemned by civil libertarians from the outset, and the zealous prosecutorial tactics of Assistant United States Attorney Thomas S. Murphy came under fire as well.[1] The Rosenbergs' multiple unsuccessful appeals gripped the public's attention. On the day of the executions, the United States Supreme Court, in emotionless prose, vacated a stay that had been issued by Justice William O. Douglas.[2] Eisenhower a few hours later denied a last-minute plea for clemency. Mary Anne would eventually come to know Tom Murphy, who was appointed to the federal district court bench in New York by President Truman only months after his prosecution of the Rosenberg case. Due to personal incompatibility and perhaps to her disapproval of his judicial and former prosecutorial style, Mary Anne had little affection for the man.[3] To Mary Anne the lawyer and prosecutor, the Rosenberg executions must have driven home the violent power of the law, and her casual remarks to friends about that "goddamn McCarthy" suggested that she distanced herself from the domestic "red-baiting" of the 1950s.[4] On the other hand, her record as Assistant U.S. Attorney shows that she was willing to fulfill the responsibilities of her office, even if the role was sometimes uncomfortable.

A few months after the Rosenberg executions, Earl Warren, governor of California, took the oath of office as Chief Justice of the United States following the death of Chief Justice Fred Vinson. Known as a moderate

---

1. For a description of the prosecutor's conduct, see United States v. Rosenberg, 195 F.2d 583 (2d Cir. 1952).

2. After a lengthy recital of the proceedings in the case, the Court, *per curiam*, wrote: "A conspiracy was charged and proved to violate the Espionage Act in wartime. The Atomic Energy Act did not repeal or limit the provisions of the Espionage Act. Accordingly, we vacate the stay entered by Mr. Justice Douglas on June 17, 1953." Rosenberg v. United States, 346 U.S. 273, 289 (1953).

3. Interview with Hon. Bernardo P. Velasco, Judge, Pima County Superior Court, Tucson, Arizona (Nov. 20, 1992).

4. Interview with William K. Richey, Nutrioso, Arizona (July 16–17, 1992); Telephone Interviews with Richey (Sept. 20, 1992, Sept. 27, 1992, Nov. 10, 1992, Sept. 21, 1994).

Republican and a skilled politician, Warren's tenure on the Court diverged dramatically from the conservative expectations of Eisenhower. A half year later, on May 17, 1954, Warren authored the unanimous yet highly controversial decision of the Supreme Court in *Brown v. Board of Education*,[5] ruling that racial segregation in public schools violated the equal protection clause of the fourteenth amendment. The opinion described the growing place of education in American life, its significance to the democratic process, and the traumatic psychological impact of segregation on the segregated minority and concluded that "in the field of public education the doctrine of 'separate but equal' has no place. Separate educational facilities are inherently unequal."[6] *Brown* and its implementing decision[7] led to a tumultuous period of resistance to the Supreme Court's mandate among die-hard segregationists and states-rights advocates. In Warren's view, the defiance could have been considerably diminished had Eisenhower put his weight more emphatically behind the decision. Instead, "no word of support for the decision emanated from the White House."[8]

Eventually, however, the President used federal power, both through the Justice Department and the military, to enforce the mandates of *Brown*. The constitutional crisis that arose in Little Rock, Arkansas, in 1957, was perhaps the most visible post-*Brown* turmoil of the 1950s. When Governor Orval Faubus called out the Arkansas National Guard to block the desegregation of Central High School, Eisenhower may first have vacillated but ultimately committed federal troops—the elite 101st Airborne—to maintain order as integration of the school proceeded. The crisis was front-page news throughout the country, and Mary Anne undoubtedly watched with interest as Attorney General Herbert Brownell and the Arkansas U.S. Attorney participated in the ensuing federal litigation to enjoin the governor from interfering with the desegregation of the school.[9] After entrenched resistance to integration continued in Arkansas, the Supreme Court issued a strongly worded decision signed by each member of the Court. In *Cooper v. Aaron*,[10] the Court declared that *Brown* was "the supreme law of the land" and that no state official could

---

5. 347 U.S. 483 (1954).

6. 347 U.S. at 495.

7. *See, e.g.,* Brown v. Board of Education (Brown II), 349 U.S. 294 (1955).

8. EARL WARREN, THE MEMOIRS OF CHIEF JUSTICE EARL WARREN 289 (1977).

9. *See* Faubus v. United States, 156 F. Supp. 220 (E.D. Ark.), *aff'd*, 254 F.2d 797 (8th Cir. 1957); TONY FREYER, THE LITTLE ROCK CRISIS (1984).

10. 358 U.S. 1 (1958).

"war against the Constitution without violating his undertaking to support it."[11] In Arizona, the legislature had repealed the laws mandating racial segregation in education shortly before *Brown*,[12] but the long process of dismantling the *de jure* segregated systems in the state extended over several decades and, in Tucson, led to litigation. In 1979, Mary Anne would encounter the evolved law of *Brown* when she presided over the implementation phase of a desegregation suit from the federal bench.

The Warren legacy, of course, was not just in the realm of civil rights. Two years after *Brown*, the Court launched its "revolution" in American criminal procedure in *Griffin v. Illinois*,[13] requiring states to provide indigent criminal defendants with free transcripts on appeal. The Court followed *Griffin* with a string of decisions in the 1960s strengthening the rights of the accused in such areas as search and seizure, police interrogation, and pretrial identification.[14] Although those decisions postdated Mary Anne's tenure as a prosecutor, her judicial record in the state court would later reveal a prosecutorial reluctance to embrace some aspects of the newly-federalized criminal procedure.

Thus, as Mary Anne began her service in the U.S. Attorney's Office, she was witnessing a sea-change in American constitutional law, one that provoked widespread criticism in some quarters as illegitimate judicial lawmaking.[15] At the same time, the responsibility of United States Attorneys to enforce federal law moved into the public eye. Mary Anne was committed to the "rule of law" as a philosophical principle, and in her of-

---

11. 358 U.S. at 18.

12. *See* Sec. 54-416(2), 1939 ARIZONA CODE (1954 Supp.) (eliminating mandate for racial segregation but substituting a provision permitting such segregation). The change in Arizona law is described in detail in Fisher v. Lohr, No. Civ. 74-90 (D. Ariz. June 5, 1978)(Findings of Fact and Conclusions of Law), at 41–43.

13. 351 U.S. 12 (1956). For an evaluation of the Warren Court's contribution to criminal procedure and a questioning of its "revolutionary" nature, see Yale Kamisar, *The Warren Court (Was It Really So Defense-Minded?), The Burger Court (Is It Really So Prosecution-Oriented?), and Police Investigatory Practices*, in THE BURGER COURT—THE COUNTER-REVOLUTION THAT WASN'T (VINCENT BLASI, ED. 1983) at 62–91.

14. *See, e.g.*, Mapp v. Ohio, 367 U.S. 643 (1961)(imposing exclusionary rule on states); United States v. Wade, 388 U.S. 218 (1967)(requiring counsel at pretrial identification of accused); Miranda v. Arizona, 384 U.S. 436 (1966)(requiring states to advise persons in custody of fifth and sixth amendment rights); Katz v. United States, 389 U.S. 347 (1967)(holding that wiretapping is subject to fourth amendment constraints).

15. For example, one of the most respected critics of *Brown* was Judge Learned Hand, who believed that the Supreme Court had assumed the illegitimate role of a "third legislative chamber" in the desegregation cases. *See* LEARNED HAND, THE BILL OF RIGHTS 55 (1958).

fice that principle translated into the rule of *federal* law, despite whatever sympathies she may have had for those who argued that the Supreme Court had violated fundamental premises of institutional restraint. Although she herself was not in a position to be the champion of civil liberties and was probably not a Warren fan, Mary Anne took seriously the new federal constitutional jurisprudence and became known among federal litigators as an aggressive but fair prosecutor.[16]

Mary Anne's formal term of service at the United States Attorney's Office began on March 15, 1954, and she remained there for seven years.[17] The U.S. Attorney's Office in that period handled a variety of civil and criminal cases. Under the formal supervision of United States Attorney General Herbert Brownell and Arizona's U.S. Attorney Jack Hays, the office represented the United States government in such civil matters as condemnations, actions arising under the Federal Tort Claims Act, civil forfeiture actions, civil deportation proceedings, and actions to recover overpayments of government benefits.[18] As Assistant U.S. Attorney in such suits, Mary Anne would frequently find herself in opposition to the monetary claims of private parties who alleged injury or death at the hands of a government actor. Finding herself quite capable of putting human sympathy to one side, she did not flinch from such representation and, as time passed, developed a preference for the civil docket.[19]

On the criminal side, the office frequently prosecuted narcotics crimes and a variety of other offenses, including violations of the liquor laws, immigration offenses, forgery, bank robbery, mail fraud, tax fraud, Dyer Act offenses (transporting stolen vehicles across state lines), Mann Act offenses (transportation of women across state lines for immoral purposes), and general crimes committed on Indian reservations and in other federal enclaves. The sheer variety of criminal cases provided Mary Anne with a

---

16. Interview with W. Edward Morgan, Tucson, Arizona (Sept. 9, 1992); Interview with James F. McNulty, Jr., Tucson, Arizona (June 24, 1992).

17. *Takes U.S. Post*, THE ARIZONA DAILY STAR, March 3, 1954 (photograph with caption).

18. Mary Anne identified her successful prosecution of an action to collect an overpayment of a government subsistence allowance, totalling $887.45, as one of the more significant cases she litigated while in the office. *See* United States v. Graves, No. Civ. 838 (D. Ariz. 1956), listed on Mary Anne Richey's Responses to Federal Biographical Questionnaire, for Nomination for Appointment to United States District Court (March 1976).

19. *Mary Ann (sic) Can Handle 'Em—Horses or Hoodlums*, TUCSON DAILY CITIZEN, June 9, 1956; Cecil James, *Smugglers Don't Faze Mary Anne Reimann*, THE ARIZONA DAILY STAR, February 9, 1958.

rich repertoire of trial experience, experience she acquired by working in tandem with Robert Roylston, the only other lawyer in the Tucson office.

In light of the fifth amendment's provision for indictment by grand jury for a "capital, or otherwise infamous crime," the Federal Rules of Criminal Procedure have long required that all felonies shall be prosecuted by indictment or, if indictment is waived, by information.[20] When Mary Anne was in the U.S. Attorney's Office, she and her colleague made a practice of presenting cases to grand juries jointly, alternating with the presentation of evidence in the closed sessions. Intended as independent screening bodies who perform investigative as well as charging functions, federal grand juries indict only upon a finding of "probable cause" that the accused committed the offense charged. Nevertheless, the grand jury system does possess characteristics that clearly produce a bias favoring indictment.[21] These include the prosecutor's *ex parte* presentation of proof, his or her role as the grand jury's primary legal advisor, and the absence of procedural protections for the accused.[22] The traditional secrecy of the grand jury proceedings continues to come under fire, at least insofar as it pertains to the grand jury's charging function. In the era in which Mary Anne was procuring federal indictments, the Supreme Court described the grand jury as a secret, roving inquiry by laymen, "unfettered by technical rules."[23] At least one lawyer perceived that Mary Anne on occasion sought indictments without reasonable basis, in an excess of prosecutorial zeal.[24] Predictably, the federal grand juries before which Mary Anne worked, composed of sixteen to twenty-three jurors and sitting a few times per year, rarely failed to return the "true bills" that the prosecutors requested. It was not uncommon for Mary Anne and Roylston to secure two dozen or more indictments in their all-day sessions before the grand

---

20. The Fifth Amendment to the United States Constitution provides, in part: "No person shall be held to answer for a capital, or otherwise infamous crime, unless on a presentment or indictment of a Grand Jury...." Implementing that guarantee, Rule 7 of the Federal Rules of Criminal Procedure provides that capital crimes and offenses "which may be punished by imprisonment for a term exceeding one year or at hard labor shall be prosecuted by indictment or, if indictment is waived,...by information." 18 U.S.C. FEDERAL RULES OF CRIMINAL PROCEDURE.

21. Grand juries have long been the subject of criticism as anachronistic and dominated by prosecutorial direction. *See, e.g.,* James P. Whyte, *Is The Grand Jury Necessary?* 45 VA. L. REV. 461 (1959)(arguing that indictment by information would be a more efficient and fairer accusatory method).

22. *See generally* WAYNE R. LaFAVE & JEROLD H. ISRAEL, CRIMINAL PROCEDURE Sec. 15.3 (2d Ed. 1992).

23. Costello v. United States, 350 U.S. 359, 364 (1956).

24. Interview with Thomas S. Chandler, Tucson, Arizona (Oct. 8, 1992).

jury. Nonetheless, on occasion a grand jury before which Mary Anne appeared returned a "no-bill," indicating at least a degree of independence from the prosecutorial hand.[25]

Mary Anne estimated that she tried two hundred cases during her years in the U.S. Attorney's Office, the vast majority of them as sole or chief counsel. About 60 percent of her cases were from the criminal docket and were tried to a petit jury.[26] Because the Tucson division of the United States District Court sat periodically in Globe and in Prescott, two outlying Arizona towns, Mary Anne tried cases in those locales as well. The Prescott assignment was particularly attractive since the sessions in that northern mining town were typically held during the summer months, away from the heat of Tucson. Mary Anne and Roylston divided up the time spent in Prescott, each staying for about a month. Frequently, Bill Richey or groups of Mary Anne's women friends, including her former roommate Jerry Kelso and other single working women, would join her for a weekend of fishing.[27] Those summer tours, with the cool weather and accessible lakes, might have been viewed as vacations but for the heavy trial docket of criminal cases from nearby Indian reservations.

Working with Robert Roylston was a joy for Mary Anne. The two former law school classmates took their jobs very seriously, laboring long hours in investigations, legal research, grand jury presentations, trials, and appeals. Mary Anne and Roylston, along with the sole secretary in the office, Agnes Hauenstein, sometimes worked from seven in the morning until ten at night when trial dates approached. The atmosphere in the office was convivial, with much laughter caused by Roylston's Tennessee humor, but a sober dedication to the job was apparent as well.[28] Mary Anne pursued the cases that came in with seeming dispassion and skill. Consistent with the existing ethical rules regarding the prosecutor's duty,[29] she viewed her role as representing fairly the government's interests rather than "winning" a conviction for the government. Despite the fact that the

---

25. *19 Are Indicted By Grand Jury Meeting Here*, THE ARIZONA DAILY STAR, November 23, 1964 (nineteen indictments were returned by grand jury, but four other indictments sought by prosecutors Reimann and Roylston were dismissed and a fifth passed for future consideration).

26. Responses to Federal Biographical Questionnaire, *supra* note 18.

27. Telephone Interview with Lois Dusenberry (Jan. 11, 1993).

28. Telephone Interview with Agnes Hauenstein (Sept. 15, 1992).

29. *See* AMERICAN BAR ASSOCIATION, CANONS OF PROFESSIONAL ETHICS CANON 5 (1908)("The primary duty of a lawyer engaged in public prosecution is not to convict, but to see that justice is done.").

Federal Rules of Criminal Procedure required little formal pretrial discovery at that time,[30] Mary Anne continued the open file policy in criminal cases that she had learned under Morris Udall at the Pima County Attorney's Office, and she attempted to cooperate with defense counsel in pretrial proceedings. In addition to fostering a sense of fair dealing by the government, Mary Anne and Roylston found that opening a complete criminal file to defense counsel would lead to more changes of plea than would other more secretive tactics. Plea bargaining was not a common practice, since a plea to a reduced charge had to be approved by the Attorney General in Washington, D.C. The goal of the office, then, was to secure a plea to the actual crime charged (rather than to a reduced charge as is common today), a goal often more likely to be attained if defense counsel were aware of the strength of the government's case.[31]

But for the office secretary, the personnel with whom Mary Anne interacted in her work were male, including the many government agents representing the Federal Bureau of Investigation, the Bureau of Alcohol, Tobacco, and Firearms, the Immigration and Naturalization Service, and other federal agencies. In general, she was accepted in that milieu by the force of her personality, and she was quick to rebuke anyone who might suggest that her gender required special sensitivity. Even veiled references to her gender were met with disapproval. One lawyer recalled overhearing an exchange in the federal courthouse when Mary Anne was trying a difficult civil case against two attorneys from out of state. Throughout the proceedings the lawyers had treated her with polite gentility in exaggerated deference to her womanhood. Their sweetness, however, was not to last. Midpoint in the trial, Mary Anne forcefully argued against an evidentiary ruling by the judge, and she prevailed. During recess, one of the opposing counsel remarked, "Well, we are mighty feisty today, aren't we, Miss Reimann?" Mary Anne purportedly responded, "You bet your bottom we are, you sanctimonious son of a bitch."[32] Thus, in characteristic style, Mary Anne let it be known that she was to be accepted as an equal.

---

30. Rule 16 of the Federal Rules of Criminal Procedure, as originally adopted in 1946, allowed the defendant access, on a showing of materiality, to documents obtained by the government. It was amended in 1966 to provide for trial court discretion to order broader discovery and again in 1975 to make certain prosecutorial disclosure mandatory. *See* LaFave & Israel, *supra* note 22, at Sec.20.1. Also, the seminal constitutional case of Brady v. Maryland, 373 U.S. 83 (1963), requiring the government to disclose evidence favorable to an accused as a matter of due process, was still a decade away.

31. Interview with Hon. Robert O. Roylston, Former Judge, Pima County Superior Court, Tucson, Arizona (Aug. 19, 1992, Aug. 24, 1992, Oct. 5, 1992).

32. Chandler Interview, *supra* note 24.

The sole United States District Judge in Tucson then was James A. Walsh; the Chief Judge of the District, David W. Ling, sat in Phoenix. Judge Walsh, for whom the federal courthouse in Tucson was later named,[33] was a highly-regarded jurist who was appointed to the federal bench in 1952 by President Truman. His was one of the last judicial appointments made by Truman, and his nomination and confirmation went through in record speed in July of 1952.[34] Walsh had enjoyed a distinguished career in state and federal governmental practice as well as private practice, and had served for two years as superior court judge in Maricopa County.[35] His judicial manner was subdued, thoughtful, and deliberate, but occasionally his Irish blue eyes would light up in laughter. He maintained close control in his courtroom but in a softspoken, restrained manner. In the tradition of some federal judges, Walsh engaged in the proceedings in his courtroom to ensure that they were fair; on occasion that meant that he would do the lawyers' work for them. He was known to cut off questioning, even without an objection from opposing counsel, if he believed the examination had gone on long enough, and he sometimes would ask questions that the defense lawyer failed to ask.[36] Walsh, who enjoyed a reputation for absolute integrity, became Mary Anne's model for the ideal judge.

When Mary Anne joined the U.S. Attorney's Office, she and Judge Walsh began an enduring friendship based on mutual respect and affection. Judge Walsh, who was only in his forties when Mary Anne became a federal prosecutor, may nevertheless have functioned as a father-figure for the thirty-six-year-old woman. Their relationship extended beyond the courthouse, for an occasional social dinner, and Mary Anne became close to Walsh's family. Walsh's opinion of Mary Anne's abilities was always high, and he seemed to take special pride in her achievements. He watched

---

33. *U.S. courthouse named after Judge James Walsh*, THE ARIZONA DAILY STAR, March 1, 1986.

34. Walsh was nominated by Truman on July 3, 1952, on the recommendation of Senator Ernest W. McFarland, a powerful Democrat and a Truman ally. Walsh had worked for McFarland in Washington, D.C., in his senatorial offices, and he had assisted with McFarland's political campaign in Arizona. McFarland's position as Democratic majority floor leader assured a swift confirmation, which came just three days later. *Senate Approves Walsh for Judge*, THE ARIZONA DAILY STAR, July 6, 1952. Walsh was officially appointed on July 7, 1952. *See* 415 F. Supp. xx (1976)(Table of Senior District Judges for the Ninth Circuit).

35. WHO'S WHO IN AMERICA, VOL. 32, at 3264 (1962–63).

36. Interview with Hon. Michael A. Lacagnina, former Judge of the Arizona Court of Appeals, Tucson, Arizona (Aug. 19, 1992).

her evolve into a tenacious and confident prosecutor over time, and one day told her what he thought of her, using words that were later repeated by others. "Mary Anne," he said, "you try a lawsuit like a man."[37] Mary Anne, after returning to her office, wondered aloud how she should take the judge's characterization. Robert Roylston, with characteristic good cheer, assured her that Walsh intended the statement to be favorable. "The judge means you try a good case and handle yourself well," Roylston told Mary Anne. "You better believe that was a compliment."[38]

Undoubtedly, Judge Walsh did intend the comment as a compliment; the comparison of the new woman lawyer to a male trial lawyer evoked an image of tough aggressiveness, professionalism, and unflinching dedication to the job. Judge Walsh's comparison is telling, moreover, for its assumption that males provided the standard by which women must be measured. Because of the almost complete absence of women in the practicing bar, such comparisons, while laden with gender stereotypes, were inevitable. Indeed, the same was said of Florence Allen, the first woman in the United States appointed to an Article III court, when she graduated from the University of Chicago Law School in 1909.[39] Since so few women in the 1950s had become litigators, the model of the good trial lawyer was necessarily male. Not only were Mary Anne's role models male, but her unique life experiences enabled her to feel comfortable and perform well in the male domain. In light of her indisputable competence in the trial arena, she was, by definition, trying cases "like a man."[40] Mary Anne's early success as a trial lawyer gave her confidence that

---

37. Similarly, Raul Castro's impression was that Mary Anne "thought and worked like a man." Telephone Interview with Hon. Raul Castro, former Judge of the Pima County Superior Court, former Governor of Arizona, former Ambassador (July 28, 1993).

38. Roylston Interviews, *supra* note 31.

39. *See* Ruth Bader Ginsburg & Laura W. Brill, *Women in the Federal Judiciary: Three Way Pavers and the Exhilarating Change President Carter Wrought*, 64 FORD. L. REV. 281, 282 (1995). A similar "compliment" had been paid to another early woman lawyer, Rose Silver, upon her graduation from the University of Arizona College of Law in 1931. On that occasion, the law school dean was said to have remarked, "Mrs. Silver, you think like a man." *See* Stephen J. Silver, *Legal Pioneer Rose Silver*, 14 UNIVERSITY OF ARIZONA LAW RECORD 2 (1992).

40. The centrality of the idea of "male" as a neutral standard or norm has been labeled "androcentrism." *See* SANDRA LIPSITZ BEM, THE LENSES OF GENDER 42 (1993): "[T]he central image underlying the concept of androcentrism is males at the center of the universe looking out at reality from behind their own eyes and describing what they see from an egocentric—or androcentric—point of view. They divide reality into self and other and define everything categorized as other—including women—in relation to themselves."

women could compete on equal terms with men in the courtroom, as in other venues, and the message of her admirers confirmed that she, at least, had measured up.

Mary Anne's strong presence in the courtroom even attracted media notice. When she perceived witnesses to be lying, for instance, her normally controlled demeanor could flare into anger. One newspaper account reported that her voice "roared throughout the U.S. District Court room" when she questioned a defendant charged with transportation of narcotics. "You mean to tell me," she asked, "that you traveled 900 miles just to spend a weekend vacation in Nogales?" The jury and spectators, according to the report, "were briefly stunned by the outbreak of the usually quiet young lady." Mary Anne explained to the reporter the reason for her obvious anger: "That guy was lying to me. I can't stand people who deliberately lie. I was sorry that I raised my voice in court, but that guy's lying made me a little mad. I rarely become angry in court. And it isn't dignified either."[41] Her comment evinced her desire to maintain self-control and to avoid shows of emotion. Dishonesty before a court, however, could trigger an outburst from Mary Anne. When revealed, her anger was powerful and intimidating.

The Tucson branch of the U.S. Attorney's Office handled several high profile cases during Mary Anne's tenure. One case that attracted great public attention was the prosecution of Floyd Baptista for bank robbery.[42] Baptista had been indicted for the February 1956 robbery of the Southern Arizona Bank of about $16,000. Mary Anne and Roylston jointly prosecuted Baptista, referred to by the Tucson press as the "lone bandit."[43] In general, in team-trying a case, the two would take turns on witnesses, and Mary Anne preferred witness examination to opening or closing statements. Her forte, according to Roylston, was cross-examination. "She was concise and to the point, and went for the big picture," he explained. "She didn't get mired down in detail, and she didn't have to practice in advance."[44]

In the Baptista case, eye witness identification came from two women, a teller and a manager, who were working at the bank at the time of the midday robbery. The case was challenging to prosecute, however, for several reasons. The bulk of the money taken from the bank was never discovered, but a marked twenty dollar bill did surface at a local drive-in

41. Cecil James, *Smugglers Don't Faze Mary Anne Reimann*, THE ARIZONA DAILY STAR, February 9, 1958.

42. United States v. Floyd Baptista, No. C-17275 (D. Ariz. 1956).

43. *Baptista Faces Robbery Count*, THE ARIZONA DAILY STAR, May 3, 1956.

44. Roylston Interviews, *supra* note 31.

theater during the pretrial period when Baptista was in jail. Also, much to Mary Anne's disgust, a government witness turned hostile on the stand with allegations that he had been threatened by FBI agents. Moreover, after firing his original lawyer, Baptista retained Benjamin Lazarow, an experienced criminal defense lawyer who chipped away at the government's case at every turn.[45]

The case had its comic moments. Witness testimony revealed that Baptista, brandishing a revolver, entered the bank and shoved a demand note and envelope at the teller. The note stated, "Put all cash in hear (sic)." After Baptista was arrested, he was asked to give a handwriting sample by writing on a piece of paper that he lived "here in Tucson." Baptista, as expected, wrote "hear" for "here". Mary Anne and Roylston enjoyed explaining to the jury that not only was the handwriting the same but also the misspelling in the sample matched that of the demand note.[46] Although substantial evidence existed connecting Baptista with the robbery, the government's case was undermined by the fact that Baptista's accomplice had not been discovered and the whereabouts of the stolen cash remained a mystery. Nevertheless, after a five-day jury trial and twenty hours of closely-watched jury deliberations, Baptista was found guilty and sentenced to twelve years in prison.

A day after sentencing, Baptista tried to lay the groundwork for a reduction in his sentence by cooperating with the government. Under the urging of attorney Lazarow, he finally admitted his participation in the robbery, and he named an alleged accomplice. He then promised federal authorities that he could retrieve the stolen cash. In the custody of the United States Marshall, Baptista led an FBI agent, Roylston, and Mary Anne to an area in the desert east of Tucson where he and his partner had purportedly buried the cash. The group did indeed find a hole in the ground lined with roofing tiles, as Baptista had predicted, but no money. On discovering that his partner had apparently taken the cash, Baptista, embarrassed in the hot July sun, uttered in dismay, "There's no honor among thieves, I guess."[47] Although the government did apprehend and convict the accomplice, Walsh later denied Baptista's requested reduction in sentence. In Roylston's view, Mary Anne showed an intuitive sense for sharp presentation of evidence and a "good ear" for witness testimony in prosecuting the *Baptista* case.[48]

---

45. *Baptista Asks New Counsel*, THE ARIZONA DAILY STAR, May 23, 1956; "Baptista Defense Tries to Shake Tellers' Stories," THE ARIZONA DAILY STAR, June 23, 1956.

46. Roylston Interviews, *supra* note 31.

47. *Id.* Baptista repeated his story for an exclusive interview with The Arizona Daily Star, reported at *Hold-Up Man Tells How Bank Robbed*, July 4, 1956.

48. Roylston Interviews, *supra* note 31.

Mary Anne tried a less colorful case early in her tenure with equal vigor. The case involved Dr. Louis Lutfy, a prominent surgeon from Phoenix, Arizona.[49] The indictment charged Lutfy with underpaying his income taxes over a period of three years by about $14,000. The case had been referred to the Tucson office by Judge Ling because of the crowded docket in Phoenix.[50] Although the prosecutors had expected that the U.S. Treasury Department would provide them with significant assistance in establishing Lutfy's guilt, at the last minute Mary Anne and Roylston learned that they would have to prepare and try the complicated case without Treasury's help. Consequently, they poured over the defendant's financial records and worked long hours in developing a theory for proving his guilt.

In court Mary Anne and Roylston established that Lutfy's own books were inadequate and did not reflect his true income. Relying on the "net worth and expenditure" method, the prosecuting team argued that Lutfy's actual income exceeded his reported income for each year in question and that the excess income was not, as he contended, the result of gifts or loans. The thrust of the Government's case was that Lutfy's reported income could not account for his yearly increase in net worth, and Roylston and Mary Anne relied on circumstantial evidence, focusing on Lutfy's assets and liabilities at the beginning and end of each year, to establish his guilt. Introducing "a small mountain of evidence" through almost thirty other witnesses, the prosecution and defense debated technical questions of appropriate depreciation schedules, capital gains taxation rates, accounting and record-keeping techniques, and intricacies of federal income tax law.[51]

Mary Anne second-chaired Robert Roylston in Lutfy's prosecution, and she examined two witnesses (each of them a female). One witness was a woman who had worked as Lutfy's medical stenographer and bookkeeper, a woman who presumably retained loyalties to her former employer. Mary Anne methodically led her through a discussion of her role in Lutfy's office accounting, taking care to clarify points for the jury where she thought necessary:

---

49. United States v. Lutfy, Case No. C-14630 (D. Ariz. 1955), aff'd, 230 F.2d 643 (9th Cir. 1956). The case was closely followed by the local press. See Surgeon Is Tried On 5 Tax Counts, THE ARIZONA DAILY STAR, September 8, 1954; Physician's Books Under Scrutiny, THE ARIZONA DAILY STAR, September 9, 1954; U.S. Agent Testifies at Trial, THE ARIZONA DAILY STAR, September 12, 1954.

50. Roylston Interview, supra note 31.

51. Lutfy Case Going To Jurors, THE ARIZONA DAILY STAR, September 16, 1954.

Q. Can you elaborate on [your job] just a little, what your duties completely consisted of?

A. Taking all dictation, medical dictation and any other dictation that the doctor had to give me; keeping the bookkeeping, doing the bookkeeping, which was a daily log book, and acting as receptionist. When the patients came to the office they came to me first.

Q. You referred to this daily log book. Will you explain what type book it was and what you kept in that book, what you did yourself?

A. It was a doctor's daily log book....

Q. All right. If I may I would like to show the Jury the way this is put on. Will you explain to the Court and Jury just what method you used in compiling these figures on here, where you did it, what you did? I want you to remember it to the best of your ability, the way you did it and what the doctor did?

A. Before income tax the doctor instructed me to make out headings on different sheets of paper.

Q. Can you recall the different headings?

A. Some I can recall because I used some of these headings in this daily log. There is a sheet at the end of each month that has expenditures listed and there are titles. I can remember stationery, surgical supplies, lights, telephone.

Q. Automobile?

A. Automobile.

Q. If these are yours maybe you can refresh your memory and read them off?

A. Office headings the doctor would give me, automobile upkeep, I could get that from the back of the book—

Q. Just a minute. When you say "from the back of the book"—

A. I don't mean from the back of the book. I mean every month there was a sheet in that daily log book that had all the expenses that were in headings that were made throughout the month.[52]

The exchange shows the very deliberate style of Mary Anne's examination and her ability to recognize ambiguities in the witness's responses to her questions. She listened carefully to the evidence and tried to put herself in the jury box to measure the impact of testimony. Because Lutfy's prosecution involved a re-creation of the doctor's recent financial life in mind-numbing detail, Mary Anne's attuned courtroom ear was useful.

---

52. Lutfy v. United States of America, No. 14630 (9th Cir. 1955), Transcript of Record, at 102–03.

At the conclusion of the two-week trial, the jury deliberated for less than two hours before returning a guilty verdict on all five counts of the indictment. Although Lutfy strenuously argued post-trial and on appeal that the case was unsuitable for the "net worth" method and that he lacked criminal intent, the conviction was affirmed by the Ninth Circuit.[53]

The Treasury Department was evidently so impressed with Mary Anne's and Roylston's trial work that they sent a formal commendation to U.S. Attorney Jack Hays in March 1956. The commendation acknowledged that the case was of "considerable importance to the Treasury Department," and praised the two for their "intelligent handling" of the prosecution. The *Lutfy* case, while not an exciting prosecution, demonstrated the sheer determination with which Mary Anne and Roylston approached their work. Although Mary Anne could be steely-eyed and aggressive in prosecuting violent crimes, she could also be fiercely single-minded when confronted with the dishonest taxpayer or other defrauder of the government purse. Crimes of dishonesty, especially white-collar crimes by individuals who seemed to have had access to life's advantages, especially provoked Mary Anne's prosecutorial ire.

Mary Anne represented the United States in two unrelated actions against alleged Communist Party members,[54] at least one of which became a cause celebre among local civil rights activists. Her representation in each case shed light on her philosophy of government lawyering. The more notorious case involved a habeas corpus action by Jose Munoz, a Mexican national whom the government intended to deport. Munoz, who had been a lawful resident of the United States since childhood, was a miner in Clifton, Arizona, and was active in union work. Through his union activities he had become acquainted with members of the Communist Party and had been given a membership card. Munoz was "befriended" by FBI agents during their monitoring of union activities in the Clifton-Morenci area, and his connection with the Party was discovered when the agents were ostensibly helping Munoz apply for United States citizenship.

Armed with evidence of Communist Party membership, the Immigration and Naturalization Service had proceeded against Munoz under recent amendments to the Immigration and Nationality Act that rendered aliens who were Party members subject to deportation. The hearing offi-

---

53. *See* Lutfy v. United States, 230 F.2d 643 (9th Cir. 1956).

54. *See* Munoz v. Kelley, 231 F.2d 381 (9th Cir. 1955) (deportation of resident alien who was member of Communist Party); United States v. Webster, C-15291 (D.Ariz. 1954)(criminal prosecution for making false affidavit as to Communist Party membership).

cer, in a ruling that was affirmed by the Board of Immigration Appeals, found that Munoz had been a voluntary and knowing member of the Communist party and was therefore subject to deportation. Desperate to remain in the United States with his family, Munoz challenged the finding of voluntary membership through a habeas corpus action in federal district court in Tucson.[55]

Although Munoz was vigorously represented by W. Edward Morgan, a civil rights activist and self-described as "the best free lawyer in Arizona," he lost in his effort to avoid deportation.[56] Munoz through his counsel argued that the evidence of Munoz's membership in the Communist Party was insufficient, but the Government called the court's attention to portions of Munoz's own lengthy and damaging testimony before the hearing officer. Judge Walsh, who was "upset and saddened by the case," ruled that there was "reasonable, substantial and probative evidence" of Munoz's Party membership.[57] That ruling, in turn, was affirmed by the Ninth Circuit Court of Appeals.[58]

Mary Anne was not yet a member of the U.S. Attorney's Office when Munoz filed his habeas corpus petition, but she had already been appointed by the time of Munoz's appeal, and the appeal was assigned to her. On appeal, Munoz had originally intended to challenge the constitutionality of the Immigration and Nationality Act on a variety of grounds, including freedom of speech and association.[59] An intervening United States Supreme Court decision, however, had effectively disposed of Munoz's constitutional objections.[60] He was left to argue on appeal only that there was no "reasonable, substantial and probative evidence" of Communist Party membership.[61] As such, Munoz's appeal was an easy win for Mary Anne, whose short opposition recounted Munoz's testimony before the INS and his personal history as a union leader. She concluded, "A man of this caliber would not appear to be the type of individual that could be duped into membership of any organization or party unknowingly or could be forced into the payment of dues if he did not believe he was obligated for their payment as a member of that organiza-

---

55. See Munoz v. Kelley, 231 F.2d 381 (9th Cir. 1955)(affirming district court's conclusion that there was sufficient evidence of Communist party membership to support order of deportation).

56. Morgan Interview, *supra* note 16.

57. Id.

58. Munoz v. Kelley, 231 F.2d 381 (9th Cir. 1955).

59. Munoz v. Kelley, No. 14075 (9th Cir. 1955), Transcript of Record at 107–08 (Appellant's Designation of Points of Error on Appeal).

60. See Galvan v. Press, 347 U.S. 522 (1954).

61. Munoz v. Kelley, No. 14075 (9th Cir. 1955), Brief for the Appellant.

tion."[62] Mary Anne took on the case reluctantly, since success for her office would mean the deportation of a man with several young children, a man who had lived almost all of his life in Arizona. According to Morgan, "Mary Anne didn't like handling the case, but she did her job. The law was on her side."[63] Mary Anne's "victory" in *Munoz* must have been emotionally difficult for her, but she focused on the task at hand: enforcement of the federal immigration laws. As she saw it, she had no discretion to do otherwise.

In another case that arose during the early 1950s, a federal grand jury indicted Flora Webster for falsely stating by affidavit that she was not a Communist Party member.[64] Webster, who had filled out the affidavit in the course of applying for employment with the United States Post Office, denied membership in the Party and pleaded not guilty to the charge. According to Ed Morgan, who represented her in the criminal action, her brother had been a Communist and she had been drawn into Party activities only by association with her brother. Robert Roylston initially handled the case for the government, and court records reveal procedural skirmishes between Roylston and Morgan as the trial date approached. After Mary Anne became involved, however, she negotiated an acceptable plea offer with Webster and Morgan. Webster changed her plea to guilty in exchange for a suspended sentence and two years probation. According to Morgan, "Mary Anne stood up to the FBI on behalf of Webster and struck a fair plea that the FBI didn't want. She was sympathetic to her. Mary Anne had a great deal of personal humanity and respect for the Bill of Rights."[65] In *Webster*, in contrast to *Munoz*, Mary Anne had some influence over the outcome, and she was able to achieve a result that served the interest of the government while minimizing the personal impact on Flora Webster.

Mary Anne and Roylston each had a vision of life that included hard work combined with intense play, and their social lives were as intertwined as their professional lives. A core group of friends, including Mary Anne and Bill Richey, the Roylston brothers and Robert's wife Edith, and Norval Jasper and his wife, often gathered for cocktails and dinner at local steak houses and periodically would travel south to Guaymas, Sonora, Mexico, for short fishing trips. Their parties were boisterous and filled with laughter; they consumed large quantities of alcohol as they entertained each other with tales from the trenches of their law practice. Frequently, someone would bring along a guitar to strum while belting out notoriously bawdy lyrics.

---

62. Munoz v. Kelley, No. 14075 (9th Cir. 1955), Brief for the Appellee, at 5.
63. Morgan Interview, *supra* note 16.
64. United States v. Webster, C-15291 (D. Ariz. indictment filed May 25, 1954).
65. Morgan Interview, *supra* note 16.

On one occasion Mary Anne and Roylston actually obtained a court order enabling them to host a party for their delighted friends. The unusual order followed the prosecution of a downtown night club, the Club La Jolla, and its owner Nicholas Abosketes for unlawfully refilling stamped liquor bottles without destroying the required internal revenue stamps.[66] Abosketes had devised a scheme of reusing large stamped bottles, originally containing "well whiskey," in order to more profitably move a backlog of other whiskey. The evidence was confiscated and sent to San Francisco by train for testing with the Alcohol, Tobacco, and Firearms Bureau. There, agents determined that the bottles contained whiskey that, while quite drinkable, was not the whiskey for which the bottle was labeled. Roylston promptly secured an indictment against Abosketes on November 22, 1954, and the case was set for a March 1955 trial date. When the day of trial approached and the crates of whiskey had not yet arrived back in Tucson, Roylston and Mary Anne wanted to avoid a continuance. Hoping for a last-minute change of plea from Abosketes, the prosecuting team did not reveal to defense counsel Edward Scruggs (Mary Anne's former employer) or to Judge Walsh that the primary evidence was still in transit. The ruse worked, and the defendant entered a plea of guilty on the morning of the trial.[67]

According to Roylston, the whiskey finally arrived around noon that same day, posing immediately the question of its disposal. The plan had been for the evidence to be returned to San Francisco for destruction by Alcohol, Tobacco, and Firearms agents after the trial. Roylston and Mary Anne, however, had other ideas. After Judge Walsh sentenced the club owner and the file was closed, the two approached Judge Walsh and asked for an order turning the whiskey over to them for disposal. Roylston's recollection was that Walsh "grinned from ear to ear and said 'I don't see why not.'" After Walsh signed the order that Roylston had drafted, the whiskey was carted up and delivered to Mary Ann and Roylston by the U.S. Marshalls. With the confiscated whiskey, the two prosecutors hosted a large impromptu party for their friends. "It was a great joy," Roylston explained, "to give such a big party. Neither of us had much money, and nobody knew how we got the whiskey. After the party, Mary Anne and I divided up what was left of it, and that was the way we disposed of the evidence."[68]

---

66. United States v. Club La Jolla, C-15857 (D. Ariz. 1955).

67. The indictment and plea were reported in the local press. *See 19 Are Indicted By Grand Jury Meeting Here*, THE ARIZONA DAILY STAR, November 23, 1954; *Liquor Count Faces Night Club Owner*, THE ARIZONA DAILY STAR, March 5, 1955; *Guilty Pleas Made in Club Liquor Case*, THE ARIZONA DAILY STAR, March 12, 1955.

68. Roylston Interview, *supra* note 31.

In 1958, Robert Roylston decided that after more than five years as a federal prosecutor, the time had come for him to make a change. His goal was the judiciary, and he intended to resign from his position as Assistant U.S. Attorney in order to run for a judgeship in the newly-created Division Five of the Pima County Superior Court. When Roylston first mentioned his plans to Mary Anne, the two began to consider the question of his successor. Because of the close working relationship in the office, the selection of the next Assistant U.S. Attorney was of utmost importance to Mary Anne, and, characteristically, she wanted her voice to be heard. After some reflection, she decided to approach Michael Lacagnina, a lawyer then in his mid-twenties who had graduated from law school in 1957 and with whom she had become acquainted. During law school Lacagnina had socialized with Mary Anne, Bill Richey, and Lacagnina's father-in-law, Jack Mantle, then Chairman of the Arizona Game and Fish Commission. The group shared an enthusiasm for game and bird hunting. After graduation, Lacagnina had handled occasional work for Richey and had impressed Richey with his legal talents. Lacagnina had already distinguished himself as defense counsel in a few highly-publicized criminal cases and was acquiring a reputation as a formidable trial lawyer.

In the summer of 1958, Roylston and Mary Anne met with Lacagnina at a restaurant downtown and told him of Roylston's plans. Mary Anne asked if Lacagnina were interested in the position. When his response was an emphatic "Yes," she reminded him that the Administration in Washington was Republican, that U.S. Attorney Jack Hays was Republican, and that she was Republican. Lacagnina, then a registered Democrat, understood her point. Lacagnina recalled, "I said I would correct that right now, and I left the restaurant. I walked right across the street into the Recorder's office and registered as a Republican. I came right back and said, 'It's been taken care of.'"[69] As expected, Hays followed Mary Anne's and Roylston's recommendation and named Lacagnina as Roylston's successor immediately after announcing that Roylston was leaving the office.

After his resignation, Roylston threw himself into the campaign for the judgeship. At that time, all superior court judgeships were elective offices, and the judicial candidates participated in partisan primaries. In the general election, the judicial races were ostensibly "non-partisan" in the sense that party affiliation of each candidate was not identified on the ballot. Although Roylston won the Republican primary, he lost in the general election in November to Democrat Raul Castro, who had twice been elected Pima County Attorney. Roylston, nevertheless, secured an appointment only weeks later from the newly-elected Republican governor,

---

69. Lacagnina Interview, *supra* note 36.

Paul Fannin, to fill a vacancy in Division Three created by a sitting judge's departure. Roylston, who was thirty-two years old at the time, was an attractive choice for Fannin because of his impeccable Republican credentials, his experience as a government lawyer, and his relative youth. Because of the rapid appointment, Roylston took office only one week after Castro, his victorious opponent, assumed the bench.[70] His successful quest for the judgeship surely triggered thoughts of similar career changes for Mary Anne.

Mary Anne worked as easily with Lacagnina as with Roylston, although the two men were very different. In contrast to Roylston's relaxed demeanor and homespun Tennessee humor, Lacagnina, an Italian with a flamboyant temperament, was out-spoken and irascible. "My life has been spent just quarreling for the sake of quarreling," Lacagnina explained. "Even if there is no reason. Just to do it. Just to start trouble." He and Mary Anne, however, did not quarrel. "We got along perfectly. We just knew, without even saying, what the other person wanted or didn't want done. It was smooth."[71] Lacagnina, moreover, learned from Mary Anne. Always an intense and excitable courtroom lawyer, the young man was advised by Judge Walsh "to watch Mary Anne try a case." In front of a jury, Mary Anne, in Lacagnina's view, was "a rock, calm, just beautiful," while Lacagnina would get excited and his voice would reveal every emotion.[72] Lacagnina was particularly impressed with Mary Anne's careful approach to cross-examination. Her style was to methodically lead the witness through a series of questions, listening closely to the responses as they came. By taking into account the witness's answers and shaping her follow-up questions accordingly, Mary Anne made sure that the least attentive member of the jury understood what she was trying to draw out from the witness. Mary Anne also revealed to Lacagnina her view of prosecuting. "She taught me that our job was to lay the foundation, to get our evidence admitted, to examine our witnesses and cross-examine theirs, to make our best logical arguments, and then to forget about it," Lacagnina recalled. "If the guy was acquitted, that's ok. As she saw it, our job was simply to put on the government's case. When it's over, it's time to go on to the next file."[73]

Mary Anne shared responsibilities in the office with Lacagnina much as she had done with Roylston, jointly presenting cases to the grand jury for indictment; trying criminal and civil cases, sometimes jointly, sometimes

---

70. Roylston Interview, *supra* note 31.

71. Lacagnina Interview, *supra* note 36.

72. *Id.*

73. *Id.*

individually; traveling to the Ninth Circuit Court of Appeals in San Francisco for appellate arguments; and dividing the Prescott court time. The friendship and mutual respect between Mary Anne and Lacagnina was forged by their team work as prosecutors. One case of some notoriety that the two tried jointly was the prosecution of John F. ("Lil John") Giuffre for income tax evasion.[74] Giuffre, the former owner of "Little John's Cafe" in Tucson, was indicted on five counts of tax evasion from 1950 through 1954. Giuffre apparently kept two sets of books for the restaurant, one maintained by accountants for tax purposes, and one for his personal use. Mary Anne and Lacagnina, contending that Giuffre had underpaid his taxes by about $24,000, relied in large part on Giuffre's personal books which indicated a much larger gross income than the accounts kept by the employed bookkeepers. Giufffre's counsel was Lawrence D'Antonio, a well-known lawyer who over the years successfully defended several individuals suspected of participation in organized crime.

Knowing D'Antonio's reputation for stratagem, Mary Anne did not enjoy litigating against him. One defensive strategy used by Giuffre and D'Antonio was to argue that Giuffre, a naturalized citizen who had immigrated from Italy, did not read or write English and did not understand bookkeeping. During an effective cross-examination of Giuffre, Mary Anne brought out for the jury that Giuffre must have known how to read and write in order to become naturalized and to pass written tests for a driver's license.[75] The trial lasted four days and culminated in a parade of character witnesses for Giuffre, including a Catholic priest and civil rights attorney Ed Morgan.[76]

After three hours of deliberation, the jury returned a verdict finding Giuffre guilty of only one count, tax evasion in 1954 for an amount less than $300. Exercising his discretion in the direction of leniency, Judge Walsh sentenced Giuffre to six months imprisonment and a $1,500 fine, but suspended the sentence prospectively on payment of the fine. The case may have represented an excess of governmental exuberance, given the resources devoted to the prosecution in contrast with the end result. The jury verdict may also have been simply the product of Giuffre's status as a sympathetic, likeable figure and well-known restauranteur, and of D'Antonio's skillful defense. In any event, Mary Anne followed the advice she had given Lacagnina and put the case behind her. She had presented the government's proof as effectively as she could, and she accepted the verdict with stoicism.

---

74. United States v. John F. Guiffre, Case No. C-17428 (D. Ariz. 1957).

75. *Giuffre Denies He Owes Taxes*, THE ARIZONA DAILY STAR, December 4, 1958.

76. *Giuffre Guilty of Tax Evasion Says U.S. Jury*, THE ARIZONA DAILY STAR, December 5, 1958.

On the civil side, Mary Anne frequently was called upon to defend the government in actions brought pursuant to the Federal Tort Claims Act. In that role, she became known for an ability to achieve favorable settlements for the government, despite the undeniably tragic circumstances of particular cases, and to cooly put on the government's defense in disputes that went to trial. Her own description of one such case is illuminating. In summarizing her performance in the law suit, where she represented the United States at all proceedings, she wrote, "Wife of Plaintiff was killed when a wing tank dropped from a B-47 jet bomber onto a street in Tucson. The explosion killed the wife of Plaintiff who was riding a bicycle along the street. Plaintiff sued for $100,000 plus punitive damges. Case settled just prior to trial for $24,000."[77] She received commendation for achieving an "excellent final settlement" in another case brought by a minor plaintiff who had been struck by a mail truck.[78] In such contexts, Mary Anne apparently was able to persuade opposing counsel to accept her compromise offers by the force of her personality and through diligent case preparation.

Mary Anne's forceful presence as defense counsel similarly surfaced in a tort suit that went to trial in early 1959. The case, *Wales v. United States*, involved the death of a fifteen-year-old boy from Tombstone, Arizona, who had been playing in an abandoned bombing range belonging to the Fort Huachuca military base early in 1957. The teenager discovered a 37 millimeter anti-tank shell in the field and knocked it against a telephone pole. The shell exploded, and the boy was killed. Glen Wales, the boy's father, filed a wrongful death action against the United States government under the Federal Tort Claims Act, claiming that the U.S. Army had been negligent in leaving the premises unguarded and that the negligence had caused the death of his only son.[79] Although the facts of the case were wrenching, Mary Anne methodically set about protecting the government's interests. Putting aside her natural sympathy for the father, she brought out at trial his role in failing to supervise his teenaged son's activities and in allowing the son to trespass on fenced property. In the two-day trial before Judge Walsh, Mary Anne argued on behalf of the government that the father had been contributorily negligent. At the conclusion of the trial, Judge Walsh ruled in the government's favor, finding that the father had been guilty of negligence which was the proximate cause of the accident. As a result, Wales recovered nothing; devastated by

---

77. Responses to Federal Biographical Questionnaire, *supra* note 18, at 13 (referring to Mary Anne's defense in David v. United States).

78. *Id.* (referring to Mary Anne's defense in Flannery v. United States, Case No. Civ. 1217).

79. Wales v. United States, Case No. Civ. 1003 (D.Ariz. filed Nov. 12, 1957).

the ruling, the parents did not appeal. According to James McNulty, plaintiff's counsel, the case was tragic from beginning to end, and he was deeply saddened by his clients' loss. On the other hand, he did not begrudge Mary Anne her handling of the case. "She called the thing right," he said, "and she did her job. She focused on the issue of parental responsibility and Judge Walsh took her arguments very seriously."[80] Mary Anne's successful defense in *Wales* on the ground of parental contributory negligence was an example of her ability to dispassionately defend her client, the federal government, despite circumstances laden with human emotion.

One of Mary Anne's last major federal prosecutions was a highly publicized criminal trial in late 1959 during which the *pro se* defendant tested the patience of Judge Walsh and monopolized the time of the federal prosecuting team. In early 1959, Frank Robles, a well-known community figure who was a newspaper editor and former state legislator from Tucson, was indicted for forging signatures on employment contracts and other documents needed by Mexican nationals to become resident aliens.[81] The defendant had had two years of law school and insisted on representing himself at trial and on appeal, despite Judge Walsh's advice to the contrary. He and his wife sat at the defense table during trial as he struggled through voir dire, opening statements, witness examination, and evidentiary objections. Robles was an obstreperous litigant from the beginning whom Walsh admonished several times during the trial and held in contempt twice. Prior to Lacagnina's opening statement, for example, Robles asked, "Is Mr. Lacagnina going to make an opening statement or opening argument?" Walsh replied, "He's going to make an opening statement, Mr. Robles. You can depend on me for that."[82] After Robles was late for the afternoon session the first day of trial, Walsh reprimanded him and directed that "[w]hen the hour for reconvening comes, you be here."[83] During the afternoon session, Mary Anne conducted the direct examination of Antonio Vergara, a key government witness, whose signature was allegedly forged on three government exhibits. Robles objected that he did not know what the exhibits contained, and Judge Walsh responded, with some impatience, "I told you before that you would have to follow the

---

80. McNulty Interview, *supra* note 16.

81. United States v. Frank G. Robles, Case No. C-17965 (D. Ariz. 1959), *aff'd*, 279 F.2d 401 (9th Cir. 1960).

82. *Robles Jury Ready to Hear Case*, THE ARIZONA DAILY STAR, October 2, 1959.

83. *Witness's Story Challenged By Defendant*, THE ARIZONA DAILY STAR, October 2, 1959.

rules of procedure. Don't tell me about your position. I don't want any argument about your handicap. Let's proceed."[84]

Robles was clearly at a disadvantage in opposing the trial team of Mary
Anne and Lacagnina. The backfiring of his cross-examination of Vergara
makes the point, and also provides a window into the methodical approach
that Mary Anne used with witnesses. After Vergara testified on direct that
he had not signed certain documents that purportedly bore his signature,
Robles tried to suggest that Vergara was lying. Robles asked Vergara on the
stand whether the witness hadn't told Robles earlier that he would repudi-
ate his testimony. Vergara responded, "No. But you have been trying to get
me to change my testimony and I always told you I couldn't." On re-direct,
Mary Anne took advantage of the opportunity opened by Robles, and the
exchange was reported verbatim in the local press:

Q. 'Did Mr. Robles ask you to change your testimony?'
A. 'Yes.'
Q. 'When?'
A. 'Yesterday morning. He asked me if I could do anything to
lighten the burden.'
Q. 'What did he want you to do?'
A. 'He wanted me to change my testimony to the grand jury.'
Q. 'What else?'
A. 'If I could be forgetful.'
Q. 'What did you tell him?'
A. 'I told him we'll see, we'll see.'
Q. 'Have you ever been threatened by anyone in the U.S. Attorney's
office or other governmental officials?'
A. 'No.'
Q. 'Are you testifying on your own free will?'
A. 'Yes.'[85]

During the trial, Robles repeatedly refused to follow Walsh's directives
and in open court accused the prosecutors and their witnesses of a political conspiracy. He made multiple groundless mistrial motions and evidentiary objections. One that caught a reporter's attention came about when
Mary Anne was questioning a witness about several government documentary exhibits. Mary Anne elicited opinion evidence from the government's handwriting expert by establishing his expertise, identifying the
document about which he would testify, asking the witness whether he

---

84. *Id.*
85. *Id*

had reached a conclusion, and then asking him to explain his conclusion. Robles objected, unsuccessfully, to Walsh, "This piece of evidence is building a case against me in the eyes of the jury."[86] Robles' statement was an accurate characterization of Mary Anne's tactics, of course, but not a valid objection. Twice Robles pushed Walsh too far. In his first contempt citation, Robles argued emphatically with Walsh over an evidentiary ruling, refused to sit down when told to, and accused Walsh of ignorance of the Constitution. He was held in contempt a second time after he posed the following question to a government witness: "Are you aware that the reason you brought that document to this court is because this is not a trial for the charges in the indictment but a political masquerade?"[87]

An exchange between Robles and Judge Walsh regarding Robles' motion for a mistrial reveals the judicious attitude for which Walsh was famous. In his motion, Robles insisted that the Government had to prove the forged documents were valid contracts, a legal argument that Walsh had repeatedly rejected.

> THE COURT: Mr. Robles, you repeatedly make that statement that it has to be a technically valid contract. I have ruled heretofore that is not so.... As I explained to you the other day, the only issue here is whether these exhibits are false documents; were they made or caused to be made by the Defendant Frank Robles....
>
> MR. ROBLES: It is well for the Court to feel that way and I highly respect the feeling of the Court. However, Your Honor, I am making my remarks for the record, not for the Court but for the record, that I may prepare those steps that are necessary for appeal in case I am—
>
> THE COURT: Mr. Robles, I don't want to be short with you. I appreciate your situation, but you should realize that certainly it can't be proper procedure when you start out in the trial of a case and make an objection we will say on the first minute of the case, that every time the same proposition is involved again you make them stop and make that same objection over and over and over.... Once you have made your point and the Court has ruled against you your record is made....
>
> MR ROBLES: Your Honor, let me offer a word of explanation. The reason I say I have to do it my way, Your Honor, is because there is such a notion of difference between the way you think I should do

86. *Judge Walsh Not Impressed By Objection*, THE ARIZONA DAILY STAR, October 3, 1959.

87. *Robles is Cited For Contempt Second Time*, THE ARIZONA DAILY STAR, October 6, 1959.

it and the way I think I should do it. And I am the one that's going to jail if I don't do it right.

THE COURT: Unfortunately, Mr. Robles, when you and I differ about the way it is to be done, I am the one that has the say. And that is the way it has to be done. And I am trying to be as patient with you, to explain things to you so you will not think me arbitrary, and it doesn't bother me that you think I am at all, but I am trying to explain to you that there is a limit to what I can do by way of listening to the same arguments repeatedly.... [88]

The patient responses from Walsh, in spite of his evident frustration, would stay with Mary Anne. As she would later make clear when she was to assume the bench, Judge Walsh was her mentor and her model, and she tried to emulate him.

Ultimately, the difficult trial came to a conclusion. On October 10 the jury, after deliberating a total of thirteen hours, found Robles guilty on four counts of producing false documents and acquitted him on three. Walsh sentenced Robles to four two-year terms, to be served concurrently, for the falsifying documents convictions, and to six months in prison for contempt. The Robles case was not over, however, for Mary Anne and Lacagnina. Robles filed his own appeal in the Ninth Circuit, challenging the principal convictions as well as the contempt citations, and personally argued the case. Mary Anne and Lacagnina traveled together to San Francisco to represent the government, Mary Anne taking the contempt appeal, and Lacagnina arguing the forgery convictions. Since Robles, in part, attacked the impartiality of Judge Walsh as a ground for appeal, Mary Anne must have enjoyed the opportunity to defend her mentor's integrity before the Ninth Circuit panel. As it happened, the appeals court disposed of all Robles's arguments in relatively short order and affirmed the convictions and sentences. The case was of such public interest that the local newspaper reported the entire Ninth Circuit opinion verbatim the day after it was announced.[89] The tenacious Robles sought review in the United States Supreme Court, again without success.[90]

Mary Anne's conduct of the Robles prosecution revealed the qualities that pushed her to the forefront of trial litigators in the Arizona legal community. She was well-prepared and focused on the task at hand. In textbook fashion, she laid the foundation for her documentary proof and introduced it into evidence smoothly and efficiently. When she saw an opportunity to undermine the defendant's credibility, she exploited the cir-

88. Robles v. United States, No. 16717 (9th Cir. 1960), Appellee's Brief at 25–27.

89. United States v. Robles, 279 F.2d 401 (1960), reported in *Judges' Ruling In Robles Appeal Case*, THE ARIZONA DAILY STAR, June 8, 1960.

90. Robles v. U.S., 365 U.S. 836 (1961)(denial of certiorari)

cumstance, not with fireworks or hyperbole, but with straightforward, carefully chosen words. Her style remained constant, whether she was facing a polished trial lawyer or an impassioned but untutored defendant intent on representing himself.

Following in Roylston's footsteps, Lacagnina not only worked diligently alongside Mary Anne but shared her *joie de' vivir*. Once, for example, when Mary Anne and Lacagnina were in San Francisco for appellate arguments, they learned that the St. Louis Cardinals would be playing the San Francisco Giants in the newly opened Candlestick Park. Since both Mary Anne and Lacagnina were avid baseball fans, they decided to try to get tickets to the opening game. Pursuing all options, they put the word out with the FBI in San Francisco and also contacted Teamster representatives they had met through litigation; each source said that obtaining tickets was almost impossible, but that if tickets did turn up, they would be sent to their hotel. The afternoon of the game, after completing their arguments before the Ninth Circuit panel, Mary Anne and Lacagnina were returning to their hotel when they noticed a sign in front of a neighborhood tavern advertising last-chance tickets to that evening's baseball game. They went in and paid full price for a pair of tickets between third base and home plate, Mary Anne's preferred location. When they arrived at their hotel less than an hour before the game, they discovered that both the FBI and the Teamsters contacts, surprisingly, had also procured tickets and left them at the front desk. Mary Anne and Lacagnina, always eager to take advantage of unexpected opportunity, raced to the ballpark and sold their four extra tickets at the gate. Marveling at their good fortune, they then proceeded inside to enjoy the game. Afterwards, the two went to the wharf for a bottle of wine and a seafood dinner, compliments of the FBI and the Teamsters.[91]

At the end of her term in the U.S. Attorney's Office, Mary Anne's reputation among the practicing bar showed that she related to her colleagues as equals and that she expected the same level of respect in return. Having stepped beyond the traditional view of the proper sphere for women, Mary Anne was all the more intimidating as an opponent in court. In 1960, women represented only 3.3 percent of all lawyers and judges.[92] In the popular culture of the previous decade, the image of the unmarried career woman seemed almost menacing. As *Life* magazine reported in a special issue on "The American Woman: Her Achievements and Trou-

---

91. Lacagnina Interview, *supra* note 36.

92. *Employment of women in selected occupations, 1950, 1960, 1970, and 1979*, in PERSPECTIVE ON WORKING WOMEN: A DATABOOK 10 (1980) U.S. DEPARTMENT OF LABOR BUREAU OF LABOR STATISTICS (Table).

bles," psychiatric experts warned both women and men against "losing their identities." The report quoted a panel of psychiatrists who decried the "assertive and exploitative" qualities of the new American woman, the "passive and irresponsible" man, and the growing problem of "sexual ambiguity."[93] The postwar message of American middle-class society was that women should devote themselves to marriage and the care of children. In delaying her second marriage for many years and in establishing herself as a respected prosecutor and member of the legal community, Mary Anne defied society's expectations and acquired an aura of power by that very defiance.

In remembering her style as a trial lawyer, several attorneys remarked on the ways in which she moved outside the prescribed boundaries of gender. "One used to hear on occasion that some women lawyers were hard to deal with because they acted almost as if they had to prove something. If they were negotiating, they pushed too hard, and it made it difficult to deal with them. That was never a problem with Mary Anne. You never thought of her as a 'woman.'"[94] Another classmate from law school explained, "Mary Anne was competent and sure of herself in court, and she was a fighter. She was right there, ready to go fist-to-fist with her opponent. No one ever pushed her around because she would give him a blast just like a man."[95] Still another lawyer reflected, "She was just accepted, where the other women had to overcome the fact that they were women, and she did not have to do that. She was obviously a woman, but she fit right into the man's world at the same time."[96] "She had a great deal of self-confidence," another lawyer remarked, adding that "it just came through without any effort on her part to convey that image. It was just clear that you were going to deal with her as an equal."[97]

Clearly, as she neared the end of her career as a government trial lawyer, Mary Anne had proven herself in the male-dominated milieu of the courtroom. Her life experiences, beginning with her childhood devotion to her older brothers and including her stint in the WASP and her days at Bill Veeck's ranch, had enabled her to develop a sense of absolute comfort within male domains. One colleague remarked that she was a

---

93. Life Magazine 41 (December 24, 1956), discussed in Myra Dinerstein, Women Between Two Worlds: Midlife Reflections on Work and Family 3 (1992).

94. Interview with Hon. Alfredo C. Marquez, United States District Judge, Tucson, Arizona, January 26, 1993.

95. Interview with Daniel J. Sammons, Tucson, Arizona (Oct. 19, 1992).

96. Interview with Norval W. Jasper, Tucson, Arizona (Aug. 27, 1992).

97. Interview with Hon. William D. Browning, United States District Judge, Tucson, Arizona (Sept. 11, 1992).

"rawhide feminist,"[98] a characterization that aptly evoked a mental and emotional toughness, a self-confidence, and an affinity for the rugged West. Those qualities would serve her well as she moved toward the next phase of her professional life.

---

98. Interview with Hon. Richard M. Bilby, United States District Judge, Tucson, Arizona (Oct. 19, 1992).

CHAPTER SEVEN

Transition Years

As Mary Anne approached six years in the U.S. Attorney's Office, she pondered her career and her personal life. On April 3, 1959, her father Wallace Reimann died in a nursing home in Rushville, Indiana. He had suffered a stroke four years earlier and had needed constant care since that time. His death left her saddened but not grieving; she had had little contact with him since she left Indiana in 1947, and even before that time her relationship with him had been uneasy.[1] Moreover, after Reimann was confined to a nursing home, Mary Anne and her brother Bill Reimann regularly helped with their father's living expenses, only to discover later that he had continued to make contributions to the athletic program at Purdue University.[2] In contrast to the death of her mother early in Mary Anne's life, which had affected her profoundly, the loss of her father simply diminished further her connection with Indiana. Although she remained close to her brother Bill, Mary Anne's life was in Arizona.

When not at work in the prosecutor's office, Mary Anne's time centered on her responsibilities as manager of Marge Allen's racing stables on River Road and on her relationship with Bill Richey. The racing was relatively successful and provided a complete diversion from her prosecutorial duties. Allen's horses did well in regional races at Del Mar, Hollywood Park, Santa Anita, and other spots, and Mary Anne accompanied her horses to their races whenever possible.[3] At the same time, Mary Anne's relationship with Bill had grown even stronger over the years. Their shared enjoyment of hunting and fishing, their love of animals, especially horses and dogs, and the easy blend of their personalities continued to create an enduring bond. In the late 1950s, friends viewed them as inseparable.[4] Mary Anne's fundamentally independent nature may have led her to delay a decision to make a formal commitment to Richey, but after nine years of "courtship," the two finally decided to marry. During those

---

1. Interview with William K. Richey, Nutrioso, Arizona (July 16–17, 1992); Telephone Interviews with Richey (Sept. 20, 1992, Sept. 27, 1992, Sept. 21, 1994).

2. Interview with Ann Bruner, Shelbyville, Indiana (Oct. 11, 1992).

3. *Mary Ann (sic) Can Handle 'Em—Horses or Hoodlums*, TUCSON DAILY CITIZEN, June 9, 1956.

4. Interview with Hon. Michael A. Lacagnina, former Judge, Arizona Court of Appeals, Tucson, Arizona (Aug. 19, 1992).

nine years, Bill's stalwart character became clear to Mary Anne. He had endured two political defeats in the 1950s, one in 1954 and one in 1956, when he twice challenged Raul Castro for the position of Pima County Attorney. In the second election, Bill lost by only 1,089 votes out of 61,000 cast, a showing that was all the more impressive due to the three-to-one Democratic majority among Pima County registered voters.[5] He was disappointed but not embittered by his losses, and continued to build a successful civil law practice. Bill's even-natured disposition and his apparent ability to withstand life's vicissitudes with equanimity were immensely appealing to the indefatigable Mary Anne.

Almost forty-two years old and five years senior to Bill, Mary Anne was acutely conscious of the age difference between the two. She confided in a friend that Bill wanted to have children, and she was worried that her age might preclude that option.[6] She was not sure whether she could become pregnant, and if she could, she was uncertain about the implications of her age for her chances of carrying a healthy baby to term. In any event, perhaps in light of Bill's steadfast devotion to Mary Anne, she decided the age difference was not cause to forego marriage, and the two decided on a fall wedding.

Characteristically, in being the older (and more professionally prominent) of the two, Mary Anne was again departing from social convention. While alliances between older men and younger women have long been socially acceptable, the reverse has seemed to threaten society's assumptions about gender roles in marriage and has occurred much less frequently.[7] Indeed, feminist historian Lois Banner has asserted that "the privilege of aging men to form relationships with younger women lies at the heart of patriarchal inequalities between the sexes."[8] In 1970, only 3.7 percent of marrying women were five or more years older than their husbands,[9] and the percentage was presumably even smaller a decade ear-

---

5. Richey Interviews, *supra* note 1; Telephone Interview with Hon. Raul Castro, former Superior Court Judge, former Governor of Arizona, former Ambassador (July 28, 1993).

6. Telephone Interview with Virginia Pothoff Trumbull (Aug. 29, 1992).

7. *See* Lois W. Banner, In Full Flower—Aging Women, Power, and Sexuality (1992); Pamela Warrick, *The New Senior Partners*, Los Angeles Times, July 29, 1992 (reporting trend in the 1980s among women aged 35–44 of marrying younger men).

8. *See* Banner, *supra* note 7, at 5 (tracing through history the combined impact of ageism and sexism on aging women).

9. *See* Banner, *supra* note 7 at 330. The National Center for Health Statistics reported that in 1978, in only 18.5 percent of marrying couples was the woman older than the man, a number that had risen to 23.5 percent ten years later. *See* Lynn Norment, *What's Behind The Older Woman-Younger Man Trend?* Ebony 44 (May 1992).

lier. The couples who fell within that small group of cross-age relationships, like Mary Anne and Bill, were rejecting a deeply-ingrained pattern
of Western culture.

Mary Anne worked up until the day before the wedding. On October
7, 1959, she examined her last witness in the Frank Robles immigration
fraud prosecution and left Lacagnina to complete the representation of the
government in the remaining two days of trial. The following day, October 8, Mary Anne and Richey were married in an informal ceremony at
the foothills home of friend Keifer Mayer in Tucson, cohosted by Marge
Allen. Although several relatives and friends traveled to Tucson for the
wedding, including Bill Reimann, Mary Anne's brother, and Robert
Markley, the man who had hosted her early trip to India, the wedding
was a surprise to many of the local guests, since the bride and groom deliberately did not disclose their plans. Their idea was to invite their closest
friends for a party, and then get married during the event with a minimum
of ritual. Midway through the evening, Mary Anne and Bill motioned for
Reverend Edgar Guenther, a close friend and missionary from the White
Mountain Apache Reservation, to come to the center of the group. They
laughingly announced to those in attendance, "All the Reimanns on this
side, Richeys on the other!" As the guests began to realize what was hap-
pening, several gasped, "My God, they're getting married." Mary Anne,
whose father had died six months earlier, walked through the crowd on
the arm of her brother to be anachronistically "given away" in marriage.
The double-ring ceremony then was performed by Reverend Guenther.[10]

Mary Anne entered her second marriage with optimism. She cared
deeply for Bill who, over the course of their long association, had proved
himself to her. She admired his core human decency, his honesty, and his
resilience. Unlike Mary Anne's marriage to Bill Showers, which her closest friends viewed as an escape, her marriage to Bill Richey was an affir-
mation of an already strong, fulfilling, and egalitarian relationship. In contrast to her first marriage, in which she was economically dependent on
her husband and dominated by his family, in her second marriage Mary
Anne was a forceful partner. Although she did not look down on women
who were traditional homemakers and counted many as close friends, she
was unambivalently happy with her own decision to pursue a career
alongside her new husband.

Because she had established a professional identity as "Mary Anne
Reimann," Mary Anne faced the quandary that many working women

---

10. *Richey-Reimann Nuptials Said*, TUCSON DAILY CITIZEN, October 9, 1959; *Miss
Mary Anne Reimann, William K. Richey Wed*, THE ARIZONA DAILY STAR, October 9,
1959; Richey Interviews, *supra* note 1.

encountered upon marriage. The tradition of the wife's assumption of the husband's surname, rooted as it was in the common law view of marriage as a submergence of the wife's legal identity into that of the husband,[11] did not suit Mary Anne nor did it reflect the reality of her marriage to Bill Richey. She compromised, as did a few other women of her era, using "Reimann" for several years after the marriage for professional purposes, but identifying herself as "Mary Anne Reimann Richey" and, later, "Mary Anne Richey" for personal matters.[12]

Throughout their marriage, Mary Anne and Bill lived in a ranch-style house on River Road in Tucson whose property adjoined the banks of the Rillito River. The house and surrounding property reflected the couple's lifestyle. Although the Rillito can fill with turbulent flood waters during Tucson's short rainy season, for most of the year the river is a dry bed perfect for horseback riding. Dense with desert vegetation, especially mesquite and creosote, the land surrounding the home shielded it from the sight and sound of traffic. The brick structure had an open design with large rooms; shelves lined one wall of the living room, filled with books about law and about horses. Animal trophies decorated the walls, including a whitetail buck, a big horn sheep, and an antelope—all felled by Bill Richey. Both the master bedroom and the living room/dining room overlooked a patio and swimming pool.[13] The property included a corral and stables, and at any given time, Mary Anne and Bill usually had several horses, including Arabians, as well as multiple dogs and cats.[14] Mary Anne had great affection for their animals, and when one would die she cried openly. When she rode horses with her friends, she often took one of her dogs with her, and remained constantly alert to the dog's welfare, fearful that it would be taken by coyotes.[15] Mary Anne swam almost every morning, often in the nude. Always comfortable with her physical self, she liked the feeling of the Arizona sun and water on her skin and relished the privacy of their desert oasis.

In November of 1960 John F. Kennedy was elected President of the United States, and the Republican domination of national politics ended

---

11. According to the common law, the very being or legal existence of the woman was suspended during marriage, or at least incorporated into that of the husband. W. BLACKSTONE, COMMENTARIES ON THE LAWS OF ENGLAND, BOOK I, Ch. 15, pp. 430 (1765).

12. As late as 1964, Mary Anne signed an appellate brief filed in the Arizona Court of Appeals as "Mary Anne Reimann." *See* Appellees' Brief, Miller v. Boeger, No. 8032 (Ariz. App. 1964).

13. *Richey Home Reflects Family Interests*, TUCSON DAILY CITIZEN, November 18, 1961.

14. *She Didn't Plan It This Way*, TUCSON DAILY CITIZEN, July 13, 1960.

15. Telephone Interview with Lois Dusenberry (Jan. 11, 1993).

for the time being. In the final days of the Eisenhower administration, Jack Hays resigned from his position as U.S. Attorney for the District of Arizona and accepted a propitious appointment by Governor Paul Fannin to the Maricopa County Superior Court, beginning a distinguished career on the state court bench. With his resignation, Mary Anne was designated Interim United States Attorney by the Justice Department. Her appointment, on December 17, 1960, was widely heralded in the press as the first appointment of a woman to the position of U.S. Attorney in the United States.[16] In reality, two other women had served as U.S. Attorneys, the first in 1918.[17] Nevertheless, the appointment of a female was so unusual that no one recognized the error. In her written oath of office, Mary Anne signed her name as "Mary Anne Reimann," and was referred to as "Miss Reimann" in news articles, although most news accounts made a point of noting that "in private life" she was married to Bill Richey.[18]

On at least one occasion while Mary Anne was the U.S. Attorney, she faced a professional resistance because of her gender. At the time, William Browning, then a private practitioner, was retained to represent a Tucson man accused of using the mails for immoral purposes under the federal Comstock Act. Although the indictment was pending in Illinois, a plea agreement was reached through which the case was to be transferred to Arizona for purposes of entering the plea and for sentencing. To facilitate that procedure, the U.S. Attorney's Office for the District of Arizona needed the underlying materials that gave rise to the indictment—materials that consisted primarily of magazines featuring photographs of nude males. When the federal prosecutor in Illinois was asked to send the materials to Mary Anne's office, he balked. Browning, as defense lawyer, received a letter from the prosecutor explaining the delay: "We have looked up the name of the U.S. Attorney for the District of Arizona and it is 'Miss Mary Anne Reimann.' We hesitate to send this sensitive material to Miss Reimann. Would you please identify a male assistant in the office to whom we might send this material?" Browning, who had clerked for Bill Richey during law school and was friendly with Mary Anne, went directly

---

16. *Interim Post Goes to Miss Reimann*, THE ARIZONA DAILY STAR, December 15, 1960; *Tucsonan To Get Post*, TUCSON DAILY CITIZEN, December 14, 1960; *Tucsonan To be First Woman U.S. Attorney*, THE ARIZONA REPUBLIC, December 14, 1960.

17. The first woman U.S. Attorney was Annettee Abbott Adams in the Northern District of California in 1918. In 1957, Kathleen Ruddell was appointed as U.S. Attorney for the Eastern District of Louisiana. Thus, Mary Anne Reimann was the third woman in the nation to be appointed U.S. Attorney. U.S. Department of Justice, *United States Attorneys 1789-1989* (monograph).

18. *Woman Here Seen as New U.S. Attorney*, TUCSON DAILY CITIZEN, December 14, 1960; *Tucsonan To Get Post*, THE ARIZONA DAILY STAR, December 14, 1960.

to her office and showed her the letter. He remembered her response: "She went through the roof. 'Goddamn him!' she said. 'Who the hell does he think he is? And what does he think I am, some kind of flower?'" Predictably, Mary Anne insisted on receiving the magazines herself, and when they arrived, she personally reviewed the photographs.[19]

The incident is telling. Mary Anne had attained success in a professional world almost exclusively populated by males, and she enjoyed a commensurate public stature as a result of that success. The Illinois prosecutor's display of ill-timed chivalry surprised and infuriated her, since it reminded her of the persistence of paternalism and stereotypical expectations for women. She knew that such paternalism, in fact, diminished the authority of the woman being shielded, and she was not about to acquiesce. Her characteristic response—anger and an insistence on viewing the "sensitive" material herself—emanated from a core value that had shaped her life.

During her brief tenure as U.S. Attorney, Mary Anne was the formal head of both offices in Arizona and her days were filled with administrative work. As the hold-over lawyers in the offices gradually resigned, the legal work increased for those remaining, and Mary Anne was frustrated by the accumulating case load. At one point, she expressed her frustration to the press. "Miss Reimann," one article reported, "said the new administration's delay in choosing her replacement has caused cases to pile up, especially in Phoenix where only two special assistant U.S. Attorneys remain. With Lacagnina's resignation, there will be only herself in the Tucson office."[20] Moreover, Mary Anne was not fond of Robert Kennedy, the new Attorney General, whose politics and leadership style she disliked and distrusted.[21]

Lacagnina resigned March 1, 1961, to join the Tucson law firm of Boyle, Bilby, Thompson & Shoenhair.[22] Mary Anne remained in the office as U.S. Attorney until March 17, at which point the new Kennedy appointee, Carl A. Muecke, assumed control. Even then, she agreed to stay on informally on a part-time basis in the Tucson office through July of that year to assist with the transition. Her willingness to help as interim head and with the transition once Muecke's appointment occurred was a characteristic contri-

---

19. Interview with Hon. William D. Browning, United States District Judge, Tucson, Arizona (Sept. 11, 1992).

20. *U.S. Atty Reimann's Resignation Delayed, Replacement is Sought*, THE ARIZONA DAILY STAR, March 1, 1961.

21. Richey Interviews, *supra* note 1.

22. Lacagnina remained with the law firm for many years, cementing his reputation as a skillful trial lawyer. Much later, after he had retired from the practice of law, he secured an appointment to the Arizona Court of Appeals, Division 2. Lacagnina Interview, *supra* note 4.

bution by Mary Anne. She took seriously her role as public servant, and her sense of responsibilty transcended political administrations.[23]

Once Mary Anne cut her ties with the U.S. Attorney's Office, she joined Bill Richey in private practice, the two working in a partnership known as "Richey & Reimann." The local press noted the opening of their downtown law office because of the unusual husband-wife association.[24] The pace of the workday at Richey & Reimann was more relaxed than at the U.S. Attorney's Office, and Mary Anne enjoyed being able to leave the office early in the afternoon. The practice consisted of general civil litigation, including land condemnation, personal injury, domestic relations, bankruptcy, and even land fraud. In *Boeger v. Miller*,[25] for example, she represented the Boegers, husband and wife, in a land fraud case against a major Tucson real estate firm. At a trial to the judge in superior court, Mary Anne established that the agent's misrepresentation had exceeded the bounds of permissible "puffing" regarding the land in question, and she secured a judgment of rescission for her clients. Despite a vigorous appeal by the defendants, the judgment was later affirmed.[26]

Through a special contract to represent the State of Arizona, Mary Anne concentrated on land condemnation work. In that role, she worked primarily for the State Highway Department, trying jury cases against private land owners regarding the compensation due for particular takings of property in connection with the improvement of Arizona's highway system. The condemnation work was technical, tedious, and required patient, careful lawyering before a jury. She worked long hours with government appraisers to help them develop convincing testimony regarding estimated land values. Her experience in condemnation work with the U.S. Attorney's Office undoubtedly helped her in her new role as quasi-government lawyer, and her trial skills and sheer endurance, honed from her years as federal prosecutor, were invaluable.

In one case, for example, Mary Anne represented the state against property owners who challenged the state's appraisal of a strip of land that had been condemned for a frontage road.[27] The legal and factual dis-

---

23. *U.S. Atty. Reimann's Resignation Delayed, Replacement Is Sought*, THE ARIZONA DAILY STAR, March 1, 1961.

24. *Legal Firm is Formed by Husband and Wife*, THE ARIZONA DAILY STAR, July 12, 1961.

25. Cause No. 70414 (Pima County Sup. Ct. 1963).

26. Boeger v. Miller, 405 P.2d 573 (1965). Although Mary Anne wrote the appellees' brief in *Boeger*, she did not argue the case since her appointment to the Pima County Superior Court occurred while the case was pending.

27. State of Arizona *ex rel.* Herman, Director, Arizona Highway Department v. Prevo, Cause No. 81894 (Pima County Sup. Ct. 1964).

putes in the case, buttressed by expert testimony from both sides, focused on the "best use" of the property, "special benefits" caused by the condemnation, and "severage damages." Mary Anne, the seasoned trial lawyer, was a daunting adversary even for Robert Stubbs, the land owners' lawyer and an experienced condemnation attorney. At one point during the trial, by way of a general objection, she cut short the testimony of a key expert for the property owners on the damage caused by the condemnation. She managed to introduce, over objection of counsel, expert testimony regarding potential benefits to the owners from the improvements. Also, in closing argument, she reminded the jury that the people of the State of Arizona would ultimately be paying the compensation award, prompting an emphatic but unsuccessful objection from Stubbs. After a five-day trial, the jury found that the property that had been condemned was worth $50,000 (the state's original appraisal) and that there had been no damages or special benefits attributable to the condemnation. The judgment, awarding an amount the state had been willing to pay from the beginning, was affirmed on appeal.[28] Through her successful representation of the state, Mary Anne was characteristically tenacious in her lawyering. She was able to blunt the impact of adverse testimony, and she showed her willingness to appeal to juror psychology in an attempt (of debatable propriety) to keep the compensation award low.

Trial lawyering, however, was not the focal point of Mary Anne's life in the years immediately following her resignation from the U.S. Attorney's Office. Instead, she began to consider making a bid for one of the two new judgeships that had been created on the Pima County Superior Court. In 1960, the Arizona Constitution was amended by the "Modern Courts" initiative, a measure that, among other things, created an intermediate court of appeals and authorized an increase in the number of superior court judges for the Phoenix and Tucson metropolitan areas.[29] Although a merit selection system (the "Missouri plan"[30]) had been proposed in Arizona in 1959 by a state bar committee chaired by Morris K. Udall, the proposal was deleted from the bill that ultimately became

---

28. Prevo v. State of Arizona *ex rel.* Herman, 406 P.2d 238 (1965).

29. *See* ART. VI, ARIZ. CONST., 1961 Session Laws 379. The initiative measure was the subject of widespread commentary. *See* William O. Douglas, *Arizona's New Judicial Article*, 2 ARIZ. L. REV. 159 (1960); Morris K. Udall, *Modern Courts—Where Do We Go From Here?*, 2 ARIZ. L. REV. 167 (1960).

30. Merit selection of judges was pioneered by Missouri with its adoption of the first merit selection system in the United States in 1940. *See* E. HAYNES, THE SELECTION AND TENURE OF JUDGES 80-135 (1944).

the 1960 Modern Courts Amendment.[31] Not until 1974, the same year Mary Anne campaigned in her last judicial election, did Arizona voters finally approve a merit selection system.[32]

Since Pima County then had a population in excess of 210,000, Divisions 6 and 7 were established by the county Board of Supervisors in 1962 to enable the courts to handle the growing civil and criminal dockets.[33] The Democrat-dominated board mandated that the judgeships be filled by election rather than by appointment by the Republican governor Paul Fannin.[34] The timing seemed right for Mary Anne, in terms of her professional career, but she harbored at least some ambivalence because her husband Bill also wanted to try for a judgeship. In consultation with the Roylstons, the couple decided that Mary Anne had greater public visibility than Bill because of her years in the U.S. Attorney's Office and that she would therefore be the more promising candidate. Thus, in a move that was not unusual in the context of their relationship but atypical for the times, the two took a course of action that gave priority to Mary Anne's career.

The all-male composition of the bench at that time must have been somewhat discouraging. In 1962, all the sitting judges on the superior court in Arizona were men. Although pathbreaker Lorna Lockwood had been elected to the Maricopa County Superior Court in 1951, she ran successfully for a seat on the five-justice Arizona Supreme Court bench in 1961 and had thus left the state trial courts uniformly male.[35] Arizona's stark statistical profile corresponded to the picture elsewhere, with women representing between 1 and 2 percent of state trial court judges nationwide during the 1960s.[36] That decade's paucity of women judges is

---

31. *See* John M. Roll, *Merit Selection: The Arizona Experience*, 22 ARIZ. ST. L. J. 837 (1990); Hink, *Judicial Reform in Arizona*, 6 ARIZ. L. REV. 13, 16 (1964).

32. Under the plan that voters adopted, the governor appoints all appellate judges statewide and all superior court judges in Maricopa and Pima Counties from a bipartisan list of nominees submitted by a merit selection commission. Appointed judges then stand for retention in noncompetitive elections. *See* ARIZ. CONST. art. VI, Secs. 36, 37.

33. UNITED STATES BUREAU OF THE CENSUS, 1970 CENSUS OF POPULATION, VOL. I, at 4–15 (1973)(*Characteristics of the Population, Pt. 4, Arizona, Table II: Population of Urbanized Areas: 1970 and 1960*).

34. *Pima Board Creates Two More Judgeships*, THE ARIZONA DAILY STAR, March 2, 1962.

35. *See* ARIZONA SUPREME COURT, THE SUPERIOR COURT IN ARIZONA 1912–1984, at 29 (1985).

36. Beverly Blair Cook, *Women Judges: The End of Tokenism*, in WOMEN IN THE COURTS 84 (Hepperle & Crites, National Center for State Courts 1978). Interestingly,

not surprising, given the persistent resistance of law schools to the enroll-ment of women, and the difficulty women law graduates faced in obtain-ing legal positions that might lead to a judgeship.[37] Estimates of women lawyers in 1960 range from 6,500 to 7,500, or 2.6 percent to 3.5 percent of the total number of lawyers.[38]

Four candidates vied for the two newly created judgeships on the supe-rior court in Pima County, two Republicans and two Democrats. Under the system then in effect, judicial candidates could seek a partisan nomi-nation through the primary election, but in the general election, the suc-cessful nominees were listed without party identification. On the Republi-can side Mary Anne was joined by close friend Richard Roylston, Robert's twin brother. The Roylston brothers, who lived together most of their lives, managed to maintain successful parallel careers to an almost uncanny degree. Richard, a staunch Republican, had been in a successful private practice since graduation from law school and was eager to join his brother on the bench. With the support of influential Republicans, Mary Anne and Richard quickly announced for Divisions 6 and 7, respec-tively. The Democratic candidates were Alice Truman and David Wine. Truman, a graduate of the University of Illinois Law College, had come to Arizona in 1953 as a divorced mother of two. After passing the state bar examination, she went into private practice using her maiden name of Alice Nihan. With her 1955 marriage to Edgar Truman, she became "Alice Truman," a name of symbolic political clout. Truman had run suc-cessfully for Justice of the Peace in 1958 and, in 1962, turned her sights on the superior court bench. Wine, a Harvard law graduate, was a local practitioner who was then serving in the state senate.

Truman and Wine debated together which Division each should seek. Truman recalled that she and her husband decided she should run against another woman, while Wine, the other candidate, apparently had no de-

---

Arizona has been somewhat of a leader in female representation on the bench. Not only can Arizona claim the first female chief justice of a state supreme court with the selection of Lorna Lockwood in 1965, but by 1977, one year after Mary Anne was appointed to the federal bench, Arizona led the states with women constituting 7% of its state trial court judges. *Id.* at 88.

37. Historian Beverly Blair Cook has concluded that women were underrepresented on the bench because of the restricted access of women to law school and to the positions that prepare lawyers politically and professionally for the bench. *Id.* at 84. She argues, moreover, that women law students ironically were better qualified for judicial positions than their male counterparts because of the institutional barriers that the women had to overcome to be admitted to and to graduate from law school. *Id.*

38. *See* RICHARD L. ABEL, AMERICAN LAWYERS 284 (1989)(Table 26).

sire to oppose Mary Anne. Truman's decision to run against Mary Anne was in part a recognition that Richard Roylston, with a brother bearing the Roylston name already on the bench, would be a tough opponent to beat.[39] Her decision also may have reflected a sense that voters might elect one, but not two, women to the superior court—an intuition that female judicial candidates, as oddities, were best combined in one race. Although the press reports bear out Truman's version, Richard Roylston's recollection was that he and Mary Anne decided between the two of them that she would oppose Truman and that he would oppose Wine.[40] In Roylston's memory, Mary Anne believed she would have a better chance against a woman, since only one other woman (Lorna Lockwood) had ever successfully sought a state court judgeship. In any event, in the end Mary Anne faced Truman and Roylston faced Wine.

In the September primaries, Mary Anne ran unopposed for the nomination in Division 6, and Truman faced John Collins, a University of Arizona law graduate who was then engaged in private practice. The Arizona Daily Star published an editorial two weeks before the September primaries that endorsed only Alice Truman for Division Six. That endorsement focused on Truman's experience: "She has enough years of actual experience to bring wisdom to the bench." It went on to suggest that the other Democratic candidate and the Republican candidate (Mary Anne) were too young to warrant the voters' support: "[They] are fine youngsters, who have plenty of time ahead to satisfy their judicial ambitions."[41] That endorsement triggered a mixed reaction from Truman, who was five years younger than the forty-four-year-old Mary Anne. The Star's error was a common one in regard to Mary Anne's age. Just as her law school classmates had been startled to learn that she was thirty-three at graduation, the public perceived Mary Anne as younger than she was. Her athletic bearing, her lack of interest in using cosmetics other than lipstick, and her often irrepressible laughter contributed to her aura of youth.

The Pima County Bar Association conducted a preferential poll among its members prior to the primary election. Of the valid ballots cast, Collins led the candidates for Division 6. As between Mary Anne and Truman, Mary Anne received slightly more total votes, but Truman earned more "first-place" votes. Interestingly, a Truman supporter alleged

---

39. Interview with Hon. Alice N. Truman, former Pima County Superior Court Judge, Tucson, Arizona (July 6, 1992).

40. Interview with Hon. Richard M. Roylston and Hon. Robert O. Roylston, former Pima County Superior Court Judges, Tucson, Arizona (Aug. 19, 1992).

41. *The Star's Primary Election Endorsements,* THE ARIZONA DAILY STAR, August 26, 1962.

that half of the ballots that had been rejected as "spoiled" had favored Truman, an estimate that would have put Truman well ahead of Mary Anne in total votes. Norval Jasper, Mary Anne's former classmate and close friend who was then chair of the Bar committee handling the poll, informed the press that there was no available evidence to support such a conclusion.[42]

In the actual primaries, Mary Anne and Roylston, each running unopposed, received the Republican nomination for Divisions 6 and 7, respectively. Truman won the Democratic nomination, showing perhaps that the public could more readily accept the idea of a female judge than could the members of the legal profession itself. (Collins, the unsuccessful Democratic candidate for Division 6, was appointed to the superior court by Democratic governor Samuel Goddard three years later.[43])

Mary Anne's campaign for the general election was a collective effort with her husband and friends. Michael Lacagnina was her treasurer, and her husband, the Roylstons, and Jasper provided friendly counsel. She was unsure of what public name to use. Although she was known professionally as "Mary Anne Reimann," she worried that the public would not accept a married woman who used her maiden name. Notwithstanding Bill Richey's advice to continue using "Reimann," Mary Anne decided to identify as "Mary Anne (Reimann) Richey." That compromise still left the campaigners worried that the name was "too long."[44]

The electoral contest between Mary Anne and Truman was low-key and non-adversarial. The modest tone of their campaigning was not surprising, in light of ethical restrictions on the activities of judicial candidates. Under the Canons of Judicial Ethics then in effect, judicial candidates were barred from making "promises of conduct in office which appeal to the cupidity or prejudice of the...electing power," and from announcing "conclusions of law on disputed issues to secure class support."[45] Indeed, the movement then underway in Arizona to institute

---

42. *Lawyers Prone to Spoil Ballots*, THE ARIZONA DAILY STAR, August 31, 1962.

43. ARIZONA SUPREME COURT, THE SUPERIOR COURT IN ARIZONA 1912–1984, at 57 (1985).

44. Robert Roylston Interview, *supra* note 40.

45. Canon 30 of the Canons of Judicial Ethics, reprinted in AMERICAN BAR ASSOCIATION, OPINIONS OF THE COMMITTEE ON PROFESSIONAL ETHICS WITH CANONS OF PROFESSIONAL ETHICS ANNOTATED AND CANONS OF JUDICIAL ETHICS ANNOTATED (1967). The Arizona Supreme Court adopted the ABA's Canons of Judicial Ethics on October 1, 1956. *See* Rule 45 of the Rules of the Arizona Supreme Court, 17 ARIZ. REV. STAT. ANN. (1956). Requiring even greater avoidance of controversy, Arizona's current rules bar judicial candidates from announcing their "views on disputed legal or political issues," or from making "pledges or promises of conduct in office other than the faithful and impar-

merit selection of judges was due in part to the problems inherent in judicial electioneering.[46]

As was typical of most judicial campaigns, Mary Anne and Alice did not debate issues, and to the extent that their speeches were substantive, they chose topics that were largely non-controversial. At one point, for example, Mary Anne endorsed the proposal for a court of conciliation as a branch of the superior court in Pima County, as an effective response to the rising divorce rate,[47] and Truman on another occasion opined that humility, a high standard of ethics, and objectivity rather than subjectivity were essential for judges.[48] In their stump speeches, they emphasized their own professional qualifications, without reference to partisan ideology, and did not publicly denigrate one another. "We never said a word about each other," Truman recalled. "We were very civilized, and we were friends."[49] The campaign goal was one of name recognition, and each spent money on radio and television spots, brochures, and signs. Compared to today's campaign costs, the judicial contest between Mary Anne and Truman was relatively cheap. Mary Anne expended about $4,200 of her own money and raised about $2,700 in contributions.[50] Truman estimated that she spent a similar amount.[51] The two traveled throughout the county, making public appearances at breakfast and luncheon meetings of clubs, at churches, and at community centers.

Mary Anne was an unpolished but sincere speaker who often left her audience smiling. She recounted for her audiences, for example, her conversation a decade earlier with brothel owner Alice Miller, one of Mary Anne's first clients. Mary Anne would tell the voters that even if she were to lose the election, she need not worry since Miller had promised her a

---

tial performance of the duties of the office." Arizona Code of Judicial Conduct, Canon 7B(1)(c), contained in Arizona Supreme Court Rules, 17A ARIZ. REV. STAT. ANN.

46. In 1959, a merit selection system was proposed in Arizona as part of the 1960 Modern Courts Amendment, but was later deleted. ARIZONA ACADEMY, TWENTY-SECOND ARIZONA TOWN HALL ON THE ADEQUACY OF ARIZONA'S COURT SYSTEM 35 (1973), discussed in John M. Roll, *Merit Selection: The Arizona Experience*, 22 ARIZ. ST. L. J. 837 (1990). The move for merit selection continued, however, culminating in the amendment of the state constitution in 1974 to provide for merit selection of superior court judges in counties with a population of 150,000 or more, and of all appellate court judges. ARIZ. CONST., Art. 6, Sec. 36, 37.

47. *Richey Backs Conciliation Court Plan*, THE ARIZONA DAILY STAR, September 10, 1962.

48. *Duties Outlined By Mrs. Truman*, THE ARIZONA DAILY STAR, August 31, 1962.

49. Truman Interview, *supra* note 39.

50. Mary Anne Reimann Richey, Candidate's Expense Statement for November 6, 1962 Election for Judge of Superior Court, Pima County.

51. Lacagnina Interview, *supra* note 4; Truman Interview, *supra* note 39.

job a long time ago. The story never failed to generate surprised laughter from the crowd.[52]

The Tucson community took an unusual interest in the race because of the gender of the participants. One banner headline proclaimed, "Superior Court Judge May Be Woman for First Time in County."[53] The same article noted that both women had been in the legal profession for many years and both had held offices "presumed to be 'men's jobs.'"[54] In almost comical fashion, local newspapers focused on the feminine nature of the candidates, perhaps a deliberate tactic by the candidates themselves to reassure the voters that they each embraced traditional female values. In one full-page feature in the "Women's View" section of the Tucson Citizen, for example, Mary Anne told the reporter that "Campaigning is exciting, rewarding and tiring, but at least it's not fattening!" She confided that campaigning was difficult for a woman because "[y]ou need to have your hair done almost every other day, wear a different dress every day, keep your nails manicured and your seams straight—and appear never to give such things a thought!" She also announced, "Happily, I'm blessed with a most cooperative husband."[55]

In a more serious and telling passage in the same interview, Mary Anne explained that campaigning was a lesson in humility. "You suddenly realize that other people—those you might not even know—actually decide what's going to happen to you. You realize what a little cog you are, and how much entwined with others is your fate."[56] That insight was important for Mary Anne, to whom independence and self-determination were vital. In the election, unlike many other aspects of her life, she could not control the outcome.

The Cuban missile crisis was unfolding in October of 1962 and may have eclipsed temporarily the voters' attention. On October 22, President Kennedy informed the nation over television of the Soviet missiles in Cuba and the plans for a blockade. Six days later, after the United States had not only implemented the blockade but also readied warplanes in Florida and secretly offered to remove NATO missiles from Turkey, the Soviets agreed to remove their offensive weapons in Cuba. The crisis was thus defused, but the criticism leveled at the Democratic administration for its brinkmanship was just beginning. Mary Anne saw Kennedy's action as foolhardy, and the incident cemented her dislike for him.

---

52. Richey Interviews, *supra* note 1.

53. THE ARIZONA DAILY STAR, September 30, 1962.

54. *Id.*

55. *Mary Anne Reimann Richey Campaigns For Office Of Judge*, TUCSON DAILY CITIZEN, October 27, 1962.

56. *Id.*

Toward the end of her electoral campaign, Mary Anne began to expect that she would be defeated. On the morning of the general election, she called Alice Truman. "Alice," she said, "I just called up to tell you that I think you are going to win." Alice, somewhat taken aback, was not feeling overly-confident about the race and was surprised by the call.[57] Mary Anne may have anticipated the defeat because of the heavy Democratic majority among Pima County voters, a majority that enabled Democratic gubernatorial candidate Samuel Goddard, for example, to take Pima County although he lost to incumbent Paul Fannin statewide. Even though the judicial ballots for the general election were non-partisan, informed voters were clearly aware of the party affiliation of the candidates. The final margin of Truman's victory over Mary Anne was sizeable, with Mary Anne receiving 18,782 votes as compared to 29,561 votes for Truman, and a write-in male candidate garnering 7,252 votes.[58] On the other hand, Richard Roylston defeated his Democratic opponent by 5,000 votes in the same election in which Mary Anne lost to Truman, proving that a Republican victory was not impossible. Other factors undoubtedly contributed to Mary Anne's loss, including, perhaps, the name "Truman." Not only did her opponent's name trigger the mental association with Harry S. Truman, but it also connected with a respected superior court judge of many years in Pinal County, William C. Truman.[59] Moreover, Truman benefitted from public visibility as a justice of the peace and from the campaigning experience she acquired in running for that position.[60] The comparative subjective appeal of each candidate to the voters may also have been material. Although both women were exceptional by virtue of their professional identities, Truman presented an image more consistent with that of the "ideal woman." She had been a private practitioner and a justice of the peace, but never a prosecutor; she dropped her maiden name entirely upon her marriage to Edgar Truman; and she was a mother. Perhaps the voters found her to be a more familiar, and thus more appealing, model of womanhood.

Ironically, although Alice Truman thus became the first woman judge on the Pima County Superior Court as a result of winning the 1962 election, Mary Anne's reputation as a trail blazer overwhelmed the historical record. In the Arizona Supreme Court's official history of the superior

---

57. Truman Interview, *supra* note 39.

58. *Elections Results*, The Arizona Daily Star, November 7, 1962.

59. William C. Truman was on the Superior Court of Pinal County from 1943 to 1965. James M. Murphy, Laws, Courts, & Lawyers 184 (1970). Several people acknowledged the significance of the name "Truman," including Truman herself. Truman Interview, *supra* note 39.

60. Truman Interview, *supra* note 39.

court in Arizona, Mary Anne is identified erroneously as Pima County's first woman superior court judge.[61]

Mary Anne, although anticipating the electoral result, was profoundly upset by the defeat. She had put great energy into campaigning, an activity that did not come naturally to her. And, as Bill Richey bluntly explained, "she hated to lose."[62] Up to that point in her career she had achieved her professional goals with seeming ease. She did not relish the idea of a life in private practice, and she had tired of the role of government lawyer. For several reasons, after her defeat Mary Anne's desire to become a judge was more palpable, more acutely felt, than it had been before the campaign. The months of campaigning had focused her on the single defining image of herself in judicial robes, and she had become emotionally invested in the role. She was an ambitious woman, and a judgeship would be yet another step up in the professional heirarchy. Finally, and more simply, she knew she would enjoy the task of judging. During the campaign, Mary Anne explained that she had wanted to be a judge ever since she covered trials for the Shelbyville Republican as a young woman, that she could "go into a courtroom and listen to a trial all day long, day after day, and love it."[63] That homespun campaign talk revealed a truth about her empathic interest in other people's lives. She took real pleasure in learning another person's story and would unabashedly ask probing questions of even casual acquaintances. Thus, she had an enduring curiosity about human events, surely an appropriate and necessary attribute for a trial judge.

After the election, when Truman asked Mary Anne what she was going to do, she told her, to Truman's surprise, that she planned to relax a bit and have a baby.[64] Even though she was physically exhausted and emotionally deflated, Mary Anne traveled to San Francisco to visit Ruth Markley. Reconnecting with friends from her youth always seemed to have a therapeutic and grounding effect on Mary Anne, and she maintained contact with a circle of friends from the past throughout her life. After her return from California, she did not relinquish her goal of becoming a judge. Because Republican Paul Fannin had been re-elected governor of Arizona in 1962, Mary Anne knew that she had a solid chance of getting an appointment to a judgeship if a vacancy in Pima County were

---

61. ARIZONA SUPREME COURT, THE SUPERIOR COURT IN ARIZONA 1912–1984, at 56–57 (1985)(identifying Mary Anne Richey as "first female judge on the Superior Court in Pima County—one of her many 'firsts'").

62. Richey Interviews, *supra* note 1.

63. *Mary Anne Reimann Richey Campaigns For Office of Judge*, TUCSON DAILY CITIZEN, October 27, 1962.

64. Truman Interview, *supra* note 39.

to occur during his term in office. With characteristic energy and an eye toward her future goal, Mary Anne resumed her practice with Richey & Reimann.

As she had suggested to Truman, a personal, rather than professional, transformation was on Mary Anne's mind in early 1963: she was determined to have a child. In fact, she had become pregnant shortly after marrying Bill but had suffered an early miscarriage. Now, four years later, she wanted very much to try again. Until that time in her life, she had broken with cultural norms by her focused pursuit of professional success in realms dominated by men. The emerging second wave of the women's movement did not attract her because she felt little connection with its themes. In the 1963 publication of *The Feminine Mystique*, for example, Betty Friedan wrote "We can no longer ignore the voice within women that says: 'I want something more than my husband and my children and my home.'"[65] Such words may have resonated for thousands of housewives around the nation, but they held little force for Mary Anne. Although she had a deeply-rooted belief in gender equality and opposed any notion of women as the weaker or passive sex, the rhetoric of the women's movement was not then meaningful for her.[66] For Mary Anne, the professional was a given. In contrast to the women for whom Friedan spoke, it was the experience of motherhood that presented, to Mary Anne, the prospect of radical personal change. In February of 1963, at the age of forty-five, she became pregnant.

Mary Anne and Bill were thrilled about the pregnancy, and Mary Anne did not allow her doctors' anxiety to dampen her high spirits. Despite the earlier miscarriage, she remained optimistic that she would be able to carry this pregnancy to term. As with other aspects of her life, her stubborn determination propelled her forward. Although she was fully engaged in the press of pending litigation, including the land fraud trial in the *Boeger* case, she thought constantly about the impending birth. At such an advanced maternal age, Mary Anne faced several risks in connection with the pregnancy, risks with which her obstetricians were quite familiar. Among the obstetrical complications that a pregnant woman over the age of thirty-five may face are increased risk for diabetes, hyperten-

---

65. BETTY FRIEDAN, THE FEMININE MYSTIQUE 29 (1963).

66. In a study of twentieth century feminism, Nancy Cott has suggested that feminism contains three core components: a belief in sex equality and opposition to sex hierarchy, a rejection of sex roles as biologically-determined, and an identification with women as a group. NANCY F. COTT, THE GROUNDING OF MODERN FEMINISM 4–5 (1987). Under that definition, Mary Anne embraced at least two of the three core components. Her reluctance to align herself with the women's movement may have reflected the solitary nature of her achievements.

sion, toxemia, abnormal labor, low fetal birthweight, and fetal Down's syndrome and other chromosomal abnormalities.[67] The risks associated with women over the age of thirty-five are only compounded for a woman nearing her forty-sixth birthday. Indeed, although the rate of first-time childbirth for women in their forties is now on the rise, medical literature generally assumes that women of forty-five years of age have ended their reproductive years.[68] As one researcher has put it, "[f]rom thirty to forty, the line of obstetrical complications rises slowly at first, then much more rapidly as thirty-five approaches forty—but it is a line, not a wall, until forty-five."[69] Moreover, in 1963, medical technology did not include the range of prenatal tests (amniocentesis and alpha-fetoprotein testing, for example) that can be performed today to screen for fetal abnormalities. At one point an obstetrician suggested to Mary Anne, erroneously, that the child she was carrying might have an underdeveloped cranium, a suggestion that could not be ruled out with certainty until the birth itself. In general, however, she and Bill remained confident as they proceeded down a path of "brute strength and ignorance."[70] Mary Anne continued working up until the last weeks of the pregnancy.

On October 8, the fourth wedding anniversary for the Richeys, Bill surprised Mary Anne with a home-cooked breakfast in bed and then left to represent a criminal defendant at a court appearance in front of Robert Roylston. Later in the morning, word came into the courthouse that Mary Anne's "water" had broken and that she was on her way to the Tucson Medical Center. Bill left immediately for the hospital. Because of Mary Anne's loss of amniotic fluid and the general medical concern about her pregnancy, doctors performed an emergency cesarean section in the early afternoon, complicated somewhat by Mary Anne's large breakfast earlier in the day. Despite her age and the last-minute sense of urgency, Mary Anne gave birth to a healthy baby girl. Anne Marie, or "Annie," as she came to be called by her parents, was a beautiful infant, except for a small

---

67. *See* CLARK GILLESPIE, PRIMELIFE PREGNANCY 217–43 (1987); Lisa Harker & Karen Thorpe, *'The Last Egg in the Basket?' Elderly Primiparity—A Review of Findings,* 19 BIRTH 1, 23–30 (March 1992). The risk for Down's syndrome, in particular, increases sharply as maternal age increases, rising to one in 250 for women aged 35 to 40, to one in 100 for women aged 40 to 45, and one in 40 for women over the age of 45. GILLESPIE, *supra* at 250. Harker and Thorpe question the validity of many predictions of obstetrical complications for older first-time mothers, noting that empirical studies are inconsistent and the methodology used in some may be questionable.

68. CAROLYN AMBLER WALTER, THE TIMING OF MOTHERHOOD (1986); LARRY L. BUMPASS & CHARLES F. WESTOFF, THE LATER YEARS OF CHILDBEARING (1970).

69. GILLESPIE, *supra* note 67 at 2.

70. Richey Interviews, *supra* note 1.

cut on her scalp received during the surgical birth. Although Bill had told friends that he had hoped for a boy, he was ecstatic to have a healthy, albeit female, baby.

In giving birth to Annie, Mary Anne attracted notice by virtue of her age alone. Staff at the hospital told her that she was the oldest first-time mother on record in Pima County. Available data suggests that nationwide, fewer than one percent of women aged forty-five or older give birth to first children.[71] Indeed, ninety-five percent of white women born 1910–1919 had their last child before age forty, and most of them by age thirty-five.[72] Mary Anne's insistence on going ahead despite the risks was in character. Although she and Bill faced the adventure of parenthood with determination and optimism, they knew little about the physical demands of infant care or the constancy of a parent's responsibility for a young child, and Mary Anne could not easily project herself into the future to ponder the challenges she would face as the sixty-year-old mother of a child in adolescence.

To many of her male friends, Mary Anne seemed unchanged by Annie's birth and continued without interruption in her dedication to her career. They saw her as obviously happy with the "unexpected blessing" of a daughter, but otherwise the same Mary Anne.[73] Those colleagues may have been interpreting Mary Anne's response to childbirth through their own perspectives, or, perhaps, Mary Anne may have wanted her professional colleagues to believe that her pregnancy was a surprise and that her career was still paramount. In contrast, her closest women friends were aware of the profound impact of Annie's birth on Mary Anne—-the unex-

---

71. UNITED STATES BUREAU OF CENSUS, UNITED STATES SUMMARY, DETAILED CHARACTERISTICS, at Table 214 (1970)(Women Ever Married 15 to 49 Years Old by Own Children Under 5 Years Old, Race and Age). Recent studies have shown that the number of "older women" giving birth has increased dramatically since 1970. Women in their thirties accounted for 12 percent of first births in 1986, compared with 3 percent in 1976, and the rate of first births for women forty to forty-four increased by 50 percent. *See* S.K. Ventura, *Trends and variation in first births to older women*, UNITED STATES 1970–1986, VITAL HEALTH STATISTICS, vol. 21, at 1–27 (1989). Although a few recent studies have suggested that the risk factors for pregnancies in older women have been exaggerated, the studies do not have definitive data on women in their mid-forties because the population pool is so small. *See, e.g.,* Patricia Baird, Adele D. Sadovnick, & Irene M.L. Yee, *Maternal age and birth defects: a population study*, THE LANCET, vol. 337, at 527 (March 2, 1991); Gertrud S. Berkowitz, Mary Louise Skovron, Robert H. Lapinski, and Richard L. Berkowitz, *Delayed Childbearing and the Outcome of Pregnancy*, NEW ENGLAND JOURNAL OF MEDICINE, vol. 322, No. 10, at 659 (March 8, 1990).

72. UNITED STATES BUREAU OF THE CENSUS, CURRENT POPULATION REPORTS, SERIES P-20, No. 108, Table 13.

73. Lacagnina Interview, *supra* note 4; Robert Roylston Interview, *supra* note 40.

pected rush of emotion that she experienced as well as her overwhelming sense of responsibility.[74]

The immediate effect of parenthood for Mary Anne and Bill was the pressing need to find someone to care for their newborn child. Mary Anne had not seriously considered staying home with Annie but rather had always intended to return to practice at Richey & Reimann soon after the birth. Consistent with the pattern of most dual working parents even today, the task of arranging for childcare fell on Mary Anne's shoulders. Indeed, studies suggest that among married women lawyers of all ages and in all kinds of practices, most assume a greater responsibility for childcare and managing the home than their husbands.[75] That pattern holds true, incidentally, for the few women lawyers who join the judiciary.[76] Thus, in order to return to full-time practice when Annie was about one month old, Mary Anne hired Maude ("Maudie") Piggee. Maudie, a young Black woman who was working part-time for Mary Anne and Bill already as a housekeeper, had moved to Arizona from Texas a few years earlier. She was married but had no children of her own at that time.[77]

The two women, separated by race, education, economic class, and age, nevertheless operated from a posture of mutual respect and affection. As a housekeeper, Maudie was invaluable to Mary Anne, often staying late when necessary, cooking for special occasions, and caring for Annie when Mary Anne and Bill traveled. Mary Anne was neither a fastidious home-maker nor an overly-anxious mother, and Maudie decided on her own, without detailed instructions from Mary Anne, what housekeeping tasks to do each day and what activities to do with Annie.[78] In fact, Mary Anne looked to Maudie, who had cared for children in the past, for advice about burping techniques, napping schedules, and other basic facets of infant care—facets that were foreign to Mary Anne. She confided in

---

74. Trumbull Interview, *supra* note 6.

75. CYNTHIA FUCHS EPSTEIN, WOMEN IN LAW 373–78 (2d ed. 1993).

76. *Different voices, different choices? The impact of more women lawyers and judges on the justice system*, 74 JUDICATURE 138, 141 (Oct-Nov. 1990)(72.5 percent of male judges identified spouse as person who "runs household," while about 60 percent of female judges identified themselves as running household, and only 9 percent of female judges responded that their spouses run household).

77. Interview with Maude Piggee, Tucson, Arizona (Oct. 5, 1992).

78. According to Maudie, Mary Anne paid attention to the details of housekeeping only once—when Maudie inadvertently almost disposed of the ashes of Marge Allen, who died during Maudie's employ with the Richey family. "When I started to move a vase in the livingroom for cleaning, Ms. Richey jumped and cried, 'Maudie don't touch that. That's Marge Allen!' *Id.*

Maudie that she worried about being so old and that she was bothered when strangers would ask her if Annie were her granddaughter. Maudie reassured her that she should pay them no mind. "You are healthy," Maudie told her, "and that is what matters. This is your baby and you love her. If you can keep up with those horses, you can keep up with a kid."[79]

Maudie remained as housekeeper for the Richeys for seven years. After she gave birth to a son of her own, affectionately called "John-John," she considered quitting work, but Mary Anne persuaded her to stay on as babysitter and to bring her son with her to the Richey home. John-John became Annie's constant playmate, a circumstance that pleased Mary Anne, who worried about Annie's lack of siblings. Over the course of Annie's early childhood, Maudie's presence helped provide a stable and joyful home environment. Although other babysitters succeeded Maudie after she left the Richeys' employ in 1970, Annie remembers her as the significant caregiver of her childhood. Maudie, in turn, recalls her employment with the Richeys with pleasure. "The judge never complained about anything I did," Maudie recalled. "She treated me as a co-worker, or a friend, and we stayed in touch until she died."[80]

Mary Anne's and Bill's household was chaotic in those early days of adjusting to the presence of an infant and to new constraints on time schedules. Moreover, the national tragedy of President Kennedy's assassination occurred only a month and a half after Annie was born and must have added to Mary Anne's sense that life was never going to be as it had been before Annie's birth. Bill and Mary Anne were in a coffee shop near their law office when the news came, and they were stunned at the announcement.[81] Later, with their new infant in their arms, they grimly watched the succession of events on television, from the profound image of the riderless horse in Kennedy's funeral procession to the shocking spectacle of Lee Harvey Oswald's own killing at the hands of Jack Ruby. Although Mary Anne was not a fan of Kennedy's, she was deeply saddened by his death.

A chaotic national political scene unfolded after the assassination with direct repercussions in Arizona. Senator Barry Goldwater, sensing that the national Democratic administration was vulnerable on several fronts (the Vietnam war, the "decline" of moral values, the threat of "big government"), launched a successful drive for the Republican presidential nomination. Mary Anne and Bill, as staunch Republicans, attended Goldwa-

---

79. *Id.*
80. *Id.*
81. Richey Interviews, *supra* note 1.

ter's kick-off celebration in Arizona. President Lyndon B. Johnson, with vice-presidential nominee Hubert Humphrey, began his battle to retain the White House. Governor Fannin in Arizona then set his sights on Goldwater's vacant Senate seat and announced his resignation as governor, effective at the end of the year. The Democratic nominee for the senatorial race, Roy Elson, was a young man who was first administrative assistant to powerful Senator Carl Hayden, then Chairman of the Senate Appropriations Committee, but Elson had little political visibility of his own. Fannin's action, in turn, produced a scramble between the parties for Arizona's state house. Sam Goddard, the Tucson lawyer who only two years earlier had run unsuccessfully for governor, received the Democratic nomination for a second attempt. Richard Kleindienst, an attorney from Phoenix who was a field director in Goldwater's nomination drive, captured the Republican nomination for governor.[82] Kleindienst, who was not yet tainted by association with the Watergate scandal in the Nixon White House, ran on a platform of "morality in government."[83] Mary Anne and Bill threw their support behind the Goldwater ticket and supported Fannin and Kleindienst as well in their respective races. Mary Anne knew that her chances for a judicial appointment would be foreclosed for all practical purposes if a Democrat were elected as governor. Moreover, Mary Anne's support for the Republican candidates was not surprising. Having identified as a Republican for more than a decade, she endorsed several themes of Goldwater conservativism. She was skeptical of the benefits of concentrated federal power and believed that local control over local problems generally produced better solutions. Thus, the "states' rights" rhetoric of the Republican platform may have touched a responsive chord in Mary Anne's understanding of social policy.[84]

Ultimately, Mary Anne's goal came more quickly than she had anticipated. In the fall of 1964, President Johnson, in the midst of his presidential election race against Barry Goldwater, was contacted by Arizona's Senator Carl Hayden. On the advice of his top staffer Elson, Hayden asked Johnson to appoint Raul Castro, then a superior court judge, as ambassador to El Salvador. Johnson was initially reluctant, in part because of Castro's name association with the Cuban dictator, but he ulti-

---

82. *Big vote Expected In Arizona*, THE ARIZONA DAILY STAR, November 1, 1964.

83. *Gubernatorial Candidates Debate Issues Before Glendale Audience*, THE ARIZONA DAILY STAR, October 1, 1964.

84. *See* BARRY GOLDWATER, THE CONSCIENCE OF A CONSERVATIVE (1960)(arguing that federal governmental excesses—through Supreme Court decisionmaking, congressional legislation, and executive enforcement—violated the intended constitutional plan).

mately agreed. Elson then tried to capitalize on the appointment in his own Senate race against Paul Fannin.[85]

Castro's ambassadorship, announced just weeks before the general election in 1964, left vacant the judgeship in Division 5 of the superior court. Notwithstanding the then-existing system of judicial election in Arizona, the majority of Arizona judges were first appointed to judicial office before ever standing for election,[86] and Mary Anne was to join that group. In contrast to the gubernatorial role under today's merit selection system, which requires the governor to appoint from the candidates suggested by the merit selection committee, the governor in Mary Anne's day was given unfettered discretion to fill unexpired terms.[87]

When Raul Castro's ambassadorship left Division 5 of the superior court vacant, Mary Anne was immediately suggested as the replacement. Just as Robert Roylston had been "rewarded" for campaigning as the Republican candidate for the superior court in 1958, Mary Anne was due such a reward from the Republican Party for her strong performance in 1962. William Frey, a Tucson attorney who was active in Republican politics, was also suggested as a possible appointee.[88] With the chance of an appointment within Mary Anne's reach, Bill Richey privately asked Frey to withdraw from consideration. "You know she deserves this, and we've got a lot of favors coming, too," Richey argued, adding, "You can get one anywhere along the line, so just back off for now."[89] As it happened, imminent political events created two vacancies instead of one, thus resolving the "competition" between Mary Anne and Frey.

The 1964 elections were close to a Democratic sweep nationwide, with Johnson winning two-thirds of the popular vote and an overwhelming 90 percent of the electoral college vote. Arizona, however, was one of the six states that Goldwater carried. In addition, the prized Senate seat in Arizona went to Republican Governor Paul Fannin. On the other hand, Democrat Sam Goddard was successful in the race for Fannin's vacant office. At the local level, two superior court judges from Pima County who had

85. ARIZONA BAR FOUNDATION ORAL HISTORY PROJECT: ARIZONA LEGAL HISTORY, *Raul H. Castro*, at 17–19 (June 7, & July 10, 1991).

86. Of the 210 judges that assumed office between 1912 and 1974, 113 were first appointed. *See* Roll, *supra* note 46.

87. At least two governors (Democrat Sam Goddard and Republican Jack Williams) created blue-ribbon committees to evaluate judicial applicants and make recommendations. *See* ARIZONA ACADEMY, TWENTY-SECOND ARIZONA TOWN HALL ON THE ADEQUACY OF ARIZONA'S COURT SYSTEM 32–33 (1973).

88. *Politics in Arizona*, THE ARIZONA DAILY STAR, November 2, 1964.

89. Richey Interviews, *supra* note 1.

run unopposed for seats on the newly created Division 2 of the Arizona Court of Appeals, were Herbert Krucker, a Republican, and John Molloy, a Democrat. Krucker immediately resigned from the superior court after the election so that Fannin, as the outgoing Republican governor, could fill his seat by appointment. Molloy, on the other hand, remained on the superior court bench through the end of 1964 in order to preserve his seat for the appointment power of Goddard, the newly–elected Democratic governor.[90]

Fannin moved quickly in making the appointments that were then available to him. On November 9, 1964, one week after he defeated Elson for the Senate seat, Fannin announced Mary Anne's appointment to Division 5 of the Pima County Superior Court to fill the seat vacated by Raul Castro.[91] Soon after that appointment, he named William Frey to fill the vacancy created by Krucker's resignation. Thus, through an ironic series of events, Mary Anne achieved her goal. A vacancy was created on the bench because of Democratic politics at the state and national levels. Her appointment to fill the vacancy was by the outgoing Republican governor who, in his own Senate race, defeated the very man who had suggested that Raul Castro be tapped for an ambassadorship. Fannin's election to the Senate, moreover, would later play a role in Mary Anne's appointment to the federal court bench.

One week later, the Roylston twins, now both superior court judges themselves, performed a joint swearing-in ceremony at the Pima County Courthouse. Mary Anne repeated the oath of office as it was said in unison, sentence by sentence, by the Roylstons. A newspaper account explained that moments before the ceremony, Mary Anne was "soundly kissed on each cheek by her husband...as he helped her don her black judicial robe for the first time." At the ceremony, J. Mercer Johnson, a close friend of Mary Anne's who had served both as superior court judge and supreme court justice in Arizona, described her as "an experienced trial lawyer" and stated that in her courtroom lawyers would know exactly how she stood "with no mincing of words." Mary Anne made a short talk using simple language. She promised "to work hard and do the best I can to be the kind of judge that you expect."[92]

---

90. *Politics in Arizona*, THE ARIZONA DAILY STAR, November 2, 1964; THE ARIZONA SUPREME COURT, THE SUPERIOR COURT IN ARIZONA 1912–1984, at 57 (1985) (describing appointments of William C. Frey and John P. Collins).

91. *Tucson Woman Named Superior Court Judge*, TUCSON DAILY CITIZEN, November 9, 1964.

92. *Mrs. Richey Becomes Division Five Judge*, THE ARIZONA DAILY STAR, November 17, 1964.

Thus, at the age of forty-seven, she became the second woman to sit on the Pima County Superior Court bench and the third female trial court judge in Arizona. With her two-year-old daughter and an unabashedly supportive husband, Mary Anne embarked on the career for which she would be most remembered. She brought to the bench not only thirteen years of professional experience in the public and private domains of law practice, but also a rich store of life experiences, many of them leveling the normal constraints of gender imposed by society. Her judicial persona would inevitably reflect a complex amalgam of those experiences and the perspectives that they shaped.

Mary Anne's mother, Emma Nading, Shelbyville, Indiana, circa 1915.

Mary Anne's father, Harry Wallace Reimann, Shelbyville, Indiana, circa 1920

Emma Nading Reimann, circa 1935.

Mary Anne with brothers Charles (left) and William (right), Shelbyville, Indiana.

Mary Anne and her brothers, Charles and William Reimann, Shelbyville, Indiana.

Mary Anne with her brother Charles, far right, and unknown friends, Shelbyville, Indiana, circa 1925.

The Reimann family around their hearth: from left to right, Anna Reimann, Mary Anne's paternal grandmother; Charles, Emma, Mary Anne, Wallace, and William, circa 1929.

Mary Anne's passport photo, 1935

Mary Anne Reimann in Karachi, India, 1936.

Mary Anne with Robert and Ruth Markley in Karachi, India, December 1935.

Mary Anne's brother Charles John Reimann, shortly before his death in 1942.

Mary Anne at Purdue University, West Lafayette, Indiana, 1937.

Mary Anne Showers, in full WASP dress uniform, Sweetwater, Texas, 1944.

Mary Anne Showers, in the leather WASP flight uniform, Sweetwater, Texas, 1944.

Mary Anne, the WASP, ready to climb into an open cockpit, Sweetwater, Texas, 1944.

Mary Anne Reimann, a new lawyer at Scruggs & Rucker, Tucson, Arizona, 1951.

The Pima County Attorneys Office, Tucson, Arizona, February 1954, immediately before Mary Anne's resignation. Left to right, standing, are deputies Gordon Aldrich and Charles Ares, County Attorney Morris Udall, deputies Alfredo Marquez, Daniel Sammons, and Raul Castro, and investigator Charles Coates. Seated, left to right, are secretaries Priscilla Espiritu and Mary de la Torre (Howard), support-enforcement specialist Frances Wallace, and deputy Mary Anne Reimann.

A beaming Mary Anne and Bill Richey at their wedding, Tucson, Arizona, October 1959.

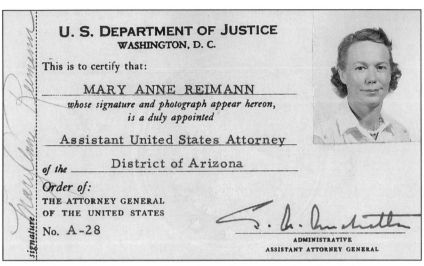

Mary Anne's identification card as Assistant United States Attorney, 1954.

Promotional flier from Mary Anne Richey's unsuccessful 1962 campaign for the Pima County Superior Court, Tucson, Arizona.

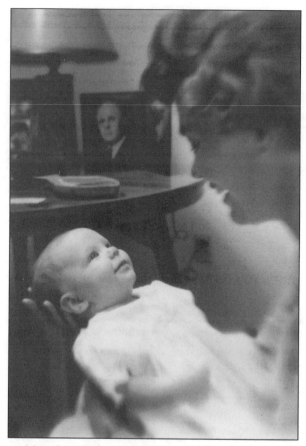

Mary Anne Richey with her new daughter Annie, December 1963.

Bill Richey and Mary Anne with their new daughter, Annie, 1964.

Three women judges at a University of Arizona College of Law function, Tucson, Arizona, 1969. Left to right, they are Judge Mary Anne Richey, Division V, Pima County Superior Court, Judge Alice Truman, Division VI, Pima County Superior Court, and Chief Justice Lorna E. Lockwood, Arizona Supreme Court.

Mary Anne and daughter Annie Richey, Tucson, Arizona, May 1970.

Judge Mary Anne Richey, United States District Court, Tucson, Arizona.

The United States District Court for the District of Arizona, 1980. Standing, from left to right, Judges Earl H. Carroll, Valdemar A. Cordova, Richard M. Bilby, Charles L. Hardy, and Alfredo C. Marquez. Seated, from left to right, Judge Mary Anne Richey, Senior Judge James A. Walsh, Chief Judge Carl A. Muecke, Senior Judge Walter E. Craig, and Judge William P. Copple.

Mary Anne Richey, Tucson, Arizona, August 1981.

Part Three
1964–1983

On the Bench—Settling In and Staying

For eleven of the twelve years that Mary Anne was on the superior court bench, her place of work was the adobe Pima County Courthouse whose multi-colored tile dome is a Tucson landmark. The courthouse, built in 1929, is a two-story structure of stuccoed brick with an elaborately-carved facade and an enclosed patio reflecting the Spanish colonial and Moorish themes of southwestern architecture. Designed by Tucson architect Roy Place, the building housed the Pima County Superior Court for forty-six years. When the court outgrew the structure, a modern concrete and glass courthouse for Pima County was constructed.[1] That relatively sterile building, which was completed in 1975 at the end of Mary Anne's state court tenure, sits directly south of the older courthouse, and the contrast in architectural styles between the old and the new is striking. Mary Anne loved the old courthouse, with its aura of grandeur and solemnity and its meld of southwestern cultural influences. The building provided a fitting backdrop for her entry into the judiciary.

When Mary Anne joined the superior court bench, Pima County had seven other judges: Lee Garrett, the senior jurist who had been appointed in 1947 to succeed John Lyons (who became dean at the College of Law and Mary Anne's mentor); Robert and Richard Roylston, the twins; Alice Truman, Mary Anne's victor in the 1962 election; William Frey, the other late-hour appointee by outgoing Governor Fannin; Jack Marks, a Democrat who was elected in November 1962 to the new Division Eight; and John Collins, a Democrat whom Governor Goddard appointed early in 1965 to replace John Molloy. Because Lorna Lockwood had left the Maricopa County Superior Court for a seat on the Arizona Supreme Court in 1961, Mary Anne's appointment brought the total number of female superior court judges statewide to two.[2] The two women, Mary Anne and Truman, may have been adversaries in the electoral battlefield

---

1. *Old Pima courthouse designated landmark*, TUCSON CITIZEN, August 5, 1978; Bonnie Henry, *Visual balm under a tiled dome*, THE ARIZONA DAILY STAR, June 21, 1989.

2. ARIZONA SUPREME COURT, THE SUPERIOR COURT IN ARIZONA 1912–1984, at 55–59 (1985).

but they became close friends and confidants as judges. They particularly enjoyed comparing their perceptions of the other (male) judges in the state and the reactions of the male judges to their presence.[3]

During Mary Anne's campaign against Truman for the superior court judgeship in 1962, each woman reportedly told a newspaper writer that she had never encountered discrimination because of her sex. Years later, Truman shook her head when reviewing the article that featured that statement and exclaimed, "How dreamy I was!" When asked if she thought she was wrong, she replied, "No, I don't. But when there were more of us...it got worse. Then there was resistance."[4] She explained that as the number of women on the superior court bench gradually increased, the men may have perceived them as a threat. In the beginning, however, the women judges were a welcome novelty, and their male colleagues treated Mary Anne and Alice with deference. In fact, both Mary Anne and Alice Truman were elected president of the State Judge's Association during their early years on the bench. The office does not carry significant authority but does indicate that the office-holder has earned a degree of respect among the state jurists. Truman became the first woman president of the Association in 1965, and Mary Anne was elected president in 1970.[5] Interestingly, women judges in Arizona had to wait until the 1990s for their ranks to supply a third president.[6]

When Mary Anne was appointed to fill Raul Castro's vacancy, she faced the immediate task of selecting her staff, including, most importantly, her secretary, court reporter, and bailiff. Through intuitive good judgment, she assembled a group of individuals who remained staunchly loyal to her and seemed to enjoy great compatibility with her and with one another. Her staff was not a somber group; rather, in chambers the talk was lively and the laughter was frequent. For six years, Kathryn Place worked for Mary Anne as secretary. A housewife who had joined the workforce only after her daughter entered college, Place was a smart woman whose personal warmth appealed to Mary Anne.[7] When Place

---

3. Interview with Hon. Alice Truman, Former Judge of Pima County Superior Court, Tucson, Arizona (July 6, 1992).

4. *Id.*

5. *Id.*

6. Pima County Superior Court Judge Leslie Miller served as president of the Arizona Judge's Association in 1992–93. *See* STATE BAR OF ARIZONA 1992–93 MEMBERSHIP DIRECTORY (Arizona Legal Organizations).

7. Place was the wife of Tucson architect Lew Place whose father had designed the Pima County Courthouse. Interview with Eleanor Robbins, Tucson, Arizona (July 13, 1992).

retired by choice in 1970, Eleanor Robbins became the new secretary and remained with Mary Anne in that position until Mary Anne's death in 1983.[8] When Robbins was hired, she was a divorced mother of two young children. Her highly competent and energetic management of Mary Anne's calendar over the years was invaluable to the judge, and Mary Anne became very dependent on Robbins' presence in the outer office. Moreover, Robbins' infectious laugh and gregarious personality made her a favorite among the practicing bar. Although about twenty years younger than Mary Anne, Robbins became one of Mary Anne's most trusted confidants—especially on matters of parenting. In later years, when Mary Anne's daughter Annie entered adolescence, Mary Anne often consulted Robbins on the challenges of raising a teenager. At the same time, Mary Anne was an influential role model for Robbins' young son and daughter, both of whom ultimately became lawyers.

Mary Anne selected Byron Stolle as her court reporter, having known him since his days as court reporter for Judge Walsh in the United States District Court. More recently, Stolle had been working as reporter for Raul Castro, and Mary Anne gladly kept him on when she filled Castro's vacancy in Division 5.[9] Stolle, a slight man who suffered from heart problems, had a soft-spoken and gentle manner, and he was an expert at the fading craft of courtroom stenography. Stolle's devotion to his work was legendary. One afternoon in superior court, the story goes, Stolle was hard at work transcribing trial testimony. He did not hear the alarm in the courthouse nor did he notice that all other employees had filed out of the building because of a bomb threat. Only after the other workers were allowed back into their offices did Stolle realize what had happened. "Do you mean to tell me," he exclaimed in dismay, "that I survived open heart surgery only to be blown up over a pile of transcripts?"[10]

Finally, Mary Anne asked Francis Copham, a ruddy-faced, white-haired diminutive man from Liverpool, England, to be her bailiff. Copham had spent twenty years as a sailor with the Merchant Marine before immigrating to the United States. It was through his position as head waiter at a local steakhouse in Tucson that Mary Anne had met him. She had been charmed by his Liverpool accent, his salty humor, and his abiding aura of personal dignity—a perfect combination for a court bailiff. As she had predicted, Francis took great pride in his job. He shepherded the jury panels with courtesy and good humor, and he intoned with a special

---

8. *Id.*

9. Letter from Judge Mary Anne Richey to Mr. R. Glen Johnson, July 12, 1976 (providing Myron Stolle's work history).

10. Robbins Interview, *supra* note 7.

flare the standard pronouncement, "All rise! Pima County Superior Court now in session, the Honorable Mary Anne Richey presiding."[11]

The selection of a courtroom was another task facing Mary Anne after her appointment, a task which ultimately generated the first public criticism of her in her judicial office. Although she temporarily occupied a small first-floor courtroom in the Pima County Courthouse, she had grander plans. In 1965, construction of a new north wing of the courthouse, including three new courtrooms, commenced. Mary Anne requested one of the three new courtrooms, and the Roylston brothers requested the other two. The Roylstons and Mary Anne looked forward to continuing their long-standing friendship in close proximity in the remodeled courthouse. Unfortunately, the three judges became embroiled in a very public battle with the Pima County Board of Supervisors, the governing body in charge of the construction project, over furniture styles for the new courtrooms. The press coverage depicted the judges as despots engaged in a power struggle with the Board of Supervisors over a relatively trivial issue, and the nature of that issue—furniture styles—left Mary Anne open to caricature.

As reported in the press, Mary Anne and the Roylstons were initially consulted on chair styles for the new courtrooms as a matter of courtesy. After spending several hours reviewing catalogues, the Roylstons accepted a standardized style recommended by the county purchasing agent, but Mary Anne requested furniture with a modern Scandinavian motif. The purchasing agent opposed Mary Anne's request on the theory that standardized chairs for the three courtrooms would be more economical. Out of loyalty to their friend and as a matter of principle, the Roylstons backed Mary Anne's right to have chairs of her own selection in the courtroom. Moreover, they contended, Mary Anne's selection would not be more expensive than the standardized chairs in a true competitive bidding process. In an unusual move, the three judges appeared before the Board of Supervisors in early April of 1966 to angrily argue their cause.[12] In the controversy, Robert Roylston accused the county purchasing agent of improperly conducting the bidding process, and the judges disputed the Board's contention that it had the final authority on chair selection.

---

11. See Old Liverpool Seafarer Appointed Court Bailiff, THE ARIZONA DAILY STAR, December 12, 1964; Copham Gets Bailiff Post, TUCSON DAILY CITIZEN, December 14, 1964.

12. A series of articles in the Arizona Daily Star in early 1966 documented the controversy. See Courts' Remodeling Still Far From Over, February 24, 1966; Pima Bench Adds Chairs to Its Judicial Cares, April 5, 1966; Board Has Final Say On Chairs, April 7, 1966.; Judge Richey Is Willing To Make Concessions On Chair Purchases, April 9, 1966.

Sarcasm abounded in the coverage by Tucson's two daily newspapers. One article, for example, began with the following passage: "Another complicated chapter unfolded today in the continuing controversy over new courtroom furniture in the renovated old Pima County courthouse, which could be styled Judges vs. Supervisors, or Swedish Modern v. Traditional."[13] An editorial pointedly opined that the furniture would outlast the judges, that "the furniture should be chosen with a view to economical long life, and not in accordance with the whim of any judge," and that to furnish a courtroom "at extra expense in a particular style when there is no assurance that the next judge...will care for the style is ridiculous."[14] In response to the editorial and other public criticism, Mary Anne told a reporter that her selection of chairs would be cheaper than those requested by the Rolystons, that Danish modern would provide greater utility space in the courtroom, and that her choice "was not a feminine whim."[15] Mary Anne evidently viewed the criticism as unjustified, and she was stung by the suggestion that she acted out of caprice and without regard to the ultimate burden on the taxpayers. Exasperated and angry, she ultimately refused to move into the new courtroom and, instead, occupied a large second-floor courtroom formerly assigned to Alice Truman. Truman, in turn, moved into one of the three newly-constructed courtrooms.

The incident and its coverage in the local newspapers revealed an irony often faced by women of prominence. On the one hand, the press routinely heralded Mary Anne's many professional accomplishments over the course of her career and especially highlighted her accomplishments as a woman. Her "firsts" as a woman lawyer were standard biographical details appended to any article containing accolades. On the other hand, when she publicly refused to back down in the furniture selection dispute, she was sharply criticized, with a veiled suggestion from the press that her position was the result of feminine fancy or selfish whim. The irony is that most women who achieve professional firsts are necessarily possessed of a strong will and independence of thought. They are praised when their personal strengths result in professional success, but when those same traits surface in a clash with traditional authority, they are disparaged.[16] Thus, in the fur-

---

13. *Roylstons Say Board Doesn't Have Last Word*, Tucson Daily Citizen, April 7, 1966.

14. *Furniture Will Outlast Judges*, Arizona Daily Star, April 7, 1966.

15. *Judges vs. Supervisors: No Appeal*, Tucson Daily Citizen, April 8, 1966.

16. *See, e.g.*, Judith Lorber, Paradoxes of Gender 243–44 (1994). Lorber notes that due to gendered assumptions about women's behavior, women leaders are often caught in a double bind. "A woman leader is expected to be empathic, considerate of other's feelings, and attuned to the personal. If she is not, she is likely to be called abra-

niture dispute, when Mary Anne's initial response to the critique was aggressive self-defense, her attitude was criticized as unseemly stubbornness.

Mary Anne thus acquired the courtroom that she was to occupy for most of her state-court tenure through a last-minute effort to mute the controversy with the Board of Supervisors. As it happened, the courtroom that Alice Truman had relinquished was an imposing place, designed in the style of the grand old courtrooms of the West. Indeed, filmmakers were a familiar presence in the courtroom during Mary Anne's tenure for the filming of Western movies and television shows, including the series known as "Petrocelli." A high domed ceiling arched above the courtroom gallery, and carved oak columns lined the walls. The jury box and the spectator bar were similarly fashioned of finely-polished wood, and the elevated, dark oak judicial bench was ornately carved in a motif matching the columns. The courtroom, with its atmosphere of formality and traditional elegance, was more imposing than the other courtrooms at the courthouse. Mary Anne became accustomed to its grandeur, and she ultimately presided over an equally imposing courtroom in the federal courthouse. According to lawyers, however, the courtroom's design could be intimidating and created acoustical problems for jury trials.[17]

Shortly after Mary Anne was appointed, she experienced vicariously another sort of public criticism. Her close friend Richard Roylston, who had been elected to the superior court in 1962, was at the center of a firestorm of controversy after he had issued a "gag order" in a notorious murder case pending before him. The case involved defendant Charles Schmid, Jr., who was accused of murdering three teenage girls in Tucson. Sensationalism abounded in the media coverage of the murders, and in November of 1965, defense counsel requested an injunction from the court to protect his client's right to a fair trial. The injunctive order that counsel sought was to prohibit police, sheriff's officers, and prosecutors from discussing with the press details of the investigation of the triple murder charges against Schmid and to bar the press from reporting anything other than information drawn from court records. In late November, Roylston granted a temporary injunction giving the defense part of what they wanted. Roylston's order, first delivered verbally in open court and then in writing, restrained the police, sheriffs, and prosecutors from discussing the case with the press. In his verbal announcement, Roylston showed the struggle he was experiencing:

---

sive....On the other hand, a more conciliatory style may be criticized by men and women colleagues as insufficiently authoritative." *Id.* at 244.

17. Interview with Richard S. Oseran, Tucson, Arizona (July 7, 1995).

It is hard to know what to do in a case like this. . . . If I were to grant any type of restraining order in this, I think, without question, I would be infringing in some way upon the question of the freedom of the press. On the other hand, I think if I fail to do anything, I would be infringing on the rights of the defendant to have an impartial jury at his trial.[18]

Roylston's limited injunction was immediately condemned as a violation of the first amendment's guarantee of a free press. Editorials in local newspapers accused Roylston of having created a "Gestapo state,"[19] and likened him to Benedict Arnold.[20] A committee of the Arizona Associated Press likewise condemned Roylston's order as an infringement of the public's right to know.[21]

Mary Anne was acutely aware of the clamor of outrage surrounding her friend Richard and felt that the public reaction, while predictable, was excessive. Her view, expressed later, was that Roylston's order was consistent with the existing code of ethics constraining lawyers' extrajudicial statements. As such, the furor over his order was "quite a bit to do about nothing." She believed, however, that the balancing of the individual's right to a fair trial with the guarantee of a free press was a problem that needed attention. She placed hope in achieving a pragmatic solution through common sense. "If we work together on this matter—the press, the bar association and judges—I think something can be worked out. . . . We need a solution which is fair to the press and to the defendant."[22]

As it happened, Roylston's stance on the protection of a defendant's right to a fair trial was vindicated within a matter of months. In *Sheppard v. Maxwell*,[23] the United States Supreme Court reversed the conviction of Dr. Sam Sheppard because of prejudicial pretrial publicity. In so doing, the Court noted that the trial judge should have exercised stricter control over the activities of the press within the courtroom, and it emphasized the responsibilities of the parties to the case not to release information to the press. With particular relevance to the *Schmid* case, the Supreme Court ex-

---

18. Ruling of Honorable Richard M. Roylston, Presiding Judge, in Order to Show Cause Entitled: Schmid v. Burr, November 22, 1965. The verbal order was put into writing the following day, Order of November 23, 1965, Schmid v. Burr, No. 93026 (Pima County Sup. Ct).

19. *What The Judge Did To You*, Tucson Daily Citizen, November 25, 1965.

20. Dick Williams, *The Window*, Tucson American, December 8, 1965.

21. *Judge's Action Condemned*, Tucson Daily Citizen, November 26, 1965.

22. Cecil James, *Frey Questions Collins' Action On Grand Jury*, Tucson Daily Citizen, October 14, 1966.

23. 384 U.S. 333 (1966).

plained that trial judges should constrain counsel and other participants in the criminal trial from releasing information to the press if the participants themselves fail to exercise such responsibility.[24]

Schmid, the sordid principal in the drama, went on to an ignominious end. In two separate trials, he was convicted of first degree murder of two of the girls, and he pleaded guilty to second degree murder with respect to the third teenager. He was sentenced to death in the first trial, and to fifty years to life on the second-degree murder charge. His convictions were affirmed on appeal, but the death sentence was reduced to life imprisonment in the wake of the United States Supreme Court's invalidation of many states' capital punishment schemes in *Furman v. Georgia.*[25] Schmid was ultimately stabbed to death by a fellow inmate at the Arizona State Prison.[26]

In the *Schmid* case, Mary Anne watched from the side as her friend and colleague received fierce public condemnation for his ruling. Roylston's commitment to the principle of a fair trial and his disregard for the possible electoral consequences of his unpopular ruling impressed Mary Anne. As a well-known federal judge with a record of controversial decisions once wrote, "When a judge has the courage of his convictions, a willingness to do what his understanding of the law tells him is right, he can in my view properly be called a judge of integrity."[27] Mary Anne, too, would experience criticism for certain actions from the bench, and she saw in Roylston's example that the stamina to withstand such criticism came largely from the judge's own sense of having made an earnest attempt to fulfill the responsibilities of the office.

Despite her discomfort with public criticism, Mary Anne had no ambivalence about her decision to become a judge, and according to Bill Richey, she "took to the work like a duck to water."[28] She felt supremely happy with her good fortune in securing a judicial appointment, and she

---

24. The Court stated, "Neither prosecutors, counsel for defense, the accused, witnesses, court staff nor enforcement officers coming under the jurisdiction of the court should be permitted to frustrate its function." 384 U.S. at 363.

25. 408 U.S. 238 (1972). *See* State v. Schmid, 509 P.2d 619 (Ariz. 1973); State v. Schmid, 484 P.2d 187 (Ariz. 1971).

26. For a report of Schmid's death, *see Schmid Dies From Wounds*, THE ARIZONA DAILY STAR, March 30, 1975. The history of the Schmid murders and his criminal trials is described, in true-crime fashion, in DON MOSER & JERRY COHEN, THE PIED PIPER OF TUCSON (1967).

27. Hon. Frank M. Johnson, Jr., *Civilization, Integrity, and Justice: Some Observations on the Function of the Judiciary*, 43 SW. L. REV. 645, 651 (1989).

28. Interview with William K. Richey, Nutrioso, Arizona (July 16–17, 1992); Telephone Interviews with Richey (Sept. 20, 27, 1992, Sept. 21, 1994).

threw herself into the job with characteristic vigor. Her transition from advocate to umpire seemingly occurred without difficulty. Although the combative and often frustrating nature of trial judging is well known,[29] Mary Anne seemed to respect the trial process more than a particular result in individual cases, and she approached the refereeing task of judging without defensiveness. A seasoned trial lawyer, she realized the truth of another jurist's words, "Along with the prestige often attached to the office, along with the rituals of deference, we view trial judges with a deep strain of mistrust and hostility."[30] Mary Anne's life experiences had equipped her to weather that hostility with equanimity.

As a superior court judge, Mary Anne's workload was intense, and the increasing backlog of cases put pressure on the system. The court administrator for the Pima County Superior Court began issuing annual reports in 1965, and each report through 1975 contains progressively more dire warnings about the case load in the superior court. In 1965, the administrator wrote, "Though the word 'backlog' has become a common term in the vocabulary of the courts and members of the legal profession, the situation is far more drastic now than it was in prior years."[31] The report shows that the judges averaged 57 civil trials and 34 criminal trials in 1965.[32] By 1971, the average trial load had increased significantly: Mary Anne presided over 177 trials, more than any other superior court judge in Pima County that year,[33] and the court experienced a 25 percent increase in civil case filings over the previous five years[34] and a 157 percent increase in criminal filings for the same period.[35] As of 1975, the trend continued, with the court experiencing a 47 percent increase in civil case filings[36] and a 71 percent increase in criminal filings.[37] During that period of sharply increasing caseloads for the superior court judges, Mary Anne became a vocal advocate of extra-judicial forms of dispute resolution, and

---

29. *See, e.g.*, Hon. Marvin E. Frankel, *The Adversary Judge: The Experience of the Trial Judge*, in VIEWS FROM THE BENCH at 47–54 (MARK W. CANNON & DAVID M. OBRIEN, EDS. 1985).

30. *Id.* at 50.

31. ANNUAL REPORT, SUPERIOR COURT OF THE STATE OF ARIZONA PIMA COUNTY at 1 (1965).

32. *Id.* at 4.

33. ANNUAL REPORT RELATING TO THE SUPERIOR COURT OF THE STATE OF ARIZONA (1971) (Chart No. 65).

34. *Id.* at 6 (Chart No. 3).

35. *Id.* at 22 (Chart No. 20).

36. ANNUAL REPORT RELATING TO THE SUPERIOR COURT OF THE STATE OF ARIZONA PIMA COUNTY 3 (1975) (Chart No. 2).

37. *Id.* at Chart No. 11, p. 11.

she took an active role in encouraging settlement in civil cases and plea agreements in criminal cases.

Although she tried to safeguard her time at home with Annie and Bill, Mary Anne spent long hours at the courthouse when necessary.[38] Annie became accustomed to her mother's hurried departure in the morning with the explanation, "I have to be on the bench by nine!" As a very young child, Annie believed that her mother was racing out of the house to take a seat on a park bench, and she did not understand why that activity was so important. Not until she was about eight years old did she finally realize that her mother's "bench" was different.[39] Mary Anne's judicial position inevitably required her to leave her daughter, even when ill, in the care of others, and she once remarked that leaving Annie alone with a housekeeper when the child was sick was harder for her than criminal sentencings.[40] Indeed, on occasion she adjourned trials because of Annie, announcing to counsel and jury, "I have a sick little girl at home and I need to be there."[41]

Through Mary Anne's state court tenure, Pima County superior court judges received cases under an assignment system, without specialization. A "master calendar," established in 1966 under the auspices of the court administrator, allocated the caseloads among the available judges. Pursuant to the calendar, available judges would be assigned to hear such matters as pending motions, civil and criminal trials, and pre-trial conferences. Unlike the federal docketing system, cases were rarely permanently assigned to a single judge. Thus, a superior court judge might be assigned a completely unfamiliar case for trial. Periodic rotations between the criminal and civil dockets, a common feature of modern judicial calendar management, was not yet in practice, and the superior court judges were forced to be generalists on a day-to-day basis. Juvenile matters, on the other hand, were viewed as appropriate for specialization, and a juvenile court judge was designated from among the superior court judges on a yearly basis.[42]

---

38. According to the Annual Report of the Arizona Judiciary, she averaged 216 days per year of holding court from 1966 through 1970, including time sitting in other counties and on appellate courts, a figure that was consistent with other judges on the superior court bench at that time. *See* ANNUAL REPORT OF THE ARIZONA JUDICIARY, 1966–70 VOLS.

39. Interview with Annie Richey, Tucson, Arizona (Aug. 22, 1992).

40. Nicki Donahue, *Judge Takes To Her Mount When Balked At The Bench*, TUCSON CITIZEN, January 24, 1969.

41. Interview with W. Edward Morgan, Tucson, Arizona (Sept. 9, 1992).

42. *See* UNIFORM RULES OF PRACTICE OF THE SUPERIOR COURT OF ARIZONA, AND RULES OF THE PIMA COUNTY SUPERIOR COURT (effective January 1, 1962).

Although Mary Anne thrived in the role of judge from the start, she did develop preferences for categories of cases. In spite of her rich prosecutorial experience, she preferred civil cases to criminal, and often said that the most difficult task she faced as a judge was criminal sentencing, so much so that she occasionally cried in chambers. "Every time I do it, it hurts," she once said, "but it's my duty. I have no choice."[43] Belying the stereotypes, Mary Anne also disliked juvenile work—delinquency matters and dependency and neglect petitions—and spent very little time in the juvenile court. Although she apparently presided over a few juvenile hearings, she was never the designated juvenile court judge during her years on the state court bench.[44] In contrast, Alice Truman found juvenile work challenging but fulfilling, and she functioned as the designated juvenile court judge for several years.[45] Mary Anne's announced disinterest in working at the juvenile court stood in contrast to her well-known commitment to helping disadvantaged youth through such programs as the YWCA and the Big Sisters program. Mary Anne may have felt impotent or ill-prepared to help the juvenile offender, and Robbins, her secretary, believed that she disliked the work from the perspective of a mother.[46] Perhaps she believed that most young offenders did not belong in the court system at all. Also, because her state court days coincided with *In re Gault*[47] and *In re Winship*,[48] she may have felt uncomfortable with the increasing constitutionalization of juvenile court procedure.

Similarly, Mary Anne cared little for domestic relations disputes. She derisively referred to divorce litigants as "people fighting over tupperware"[49] and let it be known that she had little patience for such petty quarrels. If she perceived a litigant to be whining or using the vehicle of divorce to wage an emotional battle, she would let counsel and litigants know of her displeasure. In one divorce case that came before her, a

---

43. *Judge Takes To Her Mount When Balked At The Bench*, TUCSON DAILY CITIZEN, January 24, 1969.

44. *See* ANNUAL REPORTS RELATING TO THE SUPERIOR COURT OF THE STATE OF ARIZONA PIMA COUNTY, Vols. 1966–1971. The reports show that Mary Anne presided over only three juvenile matters during the six-year period. After 1971, the court administrator compiled court-wide statistics but stopped providing workload data by division.

45. Truman Interview, *supra* note 3.

46. Robbins Interview, *supra* note 7.

47. 387 U.S. 1 (1967)(constitutional safeguards of notice of charges, right to counsel, the rights of confrontation and examination, and the privilege against self-incrimination are applicable to juvenile delinquency proceedings).

48. 397 U.S. 358 (1970)(constitutional burden of proof beyond reasonable doubt applicable to juvenile delinquency proceedings).

49. Robbins Interview, *supra* note 7.

woman litigant sought alimony from her husband. As recounted later by Mary Anne to her staff, the woman's testimony on the stand was a misguided attempt to win sympathy from the judge. The woman explained under direct examination that her husband, a rancher, had subjected her to cruelty (an existing ground for divorce) by forcing her to work in the corral with the animals and to shovel manure on weekends. At that point, Mary Anne interrupted the testimony and said, "You have come before the wrong judge. I shovel manure on weekends, too, and it is not a heinous crime."[50] Since no accessible report of the case exists, we cannot know whether the alimony request succeeded or failed, but one can surmise that it did not succeed without other evidence of hardship.

That courtroom interjection from Mary Anne sprang directly from her life experience as a horse-owner, manager of Bill Veeck's guest ranch, and stables-manager for Marge Allen. She had labored in the corrals alongside men and a few women, and she was proud of that rugged chapter in her life. Moreover, Mary Anne's own divorce had terminated without a claim for alimony. Although she had been the petitioning "innocent" spouse in the heyday of fault-based divorce, she had claimed only what she had brought into the marriage and a modest share of the property that she and Bill Showers had accumulated. Mary Anne's personal history, then, must have colored her response to the wife's ill-advised alimony request. On the other hand, as will be seen, she ruled thoughtfully and decisively when divorcing parties raised legal issues whose importance transcended the case at bar.

Mary Anne gradually established a reputation as a trial judge that was similar to her reputation as a trial lawyer. It was said that "she was a good judge because she thought like a man."[51] Just as the comments comparing her lawyering style to that of a man were intended as compliments, the similar comments about her judging style were meant to be admiring. Not one to be intimidated, she ran her courtroom with a firm hand; she treated lawyers with courtesy and respect and she expected the same in return. "You knew she was in control," one lawyer recalled, "and she wouldn't accept any foolishness in the courtroom. She'd let counsel know who was boss. She was no patsy."[52]

---

50. *Id.*

51. Interview with Hon. William D. Browning, United States District Judge, Tucson, Arizona (Sept. 11, 1992). Browning was not the source of the comment but recalled that he had heard such a description of Mary Anne.

52. Interview with Hon. Alfredo C. Marquez, United States District Judge, Tucson, Arizona (Jan. 26, 1993).

Her demeanor on the bench was generally reserved and low-key, but her eyes would narrow in anger if she sensed a lack of respect for her position or for the judicial process. One lawyer remembered Mary Anne's demeanor as "austere" and "subdued," but he had also seen her be "real angry" when attorneys were unprofessional in her courtroom, and he sensed that she would not allow counsel to engage in "histrionics."[53] Another remembered her as "businesslike and very attentive to the duties of running the courtroom."[54] In chambers, she was informal, given to loud laughter, occasional swearing, and exuberant critiques of the latest basketball or football game. One lawyer recalled that going into Mary Anne's chambers was "like walking into your aunt's house. She never made you feel like she was special because she was the judge."[55] Recognizing Mary Anne's androgynous qualities, another attorney who had appeared before her stated, "Mary Anne was one of the boys. She was always at ease in chambers, and she wasn't offended if someone used a curse word there. She would sometimes use them also. Gender was not a big issue with her."[56]

Mary Anne had little patience for petty squabbling among counsel, and she wanted lawyers to make the most efficient use of court time by eliminating non-issues from their cases. Through her many years of experience as a trial lawyer, she had acquired a shrewdness about courtroom management that she capitalized on as a trial judge. "She was obviously very experienced. By the time you got to trial, everything was resolved. There weren't any last minute surprises," recollected classmate Alfredo Marquez, who engaged in insurance defense work in her court and would later join her on the federal bench. William Browning, who appeared before her in state court and would ultimately fill her vacancy on the federal bench, described her as "firm without being autocratic or oppressive. She was somewhat impatient but not in any truly objectionable way." Her impatience, he explained, was with the process that allows lawyers to "overtry" their cases. According to Browning, Mary Anne was a "no-nonsense, let's-get-on-with-it judge."[57] As such, she was disgusted with the delaying or harassing tactics that lawyers occasionally used in her courtroom, and she was known to sharply reprimand counsel if she per-

---

53. Telephone conversation with Stephen D. Neely, Pima County Attorney (June 10, 1992).

54. Telephone Interview with Charles A. Finch (July 11, 1995).

55. Telephone conversation with Jeffrey S. Minker (Oct. 30, 1992).

56. Interview with Ruben Salter, Jr., Tucson, Arizona (May 18, 1993).

57. Browning Interview, *supra* note 51.

ceived such behavior. Ironically, innovative reforms in state and federal rules of civil procedure that were designed to give trial judges greater authority in controlling abuses by lawyers did not come about until 1983, the year of Mary Anne's death.[58]

Mary Anne also seemed to have a knack for getting adversaries to compromise and to agree. Ruben Salter, the second Black attorney to be admitted to the Arizona State Bar, litigated numerous criminal and civil cases in front of Mary Anne and remembered her as a forerunner in the matter of plea bargaining in the criminal context. "She did what judges are now authorized to do under the Arizona Supreme Court rules. With an eye on the sentence, she would suggest to the prosecutor a lesser crime than the charge in exchange for a plea."[59] As recounted in Chapter Nine, she occasionally was challenged for refusing to allow criminal defendants to withdraw their guilty pleas. One prosecutor recalled that she interjected herself into plea bargaining and in one instance "pressured" him to accept a plea agreement against his better judgment.[60] Both her ready acceptances of guilty pleas and her typical refusal to allow withdrawals reflected a belief that plea bargaining was the fairest and most expeditious method for resolving many criminal actions.

Similarly, in the civil arena, before the era of "settlement judges," Mary Anne informally encouraged counsel to settle in cases where she sensed that settlement was feasible. She was particularly persuasive in chambers, off the record, where she would give lawyers her honest appraisal of their case. As Salter bluntly put it, "Mary Anne would cut through the crap. She would tell it like it is, especially in chambers."[61] At times her demeanor on the bench may have contributed to the parties' desire to settle, where by a subtle facial expression she would communicate to counsel or the litigants her reactions to the evidentiary presentations.[62] Likewise,

---

58. The 1983 amendment of Rule 11 of the Federal Rules of Civil Procedure was designed to give trial judges greater authority to impose sanctions for abuse. In the words of the Advisory Committee, "Greater attention by the district courts to pleading and motion abuses and the imposition of sanctions when appropriate, should discourage dilatory or abusive tactics and help to streamline the litigation process by lessening frivolous claims or defenses." Rule 11 of the Arizona Rules of Civil Procedure was similarly amended shortly after the amendment of the federal rules.

59. Salter Interview, *supra* note 56.

60. Neely Conversation, *supra* note 53.

61. Salter Interview, *supra* note 56.

62. As Charles Finch recalled, "We had a big construction case settle three days into trial. I think the defendants' willingness to settle had something to do with her demeanor and the fact that we'd put on a fairly decent case." Finch Interview, *supra* note 54.

Mary Anne was an early proponent of the use of alternative methods of dispute resolution. Her tenure in the state court preceded the widespread adoption in state trial courts of rules mandating arbitration,[63] but she was an advocate of arbitration as a method of dispute resolution and served on the American Arbitration Association Advisory Council for the last five years of her state court tenure.[64] To her, arbitration promised a cheaper and faster resolution for many disputes and would relieve the courts of their backlog of cases.[65] She also saw an advantage in having cases decided by arbitrators who were experts in the field rather than a jury of lay people. Arbitrators, she once opined, can be expected to give a "much more sensible decision than a jury made up of people who know little or nothing about the issues involved."[66] Her interest in encouraging settlement and the use of alternatives to formal trials, reflected as well in her endorsement of a court of conciliation during her 1962 campaign against Alice Truman, was consistent with her general pragmatism. She valued efficiency in the civil justice system, sometimes at the expense of other values.

Mary Anne seemed to enjoy helping new lawyers with the challenge of a trial, and several recalled that she had been exceptionally patient with their ineptness. Eric O'Dowd, then a young novice lawyer, made his first court appearance before Mary Anne on a sweltering July morning in 1967. He and other lawyers hoping for a criminal appointment sat at the back of her imposing courtroom while the criminal defendants filed into the jury box. Mary Anne, sitting as the assignment judge at that time, methodically went through the informations and assigned each indigent case to an awaiting defense lawyer. O'Dowd sat nervously with the other more seasoned lawyers, hoping that he would not be the first one called. To his

---

63. In 1971, the Arizona legislature enacted a statute authorizing the state superior courts to provide by rule for the mandatory and voluntary arbitration of designated cases. ARIZONA SESSION LAWS 1971, Chapter 142, codified at ARIZ. REV. STAT. Sec. 12-133. In 1986, the statutory language was amended to require superior courts to provide for arbitration. *See* Arizona Session Laws 1986, Chapter 360, Sec. 1. In Pima County, the superior court did not adopt local rules providing for arbitration of selected disputes until 1985. *See* Rule 3.9, Local Rules of Court for Pima County Superior Court.

64. *Slump Increasing Arbitration Cases*, THE ARIZONA DAILY STAR, February 18, 1975. Her service on the Advisory Committee of the American Arbitration Association, from 1972 through 1976, is also mentioned in her submission to WHO'S WHO IN AMERICAN LAW, dated March 8, 1979.

65. *Packaging Convention Hears Judge Richey and Philbrick*, SHELBYVILLE NEWS, May 20, 1971 (reporting Mary Anne's strong endorsement of arbitration at a business convention in Indianapolis).

66. *Id.*

dismay, his was the first name Mary Anne read. "Mr. O'Dowd, would you come forward?" He walked to her elevated bench, and she handed him an information. "Do you wish to waive the reading of the information?" she asked. Thinking he should never waive any rights, he responded in the negative. He heard an audible groan from the back of the courtroom, since the other lawyers realized at that moment it was going to be a long morning. After the clerk read the information, Mary Anne asked, "Do you wish to enter a plea?" O'Dowd responded, "Yes." Mary Anne said gently, "Perhaps you should talk to your client first." O'Dowd, feeling somewhat chagrined, proceeded to hold a quick consultation with his new client in the hallway. During the conference, he determined to his own satisfaction that his client had in fact committed the crime charged. When he went back into court, Mary Anne again asked, "Do you want to enter a plea?" O'Dowd responded, "Yes, we wish to enter a plea of guilty." Aware by then of O'Dowd's complete inexperience, Mary Anne advised him, "Perhaps you should enter a plea of not guilty, since you can always change your mind." O'Dowd agreed. Finally, Mary Anne asked, "Do you wish to waive your right to proceed to trial within sixty days?" Remembering the groan that greeted his initial refusal to waive the reading of the information, O'Dowd replied, "Yes." Mary Anne, aware that the client was in jail and would remain there until trial, offered one last bit of advice: "Perhaps you want to discuss this matter with your client." O'Dowd did as suggested and requested a prompt trial date. Throughout the ordeal, Mary Anne remained impassive and respectful, but O'Dowd came away from the experience realizing he had been greatly assisted from the bench.[67]

Similarly, Fred Kay, who went on to a long career as Federal Public Defender for the District of Arizona, tried his first jury case before Mary Anne in superior court. His client was accused of theft of a guitar, and Kay recalled that he received welcome help from the bench during the trial. When he misstated the burden of proof on his motion for directed verdict, Mary Anne gently corrected him, and then denied the motion. After a hung jury, Kay tried the case again, and in that second trial his inexperience may have worked to his client's advantage: Kay delivered a brief closing argument and sat down abruptly when he had run through his points, without offering a formal conclusion. Mary Anne then looked to the prosecutor for a rebuttal statement, but the prosecutor was unprepared at that moment to do more than offer a few incoherent words to the jury. Thus, the jurors headed into deliberations with the lingering

---

67. Telephone Interview with Erik M. O'Dowd (Dec. 6, 1995).

image in their minds of the prosecutor caught off-guard. They returned in a short while with an acquittal of Kay's client.[68]

Numerous other lawyers recalled Mary Anne as a sympathetic mentor. One criminal defense lawyer remembered Mary Anne's advice to him to speak loudly and clearly so that the jury could hear each word. "She told me that my voice trailed off and the jury couldn't hear. Then she said, half-laughing, 'Of course, you may not want them to understand you some of the time.'"[69] Another lawyer recalled that he tried his first case in her court, and that she took "almost a motherly interest in me."[70] Still another remembered that Mary Anne was exceptionally patient with his faltering attempt to prosecute a theft case.[71]

Although Mary Anne sometimes expressed impatience with attorneys, she was seen as generally imperturbable in her dealings with litigants, treating even the obstreporous ones with controlled civility. On one memorable occasion, her self-control was tested but remained intact. One afternoon in the early 1970s, criminal motions had been assigned to Division 5, and Mary Anne was presiding over a hearing on a motion to suppress. Defense lawyer Bob Barber was engaged in presenting witness testimony when the doors of the courtroom opened and a young man wearing a baseball cap walked in and seated himself at the criminal defense table. Mary Anne calmly said to the man, "Sir, would you please remove your hat in the courtroom." The interloper ignored her request and leaned back in the chair, propping his feet up on the table in front of him. Mary Anne, staring down at him, said, "Sir, would you please take your feet off the table?" The man again ignored her request and mumbled that he was there to ask for a change in his appointed counsel. Mary Anne patiently waited until he was silent and then repeated her requests. At that point, the man pulled a pipe out of his shirt pocket and proceeded to light the contents with a match. Mary Anne, a bit more sharply, said, "Sir, there is no smoking allowed in this courtroom. Please extinguish your pipe." He once again ignored her request. As the smoke wafted through the courtroom, Barber realized that the man's pipe was filled not with tobacco but with marijuana. With just an edge of exasperation in her voice, Mary Anne finally announced, "Sir, having asked you to remove your hat and your having refused to do so, having asked you to remove your feet from the table and your having refused to do so, and having asked you to re-

---

68. Interview with Fredric F. Kay, Federal Public Defender, Tucson, Arizona (Jan. 30, 1993).

69. Interview with Hon. Bernardo P. Velasco, Judge, Pima County Superior Court, Tucson, Arizona (Nov. 20, 1992).

70. Oseran Interview, *supra* note 17.

71. Salter Interview, *supra* note 56.

frain from smoking and your having refused to do so, I find you in contempt of this Court. Someone get the sheriff." She abruptly adjourned the proceedings and left the bench while the man was taken into custody. According to Barber, she returned a short while later with the trace of a smile on her face and proceeded with the criminal calendar.

"A lesser judge," Barber surmised, "would have exploded at the guy. But Judge Richey was polite and calm and handled the situation admirably. She made a record and did what she had to do, without fireworks."[72] Perhaps because of her effort to emulate Judge Walsh, Mary Anne was determined to treat litigants, including the contemnor, with respect and dispassion. She seemed to view the man's misconduct not as a personal affront but rather as an affront to the state's judicial authority. As a result, her response was a measured and deliberate assertion of the state's power, with careful attention to the making of a record to support the contempt citation. Only in the privacy of her chambers did she reveal that she found humor, rather than offense, in the situation.

Because superior court judges had no law clerks, Mary Anne had to rely on the arguments of counsel and on her own analysis in resolving disputed legal issues. She frequently took matters under advisement to give herself the opportunity to reflect. "Under advisement" often meant that she would carry her work home with her mentally, to review and appraise as she rode horses with Bill and Annie through the Rillito River bed. "More decisions in my court are made in those foothills than are ever made on the bench," she explained at the time. "When I have a problem I can't solve, I get on my horse and ride. My mind seems to clear and when the ride is over, I'm ready to rule on the case."[73]

Mary Anne also made a habit of consulting more experienced jurists when novel or intellectually-challenging legal issues came before her. She wanted reassurance from other judges when she was faced with particularly perplexing questions. She regularly consulted the Roylstons because she valued their years of experience on the bench as well as their homespun wisdom. Although neither brother viewed himself as a great legal scholar, each had a reservoir of knowledge in the civil and criminal arenas that he was delighted to share with Mary Anne. Her many visits to their chambers where she sought their advice continued the camaraderie that they had enjoyed in law school and during the years after graduation.[74] In

72. Telephone Interview with Bob O. Barber, Jr. (February 13, 1996).

73. Nicki Donahue, *Judge Takes To Her Mount When Balked At The Bench*, TUCSON CITIZEN, January 24, 1969.

74. Interview with Hon. Robert O. Roylston, Richard M. Roylston, former Judges, Pima County Superior Court, Tucson, Arizona (Aug. 19, 1992); Interview with Hon. Robert O. Roylston, Tucson, Arizona (Aug. 24, 1992, Oct. 4, 1992).

addition, Mary Anne actively nurtured her relationship with Judge Walsh, whom she continued to admire and sought to emulate throughout her years on the state and federal bench. They frequently met for lunch, and Mary Anne solicited his opinion on tentative rulings, sentencings, and other aspects of judging. These informal consultations with the Roylston brothers and Judge Walsh were especially important to her in her initial years as superior court judge.[75]

Some lawyers may have deemed Mary Anne's practice of consulting other judges objectionable, since she actively sought opinions about legal issues from sources over which counsel had no control. A lawyer who had misgivings about a particular judge from whom Mary Anne sought advice might have found her actions especially problematic. On the other hand, she was seeking advice from a judicial source and not from someone with a legal interest in any case (a practice condemned under the Canons of Judicial Ethics then in effect[76]). In any event, the frankness with which she acknowledged her reliance on other judges was admired by some. Ed Morgan, who had litigated against her in the United States Attorney's Office and appeared in her court on numerous occasions after she was appointed to the state court bench, viewed the practice favorably. "I thought I would always get a fair shake in her court. I liked her manner of seeking advice from other judges. She would be very open about it. She would say, 'I don't know or I don't understand, and I'm going to ask Judge Walsh or the Roylstons.' I liked that quality of being able to admit uncertainty."[77] Thus, the very humility with which she sought out the views of other jurists may have distinguished her among her colleagues.

---

75. William Richey Interviews, *supra* note 28.

76. The American Bar Association Canons of Judicial Ethics have never prohibited judges within a single court from communicating about cases pending before them. In the 1960s, Canon 17 prohibited "ex parte communications." Although the wording of the canon was ambiguous ("A judge should not permit private interviews, arguments or communications designed to influence his judicial action, where interests to be affected thereby are not represented before him, except in cases where provision is made by law for ex parte application."), no opinion interpreting the canon had applied it to communications among trial judges. *See* AMERICAN BAR ASSOCIATION, OPINIONS ON PROFESSIONAL ETHICS (1967). Interestingly, the 1993 version of the code of judicial ethics in Arizona explicitly allows a judge to communicate with other judges about a pending case. *See* Rule 81, RULES OF THE ARIZONA SUPREME COURT, Code of Judicial Conduct, Canon 3(B)(7)(c) (1995).

77. Morgan Interview, *supra* note 41.

As a superior court judge, Mary Anne was occasionally asked to sit by designation on an appellate court or the Arizona Supreme Court when the need arose. Such assignments provided a change of pace and a chance for a more thoughtful and deliberate consideration of legal issues. Over the course of her state court tenure, she participated in fourteen appellate court cases but authored the court's opinion in only one such case.[78] That case, *Walston & Company v. Miller*,[79] came before the Arizona Supreme Court shortly after Mary Anne's appointment to the bench, and the decision was announced in February 1966. The case raised the question whether a broker of a commodity account owed his customer a fiduciary duty to inform the customer of events that would affect trading in the account. Walston, the brokerage house, had sued Miller, its customer, for fees still owing on the account, and Miller had counterclaimed for damages for breach of fiduciary duty. Miller alleged that Walston owed a duty to notify him in a timely manner of information that might affect prices on the world sugar market, and that the failure to provide such information caused his loss in commodity contracts of sugar. The trial judge ruled that Walston was entitled to its fees, totalling about $1,100, but also awarded Miller over $18,000 in damages for breach of fiduciary duty.

In Mary Anne's unadorned writing style, the supreme court reversed, holding that the broker was under no fiduciary duty to inform his client of information which might affect the price of the commodity contracts. As she put it, the main question raised "was when, in fact, the principal-agent relationship existed."[80] She treated the case as turning on black-letter law, and supported the decision with citation to the Restatement (Second) of Agency as well as to policy. Her opinion explained:

> The agency relationship between customer and broker normally termi-
> nates with the execution of the order because the broker's duties, unlike

---

78. Cases in which Mary Anne participated on request of the appellate tribunal included State v. Clayton, 514 P.2d 720 (Ariz. 1973); State v. Brierly, 509 P.2d 203 (Ariz. 1973); Quimby v. School District No. 21, 455 P.2d 1019 (Ariz. App. 1969); Morris v. Southwest Sav. & Loan Ass'n, 449 P.2d 301 (Ariz. App. 1969); Kitchell Corp. v. Hemansen, 446 P.2d 934 (Ariz. App. 1968); Saylor v. Southern Ariz. Bank & Trust Co., 446 P.2d 474 (Ariz. App. 1968); Secrist v. Diedrich, 430 P.2d 448 (Ariz. App. 1967); Midway Lumber, Inc. v. Redman, 421 P.2d 904 (Ariz. App. 1967); Flecha Caida Water Co. v. City of Tucson, 420 P.2d 198 (Ariz. App. 1966); Walston Co. v. Miller, 410 P.2d 658 (Ariz. 1966); Patterson Motors, Inc. v. Cortez, 408 P.2d 231 (Ariz. App. 1965); Brown v. White, 408 P.2d 228 (Ariz. App. 1965); Lantay v. McLean, 406 P.2d 224 (Ariz. App. 1965); City of Tucson v. Arizona Corp. Comm'n, 399 P.2d 913 (Ariz. App. 1965).

79. 410 P.2d 658 (Ariz. 1966). Mary Anne was requested to sit on the supreme court in *Walston* because Chief Justice Struckmeyer disqualified himself from participating.

80. 410 P.2d at 660.

those of an investment advisor or those of a manager of a discretionary account, are only to fulfill the mechanical, ministerial requirements of the purchase or sale of the security or future contracts on the market.[81]

Mary Anne reasoned, in addition, that a general duty to report price fluctuations would be extremely burdensome on the brokerage industry. Her analysis showed little sympathy for the claims of the disappointed customer but was receptive to the policy arguments of the commercial brokerage firm.

Mary Anne's entry into the world of opinion-writing was auspicious. *Walston* would be cited numerous times by later courts addressing the question of fiduciary duty of brokers, and its rationale would be adopted in several decisions, both in and outside of Arizona.[82] The opinion revealed Mary Anne's competence to engage in logical clear analysis and to articulate it in plain language. She avoided verbal flourishes, and tried to explain the legal problem and its resolution in few words. Although Mary Anne was not a rhetorician and at times expressed insecurity about her writing skills, *Walston* demonstrated that she was able to write a convincing opinion when forced to do so. For the remaining ten years in state court, however, she did not author another opinion for an appellate tribunal.

A year and a half after Mary Anne was appointed to fill Castro's vacancy in Division 5, she had to win the primary and general election to retain her seat for a full four-year term. Although incumbent judges rarely faced opposition, Mary Anne was challenged by Democrat Arthur Goldbaum for the Division 5 seat. (She would face no opposition, however, in the 1970 or 1974 judicial elections.) A graduate of Brooklyn Law School, Goldbaum had moved to Arizona in the late 1940s and had established a solid reputation among the practicing bar. He had served as president of the Pima County Bar Association five years earlier and thus had at least modest name recognition. Although the general election for judges was nonpartisan, the party affiliation of the candidates was well-known to the voters, and Goldbaum may have been counting on the continuing Democratic advantage in Pima County among registered voters. Of the 120,000 registered voters in the county at that time, approximately 71,400 were Democrats, and 45,000 were Republicans.[83] Bill Richey was outraged that

---

81. 410 P.2d at 661.

82. *See, e.g.,* Jennings v. Lee, 461 P.2d 161, 167 (Ariz. 1969); Carras v. Burns, 516 F.2d 251, 257 (4th Cir. 1975); Robinson v. Merrill Lynch, Pierce, Fenner & Smith, 337 F. Supp. 107, 111 (N.D. Ala. 1971); Cecka V. Beckman & Co., 104 Cal. Rptr. 374, 377 (Cal. App. 1972).

83. *Arizona Candidates Start Final Push As 1966 General Election Date Nears,* THE ARIZONA DAILY STAR, Sunday, October 23, 1966.

Goldbaum had challenged his wife in the election. Convinced that Mary Anne would easily beat Goldbaum, Richey knew that the cost of the necessary campaigning would be significant. Richey recalled saying to Goldbaum, "Goddam it, Art, you're running against her for no reason. She'll beat you four to one, and all you're doing is making us spend money."[84] As it happened, Richey's analysis was accurate.

As in her previous electoral run, Mary Anne's network of highranking friends in the legal profession helped with her campaign. Michael Lacagnina served as treasurer, and Norval Jasper, who had recently stepped down as president of the Arizona State Bar, managed the campaign. Facing Goldbaum, Mary Anne did not want to take any chances of losing, and she hired a public relations director for the campaign. Jasper's records show that many of Arizona's most prominent attorneys, including members of the Democratic Party, gave financial assistance to Mary Anne's campaign.[85] With the endorsement of the Pima County Bar Association[86] and both daily newspapers,[87] Mary Anne did succeed in defeating Goldbaum by a wide margin (50,799 votes for Mary Anne, compared to 14,382 for Goldbaum[88]), but not without spending several thousand dollars on campaign activities.

Press coverage of the 1966 election showed that Mary Anne was a cautious campaigner who avoided pointed critiques of other judges. Appearing with Judge Frey before the Tucson Press Club, for example, Mary Anne refused to join Frey in criticizing a recent ruling by Judge John Collins that had invalidated numerous indictments of a Pima County

---

84. William Richey Interviews, *supra* note 28.

85. A file maintained by Norval Jasper shows that contributors to Mary Anne's 1966 campaign read like a "who's who" list among Arizona lawyers. The all-male "Mary Anne Richey for Judge Committee" included, among others, Stanley Feldman, who would become Chief Justice of the Arizona Supreme Court; William Browning, and Alfredo Marquez, both of whom would ultimately join Mary Anne on the federal bench; Lawrence Ollason, who went on to become a federal bankruptcy judge; Lewis Murphy, who would be elected mayor of Tucson; Richard Hannah, who would join Mary Anne on the superior court bench; and a number of leading members of the Tucson bar, such as Ed Scruggs, Robert Lesher, Robert Tullar, J. Mercer Johnson, Dean Burch, William Kimble, Jack Ettinger, and Henry Zipf. At least three prominent Democrats declined to be a formal part of her campaign committee: Thomas Chandler, Marvin Cohen, and John Claborne. *See* Mary Anne Richey Campaign, Norval Jasper File.

86. *5 Candidates Endorsed By County Bar*, THE ARIZONA DAILY STAR, Sunday, October 14, 1966.

87. *General Election Recommendations*, THE ARIZONA DAILY STAR, Sunday, October 23, 1966.

88. *How Pima Voted*, THE ARIZONA DAILY STAR, Thursday, November 10, 1966.

Grand Jury, including the bribery charge of a state senator. Collins, whose judicial career was plagued by controversy, had held that the grand jury had been illegally constituted because the jurors were not properly questioned as to their qualifications as required by state law. The ruling sparked front-page news coverage and sharp controversy[89] but was ultimately affirmed by the Arizona Supreme Court.[90] Although Collins represented a political view Mary Anne did not endorse, she declined to publicly comment on Collins's order, stating "I don't think one Superior Court judge should question another judge's ruling." In the same appearance, Goldbaum, Mary Anne's challenger, submitted a prepared statement to the effect that, if elected, he would lend the weight of his office to the strengthening of criminal laws and the improvement of the administration of justice. In response, Mary Anne reminded the audience of the limits to a judge's authority: "We can not change laws. We are bound to follow the laws even though we may disagree with them…But if there are inequities in the law, I might lend the weight of the office toward having them changed."[91] Thus, in her campaigning, Mary Anne seemed to realize that judges, as public figures, were easy targets of criticism, and she preferred to restrain her own voice. Her comments revealed, as well, a pragmatic awareness of the institutional constraints on the judicial office.

Mary Anne's gender may have helped her in her contest against Goldbaum. While the race between Alice Truman and Mary Anne four years earlier had attracted attention because of the novelty of two female judicial candidates running head-to-head, Mary Anne in 1966 had the prestige of incumbency behind her and no longer attracted media attention solely because she was a woman. On the other hand, her accomplishments as a woman did surface. In a "Voters' Guide" compiled by the League of Women Voters and published shortly before the election, voters received a synopsis of each candidate's education and experience. The synopses were based on the candidates' responses to standardized questions propounded by the League. Mary Anne's description stated, in part: "Now Superior court Judge; first woman in nation to be a U.S. attorney…."[92] In addition, the only public service activities listed for Mary Anne in the Guide were women-oriented: board of directors for the YWCA and the newly-established Big Sisters program.

89. Jim Johnson, *Court Quashes Ahee Charges*, TUCSON DAILY CITIZEN, October 11, 1966; Vince Davis, *Sol Ahee Indictment Quashed; Pima Jury ordered Discharged*, THE ARIZONA DAILY STAR, October 12, 1966.

90. State v. Superior Court, 430 P.2d 408 (1967).

91. Cecil James, *Frey Questions Collins' Action On Grand Jury*, TUCSON DAILY CITIZEN, October 14, 1966.

92. *Voters' Guide*, THE ARIZONA DAILY STAR, Friday, November 4, 1966.

Similarly, in another publication shortly before the election, Mary Anne was quoted at length on the role of women in public life. "I feel that women can keep a watchful eye on community life," she was quoted as saying, "in order to properly propagandize measures for reform or improvement in the field of education, morals, health." Reflecting her belief in reform through democratic processes, she added that "women should be conscious of the political climate in which we live...and should help improve women's voting record. More than 52% of the registered voters are women, but in general they have a poor voting record."[93] She noted that Arizona had granted women the right to vote in 1912, several years before the right had been secured on a national level by the nineteenth amendment. As examples of what could be accomplished through the democratic processes, she mentioned with approval two state laws recently enacted that were designed to improve the legal status of women, one relating to working hours,[94] and the other mandating equal pay for equal work.[95] Expressing her strongly-held belief in community service, she

---

93. *Women Can Strengthen Government*, THE WOMAN'S REVIEW, November 1, 1966.

94. Interestingly, the "working hours" law that Mary Anne mentioned was a statutory amendment that lifted some but not all of the restrictions imposed on women laborers. Reminiscent of the early paternalism memorialized in *Muller v. Oregon,* 208 U.S. 412 (1908)(upholding Oregon's limitation on working hours of certain categories of female laborers to 10 hours daily), the Arizona legislature for years had limited the number of hours women could work, with notable exceptions. *See* ARIZ. REV. STAT. Sec. 23-281 (limiting females to eight hours per day and forty-eight hours per week) (1953). Significantly, by 1962, the statute had been amended to exclude women "engaged in work which is predominantly intellectual, managerial, or creative..." and to women licensed to practice law, medicine, and other professions. *See* ARIZ. REV. STAT. Sec. 23-281(B)(5)&(6), Statutory Supplement (1962). In March 1966, the statute was again amended to exclude women employees of manufacturing or industrial concerns "while engaged in performing services required to meet an emergency or extraordinary need." Moreover, the statute required that women performing such overtime work be paid a wage of at least one and one-half times the regular wage. *See* Ariz. Session Laws 1966, Chapter 17, codified at ARIZ. REV. STAT. Sec. 23-281(B)(7). Mary Anne's approving reference to the statutory change showed her belief that a relaxation in working-hour limitations and a mandate for increased overtime pay were an improvement in women's legal status.

95. Mary Anne's reference to "equal pay for equal work" may have been to the 1965 legislation creating the Arizona Civil Rights Commission and prohibiting discrimination in employment on the basis of "race, sex, religious creed, color, national origin or ancestry." *See* Arizona Session Laws 1965, Chapter 27, codified at ARIZ. REV. STAT. Sec. 41-1462. On the other hand, four years earlier the legislature had enacted Secs. 23-340 and 23-341, mandating equal wages for women and men engaged in the same classification of work, and she may have been referring to that earlier enactment. In either case, she clearly endorsed statutory changes designed to achieve equality for women in the workforce.

urged women to "become candidates for offices where they can be useful and effective" and to "let others know of their interest in working for the community." She also endorsed membership in women's organizations that engage in "civic works," an orientation she held throughout her professional career.

Mary Anne's statements during the campaign revealed not only an emphasis on her own accomplishments as a woman, but also an interest in women's political and legal gains generally. Although she never endorsed the resurgent women's movement of the 1960s and 1970s and would privately express impatience with what she viewed as the superficial concerns of many feminist leaders,[96] she believed in equality of opportunity for women. Viewing social reform through the eyes of a traditionalist, she was convinced that women had to better their legal status by their own political participation. Her willingness to identify as a women's leader and to discuss women's legal issues in the campaign showed a consciousness of the role of gender in her own life.

Interestingly, gender-based stereotypes may have operated in a minor way during the campaign to deprive the public of certain factual information. All judicial candidates except for Mary Anne and Alice Truman provided their chronological ages for the Voters' Guide. Mary Anne, who was forty-nine, and Truman, who was forty-four, apparently saw their ages as an embarrassment or a liability in the eyes of voters and preferred to keep that information confidential, even though Mary Anne's challenger was seven years her senior.[97]

Nationally and locally, the 1966 elections heavily favored the Republican Party. Despite some late-campaign stumping by President Johnson and Vice President Hubert Humphrey, voters displayed widespread dissatisfaction with the Democratic leadership. The political mood swing was attributed by local leaders to the inconclusive war in Vietnam and the high national rate of inflation, but tensions in race relations within the United States also contributed to a sense of social malaise. President Johnson held on to his Democratic majority in both Houses of Congress, but there was a net gain of forty-seven House seats and four in the Senate for the Republican Party. Republican victories in gubernatorial elections were led by Ronald Reagan's landslide triumph in California, and the Republicans retained control in other big states, including Michigan, Pennsylvania, New York, and Ohio. Newcomer Spiro Agnew was victorious in Maryland. On the homefront, Republican Jack Williams defeated Democratic incumbent Sam Goddard for the governorship of Arizona, and Re-

---

96. Robbins Interview, *supra* note 7.
97. *Voters Guide, supra* note 92.

publicans gained control of the Arizona state legislature for the first time in history.[98]

Mary Anne's chosen party was clearly on the rise, and she endorsed the Republican goals of achieving a decisive and successful conclusion to the war in Vietnam and implementing a conservative fiscal policy at home. She shared the Republican Party's concerns about certain aspects of Johnson's "Great Society" program because they seemed to undermine the notion of individual self-reliance. Over time, however, she would depart from the Republican Party's evolving views on such social issues as the Equal Rights Amendment and the legality of abortion. In her politics, as in other dimensions of her life, she was not susceptible of easy categorization.

As Mary Anne embarked on her judicial career, transformations in American law were ongoing. Six months before his assassination, President Kennedy had signed into law the Equal Pay Act, requiring equal wages for equal work without regard to sex.[99] Carrying forward the work begun by Kennedy, President Lyndon Johnson lobbied hard for several civil rights measures in Congress. On July 2, 1964, he signed into law the Civil Rights Act of 1964, outlawing discrimination on the basis of "race, color, religion, sex, or national origin" in public accommodations.[100] The Act also set up the federal Equal Employment Opportunity Commission to combat employment discrimination, authorized the United States Department of Justice to file suits to facilitate school integration, and outlawed discrimination in federally-funded projects. One year later, Title VII of the same Act went into effect, prohibiting discrimination on the enumerated grounds in private employment.[101] The Voting Rights Act was signed into law August 6, 1965, dramatically increasing the federal government's authority to monitor state and local elections to prevent race discrimination in voting.[102] Civil libertarians were succeeding in the courts as well. Indeed, two seminal cases from the Warren Court originated in Arizona: *Miranda v. Arizona*,[103] mandating that persons in custody be informed of their rights under the fifth and sixth amendments before police interrogation may proceed, and *In re Gault*,[104] extending various constitutional protections to juveniles in delinquency proceedings.

---

98. *GOP Chooses Leaders For 28th Legislature*, THE ARIZONA DAILY STAR, November 10, 1966.

99. Equal Pay Act of 1963, Pub. L. 88-38, Sec. 3, 77 Stat. 56, June 10, 1963, codified at 29 U.S.C. Sec. 206(d).

100. Pub. L. 88-352, 78 Stat. 241, codified at 42 U.S.C. Sec. 2000a–2000e17.

101. *See* 42 U.S.C. Sec. 2000e *et seq.*

102. Pub. L. 89-110, Sec. 15, 79 Stat. 445, codified at 42 U.S.C. Sec. 1971–1974e.

103. 384 U.S. 436 (1966).

104. 387 U.S. 1 (1967).

As a political moderate, Mary Anne may have viewed the expansion of federal power with skepticism, but she did not vocalize such misgivings. In contrast to some of her colleagues on the state court bench, she rarely engaged in public criticism of the Warren Court or the Democratic administration in Washington.[105] Although she once speculated in a public speech that the Warren Court's criminal procedure decisions might render all confessions inadmissible, such outspokenness was rare.[106] Also, as a woman who competed throughout her life as an equal with men, she staunchly endorsed the principle of "equal pay for equal work" embodied in the 1963 Act. Regardless of her personal responses, these changes in the legal landscape would inevitably affect Mary Anne, and, as a jurist, she would be required to incorporate them into her decisionmaking. The federal civil rights legislation, primarily cognizable in the federal courts, would have less significance for her as a state court judge than as a federal judge. The expansion of constitutional protections for criminal defendants, however, would have direct relevance for her state judicial work. In future rulings she would establish a mixed record with respect to individual liberties and the protection of the constitutional rights of persons accused of crime.

---

105. Judge William Frey, Mary Anne's colleague on the superior court, and later on the federal bench, was an outspoken critic of the "excesses" of the Warren Court. *See Frey Blames High Court For Rising Crime,* TUCSON DAILY CITIZEN, January 1, 1968. In that article, Frey condemned the Supreme Court for what he viewed as judicial legislation: "In Gault and Miranda, the court has declared itself the supreme law of the land by legislating specific rules of conduct for the police and the courts in all cases.... [T]he Supreme Court is enlarging the rights of the criminals at the expense of the rights of the people to be secure in their homes and remain free from criminal intrusions on them." Frey explicitly blamed the Court for the rising crime rates and described the situation in dire terms: "In the last seven years—after the court began its crusade—the crime rate has gone up an incredible 88 per cent.... Our society and our government can be destroyed. it can and will happen unless we cease being tolerant with those who incite and perpetuate civil disobedience and those who deal with racketeers."

106. As the featured speaker at the annual meeting of the Shelby County Chamber of Commerce in 1966, Mary Anne reportedly referred to "certain difficulties that have arisen nationally" concerning criminal confessions and expressed the "personal belief that eventually there will be no confessions as such admissible in evidence." *See Oscar Fisher Gets Top Citizen Award,* THE SHELBYVILLE NEWS, Feburary 11, 1966.

CHAPTER NINE

Of Crime and Retribution

Mary Anne's legacy as a judge on the Pima County Superior Court consists of a discrete written record and a large unwritten history. Like other trial judges in Arizona, she rarely wrote lengthy opinions in the course of ruling on motions, presiding over trials, and otherwise carrying out the duties of the trial court. Instead, her rulings were typically in the form of brief minute entries that announced the decision and only tersely alluded to underlying rationale. To the extent that she did issue long opinions, they were invariably prepared by counsel for the prevailing party and reflected the attorney's explanation of the case rather than Mary Anne's independent analysis. Thus, the pattern of her decisionmaking, rather than her own articulation of legal reasoning, provides the source for many of the conclusions set forth here about her judicial philosophy. In this regard, the fate of her trial court rulings in the appellate courts and in the United States Supreme Court has provided the primary source of information about her judicial work.[1] Her many judicial acts that were not appealed to a higher court remain for the most part unreported and effectively unrecoverable.[2]

A judge's affirmance/reversal record provides some indication of the soundness of her reasoning in particular cases. On a purely numerical basis, Mary Anne's record of affirmances and reversals on the state trial court was consistent with that of her peers, and her rulings did not result in significantly more appeals, or significantly fewer appeals, than the rulings of her colleagues. Over the entire span of her state court tenure, 62 out of a total of 78 criminal appeals from her court, or 79 percent, re-

---

1. During most of Mary Anne's tenure on the state court bench, Arizona appellate courts published all written opinions. The state did not move to a system of selective publication of appellate court opinions until September 1, 1973. See Rule 48, RULES OF ARIZONA SUPREME COURT (1973).

2. Pima County Superior Court judges did not have a docket of cases permanently assigned to their division; rather, they were assigned trials, motions, and other proceedings on the basis of availability. See UNIFORM RULES OF PRACTICE OF THE SUPERIOR COURT OF ARIZONA (1975). That assignment system makes the reconstruction of a particular judge's historical docket virtually impossible. The archives of closed case files are accessible by case number, not by the identities of the several judges that might have had a connection with a particular case.

sulted in unqualified affirmances by the final appellate court, and 16 out of the total criminal appeals, or 21 percent, resulted in partial or complete reversals. Her affirmance rate was lower in civil appeals: 33 out of a total of 53 civil appeals, or 62 percent, resulted in unqualified affirmances by the appellate court, while 20 out of the total, or 38 percent, resulted in partial or complete reversals.[3] The affirmance/reversal records for colleagues Alice Truman, Robert Roylston, Richard Roylston, and Jack Marks during a similar time period were comparable, suggesting that neither the political affiliation nor the gender of the judges produced consistent patterns.[4] Thus, based on the numbers alone, Mary Anne did not ex-

---

3. The data is based on all dispositions, published and unpublished, in the Arizona appellate courts of appeals from Mary Anne Richey's court. The appellate cases date from March 1965 through February 1979, and include "memorandum decisions" from 1973 forward, the year in which unpublished dispositions were authorized by rule of the Arizona Supreme Court. *See* Rule 111(d), RULES OF THE ARIZONA SUPREME COURT.

4. The statistics for the judges are based on published and unpublished dispositions from the indicated time periods:

Robert Roylston (Based on published opinions from February 1960 through November 1979, and memorandum decisions through 1978):

    138 total criminal appeals
    78 percent affirmances
    136 total civil appeals
    63 percent affirmances

Richard Roylston (Based on published opinions from September 1964 through December 1979, and memorandum decisions through 1978):

    109 total criminal appeals
    89 percent affirmances
    106 total civil appeals
    62 percent affirmances

Jack Marks (Based on published opinions from February 1964 through September 1982, and memorandum decisions through 1978):

    25 total criminal appeals
    84 percent affirmances
    77 total civil appeals
    70 percent affirmances

Alice Truman (Based on published opinions from December 1963 through September 1981, and memorandum decisions through 1978):

    80 total criminal appeals
    81 percent affirmances
    97 total civil cases
    60 percent affirmances

hibit extraordinary caution or an extraordinary propensity for error, as compared to her colleagues on the bench.

All of the judges studied had higher affirmance rates in criminal cases than in civil cases, most likely the result of the fact that criminal appeals involving indigent defendants were financed at public expense. Where cost was not a factor, a litigant could decide to pursue a doubtful appeal more readily than where cost was a factor. In the civil arena, where the parties had to finance their own appeals, the decision to appeal reflected a more objective determination that the case contained reversible error.

Mary Anne's responses to the individual issues and parties that came before her from the criminal docket provide a nuanced, if incomplete, picture of her judicial persona. Her prosecutorial experience in the County Attorney's Office and later in the U.S. Attorney's Office undoubtedly created an ideological bond with the prosecution that informed her rulings as trial judge. Lawyers who appeared before her viewed her as fair but, in a close case, more likely to align herself with the government's position. One criminal defense lawyer explained, "She obviously had a prosecutorial bias. She'd believe a policeman's story over anybody else's. The system had worked for her, and she was going to work for the system. On the other hand, she had compassion, and she had integrity. She was no rubber-stamp."[5] Another said, "Even though she was pro-government, you always felt like you had a fighting chance in her courtroom."[6] That sentiment was echoed by still another criminal defense lawyer, "If I had a case assigned to her court, I knew I was going to get a straight shot, the best that I could hope for in any court. If the evidence wasn't there, I felt comfortable that she would rule accordingly, and she did."[7]

The reversal record itself is a useful window into a judge's philosophy, since the rulings that arguably misconstrue established legal doctrine, or that fail to intuit emerging themes in the law as seen by a higher court, may reveal the trial judge's individuality more sharply than the record of affirmances. This chapter therefore focuses primarily on the cases in which Mary Anne's rulings were overturned or questioned by higher courts. Her judicial record in the criminal arena reveals numerous instances in which she was found to have committed error against the interests of the defendant, including rulings on speedy trial claims,[8] challenges

---

5. Interview with Richard S. Oseran, Tucson, Arizona (July 7, 1995).

6. Interview with Hon. Bernardo P. Velasco, Judge, Pima County Superior Court, Tucson, Arizona (Nov. 20, 1992).

7. Telephone Interview with Howard A. Kashman (July 11, 1995).

8. Rockmore v. State, 519 P.2d 877 (Ariz. App. 1974); State v. Harris, 541 P.2d 402 (Ariz. App. 1975).

to errors in the information,[9] motions to suppress,[10] evidentiary questions raised during trial,[11] questions relating to the general conduct of the trial,[12] and voluntariness of plea agreements.[13] Nevertheless, consistent with her reputation among the practicing bar, she sustained the arguments of defense counsel on pivotal motions in some cases,[14] and in a few cases was reversed for doing so.[15]

One of Mary Anne's earliest cases posed a novel issue of criminal law in Arizona—whether a person accused of driving while intoxicated was entitled to a jury trial. The crime, punishable according to state statute by up to six months in jail, a fine of up to $300, and a possible suspension of the defendant's driver's license for up to ninety days, was triable in city court with a trial de novo in superior court. Charles Rothweiler was tried and convicted in Tucson City Court, appealed to superior court, and requested a jury trial. The case was assigned to Mary Anne who, perhaps after consultation with the Roylstons, denied the request for a jury trial. Requiring a jury trial would have meant a change in existing practice, and Mary Anne, a newcomer to the bench, opted for the preservation of the status quo. Rothweiler petitioned the court of appeals for a writ of prohibition, basing his argument on the sixth amendment to the U.S. Constitution and its state law counterpart. The case attracted widespread attention and both the Arizona State Bar and the Arizona League of Cities and Towns participated on appeal as amici curiae.

---

9. *See* State v. Bollander, 484 P.2d 219 (Ariz. App. 1971).

10. Mincey v. Arizona, 437 U.S. 385 (1978); State v. Miller, 520 P.2d 1115 (Ariz. 1974).

11. *See, e.g.,* State v. Swinburne, 569 P.2d 833 (Ariz. 1977) (reversing conviction because of erroneous restriction on defense counsel's cross-examination of key prosecution witness); State v. Shaw, 471 P.2d 715 (Ariz. 1970)(reversing conviction because, in part, of erroneous admission of psychiatric testimony in violation of doctor-patient privilege); State v. Jorgenson, 502 P.2d 158 (Ariz. 1972)(reversing conviction because of erroneous failure to hold hearing on voluntariness of defendant's out-of-court statements); State v. Hill, 469 P.2d 88 (Ariz. App. 1970)(reversing conviction because evidence insufficient to show burglary).

12. *See, e.g.,* State v. Reid, 559 P.2d 136 (Ariz. 1976)(shackling of defendant); State v. Swinburne, 569 P.2d 833 (Ariz. 1977)(restriction on cross-examination).

13. *See, e.g.,* State v. Carr, 495 P.2d 134 (Ariz. 1972) (reversing conviction based on plea where record failed to disclose that defendant had been advised or knew of the maximum range of sentences; supreme court noted that problem was one of form and not substance).

14. State v. Edwards, 529 P.2d 1174 (Ariz. 1974).

15. State v. Curlin, 560 P.2d 62 (Ariz. 1977)(reversing Mary Anne's order of suppression); State *ex rel.* Murphy v. Superior Court, 470 P.2d 486 (Ariz. App. 1970)(reversing Mary Anne's allowance of an appeal from city court).

The court of appeals and ultimately the supreme court disagreed with Mary Anne. Resolving the issue of first impression in the state, the supreme court held that Rothweiler was entitled to a jury trial. The court reasoned that the severity of the possible penalty brought the charge into the "serious offense" category, thereby triggering the jury trial guarantee under Article II, section 24 of the Arizona state constitution. "The power to imprison, fine and suspend the right to use the public highways," wrote Justice Jesse Udall for the supreme court, "must be considered today as the ability to impose grave criminal sanctions not comparable to petty crimes at common law which were tried summarily."[16] Mary Anne's erroneous call on the jury trial question, occurring just months after she assumed the bench, must have been a matter of regret for her. To be subject to the extraordinary writ of prohibition meant that she had violated a legal duty owing to the petitioner, not simply that she had abused her discretion. The fact that she had miscalled an undecided question of law was not a cause for shame, but the early visible "correction" from the higher courts was disquieting.

The first-degree murder trial is a useful measure of justice, since the trial by definition involves simultaneously a charge of the most serious crime and a threat of the most severe penalty under law. In presiding over such trials, the judge must be constantly on the alert to avoid error, both out of fairness for the accused and to ensure that any conviction and sentence will withstand constitutional scrutiny from the higher courts. Several notorious murder cases were assigned to Mary Anne during her state court tenure, and her rulings met with mixed responses from the appellate courts. In one highly visible murder trial during her state court tenure, Mary Anne's handling of the case garnered reversals from both the Arizona Supreme Court and the United States Supreme Court. In late 1974, Rufus Mincey, an airman from Davis Monthan Air Force Base, was charged with murder, assault with a deadly weapon, and possession and sale of narcotics. The notoriety of the case stemmed from the fact that the murder victim was undercover agent Barry Headricks, the first Tucson police officer to be killed by gunfire in the line of duty. Headricks had led

---

16. Rothweiler v. Superior Court of Pima County, 410 P.2d 479, 485 (Ariz. 1966). Interestingly, in 1989, the United States Supreme Court reached the opposite result in Blanton v. City of North Las Vegas, 489 U.S. 538, holding that a defendant in a misdemeanor DUI case had no sixth ammendment right to jury trial where the maximum penalty was a six-month jail term, driver's license suspension, and a $1,000 fine. At least two critics have called for the overruling of Rothweiler. See Hon. B. Robert Dorfman & Hon. George T. Anagnost, Revisiting the Right to Trial by Jury in Misdemeanor DUI Cases, 32 Ariz Attorney 28 (1996).

a group of officers on a "buy-bust" drug raid into Mincey's apartment, and in the resulting shootout, Mincey and a codefendant were wounded and Headricks was killed. Immediately after the event, Mincey was hospitalized for his injuries, and he was later questioned by an officer while in the intensive care unit. Over a four-day period, police conducted a warrantless search of Mincey's apartment and recovered evidence relevant to the murder and narcotics charges.

Mincey's attorney was Richard Oseran, a young man only four years out of law school and brazen enough to take the case. Oseran had recently left the Pima County Public Defenders' Office for private criminal defense work and was known as a tenacious fighter in the courtroom. "I believed strongly in the case," he recalled, "and I never gave up. I thought there were problems in the search and the treatment of my client generally, and I just kept making the arguments."[17] Oseran moved to suppress the evidence seized during the search of Mincey's apartment and the written statements taken from Mincey at the hospital. At the hearing on his motion, Oseran challenged the warrantless search of Mincey's apartment as unconstitutional since there were no exigent circumstances justifying the failure to obtain prior judicial authorization. He argued that Arizona's "murder scene" exception to the warrant requirement was invalid in these circumstances. As to the hospital interrogation, Oseran brought out the fact that at the time Mincey was on an oxygen tube, a feeding tube, and a catheter to his bladder. Although the police officer at the hospital had given Mincey his *Miranda* warnings, he had repeatedly ignored Mincey's indications that he wanted to consult a lawyer and that he wanted to stop answering questions. During the hearing before Mary Anne, the prosecution stipulated that Mincey's statements would be used only to impeach him if he took the witness stand. Thus, the sole issue became whether Mincey's statements were sufficiently voluntary to be admissible for impeachment purposes. Oseran vehemently contended that Mincey's pain and confusion rendered him incapable of giving a voluntary statement and that his written words were inherently untrustworthy. The prosecution, however, put on evidence that Mincey was alert and cooperative and was able to understand the officer's questions. That evidence apparently satisfied Mary Anne.

At the close of the hearing, Mary Anne refused to suppress the evidence taken from Mincey's apartment, presumably in reliance on Arizona's murder-scene exception to the warrant requirement. In light of the violation of *Miranda* and the State's stipulation, she ordered that Mincey's statements from his hospital bed could not be used in the prosecution's

---

17. Oseran Interview, *supra* note 5.

case in chief, but she denied the motion, without making any findings, as to use of the statements for impeachment. She therefore implicitly accepted the State's evidence and found that Mincey's statements were voluntary. Oseran believed Mary Anne struggled with the case, but he was not surprised by her ruling in light of her prosecutorial background. He intended to pursue all avenues of appeal, if necessary, to vindicate his client's rights.

The two-week criminal trial, the last felony trial to be held in the old Pima County Courthouse, was closely followed by the local press[18] and was crowded with spectators each day. At the trial, prosecutor Jim Howard, a physically-imposing bearded veteran of the Pima County Attorney's office, effectively presented the State's case to the jury. Mincey took the stand and contended that he had acted in self-defense after Headricks first shot him and that he had not known that Headricks was an undercover agent. Because Mincey was charged with murder "committed in avoiding or preventing lawful arrest," his knowledge of Headricks's identity thus became a central issue at trial. His defense, and the case itself, raised raw emotion in the Tucson community and especially among members of the police force. The tone of the trial was exemplified by a statement from Howard's closing argument to the jury: "Don't tell every heroin pusher in town that he can have a gun; that he can have it loaded; that he can shoot a pig if he feels hassled and that all he need do is take the witness stand and say, 'Yes, sir; no sir,' and claim that he had no idea that he was shooting a cop."[19]

In her instructions to the jury, Mary Anne grappled with the degree of scienter required for the particular category of first degree murder charged. Suggesting on the one hand almost a negligence standard, she stated to the jury, "If a person has knowledge, or by the exercise of reasonable care should have knowledge, that he is being arrested by a peace officer, it is the duty of such a person to refrain from using force...to resist such arrest."[20] In contrast, she also told the jury, "A murder which is perpetrated...in knowingly avoiding a lawful arrest is murder in the first degree."[21] Thus, the requisite degree of knowledge was left somewhat confused by the nature of Mary Anne's instructions. After thirteen hours of deliberation, the jury returned guilty verdicts against Mincey on all

---

18. *Three Men Indicted In Drug Shootout*, THE ARIZONA DAILY STAR, November 2, 1974; *Jury May Get Mincey Case Late Today*, THE ARIZONA DAILY STAR, June 11, 1975; *Jury Gets Mincey Killing Case*, THE ARIZONA DAILY STAR, June 12, 1975; *Mincey Convicted in Officer's Death*, THE ARIZONA DAILY STAR, June 13, 1975.

19. State v. Mincey, 566 P.2d 273, 284 (Ariz. 1977).

20. 566 P.2d at 278.

21. 566 P.2d at 279.

counts. Mary Anne later sentenced Mincey to life imprisonment on the murder count, a concurrent sentence of ten to fifteen years for assault, and sentences ranging from two to fifteen years on the narcotics counts, to be served consecutively to the life sentence.

The conclusion in Division 5 of Mincey's first trial was only the beginning of the legal system's consideration of Rufus Mincey. In the Arizona Supreme Court, Oseran raised numerous claims of error and succeeded on only one: resolving an issue of first impression, the court held that the first degree murder statute under which Mincey was convicted required proof of actual knowledge that the victim was a law enforcement officer. Although actual knowledge was not explicitly mentioned in the statute, the court found such a requirement implicit: "[W]e are dealing with a first degree murder statute which carries the most drastic penalty in our system of criminal justice—death. Such a penalty has traditionally required criminal intent as the *mens rea....*"[22] Since some of Mary Anne's instructions could have led the jury to convict on the basis of negligence rather than knowledge and those instructions were emphasized by the prosecutor in closing argument, the state supreme court reversed Mincey's murder conviction, his related conviction for assault with a deadly weapon, and his life sentence.[23] The court, on the other hand, rejected Oseran's claims of error regarding the use of Mincey's hospital statements for impeachment and the admission of evidence seized from his apartment.

Predictably, newspapers featured the supreme court's reversal prominently, the headlines announcing, "Conviction voided in police killing."[24] The case had been difficult for Mary Anne, both because of the public attention focused on her courtroom and because of the legal issues involved. She was glad when the case left Division 5, but she knew, in light of the tenacity of Mincey's lawyer, that it was far from over. Before the appellate courts announced their rulings in *Mincey*, Mary Anne was appointed to the federal bench by President Gerald Ford. Thus, when the Arizona Supreme Court's ruling came down in May of 1977, Mary Anne read about it in her chambers in the United States Courthouse. Although she was removed in time and position from the hot June days in 1975 when Mincey's trial was in progress, she was visibly upset by the reversal.

The case, however, continued past the state court level. "The state supreme court ducked the really hard issues," Oseran remembered, "and

22. 566 P.2d at 279.
23. 566 P.2d at 280.
24. Betty Beard, *Conviction voided in police killing*, THE ARIZONA DAILY STAR, May 13, 1977.

I was prepared to keep fighting. I still wanted to press the question of the search and the hospital interrogation."[25] The United States Supreme Court granted certiorari on the federal constitutional questions that remained following the Arizona court's disposition. One year later, the high Court announced its opinion in *Mincey*, and Mary Anne was again bothered by the very public nature of her errors. In *Mincey v. Arizona*,[26] the Supreme Court addressed the questions whether the warrantless search of Mincey's apartment was constitutional and whether his statements from his hospital bed had been voluntary. On the first issue, the Court rejected the State's argument that the search of a homicide scene should be recognized as an exception to the warrant requirement. The murder-scene exception on which Mary Anne relied was well-established under Arizona law at the time, but the Supreme Court found none of the justifications for it to be convincing. "If the warrantless search of a homicide scene is reasonable, why not the warrantless search of the scene of a rape, a robbery, or a burglary?" Justice Potter Stewart's majority opinion asked rhetorically.[27] Overturning the Arizona doctrine, Stewart wrote, "We hold that the 'murder scene exception' created by the Arizona Supreme Court is inconsistent with the Fourth and Fourteenth Amendments—that the warrantless search of Mincey's apartment was not constitutionally permissible simply because a homicide had recently occurred there."[28]

As to the second issue, Justice Stewart's opinion strongly condemned Mary Anne's decision to allow the use of Mincey's hospital statements to impeach his credibility. Examining the record, the Court remarked that "[i]t is hard to imagine a situation less conducive to the exercise of 'a rational intellect and a free will' than Mincey's."[29] Characterizing Mincey's statements as "the result of virtually continuous questioning of a seriously and painfully wounded man on the edge of consciousness," the Court concluded that Mincey's statements were not voluntary. Drawing selectively from the record, the Court down-played testimony in the trial court that suggested that Mincey cooperated with the police officer voluntarily.[30] The final passage in the opinion again deplored Mincey's treatment. "Mincey was weakened by pain and shock, isolated from family, friends, and legal counsel, and barely conscious, and his will was simply over-

---

25. Oseran Interview, *supra* note 5.

26. 437 U.S. 385 (1978).

27. 437 U.S. at 393.

28. 437 U.S. at 395.

29. 437 U.S. at 398.

30. As Justice Rehnquist noted, "The Court…ignores entirely some evidence of voluntariness and distinguishes away yet other testimony." 437 U.S. at 408 (dissent).

borne. Due process of law requires that statements obtained as these were cannot be used in any way against a defendant at his trial."[31]

The *Mincey* decision from the high Court was headline news in Arizona and elsewhere.[32] The newsworthiness of the case stemmed from the Court's doctrinal clarification regarding the constitutionality of warrantless searches, which, unlike the vountariness holding, had general applicability beyond Mincey's individual case. Mary Anne, however, knew she had been justified in following established Arizona law at the time of Mincey's motion to suppress and she felt no embarrassment about that holding. For her, the Court's other conclusion that Mincey's statements were involuntary was the more salient part of the case, and the more painful. She viewed the case as a stinging disapproval of her ruling on Mincey's motion to suppress three years earlier. Although appellate courts ordinarily give great deference to trial court findings, here Mary Anne had made no specific findings, oral or written, on the question of voluntariness. Without any findings before it, the Supreme Court engaged in an independent evaluation of the record.[33] The Court's vivid description of Mincey's questioning and its resounding references to "due process of law" created the impression that any competent trial judge would have suppressed Mincey's statements for all purposes. Mary Anne, by then a two-year veteran of the federal judiciary, felt humiliated and somewhat angered by the tone of her elite colleagues' decision in Washington, D.C.

The *Mincey* case lingered in the courts for another six years. On remand from the United States Supreme Court, Mincey was tried and convicted of second degree murder before Alice Truman, but his conviction was reversed because of error in Truman's instructions.[34] He was tried and convicted a third time, and that conviction and sentence of twenty-five years to life was affirmed in 1984.[35]

In two other murder cases, the Arizona Supreme Court determined that Mary Anne committed error in the conduct of the criminal trial itself.

---

31. 437 U.S. at 402.

32. Linda Greenhouse, *Murder Site Is Ruled No Exception To the Need for a Search Warrant*, THE NEW YORK TIMES, June 22, 1978; *Justices insist on warrants in murder cases*, THE ARIZONA REPUBLIC, June 22, 1978; *Murder search is voided*, THE ARIZONA DAILY STAR, June 22, 1978.

33. On this point, then-Associate Justice William Rehnquist dissented, arguing that the trial court's finding of voluntariness should have been affirmed. *See* 437 U.S. at 407–410 (Rehnquist, J., dissenting).

34. *See* State v. Mincey, 636 P.2d 637 (Ariz. 1981)(reversing second-degree murder conviction for faulty instructions by Alice Truman).

35. *See* State v. Mincey, 687 P.2d 1180 (Ariz. 1984)(affirming second-degree murder conviction).

In *State v. Reid*,[36] Mary Anne, then a ten-year veteran of the state bench, presided over a difficult murder trial and, in her handling of the case, may have revealed a somewhat hardened judicial demeanor. In the summer of 1974, a sequence of violent events in southwest Tucson led to charges against Timothy Reid and Spencer Watson of first-degree murder, armed robbery, armed burglary, and theft of a motor vehicle. As described in news articles, Reid and his companion were accused of having broken into the home of a federal border patrol agent, terrorizing the man's wife and teenage daughter, and then killing him by gunfire.[37] At their separate trials, each defendant claimed that the other fired the fatal shots. Reid was found guilty in Mary Anne's court of the crimes charged, and she sentenced him to life imprisonment on the murder count, and to concurrent lesser sentences on the other charges. Watson was similarly convicted in Robert Roylston's court, but received the death penalty.[38] Despite Reid's assertion through counsel of numerous errors on appeal, the supreme court affirmed his conviction and sentences. Nevertheless, the state high court did note that Mary Anne had committed error, though not reversible error, on two separate occasions during the trial.

One point of contention at the outset of Reid's six-day trial was Mary Anne's order that Reid be kept in leg irons during his trial for security reasons. The supreme court concluded that the shackling of the defendant was error, albeit harmless error in light of the overwhelming evidence of defendant's guilt: "Manacling a person when there is no necessity to do so, and bringing him into court in the presence of the jury could not be too strongly condemned."[39] The supreme court's language troubled Mary Anne, since Reid's case had been challenging from the beginning and she believed she had expended extra effort to be fair. Before Reid's trial, Mary Anne had consulted security at the courthouse regarding the defendant's request to have his handcuffs removed so that he could take notes during his trial. The transcript of the discussion regarding shackles shows Mary Anne's impression that Reid did not object to the leg irons.

> THE COURT: I want to speak to the Sheriff's Deputies in the presence of Mr. Reid. Mr. Reid has requested the right to take notes, and it

---

36. 559 P.2d 136 (Ariz. 1976).

37. Betty Beard, *Two Held in Agent's Death*, THE ARIZONA DAILY STAR, June 1, 1974.

38. *See* Sam Stinson, *Watson Receives Death Sentence; Brother Found Guilty in Robbery*, THE ARIZONA DAILY STAR, November 26, 1974. Watson's own appeal led to a reduction of the death sentence to life imprisonment. State v. Watson, 559 P.2d 121 (Ariz. 1976).

39. State v. Reid, 559 P.2d 136, 142 (Ariz. 1976), quoting State v. Robinson, 433 P.2d 70, 73 (Ariz. App. 1967).

is my understanding, and I may be wrong again, Mr. Reid, I am quoting you, that there will be no objection made to leg irons rather than handcuffs. Is there any problem with that?

THE DEPUTY SHERIFF: No, Your Honor.

THE COURT: So he can have his hands to use to take notes?

THE DEPUTY SHERIFF: We can replace them with leg irons, Your Honor.[40]

Later, defense counsel stated that his client now wanted permission to have the shackles and handcuffs removed while in the courtroom. Mary Anne responded that she would take the matter under advisement, adding "I do not make these rulings. I have to consider it with Security in this matter."[41] Mary Anne's minute entry on the matter reveals her impatience with the defendant and her concern for the safety of people in the courtroom:

> When the defendant was originally brought into the Court, the defendant was handcuffed and he did not have any leg irons on; however, he made a request to be able to write and his counsel indicated that he, the defendant, was willing to have leg irons on if he was allowed to have the handcuffs taken off in order to write, and that this was done and the Court also ordered that the defendant not be brought through the hallway in the presence of the jury in leg irons but only by handcuffs and then to have them removed in the courtroom and irons put on outside the jury's presence. The Court states that it feels that some restraint is necessary for the protection of the people in the courtroom, based upon the nature of the crime, psychiatric reports, and based upon even a request from counsel for the defendant that precautions be taken.[42]

Thus, Mary Anne's decision to have Reid shackled during the trial stemmed from her sense that the defendant originally had agreed to the use of leg irons, and from her concern for the safety of people in the courtroom, including perhaps her own safety. The supreme court's notation of error was a stark reminder to her that the myriad rulings required of a trial judge, though supported by apparent justifications at the time, are often viewed differently on the cold record.

A second error in *Reid* was Mary Anne's failure to grant the defendant a hearing to determine if an eye witness's in-court identification was tainted by pretrial procedures. The witness, the wife of the murder victim, had identified Reid at the preliminary hearing after having been told by the county attorney that the defendant would be there in shackles. When

---

40. The transcript references are from *State v. Reid*, 559 P.2d 136, 142 (Ariz. 1976).

41. *Id.*

42. Minute Entry, State v. Reid, Cause No. 25732 (Pima County Sup. Ct. September 27, 1974).

defense counsel objected to the reliability of the witness's identification before trial, Mary Anne rejected the argument categorically and refused to allow a hearing on the matter. The supreme court disapproved, ruling that she should have conducted a factual hearing about the circumstances of the witness's identification. But again, in light of other evidence of guilt, the court concluded that the error was harmless.

Throughout his trial, Reid repeatedly challenged his lawyers's authority and undoubtedly provoked Mary Anne's anger. She was particularly put off by his frequent requests for a change of appointed counsel. When Reid had belatedly sought new counsel, the following exchange took place:

> MR. REID: (interrupting) How do I have to accept him as my attorney when I don't want him?
> THE COURT: Because, Mr. Reid, he is appointed by the Court.
> MR. REID: I want to know the reason behind this.
> THE COURT: Very well. If you keep quiet a minute, I will tell you the reason. He is appointed by the Court to represent you.
> MR REID: When was he appointed? They didn't bring me over here in court when they appointed him....[N]o judge appointed him to me.
> THE COURT: The record shows, and I have gone over it, that he was appointed attorney, and when you have an attorney appointed, Mr. Reid, you don't have the right to pick and choose your attorney. The Court appoints an attorney to do this....
> MR. REID: My opinion don't mean nothing then, huh?
> THE COURT: No, sir, other than at the time we have a hearing, if you can raise specific points, then the Court will listen to you at that time.[43]

Mary Anne did in fact appoint additional counsel to assist Reid's original lawyer, but her controlled anger in dealing with Reid was apparent.

In the same trial, Mary Anne allowed the testimony of the coroner's pathologist to be videotaped before trial because the witness was scheduled to be outside the country during trial. The defendant was present during the taping in the courtroom, and defense counsel cross-examined the doctor. The defendant had objected to the procedure, however, and had argued to Mary Anne that she should require the expert to appear at trial so that he could be cross-examined before the jury. Her denial of the defense motion evinces, again, the elevation of expediency over the defendant's interest in confronting the witness before the jury. Although a majority of the Arizona Supreme Court found no infringement of the defendant's sixth amendment right of confrontation, Vice Chief Justice Fred

---

43. State v. Reid, 559 P.2d 136, 143–44 (Ariz. 1976).

Struckmeyer wrote a strong dissent, accusing the majority of misconstruing the value of the right of confrontation.[44]

The *Reid* case reveals contrasting dimensions to Mary Anne's judicial approach. On one hand, she responded evenhandedly to Reid's request for new counsel, though obviously irritated by the defendant's complaints. She imposed the lesser of the two possible sentences for Reid's crime—life imprisonment as opposed to death. By contrast, Reid's codefendant Watson had received the death penalty from Robert Roylston. In *Reid*, as in other cases where the death penalty was an option, she consistently avoided the imposition of capital punishment. On the other hand, the shackling of the defendant, the refusal to hold a hearing on the identification testimony, and the willingness to allow videotaped testimony of the pathologist over defense counsel's objection suggest a prosecutorial orientation or, perhaps, her sense that she should not let the trial be detoured by defense tactics where evidence of guilt was overwhelming.

A first-degree murder case towards the end of Mary Anne's state court tenure resulted in a reversal and, as in *Mincey*, the reversal came down after Mary Anne had left the state court bench. In *State v. Swinburne*,[45] the defendant was charged with murder, kidnapping, and burglary. The ten-day criminal trial was held in January of 1976, just months before Mary Anne's appointment to the federal court, and resulted in a conviction on all counts. Mary Anne imposed concurrent sentences of life imprisonment on the murder and kidnapping charges and from ten to fifteen years on the burglary charge.

Although Swinburne raised some seventeen issues on appeal from his conviction, his main argument centered on Mary Anne's order restricting his right to cross-examine a government witness. Before trial, Mary Anne granted the state's motion to suppress a tape recording of an interview between the witness and a detective during which the detective impliedly promised not to disclose damaging information to the witness's out-of-state probation officer if the witness testified at trial. The witness provided important and extremely damaging testimony at trial implicating the defendant in the murder. The witness had two apparent motives for cooperating with the prosecution: he did not want to be arrested as an accessory to the murder, and he did not want Tucson authorities to contact his probation officer about his involvement in the Tucson events. Taking a narrow approach to the permissible scope of cross-examination, Mary Anne suppressed the tape and refused to allow the defense counsel to cross-examine the witness regarding the second motive. At trial, she

---

44. 559 P.2d at 151–52.
45. 569 P.2d 833 (Ariz. 1977).

stated: "The Court is of the opinion that in the context that this was said, that it is not a promise that could come into evidence. It would open up a new collateral matter."[46]

In reversing, the state supreme court emphasized the traditionally wide latitude given to criminal defendants in cross-examining witnesses for the purpose of impeaching their credibility. The court reasoned that defense counsel should have been allowed to bring out both motives underlying the key witness's cooperation with the state. The possibility that such cross-examination would reveal other crimes or that the witness mistakenly believed the State had made him a promise was irrelevant, since the test is the witness's expectation or hope of a reward. The court concluded that Mary Anne's restriction on the cross-examination of a key witness was reversible error.[47]

Although Swinburne's reversal was not the media event that Mincey's had been,[48] the error was one which called into question Mary Anne's objectivity as a trial judge. Directing the scope of cross-examination, like ruling on an evidentiary objection, is the bread and butter of trial work. In those areas, the seasoned trial judge reacts not from protracted deliberation but from experience. Mary Anne, a very experienced judge by the time of *Swinburne,* did not give sufficient weight to the defendant's tactical need to freely question the adverse witness. Her empathy seemed directed not to the defendant's side of the courtroom but to the prosecution's chair. Mary Anne's willingness in *Swinburne,* a first-degree murder case, to curtail the defendant's right to cross-examine an important prosecution witness reflected her intuitive alignment with the State.

In one other murder case, Mary Anne's experience as a prosecutor may have informed her controversial ruling on an evidentiary question. In *State v. Skinner,*[49] Mary Anne presided over the trial of one of four men charged with the crimes of armed robbery and murder in connection with the robbery of a liquor store in Tucson. Before Skinner's trial, a key government witness provided a statement that implicated Skinner, but the witness later refuted the statement. At trial, when the witness failed to testify consistently with his earlier statement, the prosecution sought to introduce the statement substantively to prove the truth of the facts recited.

---

46. 569 P.2d at 837.

47. On remand, Swinburne pleaded guilty to second-degree murder and received a sentence of from ten to twelve years in prison. The sentencing judge, Thomas Meehan, was impressed by evidence of Swinburne's rehabilitation. *See Second trial for murder brings lighter sentence,* THE ARIZONA DAILY STAR, October 13, 1978.

48. The articles recounting the trial were not front page news. *See Swinburne Found Guilty Of Murder,* THE ARIZONA DAILY STAR, January 17, 1975.

49. 515 P.2d 880 (Ariz. 1973).

Mary Anne granted the prosecution's motion and admitted the statement as substantive evidence.

Although her evidentiary ruling was affirmed on appeal, Mary Anne had contravened existing Arizona law when she granted the state's motion for the substantive use of the witness's out-of-court statement. In so ruling, she had relied on indications that the federal courts and other states were changing their evidentiary rules to allow such use.[50] In affirming her decision, the Arizona Supreme Court expressly overruled existing precedents and used the case to announce new law.[51] In dissent, Justice William Holohan expressed grave misgivings about the holding. "My fear is that [the holding] provides a tool for the unscrupulous, dishonest, and crafty to obscure the truth. The temptation to get a favorable unsworn statement from a witness at any cost will be tremendous.... What was advertised as the cure for the turncoat witness may turn out to be a plague on the rest of our system of evidence."[52]

Mary Anne's acceptance of the State's position on the substantive use of the witness's prior statement, notwithstanding the existence of contrary Arizona law, is significant. Although she was generally reluctant to establish new law, here she did so willingly. Perhaps, as a trial judge, she realized the futility of instructing a jury to consider evidence for a limited purpose. Her ruling may also have reflected her own prosecutorial experience. She had faced the problem of the "turncoat witness" in her days in the Pima County Attorney's Office and in the U. S. Attorney's Office, and she knew first-hand the angry frustration felt by prosecutors when key witnesses reneged on promised testimony. Her approach in *Skinner* decidedly strengthened the hand of the prosecution in dealing with unpredictable witnesses.

In one final murder case, Mary Anne's independence surfaced in an uncharacteristic ruling. In *State v. Edwards*,[53] Mary Anne's suppression of pivotal incriminating evidence led to the dismissal of charges against the defendant. The case involved a murder arising out of a love-triangle, and the circumstances were described in vivid detail in the daily newspapers.[54]

---

50. At that time, Rule 801 had been proposed for the Rules of Evidence for United States Courts and Magistrates. *See also* California v. Gree, 399 U.S. 149 (1970)(upholding the constitutionality of Sec. 1235 of the California Evidence Code).

51. "We therefore hold that the prior decisions of this court...which hold that such statements may not be used substantively are by this decision overruled." State v. Skinner, 515 P.2d at 887(citations omitted).

52. 515 P.2d at 895.

53. 529 P.2d 1174 (Ariz. 1975).

54. *See* Sam Stinson, *City Woman Found Slain While Her Home Burns*, THE ARIZONA DAILY STAR, July 13, 1973; *Motive, Suspect Sought in Eastside Murder*, THE ARIZONA DAILY STAR, July 14, 1973; *Nurse Held In Slaying Of Woman In Home*, THE ARI-

Yvonne Edwards, a thirty-one-year-old nurse and the apparently-spurned member of the triangle, was accused of murdering the fiancee of her former lover. Death occurred by five point-blank gunshots to the victim in the victim's own bedroom, and then the murderer partially burned the victim's body. In the course of investigating Edwards's involvement in the crime, the Tucson police arrested Edwards based on information from her former lover and then repeatedly ignored Edwards' requests to speak with counsel and her assertions of her right to remain silent. During the investigation, police administered a polygraph test to Edwards and seized physical evidence from her. Ultimately, after detention in jail for three days and intermittent questioning by police, Edwards confessed to the murder.

David Hoffman, a flamboyant but respected criminal defense lawyer representing Edwards in Mary Anne's court, moved to suppress the test results, the physical evidence, Edwards' statements to police, and her confession. In his fifty-page motion, Hoffman argued eloquently that his clients' fifth and sixth amendment rights had been flagrantly violated by the police investigation. He reminded Mary Anne that "the quality of a nation's civilization can be largely measured by the methods it uses in the enforcement of its criminal law."[55] In the nine-day hearing on the motion in December of 1973, Hoffman established that police had arrested Edwards without probable cause and then had relentlessly pressured her to confess, ignoring her requests to speak to counsel. After the close of the hearing, Mary Anne took the matter under advisement and pondered the case over Christmas and into the new year. Finally, on April 10, 1974, she announced her ruling, granting the defendant's motion to suppress in totality. She found that the warrantless arrests of the defendant had been without probable cause and that the statements and confession of the defendant were not voluntary within the meaning of the fifth amendment.

In language strongly condemning the conduct of the Tucson police, the Arizona Supreme Court affirmed Mary Anne's ruling. Chief Justice Jack Hays, Mary Anne's longtime friend, wrote for the court:

> We thought that it had long ago become unnecessary to remind the police departments of this state of the requirements of the United State Constitution as interpreted by the United States Supreme Court, particularly with regard to the privilege against self-incrimination and the right to counsel.... It is...basic to our system that the State which proposes to convict and punish an individual must produce the evidence against him

---

ZONA DAILY STAR, August 4, 1973; *Suspect's Arrest Detailed*, THE ARIZONA DAILY STAR, December 6, 1973.

55. Defendant's Motion to Suppress, Yvonne v. Edwards, Cause No. A-23950 (Pima County Sup. Ct. filed November 19, 1973).

through the independent efforts of its officers and not by inducing the individual to incriminate himself.[56]

Again, the high court's ruling was headline news in the press.[57] Shortly after the supreme court's affirmance, Mary Anne approved of the State's dismissal of the indictment against Edwards based on inadequate evidence. A final legal dispute arose over whether the dismissal should be "with" or "without" prejudice, the State arguing that it wanted to preserve the opportunity to refile in the future. Unimpressed, Mary Anne found no authority for the State's request and entered the dismissal with prejudice.[58]

In *Edwards*, Mary Anne was repelled by the flagrant police misconduct and called the constitutional issues as she saw them, notwithstanding the sensational and gruesome nature of the crime. Her prosecutorial background, however prominently it figured in other rulings, did not overwhelm her ability to objectively respond to Hoffman's suppression motion. To the contrary, her experience as a prosecutor may have made her particularly impatient with shoddy or reckless police work. In any event, Mary Anne's reputation among criminal defense lawyers enjoyed a lift after *Edwards*.[59]

Motions to suppress, the workhorse of the criminal defense lawyer, were often the subject of appeal from Mary Anne's court. In contrast to the reputation of some of her colleagues, most criminal defense lawyers felt that their clients would be treated fairly by Mary Anne. Howard Kashman, a criminal defense lawyer who appeared before her numerous times in state court, remembered that Mary Anne once granted a motion to suppress after the same motion had been denied by another judge. The case involved the alleged kidnapping and rape of a white woman by two young black men. Kashman moved to suppress a gun found in one defendant's home because of a defective affidavit supporting the search warrant. Judge Herbert Krucker, sitting by designation from the court of appeals to hear pretrial proceedings in the case, denied the motion to suppress. Hoping for a better result from Mary Anne, Kashman raised the same motion at trial in Division 5. "It took her no time to say that the af-

56. State v. Edwards, 529 P.2d 1174, 1175, 1178 (Ariz. 1975).

57. Alex Drehsler, *Court Rejects Confession, Cites Threats*, THE ARIZONA DAILY STAR, December 27, 1974.

58. Minute Entry, State v. Edwards, Cause No. A-23950 (Pima County Sup. Ct. March 10, 1975).

59. Telephone Interview with David Hoffman (May 13, 1993).

fidavits were based on guesswork, and she suppressed the gun. She did this notwithstanding the fact that it had already been ruled on, and by a court of appeals judge. Both defendants were later acquitted."[60] Mary Anne's response in the case cemented Kashman's belief that if a case of his were assigned to her court, he would get an objective appraisal of the evidence, without regard for the result.

Mary Anne's record on motions to suppress reveals her efforts to apply the protean law then developing under the fourth amendment. In a case arising at the end of her state court tenure, she granted the defendant's motion to suppress, only to be met with reversal from the court of appeals. In *State v. Curlin*,[61] the defendant, a Tucson police officer, was charged with auto theft. During investigation of the case, police performed a warrantless limited search of a car that had been seen in the defendant's possession to determine the ownership and registration of the car. In his criminal case, defendant filed a motion to suppress all evidence flowing from the search and seizure of the car, and Mary Anne presided over a one-day hearing on the motion in December of 1975. The evidence at the hearing showed that law enforcement investigators had checked the license plate of the locked vehicle and found that the license number was not on the list of recently stolen cars. They were unable to see the vehicle identification number because it was covered by a road map. Thus, they continued to investigate by unlocking the car door with a coat hanger, ascertaining the vehicle identification number, and checking for registration papers. With the information gleaned from the search, law enforcement determined that the car had been stolen, and the car was later seized.

Early in 1976, Mary Anne granted the defendant's suppression motion, finding a lack of probable cause to support the search. Presumably, her ruling reflected her belief that the officers lacked probable cause to pursue the search. The court of appeals, however, viewed the evidence as establishing a "well-founded suspicion" that the car was stolen and reversed her ruling. "The fact that a check of the license plate did not disclose the vehicle as stolen was no reason for the officers to drop the investigation," the court reasoned, since the check "did not vitiate their suspicions."[62] Moreover, no warrant was required since the United States Supreme Court had only recently held that automobiles by their nature present exigent circumstances justifying warrantless searches. In *Curlin*, Mary Anne erred on the side of the defendant (perhaps rendered more sympathetic to

60. Kashman Interview, *supra* note 7.

61. 560 P.2d 62 (Ariz. App. 1977).

62. 560 P.2d at 64.

her because of his status as a police officer), but the appellate court read the evidentiary record differently. Although the motion to suppress in *Curlin* did not raise far-reaching legal issues, it demonstrated the difficulty facing trial judges in applying the evolving fourth amendment jurisprudence to concrete facts.

Although Mary Anne's record of reversals in criminal cases is intriguingly suggestive of a judicial worldview, one must remember that she was more often affirmed than reversed, and the record of affirmances showed that her rulings were squarely within the mainstream. For example, she believed in holding people responsible for the predictable consequences of their acts, a theme of her challenged instructions in *Mincey*, and she was affirmed in applying that principle in diverse factual contexts. In *Drury v. Burr*,[63] the defendant had broken another man's jaw in an altercation. The man died as a result of suffocation, apparently caused by inhaling his own vomit. The defendant challenged the finding of probable cause before Mary Anne in a habeas corpus action, arguing that the death might equally have been caused by the victim's intoxication and that he had not intended to kill the victim. Mary Anne denied relief, and she was ultimately affirmed by the Arizona Supreme Court. The supreme court's reasoning, and that of Mary Anne, was that the evidence was sufficient to establish probable cause based on the severity of the beating and the occurrence of the death "through a chain of natural effects and causes unchanged by human action."[64]

In a related vein, Mary Anne was affirmed in her rejection of the defense of insanity in at least two murder cases where she imposed lengthy prison terms.[65] In that era, predating Arizona's present "guilty but insane" alternative,[66] Mary Anne may have disliked the possibility that a violent person, if acquitted on the ground of insanity, might be released from a psychiatric hospital within a few years. A criminal conviction and lengthy sentence would ensure that the defendants, even if mentally ill, would not pose a danger to society.

---

63. 483 P.2d 539 (Ariz. 1971).

64. 483 P.2d at 541.

65. *See* State v. Billhymer, 561 P.2d 311 (Ariz. 1977)(in bench trial, Mary Anne found defendant was not legally insane, found him guilty of two counts of first degree murder, and imposed two consecutive life sentences); State v. Makal, 480 P.2d 347 (Ariz. 1971)(Mary Anne imposed life sentence for first-degree murder, refusing defendant's motion to set aside plea on ground of his incompetence).

66. *See* ARIZ. REV. STAT. Secs. 13-502 & 13-3994, enacted in 1993, authorizing a verdict of "guilty except insane," and placing defendant under jurisdiction of "psychiatric security review board" for period equal to criminal sentence that could have been imposed but for defendant's insanity.

In another case, Mary Anne similarly manifested the desire to hold defendants to the consequences of their acts, and she was willing to overlook a defect in the charging information to achieve that end. In *State v. Bollander*,[67] the defendant had been charged with credit card forgery under Ariz. Rev. Stat. Sec. 13-1074 for numerous acts committed in June of 1969. Defense counsel Howard Kashman, in researching the case, discovered that Sec. 13-1074 had not become effective until July of that year. Hoping to achieve a permanent dismissal for his client, Kashman delayed raising the defect until trial. "I wanted to wait until jeopardy had attached," he explained, "so that the State couldn't start the whole thing all over again." On the opening morning of trial, Kashman stood up and moved to dismiss the information, but Mary Anne was unamused. "She went through the ceiling," he recalled. "She was furious. Then she looked at [the prosecutor] and said, 'I want you to go back to your office and figure out how to fix this thing. I'll give you until 1:30 this afternoon.'"[68] When the prosecutor returned in the afternoon, he moved to amend the information to charge a violation of the general forgery statute, which carried a longer maximum sentence. Despite the irregularity, Mary Anne granted the State's motion and proceeded to try the case, and the jury returned a verdict of guilty. On appeal, however, Kashman succeeded in obtaining a short-lived victory for his client. Bollander's conviction was thrown out by the court of appeals, the court reasoning that the original information had been fatally defective and could not be cured by amendment.[69] Mary Anne's angry refusal to reward the tactic used by Kashman had thus garnered a reversal, but the appellate court noted that on remand the information was to be dismissed with leave to refile.[70] Thus, Kashman's gambit succeeded only in temporarily delaying the inevitable for his client.

Mary Anne's judicial response in *Bollander* was revealing of two prominent qualities. First, she had a distinct dislike for gamesmanship in the courtroom. She reacted with raw anger if she perceived that counsel were engaging in disingenuous tactics *vis a vis* the court to achieve an advantage for their clients. In *Bollander* that anger was palpable. Some would come to believe that her anger was less repressible once she made the transition to the federal bench. Second, Mary Anne strongly believed in holding individuals to answer for their wrongful conduct, and she therefore was reluctant to allow a technical defect to derail the prosecu-

67. 484 P.2d 219 (Ariz. App. 1971).
68. Kashman Interview, *supra* note 7.
69. 484 P.2d at 220.
70. *Id.*

tion of an apparently guilty defendant. Since the general forgery statute had been on the books at the time of Bollander's offenses, the belated amendment seemed to her to pose no fundamental obstacle to his prosecution. Interestingly, the holding in *Bollander* was expressly overruled some fifteen years later. In *State v. Dungan*,[71] the appellate court concluded that, absent a showing of prejudice, a miscitation of a criminal statute in an information or indictment is merely technical and does not require reversal of a conviction. Thus, Mary Anne's original position in *Bollander* was vindicated and became the operative principle for evaluating charging errors committed by the prosecution.

Mary Anne was unsympathetic to post-conviction claims of inadequacy of legal representation and was not impressed by belated attempts to withdraw guilty pleas, and her judicial responses to such petitions generally met with affirmance.[72] In *State v. McKesson*,[73] for example, the defendant attempted to withdraw a guilty plea to second-degree murder that he had entered pursuant to a plea agreement. Significantly, the defendant had not moved to withdraw the plea until after a key witness for the state had been murdered. Mary Anne was not amused by the defendant's argument that she had never formally "accepted" the plea. Somewhat impatiently, she commented to defense counsel in open court, "Once you enter that plea of guilty and I put in on the record that...the Defendant has entered a plea of guilty and the Court finds it is voluntary and knowledgeable and that there is a factual basis, I think it would be ludicrous to say that that is not an acceptance of the plea."[74] Thus, she revealed her cynicism about belated attempts to change voluntary pleas.

A trial court's instructions to the jury are frequently the focus of appeal, sometimes successfully, as in *Mincey*, but more often unsuccessfully. Mary Anne recognized the great importance of jury instructions and labored hard to make them accurately reflect the law in language that a juror could understand. Indeed, her interest in improving standardized jury instructions led to her appointment as co-chair of the Arizona Supreme Court Committee to Revise Civil Jury Instructions in 1971. In the criminal cases before her, she would select, reject, or modify proposed instructions from defense counsel and from the prosecution; her superior court case files do

---

71. 718 P.2d 1010 (Ariz. 1986).

72. *See, e.g.,* State v. Rogers, 545 P.2d 930 (Ariz. 1976) (affirming Mary Anne's denial of post-conviction relief on ground of inadequate representation); State v. McKesson, 556 P.2d 801 (Ariz. App. 1976)(affirming Mary Anne's denial of motion to withdraw plea).

73. 556 P.2d 801 (Ariz. App. 1976).

74. 556 P.2d at 802 (quoting from trial court transcript).

not reveal a greater willingness on her part to accept the State's proposed instructions than those proposed by the defense. Predictably, the appellate courts generally found no error in her jury instructions.[75]

In one case, her instructions and the resulting appellate litigation must have reminded her of Professor Barnes's criminal law class at the University of Arizona College of Law. In *State v. Hughes*[76] the defendant was convicted in Mary Anne's court of first-degree rape. On appeal, defense counsel frankly conceded that he had searched the record and had found no error in the trial court proceedings, but he identified matters that "might arguably support the appeal." One such argument was that Mary Anne wrongly instructed the jury as to the requisite "penetration" necessary to establish rape. The instruction that she gave was: "Any sexual penetration however slight is sufficient to complete the crime of rape if the other requisite facts are present." The contention by defense counsel was that the instruction did not "sufficiently specify that the penetration required has to be that of a penis." The court of appeals rejected the argument, reasoning that the words "sexual penetration" in Mary Anne's instruction sufficiently implied that the penetration must be that of a penis.[77] Thus, the question that Mary Anne had fielded in her criminal law class twenty years earlier had surfaced in her courtroom, and just as her law professor had been satisfied with her straightforward answer in law school, the appellate court was satisfied with her common sense instructions for the jury.

Despite an arguable prosecutorial bias in her conduct of criminal trials, Mary Anne was acutely sensitive to the unnerving responsibility of criminal sentencings. She found sentencings to be the hardest part of her judicial work and struggled internally for the just disposition. One lawyer described her as somewhere between William Frey, a judge known for his unyielding severity *vis a vis* criminal defendants, and John Collins, a judge known for his leniency.[78] Another remarked that he had seen her exercise real compassion in the course of sentencings. "Her world experience helped her as a judge," he explained. "She understood hard times."[79] One attorney, characterizing her as "moderate in sentencings," stated that

75. *Mincey* is perhaps the most significant case finding error. In numerous other cases the appellate courts rejected claims of error in Mary Anne's jury instructions. *See, e.g.,* State v. Collins, 528 P.2d 829 (Ariz. 1975); State v. Richmond, 540 P.2d 700 (Ariz. 1975).

76. 456 P.2d 393 (Ariz. 1969).

77. 456 P.2d at 395.

78. Interview with Ruben Salter, Jr., Tucson, Arizona (May 18, 1993).

79. Interview with Fredric F. Kay, Federal Public Defender, District of Arizona, Tucson, Arizona (Oct. 31, 1992).

"[s]he wouldn't let a convicted guy walk, but she also wouldn't send him away to the slammer forever."[80] Ed Morgan, who represented a man convicted in Mary Anne's court of attempted murder of his stepdaughter, recalled that Mary Anne "showed moderation" in sentencing the defendant to ten to fifteen years in prison.[81] Although Mary Anne's criminal sentencings were frequently the subject of challenge on appeal under the eighth amendment, none of her sentencings was set aside on that ground.[82]

Mary Anne never sentenced a criminal defendant to death, although she had the opportunity on several occasions. Prior to the United States Supreme Court's 1972 decision in *Furman v. Georgia*[83] declaring the existing practice of capital punishment unconstitutional, juries rather than judges had the authority under Arizona law to impose the death penalty after a jury-trial conviction for first-degree murder. Charles Schmid, for example, had been sentenced to death by a jury, a sentence that was reduced to life imprisonment in light of *Furman*.[84] Although judges had the authority to impose death where the conviction was based on a guilty plea,[85] Mary Anne chose not to do so even for the most sensational of crimes. While colleagues and friends cannot recall discussing the subject with her, some believed that she was opposed to capital punishment;[86] others felt that she was not opposed philosophically but did not want to

---

80. Interview with W. Edward Morgan, Tucson, Arizona (Sept. 9, 1992).

81. *See* State v. Hughes, 475 P.2d 511 (Ariz. App. 1970) (affirming trial court's denial of motion for new trial and for change of judge).

82. *See* State v. Guthrie, 532 P.2d 862 (Ariz. 1975)(five-year minimum sentence for sale of heroin); State v. Collins, 528 P.2d 829 (Ariz. 1974)(40 to 50 years imprisonment for felony murder); State v. Miller, 522 P.2d 23 (Ariz. 1974)(30 to 50 years imprisonment for beating death of child); State v. Hughes, 456 P.2d 393 (Ariz. 1969)(10 to 12 years imprisonment for rape of ten-year-old girl); State v. Nagle, 452 P.2d 99 (Ariz. 1969)(12–15 years imprisonment for kidnaping while armed with gun); State v. Espinosa, 421 P.2d 322 (Ariz. 1966)(5 to 6 years imprisonment without parole for sale of heroin).

83. 408 U.S. 238 (1972).

84. *See* State v. Schmid, 509 P.2d 619, 626 (Ariz. 1973).

85. *See* ARIZ. REV. STAT. Sec. 13-453 (1956)("A person guilty of murder in the first degree shall suffer death or imprisonment in the state prison for life, at the discretion of the jury trying the person charged therewith, or upon a plea of guilty, the court shall determine the punishment."). Under the pre-1972 laws in Arizona, capital crimes other than murder included assault with a deadly weapon by a prisoner, ARIZ. REV. STAT. Sec. 13-250, kidnapping for extortion, robbery or ransom, ARIZ. REV. STAT. Sec. 13-492, perjury resulting in the death of an innocent person, ARIZ. REV. STAT. Sec. 13-572, and treason, ARIZ. REV. STAT. Sec. 13-701.

86. Morgan Interview, *supra* note 80.

have to impose the death sentence herself.[87] The fact remains that she opted for life imprisonment whenever given the choice.

In *State v. Makal*,[88] for example, Mary Anne accepted James Makal's guilty plea to first-degree murder pursuant to a plea bargain and sentenced him to life imprisonment. Makal had been previously tried and convicted in the strangling deaths of his wife and two young children and sentenced to death. That conviction was set aside on appeal because of error committed at trial,[89] and Mary Anne was assigned the case on remand. Although Makal, through his lawyer Ed Morgan, challenged Mary Anne's acceptance of the plea due to Makal's alleged incompetence, the Arizona Supreme Court affirmed her handling of the case in all respects. The court noted that Mary Anne "was careful and thorough in her questioning of the defendant in order to determine that his guilty plea was entered into knowingly and voluntarily."[90] As to imposition of life imprisonment, the court explained that Mary Anne, "after careful consideration of circumstances in mitigation of punishment, sentenced defendant Makal to life imprisonment rather than death."[91]

Similarly, after Arizona's capital sentencing law was revised in 1973 to place the authority in the judge rather than the jury,[92] Mary Anne continued to opt for life imprisonment in the cases that came before her. Her treatment of Willie Lee Richmond is illustrative. Richmond was involved in a notorious robbery-murder spree in the summer of 1973 in Tucson. He was tried separately on three different murder charges, resulting in two convictions and one acquittal. Mary Anne imposed life imprisonment for Richmond's first-degree murder conviction in her court, as well as a concurrent lesser sentence for burglary.[93] In contrast, her colleague Richard Roylston imposed the death sentence on Richmond[94] for the sep-

---

87. Interview with Eleanor Robbins, Tucson, Arizona (July 13, 1992) ("She prayed that she would not get a case where the death penalty was required"); Interview with Hon. Robert Roylston, former Judge, Pima County Superior Court, Tucson, Arizona (Oct. 5, 1992) (Mary Anne may not have ever imposed the death sentence in fact but she was not opposed to it).

88. State v. Makal, 480 P.2d 347 (Ariz. 1971).

89. 455 P.2d 450 (Ariz. 1969).

90. 480 P.2d at 350.

91. 480 P.2d at 351.

92. *See* ARIZ. REV. STAT. Sec. 13-454 (describing separate sentencing hearing to determine sentence for first degree murder, and mandating sentence of death where court finds one or more aggravating circumstances to be present and the absence of mitigating circumstances).

93. State v. Richmond, 540 P.2d 700 (Ariz. 1975).

94. State v. Richmond, 560 P.2d 41 (Ariz. 1976), *cert. denied*, 433 U.S. 915 (1977)(affirming conviction and sentence).

arate murder conviction. As it happened, the saga of Richmond's efforts to avoid the death penalty would last more than twenty years in the state and federal court systems, including the United States Supreme Court; he ultimately succeeded in having his sentence reduced to life imprisonment in 1994.[95] Mary Anne's reluctance to impose the death penalty probably stemmed from a combination of factors: her sense that the statutory "aggravating factors" were not sufficiently present to justify death, her intuitive repulsion at the idea of pronouncing the death sentence, and, perhaps, her recognition that seemingly endless appeals and collateral proceedings were the inevitable consequence of such a sentence.

Mary Anne's state-court record in the criminal arena reflected the complexity of her character. Her plain-spoken style and her grounding in common sense surfaced not only in jury instructions but also in her interpretation of questions of criminal law. Her emphasis on "law and order" and her discernible affinity for the prosecution did not manifest the feminine "compassion" that has spawned grand theory. A drug-dealing or violent defendant could expect little sympathy from her, and she erred several times in failing to give sufficient protection to the defendant's fair trial rights under the fifth and sixth amendments. Her belief in holding people to the consequences of their intentional acts persuaded her on occasion to move too quickly toward the goal of conviction. On the other hand, her internal struggles as a sentencing judge and her reluctance to impose the death penalty did show that she was acutely sensitive to the power she possessed over the lives of the criminal defendants in her courtroom. Finally, her independence of thought allowed her to rule at times in favor of the unpopular defendant, notwithstanding the spotlight of public attention.

---

95. After its initial affirmance of the death sentence, the Arizona Supreme Court later vacated the sentence in light of its intervening decision in *State v. Watson*, 586 P.2d 1253 (Ariz. 1978), *cert. denied*, 440 U.S. 924 (1979), which held that it was unconstitutional to restrict mitigating circumstances to those enumerated by statute. After Richmond was sentenced to death the second time by the trial court, the sentence was again affirmed. State v. Richmond, 666 P.2d 57 (Ariz. 1983)(Feldman, J., dissenting). Richmond's death sentence, however, was overturned by the United States Supreme Court on Richmond's habeas corpus petition in Richmond v. Arizona, 113 S. Ct. 528 (1992), because the state supreme court had failed to reconsider defendant's sentence after the trial judge gave weight to an unconstitutionally vague aggravating factor. The factor, "especially heinous, cruel or depraved," had not yet been adequately narrowed at the time of defendant's second sentencing. Finally, the Arizona Supreme Court itself reduced Richmond's death sentence to life imprisonment in Richmond v. State, 886 P.2d 1329 (1994), in light of the fact that defendant had been on death row for more than twenty years and there was evidence that defendant had changed since the crime.

Chapter Ten

Logic and Experience on the Civil Bench

Mary Anne's unique personal history as well as her professional experiences shaped her judicial identity on the civil bench. Beyond doubt, she had acquired an abiding self-confidence as a pathbreaker in law and in other domains. That confidence manifested itself in her judicial bearing, especially noticeable in cases that placed her in the eye of public controversy. In her demeanor and her substantive rulings, she often displayed a willingness to do the unpopular thing, to take a controversial stand; she was perhaps strengthened in that direction by her observations of Richard Roylston's resolve in the Charles Schmid case at the beginning of her state court tenure.

The civil docket in the Pima County Superior Court covered a broad spectrum of litigation, with the heaviest filings in the areas of tort, contract, and domestic relations, and occasional filings in the realm of civil rights, eminent domain, and review of agency actions.[1] Mary Anne's record in the civil arena is an amalgam of rulings that suggest the operation of quite distinct values: a deep regard for individual liberty and for equality of opportunity in dealings with the government; a respect for the obligations of contract; a sympathy for the rights of private property owners; a desire for efficiency in litigation and an impatience with misuse or delay of the litigation process; and a skepticism, if not arrogance, in regard to the decision-making of administrative agencies. As noted earlier, her rate of affirmances in the appellate courts for civil cases (62 percent)

---

1. The annual reports for the Pima County Superior Court categorized civil cases into the following types: prayer under $500, tort-motor vehicle, tort non-motor vehicle, contract, domestic relations, eminent domain, appeals, non-classified civil, habeas corpus. The actual docket for the court reflected the increase in caseload over the course of Mary Anne's state court tenure. As of January 1, 1966, for example, superior court records showed the numbers of pending cases in various categories: 546 tort motor vehicle, 422 tort non-motor vehicle, 1,528 contract, and 763 domestic relations actions. ANNUAL REPORT RELATING TO THE SUPERIOR COURT OF THE STATE OF ARIZONA PIMA COUNTY 3 (1966). By January 1, 1976, those numbers had increased to 1,543 tort motor vehicle, 1876 tort non-motor vehicle, 2,474 contract, and 2,226 domestic relations/dissolutions. ANNUAL REPORT RELATING TO THE SUPERIOR COURT OF THE STATE OF ARIZONA PIMA COUNTY 2 (1975)(Chart No. 1).

was lower than for criminal appeals (79 percent); thus, the record of her civil rulings may provide a richer window into her individuality as a judge. In particular, her reversals in the court of appeals and the Arizona Supreme Court reveal an independent adjudicator whose errors, although sometimes the result of apparent misunderstanding of the applicable law,[2] were at other times more forward-looking decisions presaging a change in the law.[3] Although she was generally a judicial moderate who disliked cre-

---

2. In *Kalav v. Pitt*, 503 P.2d 833 (Ariz. App. 1972), for example, a case was filed in Pima County Superior Court alleging violations of state and federal securities laws in connection with the sale of stock by an owner. Mary Anne, sitting without a jury, found in favor of the plaintiff and issued lengthy findings of fact and conclusions of law to the effect that defendants had failed to register the securities as required by state and federal law. She ordered rescission of the contracts of sale and a return to the plaintiff of the stock that had been sold.

Mary Anne's written order, however, contained inadequate findings and miscitations of law (a reference, for instance, to the nonexistent "Securities and Exchange Act of 1935"). Interestingly, the findings and conclusions were adopted verbatim from proposed findings and conclusions submitted by plaintiff's counsel, as is customary among trial judges. *See* Pitt v. Kalav, Cause No. 115615 (Pima County Sup. Ct. Sept. 28, 1971)(Court's Finding and Conclusions, prepared by Attorneys for Plaintiff). Mary Anne was reversed by the court of appeals, the court reasoning that the transactions that were the target of the action were exempt from registration under the relevant securities laws and that Mary Anne's conclusion to the contrary was "clearly erroneous." The appellate court wrote, "There being no findings of fact to support the trial court's conclusions of law, it is ordered that the judgment be reversed...." 503 P.2d at 838. Thus, in *Kalav*, Mary Anne seemed to simply misunderstand the securities laws.

3. In *Ashton Co. v. City of Tucson*, 441 P.2d 275 (Ariz. App. 1968), Mary Anne faced an issue of first impression in Arizona early in her tenure. The issue in *Ashton* was whether the city of Tucson could impose its business privilege tax on contracts to be performed on the campus of the University of Arizona. Ashton Company, a construction company that was under contract with the University, had paid the taxes under protest. In its refund action in court, the company argued that any tax by the city would necessarily be passed on to the University. The city, Ashton contended, would be effectively taxing another governmental agency. After a trial to the court, Mary Anne rejected Ashton's logic and ruled that the city could lawfully impose the tax, since the tax was the obligation of the contractor and not the University. The special immunity sought by the contractor likely offended Mary Anne's sense of even-handed justice.

On review at the Arizona Court of Appeals, Mary Anne's decision was reversed. Accepting the contractor's argument, the appellate court, over a dissent by Chief Judge Hathaway, held that the state constitution prohibited the city's imposition of its business privilege tax under the circumstances, since the tax "in effect...is a direct tax on the University." 441 P.2d at 277.

Mary Anne's resolution of the legal question in *Ashton* was thus short-lived. Her view of the question, however, was vindicated four years later. In City of Tempe v. Del. E. Webb Corp., 480 P.2d 18 (Ariz. App. 1971), the court of appeals overruled *Ashton* and

ating new doctrine in her courtroom,[4] she did not shy away from novel or controversial rulings when she deemed the case to call for a more activist stance.

Several cases assigned to Division 5 raised issues related to civil liberties and equality of opportunity, and Mary Anne's dispositions showed a marked sensitivity to the litigants' claims. After she had been on the bench for six years, she presided over a civil rights case that she later identified as one of the most significant cases of her state court tenure.[5] In 1970, a class action was filed on behalf of indigent chronic alcoholics in Pima County against the county's governing body. The lawsuit, captioned *Sexton v. Board of Supervisors*,[6] sought an injunction under Arizona statutory law requiring the county to provide plaintiffs, as persons suffering from a "medical sickness," with medical treatment at public expense, including detoxification on an in-patient basis. The three named plaintiffs were individuals who had suffered from chronic alcoholism over a period of years and had never received significant medical help. Instead, as they would eventually testify, whenever they were observed by law enforcement to be in a state of drunkenness, they were arrested pursuant to county policy and temporarily jailed. County policy did not entail any detoxification treatment, and the named plaintiffs had sought admission to the county hospital on several occasions but had been turned away.

The plaintiffs' counsel were Mark Raven and Peter Axelrod, two young legal aid lawyers who were fueled more by idealism than by experience. Axelrod recalled being impassioned by the plight of his clients. "The named plaintiffs were people who had been drinking for a long time and were not able to control it. They were chronic alcoholics and they weren't getting any help. Basically, they were in a box and they weren't able to

---

held that private contractors were subject to municipal business taxes even when performing contracts for state universities. The court reasoned that even if the tax were passed on to the state agency, the legal incidence of it fell only upon the private contractor. Leaving no doubt as to the import of its decision, the court stated, "Since judicial surgery is appropriate to excise a palpably wrong decision, we expressly overrule Ashton Company v. City of Tucson...." 480 P.2d at 20. Hence, the appeals court in 1971 emphatically returned to the approach that Mary Anne had decreed in 1967.

4. One lawyer who appeared before her, for example, stated that she was not the judge you wanted if your client's success depended on a novel constitutional interpretation from the court. Interview with W. Edward Morgan, Tucson, Arizona (Sept. 9, 1992).

5. In providing background information to the Senate Judiciary Committee in connection with her nomination to the United States District Court in 1976, she was asked to identify ten of the "more significant opinions" she had authored as a state court judge. The *Sexton* case was one of those she listed. *See* Personal Data Questionnaire for Nomination of Mary Anne Richey to United States District Court (March 5, 1976).

6. *See* Complaint, Civil Cause No. 121995 (Pima County Sup. Ct. Sept. 9, 1970).

climb out of it."[7] The defendant Board of Supervisors, represented by Robert Hillock, fought the *Sexton* plaintiffs' demands vigorously, since considerable public funds were at stake. Moreover, the requested characterization of alcoholism as a disease carried great symbolism at the time, since the prevailing social view was that alcoholics were weak-willed and morally to blame for their addiction. Indeed, as late as 1988, the United States Supreme Court upheld the Veterans' Administration's categorization of primary alcoholism as "willful misconduct,"[8] and commented, "This litigation does not require the Court to decide whether alcoholism is a disease whose cause its victims cannot control. It is not our role to resolve this medical issue on which the authorities remain sharply divided."[9] In the early 1970s, the categorization of alcoholism as a disease was even more controversial, but Mary Anne stepped into the fray with a definitive pronouncement.

The four and one-half day trial before Mary Anne on the requested declaratory judgment and injunction generated five hundred pages of testimony. The named plaintiffs testified at length about their struggles with alcoholism; because of their visible personal degeneration, they were effective, albeit inarticulate, witnesses. According to Axelrod, "[t]hey were fairly pathetic because of their condition. They were pretty rough and were basically street people. They told of being locked up repeatedly at the county jail and never receiving any help."[10] In one bit of compelling testimony, the wife of a named plaintiff said that when her husband was shaking badly and showing other symptoms of withdrawal, she took him to the county hospital and asked if he could be admitted. She said a nurse told her, "Hell no, we don't admit alcoholics."[11]

Much of the trial time was consumed by expert witnesses testifying as to the nature of alcoholism and the medically-indicated course of treatment. Plaintiffs' experts characterized Pima County as "behind the times" in its approach to alcoholism and testified that detoxification was essential treatment for a chronic alcoholic undergoing withdrawal.[12] Defense experts, on the other hand, disputed the need for immediate hospital-

---

7. Interview with Peter D. Axelrod, Tucson, Arizona (Aug. 14, 1995).

8. *See* Traynor v. Turnage, 485 U.S. 535 (1988)(denying veterans' argument that alcoholism was a disability under the Rehabilitation Act entitling them to continue receiving benefits after statutory period had expired).

9. 485 U.S. at 552.

10. Axelrod Interview, *supra* note 7.

11. Judy Donovan, *Hospital Rejection Alleged*, THE ARIZONA DAILY STAR, March 18, 1971.

12. Judy Donovan, *Alcoholism Treatment 'Behind Times'*, *Expert Says*, THE ARIZONA DAILY STAR, March 19, 1971.

based detoxification. Axelrod remembered that Mary Anne took the case very seriously and paid close attention to the testimony. "She listened intently to all of the witnesses, and never ever smiled, not even when a witness said something that was genuinely funny. She was just dead serious the entire time."[13]

The case involved more than a dispute about the extent of the county's legal obligation to provide medical care for indigents; it embodied a philosophical clash about the role of government in providing for the poor. In their opening statements, lawyers for both sides gave their views of the debate. Raven and Axelrod, believing strongly in their clients' cause, argued eloquently that the county's legal duty to furnish medical care to indigents extended to those who suffered from the sickness of alcoholism. Raven told Mary Anne that without treatment, detoxification will take place "in the streets, parks, flop houses or drunk tanks in jails."[14] Plaintiffs' post-trial memorandum urged Mary Anne to follow the mandate of state law and emphasized that adequate medical treatment could repair countless lives ravaged by alcoholism.[15] In contrast, Hillock, representing the county board of supervisors, contended that experts disagreed about how to treat alcoholism and that there is "no real evidence that an alcoholic is sick or suffering from a disease." He stated that "[i]t is not the county's obligation to adopt a program of social reform only to provide medical treatment."[16] In his post-trial memorandum, defense counsel argued to Mary Anne that the county was providing out-patient treatment already to indigent alcoholics and that its approach was sufficient to satisfy its legal and moral obligation. Defendants contended that the plaintiffs were seeking to force their way "into the formalized medical programs of the hospital" and suggested that the lawsuit really sought to create a form of "social programming."[17]

Mary Anne deliberated for several months after the filing of the post-trial memoranda before announcing her ruling. Although plaintiffs' counsel believed that her demeanor had been sympathetic during the hearing, they were not overly confident of prevailing. Because of the class action context and the novelty of the plaintiffs' legal theory, *Sexton* thrust Mary

---

13. Axelrod Interview, *supra* note 7.

14. *Trial Over County Aid To Alcoholics Begins*, THE ARIZONA DAILY STAR, March 17, 1971.

15. Plaintiffs' Post-Trial Memorandum, Sexton v. Board of Supervisors, Civil Cause No. 121995 (Pima County Sup. Ct. June 30, 1971).

16. *Trial Over County Aid to Alcoholics Begins*, THE ARIZONA DAILY STAR, March 17, 1971.

17. Defendant's Post-Trial Memorandum, Sexton v. Board of Supervisors, Civil Cause No. 121995 (Pima County Sup. Ct. Nov. 4, 1971).

Anne squarely, if reluctantly, into the public eye. She was quite conscious of the inevitable burden on the taxpayers of a judgment in the plaintiffs' favor, but she was also fully aware of the human costs of inadequate treatment for chronic alcoholics. Finally, one full year after the hearing, Mary Anne entered judgment in the case. Her decision, the first of its kind in Arizona, held that chronic alcoholism was a "medical sickness," that chronic alcoholics were "sick people," and that Pima County by state law had the duty to provide hospitalization and medical care for the plaintiff class, as indigent sick within the county. She went on to order that Pima County establish an interim program through which indigent chronic alcoholics could receive simple detoxification where the attending physician found it appropriate.[18] The interim order was to continue until July 1, when a community-wide program was to begin using state and federal funds. The order was both absolute in its finding of a legal duty on the part of the county, and flexible in its structure. For Axelrod, *Sexton* was the biggest public law case he ever litigated, and he was gratified that Mary Anne handed the plaintiffs a complete victory. Even Hillock, attorney for the county, reportedly complimented Mary Anne for her "diligent effort to structure the order so as to make it possible and practical for the county to comply."[19] Despite his estimate that the annual cost of treatment for indigent alcoholics would be about $50,000, Hillock thought Mary Anne's ruling was "very fair,"[20] and the county did not appeal.

Mary Anne's approach in *Sexton* illustrated several facets of her judicial temperament. She did not retreat from innovative or groundbreaking rulings if the case seemed to her to call for such action. *Sexton*, moreover, involved not just a novel legal theory but also a theory that would tax the public fisc. In spite of its inherently controversial nature, she did not back away from granting full relief to the plaintiffs. On the other hand, she was cautious. She required painstaking justification from plaintiffs' counsel, and she held the case under advisement for many months. Also, she was characteristically pragmatic: she kept in mind the fiscal impact of her ruling and structured the final order so as to afford maximum flexibility to the county. Finally, the tragic personal stories of the *Sexton* plaintiffs surely would have triggered a sympathetic reaction in most judges, but the case may have been particularly meaningful for Mary Anne because of her own memories. Her judicial attitude in *Sexton* seemed not so much a show of generalized altru-

---

18. *See* Judgment, Sexton v. Board of Supervisors, Civil Cause No. 121995 (Pima County Sup. Ct. March 27, 1971).

19. *Alcoholic-Care Ruling is Fair, Says Supervisors' Attorney*, THE ARIZONA DAILY STAR, March 3, 1972.

20. *Id.*

ism but rather the result, at least in part, of having witnessed first-hand the debilitating effects of long-term drinking in someone close to her.

In two other cases, Mary Anne likewise revealed a civil libertarian perspective but her rulings met with reversal in the court of appeals. In *Civil Service Commission v. Livingston*,[21] Mary Anne struck down as unconstitutional a Tucson civil service regulation under which a police officer had been discharged from employment by the department. Livingston was accused of having left his duties to attend a "licentious and morally unacceptable party," and of having sexual intercourse with a woman of known disrepute at the party. The Civil Service Commission upheld Livingston's discharge, finding his actions to have violated, among other rules, a regulation that proscribed "conduct unbecoming an officer." Livingston challenged the Commission's ruling in superior court by means of a special action.

By her judgment entered in October 1973, Mary Anne's struggle with the case was apparent. She found that the regulation under which Livingston was discharged was "unconstitutionally vague, indefinite, and overbroad," and she ordered that Livingston be reinstated with back pay. Nevertheless, she qualified her ruling. In her minute entry, she wrote, "In the event it is later determined that the Civil Service commission acted within its jurisdiction and legal authority, the decision of the Board was not arbitrary, capricious, or an abuse of discretion." Thus, Mary Anne quite clearly decided the proscription of "conduct unbecoming an officer" failed to give adequate notice of the precise nature of the forbidden behaviors, but her confidence in that decision was less than absolute.

The court of appeals reversed Mary Anne's ruling. Rather than relying on the specific regulation cited by the Commission, the court of appeals looked to the broader authority in the city charter and implementing ordinances to discharge city employees for "just cause." "Just cause," to the appellate court, meant the violation of "implicit standards of good behavior," such that a reasonable officer would have known that the challenged conduct was prohibited. Finding that Livingston's conduct was reasonably prohibited, the court stated that the "question of overbreadth of the regulation is irrelevant."[22] Thus, according to the court, Mary Anne erred in overturning Livingston's discharge.

In *Livingston*, Mary Anne was motivated by a libertarian inclination. As a woman who had often defied cultural mores, she was tolerant of a range of behaviors and eschewed moralistic pronouncements. Livingston arguably had caused no harm by his consensual sexual conduct, and

---

21. 525 P.2d 949 (Ariz. App. 1974).
22. 525 P.2d at 954.

Mary Anne was reluctant to affirm his discharge on that basis alone. Indeed, at the hearing before Mary Anne and on appeal, Livingston argued that he did not know his companion was a prostitute, and he emphasized that neither he nor the companion was married. Unlike the three judges on the court of appeals, Mary Anne was uncomfortable inferring standards of behavior "imposed upon one who stands in the public eye as an upholder of that which is morally and legally correct."[23] In addition, Mary Anne's reaction in *Livingston* evidenced a distrust of vague rules and a respect for the value of fair notice.

In the last of the trio of civil liberties cases, Mary Anne again condemned a governmental employment decision that she deemed unfair, but again, according to the court of appeals, she miscalled the law. In *Indian Oasis School District No. 40 v. Zambrano*,[24] two school teachers sued the Indian Oasis district for damages for the district's termination of their probationary teaching contracts without adequate notice or hearing. The plaintiffs were represented by Ed Morgan, the civil rights lawyer who had litigated against Mary Anne in the U.S. Attorney's Office and with whom Mary Anne enjoyed a relationship of mutual respect. The stipulated facts in the case showed that the two plaintiffs had been terminated mid-year for "lack of cooperation" and "insubordination" and their contracts were not renewed for the coming year. Although the plaintiffs alleged a violation of constitutionally-protected due process rights as well as a breach of state-mandated procedures, Mary Anne apparently relied only on state law grounds in the disposition of the case. She found that the school district violated state statutory law by failing to send written notice of the causes for the recommended dismissal and by failing to hold a meaningful hearing. She therefore set aside the Board's termination of the existing contracts and its non-renewal of the contracts for the future. Moreover, in Mary Anne's view, both plaintiffs were entitled to lost salary not only for the mid-year terminations but also for the Board's failure to renew the contracts.[25]

In the view of the court of appeals, Mary Anne had been too generous in her approach to the plaintiffs' claims. The appellate judges agreed that the two teachers were entitled to damages for the summary mid-year termination of their contracts under state law, reasoning that the "teachers were not afforded a 'hearing' which comports with due process requirements."[26] Nevertheless, the court held that the relevant Arizona statutory

---

23. *Id.*

24. 526 P.2d 408 (Ariz. App. 1974).

25. Minute Entry of March 1, 1973; Judgment of October 4, 1973, in Zambrano v. Indian Oasis School District No. 40, Civ. Cause No. 118374 (Pima County Sup. Ct.).

26. 526 P.2d at 411.

and decisional law did not require the school board to give the teachers a full hearing on the non-renewal of their contracts for the future. "The reasons given by the School Board for non-renewal were not subject to judicial scrutiny," the court pointedly wrote,[27] and remanded the case for a determination of damages sustained solely by reason of the wrongful termination. Thus, Mary Anne's conclusion that the plaintiffs were entitled to damages for the non-renewal of their contracts was in error. That ruling, according to the lawyer for the school board, "was very much in character for the judge. She was by nature sympathetic to the downtrodden."[28]

The plaintiffs' claims in *Zambrano* were on the cutting edge of the evolving constitutional law of procedural due process. Through a series of contemporaneous cases, the Supreme Court had expanded the notion of "property" and "due process of law" within the meaning of the due process clause of the fourteenth amendment.[29] Inevitably, the question of the due process rights of probationary employees had come before the Court. One year before Mary Anne's decision, the Court held in *Board of Regents v. Roth*,[30] that an untenured teacher at a state university did not have a due process right to a hearing prior to the university's decision not to renew his contract. There, as in *Zambrano*, the applicable state law left the renewal decision to the "unfettered discretion of university officials."[31] Despite the evident weakness of the plaintiffs' constitutional claims in *Zambrano* in light of *Roth*, Mary Anne had awarded the *Zambrano* plaintiffs full damages based on her abiding sense that they had been unfairly treated by the school board. She was quite willing to stretch Arizona's statutory law to compensate the plaintiffs even for the nonrenewal of their contracts.

Another substantive theme that surfaced in several of Mary Anne's decisions was a respect for the rights of private property owners. As a property owner herself, she took immense pleasure in the haven at the edge of the foothills where she and Bill lived throughout their marriage. She val-

---

27. 526 P.2d at 412.

28. Interview with Hon. Lawrence Ollason, United States Bankruptcy Judge, Tucson, Arizona (Feb. 27, 1996).

29. *See* Goldberg v. Kelly, 397 U.S. 254 (1970)(welfare recipient had due process right to hearing before termination of benefits); Bell v. Burson, 402 U.S. 535 (1971)(driver had due process right to hearing before suspension of his license); Sniadach v. Family Finance Corp., 395 U.S. 337 (1969)(pre-judgment garnishment of wages without a prior adversary hearing violated debtor's due process rights); Fuentes v. Shevin, 407 U.S. 67 (1972) (prejudgment replevin of household goods without prior hearing violated debtor's due process rights).

30. 408 U.S. 564 (1972).

31. 408 U.S. at 567.

ued her privacy and her freedom to use her property as she chose, without governmental intrusion. Consistent with her worldview, she granted judicial relief in a variety of contexts to petitioning property owners as against an administrative authority, only to see her decisions reversed on appeal. For example, she ruled in favor of a property owner seeking a liquor license and ordered the Arizona State Liquor Board to grant the license over the Board's objection[32]; she ruled in favor of a developer seeking to avoid the requirement of paved streets and ordered the Pima County Board of Supervisors to approve a proposed plat over its objection[33]; and she ruled in favor of a mining company seeking to lower its tax base and found a property valuation by the State Board of Tax Appeals to be excessive.[34] In each case, Mary Anne's vigorous protection of the property owner was overturned on appeal, thus suggesting that her understanding of the limits of her authority may have been skewed by her personal values. Indeed, the reviewing courts remarked on her readiness to second-guess the administrative agencies. In the dispute involving the liquor license application, the court of appeals wrote, "Just as the courts cannot sit as super zoning boards, nor as a super school board, they cannot sit as a super State Liquor Board."[35] Similarly, in the tax appeal, the Arizona Supreme Court cautioned, "a trial court in reviewing the action of the Board of Tax Appeals may superimpose its opinion only in the event that the State agency abused its legislatively-delegated duty."[36] In each of the mentioned cases, Mary Anne clearly did assume the authority to substitute her views about the issue at hand for that of the appropriate agency, fueled apparently by her view that the agency had acted unfairly *vis a vis* the property owner.

In another case involving review of administrative action, Mary Anne again came down solidly on the side of the property owner and was again reversed, notwithstanding the fact that her decision there actually supported the agency action. In *Ivancovich v. City of Tucson Board of Adjustment*,[37] the Board of Adjustment had granted a variance to Levy's, a major Tucson department store, to permit it to build a third story. The store was located in the city's first shopping "mall," a shopping center situated in an upper-income residential area. Because the proposed third

---

32. Arizona State Liquor Board v. Jacob, 511 P.2d 179 (Ariz. App. 1973).

33. Pima County v. Arizona Title Insurance & Trust Co., 565 P.2d 524 (Ariz. App. 1977).

34. *See* Mohave County v. Duval Corp., 579 P.2d 1075 (Ariz. 1978).

35. Arizona State Liquor Board v. Jacobs, 511 P.2d 179, 183 (Ariz. App. 1973).

36. Mohave County v. Duval Corp., 579 P.2d 1075, 1081 (Ariz. 1978).

37. 529 P.2d 242 (Ariz. App. 1975).

story might detract from the aesthetics of the surrounding neighborhoods and would undoubtedly increase traffic congestion, nearby residents attended the public hearings on the variance in large numbers. The Tucson code at that time conditioned the granting of a variance on a showing by the petitioning property owner that it would face "exceptional" practical difficulties and "exceptional" undue hardship without the variance. To meet that standard, Levy's put on evidence at the hearing that the store would be more profitable with a third floor and that it would decrease in value if it were not allowed to expand. Notwithstanding objections from residents of the surrounding affluent neighborhoods, the Board found that the variance was needed "to preserve substantial property rights and [would] not be detrimental to the public good or impair the purpose of the Zoning Code."[38]

After the decision of the Board, local homeowners brought a special action in superior court to challenge the variance, and the case was assigned to Mary Anne. The dispute attracted media attention, and some of the most prominent lawyers in the state were involved in the litigation.[39] After hearing objections from the homeowners in her courtroom, Mary Anne affirmed the action of the Board. In her ruling, she explicitly found that the Board had jurisdiction to grant the height variance and that the evidence presented at the hearing supported the Board's findings.[40] The court of appeals, however, reversed, emphasizing that the criteria for the variance had not been met and that the Board, contrary to Mary Anne's ruling, lacked jurisdiction. Indeed, the court characterized Levy's arguments about potential loss of value as "wholly speculative and unsupported by the evidence," and added sarcastically that such a "'hari-kari' theory of valuation is as elusive as the Scarlet Pimpernel and just as fictional."[41]

From the viewpoint of the appellate court, the Board's lack of authority was indisputable. Mary Anne's ruling in favor of the variance showed that she was convinced otherwise. She also likely believed that the variance would best serve the interests of the commercial property owner without unduly harming the goals of the zoning code. As it happened, the Tucson City Council ultimately granted a zoning change to permit Levy's to build its third story, perhaps vindicating Mary Anne's own assessment

---

38. *Ivancovich*, 529 P.2d at 246 (quoting the findings of the Board of Adjustment).

39. Representing the store were Marvin S. Cohen of Bilby, Thompson, Shoenhair & Warnock, and Thomas Chandler of Chandler, Tullar, Udall & Richmond. Gordon S. Kipps of Kipps & Salter represented the homeowners. *See* 529 P.2d at 243.

40. *Court Upholds Levy's Permit For 3rd Story*, THE ARIZONA DAILY STAR, December 4, 1973.

41. 529 P.2d at 249.

of the conflicting interests involved.[42] Her decree in *Ivancovich* paralleled her decisions in other cases involving agency action to the extent it manifested an anti-regulatory bias favoring the rights of private property owners. Although *Ivancovich* implicated the rights of property owners on both sides of the litigation, the impact of the variance on homeowners in surrounding neighborhoods was indirect. The denial of the variance, however, would have had a direct impact on the commercial owner by prohibiting it from engaging in the most lucrative use of its property. Thus, Mary Anne's decision favoring the commercial property owner again may have reflected her deep regard for ownership rights and a skepticism about the value of governmental regulation.

In the arena of tort law, Mary Anne displayed a mix of judicial attitudes. In some cases she issued rulings that arguably reflected pronounced sympathy for plaintiffs at the expense of established principles of tort law.[43] In other cases her judicial actions evinced a reluctance to extend liability to particular defendants, especially those whose alleged fault was merely passive.[44] One veteran defense lawyer believed she would favor the plaintiff in a close case and that she and other judges "would usually give the plaintiff the benefit of the doubt." On the other hand, the same attorney opined that "Mary Anne would take a case from the jury more readily than some other judges. She was willing to make that decision, if she felt that there wasn't enough evidence."[45] Mary Anne's many years as a trial lawyer equipped her to evaluate evidence with some degree of confidence, and in most cases her assessments were upheld.

A pair of rulings from Mary Anne's court suggest that her sensitivity to the rights of private property owners shaped her judgment in the tort realm as well as other contexts. The 1971 case of *Hall v. Mertz*[46] involved a personal injury lawsuit brought on behalf of a young girl who had been hit by a car and injured while bicycling through an intersection in Tucson. The plaintiff sued the City of Tucson, the driver of the car, and the property owner whose shrubbery had allegedly obstructed the driver's view. At the close of the plaintiff's evidence in a trial to the court, Mary Anne dismissed the action as against the property owner, finding that the owner owed no legal "duty" to the plaintiff. In her order, Mary Anne explicitly relied on a decision from the court of appeals barring common law liabil-

---

42. *See* 529 P.2d at 243 n.1.

43. *See, e.g.,* Chesin Construction Co. v. Epstein, 446 P.2d 11 (Ariz. App. 1968)(holding that trial court erred in imposing liability on general contractor, where general contractor had no supervisory authority over the negligent activity of the subcontractor).

44. *See, e.g.,* Rogers v. Unimac Company, 565 P.2d 181 (Ariz. 1977).

45. Interview with David Burr Udall, Tucson, Arizona (Dec. 13, 1995).

46. 480 P.2d 361 (Ariz. App. 1971).

ity of landowners for injuries caused by obstructions on their property.[47] The court of appeals reversed on a theory of negligence *per se*. According to the court, the defendant property owner had violated a Tucson city ordinance prohibiting owners from allowing obstructions on their property to interfere with traffic visibility at an intersection. Less than a year later, a similar question involving the same Tucson ordinance arose in the context of a wrongful death suit. In *Slavin v. City of Tucson*,[48] a motorist was killed in a Tucson intersection when his car was struck by another automobile traveling through the intersection. The victim's widow brought a wrongful death action against not only the other driver but also the owner of a residence at the intersection and the City of Tucson. After the close of the evidence at trial, Mary Anne directed a verdict in favor of the property owner and the city. Although her minute entry does not reveal the reasoning for the directed verdict, Mary Anne apparently accepted the defendants' arguments that the negligence per se theory of *Hall* did not apply on the facts before her. Mary Anne was again reversed by the court of appeals. Although the appellate court agreed that the city was not liable, the court held that the evidence supported a finding of a *per se* violation of the Tucson ordinance as against the property owner.

Mary Anne's ruling in *Slavin* is noteworthy because it came on the heels of a reversal on the same issue in *Hall*. Indeed, Mary Anne granted the motion for directed verdict in *Slavin* less than four months after the reversal came down in *Hall*, and court filings show that the authority of *Hall* was argued to Mary Anne.[49] In both cases, she was unwilling to extend tort liability to a landowner who unwittingly had violated the city code. Her back-to-back reversals suggest a stubborn reluctance to impose tort liability on a theory of negligence *per se* where the end result would be an incursion on the freedom of property owners.

On the other hand, two decisions from Mary Anne's court involving uninsured motorist coverage suggest a pro-compensation bias on her part. In addition, they show the earnestness with which Mary Anne approached the task of adjudicating. In *State Farm Fire & Casualty v. Rossini*,[50] Mary Anne's willingness to stretch the law to obtain a plaintiff-

---

47. Mary Anne stated in her order: "A landowner under the holding of Rodgers v. Ray, 10 Ariz. App. 119, cannot be held legally liable for injuries to persons occurring on streets adjacent to his property even if caused by a structure created or maintained by him on his property and even if such structure or planting obstructed the vision of the persons using a public street or highway." Hall v. Mertz, 480 P.2d 361, 362 (Ariz. 1971).

48. 495 P.2d 141 (Ariz. App. 1972).

49. *See* Plaintiff's Trial Memorandum; Plaintiff's Motion for New Trial, Slavin v. City of Tucson, Civ. Cause No. 119263 (Pima County Sup. Ct. 1971).

50. 490 P.2d 567 (Ariz. 1971).

favoring result was rebuffed by the Arizona Supreme Court. There, Rossini had been injured while a passenger in a car driven by his son. The injury occurred when the car was hit by another vehicle, driven by an uninsured motorist. After the accident, Rossini executed a release of the driver of the other car so that his son, who had arranged the release, could regain his driver's license. When Rossini attempted to collect on his uninsured motorist coverage with his own insurance company, the company refused to pay because of the unauthorized release in violation of the policy, prompting Rossini to file suit.

After a trial to the court, Mary Anne found that Rossini had uninsured motorist coverage, notwithstanding the release.[51] She apparently determined that the release was not supported by consideration and therefore was not binding on the parties.[52] Viewing the evidence in totality, she concluded that Rossini's signing of the release at his son's request did not void the policy. Mary Anne's ruling, however, did not survive scrutiny on appeal. The supreme court held that the release was a direct violation of the terms of the policy and thus absolved the insurance company of any liability. The opinion is devoid of any recognition of the interests of Rossini. "Although by signing the release," Jack Hays wrote for the court, "Rossini accomplished more than he had intended, the fact remains that he did bestow a benefit...on his son [the procurement of his driver's license]...and the benefit bestowed was the inducement for the signature. We find, therefore that the release executed by Rossini was a valid release fully supported by consideration."[53]

Mary Anne did not overlook the *Rossini* decision when it was announced, and her ruling on a similar question a few years later is telling. In *Dairyland Ins. Co. v. Lopez*,[54] Mary Anne again faced the question of the availability of uninsured motorist coverage, and she again sided with the insured against the insurer but not without manifest ambivalence. There, a husband and wife were injured in an automobile accident caused by two other vehicles, one insured and the other uninsured. Without the consent of their own insurance carrier, the Lopez couple settled their potential claim against the insured driver for a small sum. When they tried to collect on their uninsured motorist policy, the insurance company balked, arguing that the earlier settlement in violation of the insurance agreement had voided the policy. The company's subsequent declaratory

---

51. Declaratory Judgment, State Farm Fire & Casualty Company v. Rossini, Civ. Cause No. 109087 (Pima County Sup. Ct. filed Feb. 25, 1970). In character, Mary Anne also determined that the company's liability on the policy was subject to arbitration.

52. 490 P.2d at 570.

53. *Id.*

54. 526 P.2d 1264 (Ariz. App. 1974).

judgment action seeking determination of non-coverage was assigned to Mary Anne.

With cross-motions for summary judgment before her, Mary Anne at first ruled in favor of the insurance company. In a minute entry granting the company's motion, she stated that she was relying on *Rossini*, although it had not been cited by counsel. Nevertheless, the plaintiffs' tenacious attorney did not give up. Stanley Feldman, who was a prominent personal injury lawyer in Arizona and later would be appointed to the Arizona Supreme Court, moved for reconsideration of the order that had been entered against his clients.[55] He argued that *Rossini* was distinguishable and that his clients' coverage was still in effect. Two and half months later, Mary Anne, on reconsideration, withdrew the original order and granted the Lopez' motion for summary judgment.

On appeal to the Arizona Court of Appeals, Mary Anne's belated judgment in favor of the Lopez couple was affirmed. Like Mary Anne, the higher court concluded that *Rossini* was distinguishable. Moreover, the appeals court questioned the continued validity of *Rossini* in light of the state's move to mandatory uninsured motorist coverage. By the time of the *Lopez* appeal, Arizona had mandated coverage and had also strengthened considerably the public policy underlying uninsured motorist coverage. The amended statutes eliminated the possibility of an insured's waiving coverage and prohibited the carrier from denying coverage based solely on a contractual breach.[56] In light of the new laws, the court in *Lopez* held that the contractual provision on which the insurance company had relied in *Lopez* was void.

In both *Rossini* and *Lopez*, Mary Anne ultimately ruled in favor of compensation to the injured parties. Her decision after reconsideration in *Lopez* showed a confidence in her own ability to predict a new direction in the law. In *Lopez*, moreover, she rendered a judgment that, while ostensibly contradicting the spirit of the supreme court's opinion in *Rossini*, was in keeping with the newly strengthened public policy regarding uninsured motorist coverage. Her decisions in *Rossini* and *Lopez* together revealed her efforts to faithfully apply the established law, her willingness to heed counsel when valid reasons for reconsideration were advanced, and her readiness to move the law forward.

Mary Anne's apparent plaintiff-favoring bias did not dominate her adjudications in the tort arena by any means. To the contrary, she exhibited a

---

55. Defendant's Motion for Reconsideration, Dairyland Insurance Company v. Lopez, Civ. Cause No. 142439 (Pima County Sup. Ct. filed Sept. 10, 1973.

56. The statutes examined in *Lopez* were the newly amended Financial Responsibility Act. The strong prohibition on avoiding coverage was found in Ariz. Rev. Stat. Sec. 28-1170(F)(1).

readiness to take a case from the jury where she found an insufficient evidentiary showing or an inadequate legal theory.[57] She directed a verdict in favor of the local newspaper in a high profile libel action, for example,[58] despite her awareness that she might be perceived as currying favor with the press.[59] Her handling of another closely-watched case reveals the tension between her desire to avoid unnecessary or meritless litigation and the traditional policy of the civil justice system favoring jury resolution. In *Rogers v. Unimac Company*[60] she directed a verdict for the defense in a product liability suit but only after a somewhat unusual show of ambivalence. The case attracted attention among tort lawyers because of its implications for strict product liability doctrine.[61] The plaintiff in *Rogers* was a young man who had been injured while employed at a commercial car wash. Alleging that he had suffered injuries when his arm was caught in a washer-extractor used at the car wash, he filed suit against the manufacturer of the machine. At the trial in Mary Anne's court, held in late 1975, the plaintiff failed to produce evidence to support any available theory of liability. Instead, the evidence revealed that he was injured because the machine had not been properly maintained by the car wash operators.

Mary Anne worked diligently on the instructions on strict liability and failure to warn, and the case file shows her careful review of the instructions proposed by the parties. Because the evolving doctrine of strict

---

57. In Mather v. Caterpillar Tractor Corp., 533 P.2d 717 (Ariz. App. 1975), for example, Mary Anne directed a verdict against the plaintiff in favor of the manufacturer of a tractor on which the plaintiff's husband had been killed. In so doing, she explained that since she was going to submit the case to the jury on the basis of strict liability, the negligence count was superfluous and would tend to confuse the jurors. As it happened, the jury returned a defense verdict on strict liability. The appeals court affirmed Mary Anne's handling of the case in all respects.

58. Minute Entry Granting Directed Verdict, Tucson House, Inc. v. Star Publishing, Cause No. 90873 (Pima County Sup. Ct. filed March 3, 1967).

59. Interview with S. Thomas Chandler, Attorney for Star Publishing, Tucson, Arizona (Oct. 13, 1992).

60. 565 P.2d 181 (Ariz. 1977).

61. The Arizona Trial Lawyers Assocation filed a brief amicus curiae in the case to urge the court to not impose too onerous a burden of proof on tort plaintiffs. The legal dispute apparently centered on whether the plaintiff was required to show not only a design defect in the product but also that the product was unreasonably dangerous. *See Rogers*, 565 P.2d at 183. Because of the attention focused on the case, the Arizona Supreme Court took the unusual step of transferring the case from the Arizona Court of Appeals to the supreme court's docket. *Id.* at 182(citing to then Rule 47(e)(5) of the Rules of the Supreme Court).

products liability contained ambiguities, the compilation of accurate instructions was a challenging exercise.[62] At the close of the plaintiff's case, Mary Anne had doubts about the sufficiency of the plaintiff's evidence but she nevertheless denied the defendant's motion for a directed verdict. After the jury was unable to reach a verdict, Mary Anne declared a mistrial and then belatedly granted the defendant's motion for a directed verdict, apparently believing that a second trial would be a waste of time.[63] Mary Anne's assessment of the deficiencies in the plaintiff's case was affirmed on appeal,[64] the Arizona Supreme Court reasoning that plaintiff had not shown that the machine was unreasonably dangerous or that there had been a causative failure to warn by the manufacturer.

The sequence of events in Mary Anne's court in *Rogers* showed that she struggled over whether the case should go to the jury. According to William Kimble, who represented the manufacturer, Mary Anne denied the initial motion for a directed verdict "reluctantly." He explained, "I think she felt we were entitled to the directed verdict, but she thought she would let it go to the jury out of caution. Then, when the jury couldn't agree, she just ended it."[65] Mary Anne's initial caution in *Rogers* was pragmatic: a defense verdict from the jury would have obviated altogether the need for the judge to assess the sufficiency of the evidence. When the jury failed to reach a verdict, however, Mary Anne chose not to duck the question. At that point, she was willing to direct a verdict on the basis of insufficient evidence rather than endure a possibly futile second trial.

Although Mary Anne's dislike for domestic relations disputes was well-known, she gave the burgeoning divorce docket her full attention when cases assigned to Division 5 raised what she viewed as serious issues, and a few of her rulings became important precedents for the domestic relations bar. Her insistence on fair dealing and her conviction that people ought to meet their contractual and parental obligations surfaced in at least one noteworthy ruling in the domestic relations field fairly late in Mary Anne's tenure on the state court bench. In *Ruhsam v. Ruhsam*,[66] the Supreme Court of Arizona ultimately affirmed a ruling by Mary Anne in a

---

62. Not until 1976 did the Arizona Supreme Court make clear that a plaintiff relying on strict liability theory had to establish that the product was defective, that the defect made the product unreasonably dangerous, and that the defect was the proximate cause of the injury. *See* Byrns v. Riddell, 550 P.2d 1065 (Ariz. 1976).

63. Minute Entry, Rogers v. Unimac Company, Civ. Cause No. 145146 (Pima County Sup. Ct. Dec. 8, 1975)(declaring mistrial and then directing verdict for defendant).

64. 565 P.2d 181 (Ariz. 1977).

65. Interview with William Kimble, Tucson, Arizona (Sept. 29, 1995).

66. 518 P.2d 576 (Ariz. 1974).

bitter divorce suit that had occupied the superior court docket for years. The ruling that was at issue concerned the interpretation of a postnuptial agreement which gave custody of the divorcing couple's three minor children to the wife and obligated the husband to pay $100 per month for each child until "emancipated by marriage, majority, or…death." At the time of the divorce, Arizona law defined majority to mean "the age of twenty-one years or more," but in 1972 the legislature amended the statute to read "eighteen years or more." *Ruhsam* raised an issue of first impression in Arizona of how to interpret the contractual term "majority" after the legislative change.

After a hard-fought hearing on the matter, Mary Anne ruled that at the time of execution of the agreement, "the word 'majority' was understood by both the parties to mean twenty-one years of age." She was not persuaded by the husband's argument that he meant to obligate himself to support his children only so long as a legal obligation to do so existed, and she may have been put off by his interjection of his wife's alleged marital infidelity into the child support dispute.[67] Mary Anne concluded that the new state law lowering the age of majority to eighteen had no effect on the contract, and she therefore ordered the father to comply with the terms of the agreement.[68] In so ruling, she upheld the expectations of the mother as custodial parent and her justifiable reliance on continuing support.

Although Mary Anne's ruling met with reversal in the court of appeals,[69] that decision in turn was set aside by the Arizona Supreme Court. The high court agreed with Mary Anne that the child support obligation should be defined by the terms of the contract and the intention of the parties at the time of contracting.[70] Mary Anne was undoubtedly pleased with the affirmance in *Ruhsam* and later identified her ruling in the case as one of her "more significant opinions.[71]

---

67. *See* Affidavit of Hugh P.V. Ruhsam, Ruhsam v. Ruhsam, Civ. Cause No. 116285 (Pima County Sup. Ct. Dec. 3, 1972 (accusing wife of surreptitiously carrying on affair during marriage).

68. Minute Entry, Ruhsam v. Ruhsam, Civ. Cause No. 116285 (Pima County Sup. Ct. Feb. 1, 1973).

69. *See* Ruhsam v. Ruhsam, 515 P.2d 1199 (Ariz. App 1973).

70. *See Ruhsam*, 518 P.2d at 578: "We therefore hold that under the contract of the parties, by the use of the word 'majority,' Hugh P.V. Ruhsam became indebted to Joan M. Ruhsam for the sum of $100.00 a month for each of his three children until each reached the age of twenty-one years."

71. Mary Anne identified the case as one of her more significant opinions in her responses to the questionnaire submitted in connection with her nomination to the federal court. *See* Personal Data Questionnaire, *supra* note 5.

Mary Anne again revealed a somewhat hard-nosed approach to contractual enforcement in the context of divorce two years later in *Marshick v. Marshick*.[72] The case involved a dispute over the enforceability of a property settlement agreement that had been entered into at the time of the parties' divorce. The agreement, giving the wife custody of the minor children and obligating the husband to pay child support, alimony, and half the children's college expenses, had been approved of by the divorce court. When the agreement was executed, Mr. Marshick had been earning $40,000 annually as an engineering consultant. He unilaterally stopped his monthly payments of $900 four years later when he "fell upon hard times." He ultimately lost his job and began receiving unemployment benefits.[73] Nevertheless, after a bench trial, Mary Anne rendered judgment in favor of Mrs. Marshick for over $15,000 of past-due support and rejected Mr. Marshick's argument that his duty to perform was discharged by the doctrine of "impossibility." She also rejected the husband's argument that the agreement had been "merged" in the divorce decree and thereby rendered unenforceable as a matter of contract. Mary Anne's ruling in *Marshick*, which was affirmed in all respects in the court of appeals, showed her determined resolve to enforce agreements entered into at divorce and her lack of sympathy for arguments intending to excuse non-performance.

A third case in the domestic arena reveals a parallel insistence on respect for contractual obligation. In *Randolph v. Howard*,[74] Mary Anne refused to lower the amount of money that a father had agreed to pay for his son's college education, and her ruling was likewise affirmed. The father, represented by Ed Scruggs (who had given Mary Anne her first job as a lawyer), had agreed at the time of divorce to "pay all usual and customary expenditures which may occur in the normal four-year college education of [his child] at a school of higher learning selected by said child." Fifteen years later, after the custodial mother had relocated to Arizona, the child was accepted at Wabash College. When the father refused to pay the son's tuition, the mother went to court seeking an order compelling the father's payment. Remarried and with additional expenses of his own, the father argued that tuition at Wabash was significantly higher than at other schools and that, in light of his remarriage, his support obligation should be modified to reflect a more modest rate of tuition. Mary Anne found that father had not shown adequate justification for modifying the original order, and she noted that the agreement gave the son the right to

---

72. 545 P.2d 436 (Ariz. App. 1976).
73. *Marshick*, 545 P.2d at 437.
74. 491 P.2d 841 (Ariz. App. 1972).

choose his college. She probably shared the appellate court's perception that the father's primary reason for attacking the decree was the "feeling that he made a 'bad bargain.'"[75]

Mary Anne's decisions in *Ruhsam*, *Marshick*, and *Randolph* reflected a desire to hold people to their promises, especially within the family domain. Each case presented an economically dependent wife as custodial mother seeking relief primarily for the benefit of her children, and in each case Mary Anne found in favor of the mother. Although Mary Anne had chosen to follow a nontraditional path in her own life and in her marriage, she held no disrespect for women who adhered to the traditional model. Thus, when economically-dependent former wives appeared in her court seeking to enforce the terms of property settlements, Mary Anne readily granted relief.[76] Moreover, she may have been particularly intent on enforcing the obligations of parenthood against recalcitrant fathers.

Mary Anne displayed a somewhat erratic regard for civil process values during her tenure on the superior court. In some contexts she actively protected a litigant's right to a full hearing on his or her particular claim, but in other circumstances she seemed to disregard the value of individualized process for the sake of expediency and judicial economy. She sometimes exhibited a predilection for disposing of litigation other than on the merits. Thus, for example, she closed the courthouse door too quickly on one tort plaintiff's case on a theory of res judicata, only to be reversed by the court of appeals.[77] In that case, the appellate court pointedly reminded her that the "[the plaintiff] did not have his day in court."[78] The blend of concerns evident in her rulings reflected the disparate values that operated within her life. On the one hand, Mary Anne had deep respect for civil litigation as a means of securing redress for wrongs suffered, a respect that was first kindled when she had worked as a reporter in Shelbyville, Indiana. On the other hand, her years as a prosecutor, as a private practi-

---

75. 491 P.2d at 843.

76. Mary Anne's decision in another case may also reflect a sympathy for the economically disadvantaged wife in a traditional marriage, but the case pitted the wife against a federal credit union rather than a former spouse. In *Tucson Telco Federal Credit Union v. Bowser*, 451 P.2d 322 (Ariz. App. 1969), Mary Anne granted summary judgment for plaintiff under the federal Soldiers and Sailors Civil Relief Act of 1940, 50 U.S.C. Secs. 532–36. The act protected military personnel and their dependents from certain actions by creditors where the service person's ability to pay had been impaired by military service. Although the facts probably went beyond what Congress had intended in the statute, the literal words of the statute allowed for the result Mary Anne reached.

77. Burrell v. Southern Pacific Co., Civ. Cause No. 108758 (Pima County Sup. Ct.), *rev'd*, 474 P.2d 466 (Ariz. App. 1970).

78. 474 P.2d at 468.

tioner, and as a judge imbued her with a skepticism about the utility of litigation in certain circumstances, and she may have prided herself on having developed an ability to identify frivolous arguments and meritless claims.

In several cases, Mary Anne faced the fundamental question of whether to set aside a default judgment. Because trial judges have broad discretion in deciding the question and appellate courts rarely reverse such decisions, the fate of Mary Anne's rulings on default judgments in the court of appeals must have provoked her consternation. In an early case, *Campbell v. Frazer Construction Company*,[79] the plaintiff sued the defendant company and its chief officer for breach of contract and negligence, and personal service was effected at the company's place of business. When the defendants failed to file a timely answer, the plaintiff secured entry of default and, ultimately, a default judgment. The judgment was entered only twenty-seven days after service of the complaint. Four days later, the defendants moved to set aside the default judgment. In an affidavit submitted to Mary Anne, the individual defendant maintained that he had misread the summons and wrongly believed he had thirty days in which to answer, and he also made a showing of a valid defense on the merits. On the basis of the affidavit, Mary Anne granted the motion to set aside. Most likely, the short passage of time and the defendant's showing of plausible defenses made her quite comfortable with the decision to set aside the default and allow the case to be litigated.

In an unusual move, the court of appeals reversed, notwithstanding the broad discretion vested in trial courts on such matters and the strong policy favoring a trial on the merits. "Despite the overwhelming majority favoring the setting aside of defaults," the court explained, "we do not believe that the 'discretion' of the trial judge is unlimited."[80] The appellate court concluded that Mary Anne had abused her discretion because the defendants had failed to show unusual circumstances warranting relief. The defendants' innocent mistake, and their prompt attempt to remedy the error, were insufficient. In somewhat didactic prose, the appellate court wrote, "We believe there is more at stake than merely 'harm' to the plaintiff. Judicial proceedings merit some dignity in and of themselves.... Any delay in prosecuting a valid claim is 'harm' in some degree to the claimant."[81] The reversal, rendered over a strong dissent, clearly conveyed a message to Mary Anne. By implication, she was accused of ignoring the rule of law and adjudicating out of sympathy or a subjective sense of fairness. Referring to her

---

79. 451 P.2d 620 (Ariz. App. 1969).

80. 451 P.2d at 621.

81. 451 P.2d at 622.

disposition, the appeals court wrote, "We do not believe that a trial court should have discretion, without a standard upon which to base that discretion, to change [the prescribed time limits for answering a complaint]."[82] Thus, the appellate court effectively accused Mary Anne of having substituted her notions of fairness for the express terms of the rule.

Three years later, the same issue came before Mary Anne, and her ruling reflected the lesson she had received in *Campbell*. In *Cota v. Southern Arizona Bank & Trust Company*,[83] an individual defendant defaulted in a lawsuit brought to recover sums due on a promissory note. After the default judgment was entered, the defendant sought to have it set aside. His argument was based in part on his slight knowledge of English and his illiteracy, as well as a substantive defense on the merits. Mary Anne, no doubt still mindful of the words of the *Campbell* opinion, refused to set aside the judgment. Believing that no extraordinary showing had been made to justify setting aside the default, and perhaps doubting that the defendant had a meritorious defense, she denied relief. Indeed, the file in *Cota* revealed that the defendant had had a history of debt evasion.[84] The court of appeals, however, held that the default judgment should have been set aside. Without even citing *Campbell*, the court concluded that the defendant's illiteracy constituted a sufficient excuse for the failure to answer and that defendant's allegation of duress raised a meritorious defense. The court wrote, "There are many Spanish-speaking persons in Arizona who are unable to speak or read English or who are greatly limited in the use of the English language. When their linguistic handicap causes them to fail to answer a complaint, they should not be penalized by the extreme sanction of a default judgment, provided a meritorious defense exists."[85] Thus, the appellate court portrayed the trial judge as needlessly severe, and the condemning tone of the opinion must have stung Mary Anne. Nevertheless, Mary Anne again refused to set aside a default judgment in a later case involving human error, *Jeffreys, Inc. v. Multi-Color, Inc.*, prompting yet another reversal by the court of appeals.[86]

While Mary Anne's ruling in *Cota* and *Jeffreys* suggest that she had little patience for human mistakes that lead to litigation delays, they came after her reversal in *Campbell*. Since the appellate court in *Campbell* admonished

---

82. 451 P.2d at 622.

83. 497 P.2d 833 (Ariz. App. 1972).

84. *See* Southern Arizona Bank & Trust Co. v. Cota, Civ. Cause No. 124442 (Pima County Sup. Ct.)

85. 497 P.2d at 834.

86. 2 CA-CIV 1613 (Ariz. App. 1974)(Memorandum Decision), reversing default judgment in Multi-Color, Inc. v. Lee Jeffreys, Inc., Civ. Cause No. 140869 (Pima County Sup. Ct).

her for her misguided willingness to set aside the default, the later cases may simply reflect her good-faith attempt to interpret the meaning of the reversal: when is human error "excusable neglect" and when is it not? That she was reversed in *Cota* and *Jeffreys* may mean that in close cases she chose a route that would end the litigation rather than perpetuate it, at least after she had been rebuked for an excess of compassion in *Campbell*.

In the last year of Mary Anne's state-court tenure, a unique public controversy arose that played itself out in her courtroom, and her management of the case revealed certain fundamental qualities of her judicial identity. In September of 1975, labor groups representing Tucson police and firemen joined together to form the Tucson Police-Fire Association to press the city council for pay raises. The city council had earlier rejected the 15–20 percent pay increases that the labor groups had requested, and had also rejected a much lower pay increase that an outside advisory arbitrator had recommended for the police.[87] When ongoing negotiations ultimately reached a stalemate, the Police-Fire Association staged a massive walk-out. Close to 80 percent of the city's police and fire protection force went on strike, prompting the sheriff to declare Pima County to be in a state of emergency. According to press reports, strikers "abandoned police patrol cars and walked out of fire stations when the strike deadline arrived."[88]

When the strike was announced, Tucson City Attorney James Webb had only one option—to seek an injunction compelling the strikers to return to work in accordance with the existing contracts between the police and firefighters organizations and the city. Because Mary Anne was the assignments judge at that point, Webb drove to her home at eight o'clock on a hot September evening, armed with affidavits showing the occurrence of the strike and a hastily drawn-up temporary restraining order. In less than thirty minutes, he convinced Mary Anne that the strikers were in breach of their contracts and that the strike posed a significant threat to public safety. About 8:30 p.m., Mary Anne signed the order directing the strikers to return to their jobs pending a hearing on a permanent injunction. "She was orderly about it and swift," Webb recalled. "I don't remember even sitting down. It was all done quickly and she seemed quite calm and businesslike."[89]

The following day, Mary Anne quashed the existing restraining order after counsel for the Police-Fire Association challenged it as overly vague, but she immediately issued a new one that defined with greater specificity

87. Betty Beard, *Policemen To Plan Pay Hike 'Action,'* THE ARIZONA DAILY STAR, September 9, 1975.

88. *Police, Firemen Walk Out; Court Issues Injunction,* THE ARIZONA DAILY STAR, September 23, 1975.

89. Telephone Interview with James D. Webb (Aug. 15, 1995).

who was subject to the injunction. In announcing the new order, Mary Anne explained, perhaps with some irritation, "If there is any doubt as to whom this order applies to (sic), let me make it clear. In my mind, it applies to every individual policeman and fireman who is not on duty—on the job—when he is supposed to be."[90] She also announced the justification for the order itself. The strike, she stated, was "against state and community policy and in direct violation of contracts signed by policemen and firemen." She added, "I really don't think we can throw common sense out the window here. [The fact that] the city is virtually without fire protection and has limited police protection is of great concern to the court. I feel we are in an emergency status right now...and the court must step in."[91]

With the commencement of the strike came a flurry of activity by negotiating teams on both sides of the dispute. City council representatives offered a staggered pay increase which the strikers quickly rejected. At the same time, the mayor, worried about the risk to public safety, promised the strikers "amnesty" if they would return to their jobs within twenty-four hours. The strikers disregarded his overture. For the next seven days, members of the Police-Fire Association remained on strike, notwithstanding Mary Anne's court order and threats from the chief of police that all strikers would lose their jobs.

Although the strikers were in open defiance of the court order, Mary Anne was not eager to see contempt proceedings brought against the strikers. She explained to reporters that any violations of her order would have to be reported to her by the city before she could act on it.[92] "Mary Anne wasn't angry that her order was being flouted," Webb remembered. "She saw her order as being in service to the deal. She didn't view it one-dimensionally."[93] Webb recalled that he likewise was reluctant to initiate contempt proceedings, since he and the other participants viewed the court order as a stepping point in the negotiations and not as an end in itself.

The strike dragged on for seven days, and city officials and the public became increasingly concerned about the threat it posed to the community. Members of the South Tucson police force helped sporadically to meet Tucson's law enforcement needs, and Tucson's sanitation department personnel also assisted. "The garbage men saved the city," Webb remembered.

---

90. Diane Johnsen & Ken Burton, *Strikers Reject City Offer of Staggered 12.5% Raise*, THE ARIZONA DAILY STAR, September 24, 1975.

91. Ben MacNitt, *Both Unions' Contracts Include Ban On Strikes*, THE ARIZONA DAILY STAR, September 24, 1975.

92. Diane Johnsen & Ken Burton, *Strikers Reject City Offer of Staggered 12.5% Raise*, THE ARIZONA DAILY STAR, September 24, 1975.

93. Webb Interview, *supra* note 89.

"They were putting out fires and maintaining the public order."[94] A federal labor mediator arrived midweek to assist in negotiations, and the dispute was ultimately resolved through an agreement for across-the-board pay raises for all city employees. Pursuant to the settlement, strikers returned to their jobs but forfeited their pay for the days they were on strike.

Mary Anne remained behind the scenes in the negotiations and did not usurp the role of the mediator. Webb had the impression that she did not want to categorically end the strikers' opportunity to press their grievances and that she understood her order to be a necessary part of the process. Although Webb had in fact initiated contempt proceedings against the Police-Fire Association's twelve leaders, he made no serious effort to proceed on the contempt charges. Also, as part of the settlement, Webb requested dismissal of the temporary restraining order. In response, Mary Anne not only dismissed the TRO but also the pending contempt citations. In her minute entry, she explained that she lacked authority "to proceed in any way on the order to show cause for contempt" after the underlying restraining order had been dismissed.[95]

Thus, for a tumultuous twelve days, Mary Anne was drawn into the center of the dispute between the striking employees and city hall. Mary Anne's self-confidence was apparent through her steady management of the injunctive action. Although she had great respect for law enforcement personnel and may have believed that the strikers' request for a pay hike had merit, she also was firmly convinced that the strikers were in breach of their contracts and that the public safety of the community was at risk by virtue of the strike. With law and policy on her side, she rapidly issued the TRO that Webb requested and publicly defended the issuance of the order. When the order was attacked as being vague, Mary Anne acknowledged the shortcomings of the TRO and issued a more precise order in its stead.

Mary Anne exhibited a nuanced perspective about the role of the judicial process in the strikers' dispute. Although the strikers' flagrant violation of the TRO continued for seven days, Mary Anne remained passive. Other judges might have reacted more aggressively to the open flouting of the court order. Mary Anne, however, seemed to view the court's process as a means of getting the strikers to the bargaining table, and she cooperated to that end. Also, as a longtime supporter of arbitration, she may have felt dismay about the failure of the arbitration process that preceded the strike. She undoubtedly continued to believe that the resolution of the dispute would be through extra-judicial mechanisms and she must have

---

94. *Id.*

95. Diane Johnsen, *Pay-Raise Package Will Mean City Layoffs*, THE ARIZONA DAILY STAR, October 2, 1975.

welcomed the arrival of the federal mediator. Ultimately, by remaining firm but in the background, she allowed the strikers and the city to "bargain in the shadow of the law."[96]

Mary Anne's civil record ranged from the dramatic class judgment in *Sexton*, where she distinguished herself as a courageous voice for a marginalized segment of society, to the series of judicial review cases that evinced a somewhat arrogant readiness to second-guess administrative agencies. The same self-confidence that enabled Mary Anne to enter domains unfamiliar to women throughout her life enabled her to announce controversial decisions and, on occasion, to stubbornly adhere to her views, as in *Slavin v. City of Tucson*, even after a pointed reversal on the same question from the appellate judges. On the other hand, she was a conscientious judge who listened to counsel, sometimes changing her mind in the middle of a case, as in *Rogers v. Unimac Company* and *Dairyland Insurance Company v. Lopez*. Her compassion surfaced in many of her rulings, but it was a compassion tempered by pragmatism. In her life she had weathered challenges and setbacks, and she expected others to do the same. She admired self-sufficiency and honesty, and she expected people to live up to their bargains. Thus, she was rigorous in holding the divorcing husbands to their contractual and legal duties of support, as in *Ruhsam* and *Marshick*. Finally, her independence manifested itself in several libertarian rulings—decisions that suggested a suspicion of governmental intrusion into the private affairs of individuals, as in *Livingston*, or a hostility toward incursions on a private property owner's freedom, as in *Ivancovich*. In sum, although Mary Anne diligently attempted to "apply the law" to the cases that were assigned to Division 5, adjudication at the trial level is rarely a wooden application of clear law to clear facts. A trial judge's human responses to the disputes in her courtroom form a backdrop to the formal decisionmaking. When Holmes proclaimed that "[t]he life of the law has not been logic: it has been experience," he referred to both the experience of society and the experience of the adjudicators.[97] Inevitably, the many dimensions of Mary Anne's character informed her judicial responses to the issues that came before her.

---

96. The phrase "bargaining in the shadow of the law" was coined by Robert Mnookin in a well-known law review article about the influence of the formal law on extra-legal divorce negotiations. *See* Robert H. Mnookin & Lewis Kornhauser, *Bargaining in the Shadow of the Law: The Case of Divorce*, 88 YALE L.J. 950 (1979).

97. O.W. HOLMES, THE COMMON LAW 5 (1963).

CHAPTER ELEVEN

Attaining Article III Status

Although Mary Anne's work on the Pima County Superior Court remained the central focus of her life from 1964 through 1976, the joys and sorrows of her personal life and the social and political movements of the era gave context to that work. Her husband Bill and daughter Annie were of core importance to her, and the strong familial bonds among the three of them were very evident to others. Mary Anne and Bill had an unusually successful marriage, one that survived the inevitable strain produced by Mary Anne's own professional challenges as well as the vicissitudes of Annie's adolescence. As a couple, they seemed to operate from a foundation of deep affection and mutual respect, and they interacted with obvious consideration for one another's feelings. Mary Anne ate lunch with Bill almost every day, sometimes in chambers and sometimes at a nearby restaurant or club. Annie was a frequent visitor to Mary Anne's chambers once she was of school-age. The Richey family, along with Mary Anne's staff, gathered in her courtroom each year to watch Tucson's annual "rodeo parade" through a large arched window facing the street. The decidedly Western spectacle, tauted as the nation's longest non-motorized parade, was a favorite event for Bill and Mary Anne. Indeed, one year Annie, when still of elementary school age, rode her own pony in the parade, to the great pride of her parents.[1]

Laughter played a vital role in the Richeys' lives. Mary Anne often saw humor in the proceedings in her courtroom, and on occasion she would bring home transcripts of witness testimony and would entertain Bill and Annie with her own renditions of the witnesses' words. One criminal case in Mary Anne's court, for example, involved two women who were accused of robbery. The victim, a seventy-year-old man, testified that one of the defendants, a woman weighing about 350 pounds, sat on him while her slender companion removed money from his clothing.[2] After the trial ended in an acquittal of both defendants, Mary Anne read the transcripts to an appreciative audience at the Richey home. Mary Anne was also an accomplished hog caller, and her unique "Souiee!" was a loud reminder

---

1. Interview with Annie Richey, Tucson, Arizona (Aug. 22, 1992).

2. *Women Accused of Robbing Man Are Acquitted*, THE ARIZONA DAILY STAR, January 26, 1965.

to family and friends of her Indiana heritage.[3] Bill could be playful as well. One year when he planned on putting in a concrete basketball court near their home for his athletic wife as a Christmas gift, he wrapped a heavy piece of broken asphalt in ornamental paper and put the package under the Christmas tree. Mary Anne's befuddlement turned to laughter when she understood that she had received a piece of her future court.[4]

Recreation for the Richeys included horseback riding, hunting and fishing, camping, regular attendance at University of Arizona athletic events, and the singular pleasure of relaxing on their back patio with a cocktail in the late afternoon, watching the sunset or the gambits of a wayward jackrabbit. Swimming, golf, and tennis were three of Mary Anne's favorite sports, and she swam every morning before work in the family's pool.[5] Mary Anne, Bill, and Annie also traveled extensively, to conferences related to Mary Anne's work and for pure pleasure. Bill's law practice and Mary Anne's judicial salary gave them a comfortable combined income, allowing them to indulge their love of travel and other recreational interests. They spent time in Montreal, Canada, when Mary Anne was designated as Arizona's representative to the national state judge's conference, for example, and they visited other popular resort areas simply as tourists. Their travels took them to Disneyland and Disneyworld; Hawaii; Sun Valley, Idaho; Baja California and other coastal areas in Mexico; Europe; and the Soviet Union.[6]

Animals were an essential part of the home environment, including especially the family horses. Although Annie did not share her mother's interest in other sports, the young girl did share her mother's passion for horses and riding. Annie received a pony when she was four years old, and her devotion to the pony and to perfecting her riding skills was a source of great joy for her mother and father. Annie's interest in horses developed into a life-long avocation, and for years she rode in shows, demonstrating her horsemanship and jumping skills to the onlookers. Mary Anne tried hard to attend those events, and Annie recalled that her

---

3. Interview with William K. Richey, Nutrioso, Arizona (July 16–17, 1992); Telephone Interviews with Richey (Sept. 20, 1992, Sept. 27, 1992, Sept. 21, 1994).

4. Annie Richey Interview, *supra* note 1.

5. In 1982, when Annie Richey accepted a Rotary Club award in Shelbyville, Indiana, on behalf of her mother, she told the audience, "I want you to know that she swims every morning, rain, snow or shine, and she rides every weekend. You would not think that she is almost 65." *Judge Richey receives Arts, Humaniites Award*, THE SHELBYVILLE NEWS, July 3, 1982.

6. Annie Richey Interview, *supra* note 1.

mother rarely missed a show. Although Annie's relationship with her mother would not be smooth during Annie's adolescence, the family dynamics while Annie was a young girl were loving, harmonious, and joyful. "I had a very, very happy childhood," Annie remembered, "and I didn't really think about the fact that my mother was older than my friends' parents. She did everything with me."[7]

Bill Richey continued a successful law practice after Mary Anne was appointed to the superior court, but Mary Anne's career remained the central hub around which the family's life revolved. When her judicial work required her to remain late at the courthouse, or when her administrative work at the superior court required her to leave town, Bill was available to manage their home and care for their daughter. "We were a team," he recalled, but it was a team with Mary Anne's career as the driving force. Bill tried to secure a judicial position for himself several times after the Arizona legislature authorized merit selection of superior court judges in 1974, but he was never successful. Although he easily survived the screening process in his judicial applications and had the support of high-ranking Republicans, he was bypassed in the gubernatorial selection. His repeated failures led him to believe that his marriage to Mary Anne was a factor held against him. Indeed, in one of his first efforts, Republican Governor Jack Williams informed Bill that Mary Anne's presence on the bench was an insurmountable obstacle to his own appointment. Williams apparently believed that the precedent might have undesireable consequences. Although Bill felt a sharp regret then and each additional time that he lost in a bid for a judgeship, he did not dwell on his disappointment in conversations with Mary Anne. Her career achievements remained the focus of their professional lives, and Bill effectively subordinated his own ambitions to her career advancement.[8]

In the middle of her state court years, Mary Anne suffered a painful personal loss. On November 4, 1971, her brother Bill Reimann died unexpectedly in Shelbyville at the age of fifty-nine, and his death left Mary Anne as the only surviving member of her original nuclear family. Reimann, the president of Kennedy Car Liner Corporation at the time of his death, had become a respected business leader in Shelbyville and in the state of Indiana. A perennial fundraiser for public charities, he had been an affable, well-liked man who was known for his civic accomplishments. Mary Anne cared deeply for her brother and had remained in touch with him despite the geographic distance that separated them. Only

---

7. *Id.*
8. William Richey Interviews, *supra* note 3.

six months before his death, she had given a speech at his request at a meeting of his trade association in Indianapolis.[9] On the day of Reimann's death, Eleanor Robbins, Mary Anne's secretary, received the news from Shelbyville while Mary Anne was presiding over a trial. Robbins went into the courtroom and handed Mary Anne a note telling her that her brother had died. Robbins recalled that Mary Anne announced in a level voice to the jury that the court would adjourn temporarily. Mary Anne left the courtroom and went to her chambers, where she sat silently and alone for about thirty minutes, and then resumed her work.[10] Mary Anne later attended the funeral in Shelbyville. "Bill's death really shook her up," Bill Richey remembered. "She really loved her brother and admired him, and of course it brought back the loss of her other brother in the war."[11] With Bill Reimann's death, Mary Anne's connection to Indiana became decidedly attenuated. Although she had returned in 1966 to be honored as Shelbyville's "Favorite Son,"[12] her sense of belonging in the community clearly was diminished by Reimann's death. She maintained contact with Bill Reimann's family, but she was no longer drawn to the small town that had been her girlhood home, and her visits became rare. Thus, in 1982, when the Shelbyville Rotary Club selected Mary Anne for its Arts and Humanities Award, she did not go to Shelbyville but sent her daugher Annie instead to accept the honor on her behalf.[13]

Mary Anne's view of the "second women's movement" of the early 1970s[14] and her identification with the movement are not capable of easy

---

9. *Packaging Convention hears Judge Richey and Philbrick*, THE SHELBYVILLE NEWS, May 20, 1971.

10. Interviews with Eleanor Robbins, Tucson, Arizona (July 13, 1992, July 15, 1995).

11. William Richey Interviews, *supra* note 3.

12. *Shelbyville Picks Judge Richey As Its Favorite 'Son,'* THE INDIANAPOLIS STAR, February 2, 1966; *Oscar Fisher Gets Top Citizen Award*, THE SHELBYVILLE NEWS, Feburary 11, 1966.

13. *Judge Richey receives Arts, Humanities Award*, THE SHELBYVILLE NEWS, July 3, 1982. The award recited that Mary Anne was selected "[i]n recognition of her creative accomplishments and contributions to the Arts or Humanities and the consequent enrichment of the lives of the people of Shelby County, Indiana . . . ."

14. Women's historians generally identify the "first" women's movement in this country as the suffrage movement, beginning perhaps with the Seneca Falls Convention of 1848 and culminating in the ratification of the nineteenth amendment in 1920. Although the first proposal for an equal rights amendment was introduced in 1923, the momentum for its ratification did not materialize until the 1960s. Thus, the "second" women's movement, in the view of many scholars, dates from the mid-1960s forward. *See* JOAN HOFF, LAW, GENDER, AND INJUSTICE—A LEGAL HISTORY OF U.S. WOMEN 3–20 (1991).

categorization. She was not a self-proclaimed "feminist," and she would have bristled had someone given her that label. As a Republican, she distanced herself from the activists of the modern women's movement, the "bra burners" and sign-carriers, as she derisively called them in private conversation.[15] In Mary Anne's view, the women's movement was too frequently sidetracked by peripheral issues and left-wing politics and had lost focus of the core issue of sex equality. She occasionally referred in public to that notion of equality. "I don't want anything just because I'm a woman," she said in a 1976 interview. "I just want to be equal."[16] Similarly, she once advised a group of teenage girls that they should never expect to be treated deferentially because of their sex. "You need only to take advantage of opportunity," she said. "But you must remember that you can't push yourself simply on the pretext that you are a woman. You'll never succeed in politics if you present yourself as a sweet, feminine little thing expecting special favors because of your gender."[17] In the same speech she emphasized the importance of the right to vote and the reforms that women's suffrage had brought about. Thus, as to the core goal of gender equality, Mary Anne diverged from the women's movement in style more than substance. In that respect, she clearly departed from the Republican romanticization of traditional sex roles that was being championed by right-wing activist Phyllis Schafly throughout the 1970s.

Mary Anne's belief in equal rights was not lightly-held. She demonstrated throughout her life an aggressive determination to achieve acceptance in male-dominated realms, both professional and recreational. To Mary Anne, true equality of opportunity should have been the central focus of the women's movement. Not suprisingly, she was an early supporter of the Equal Rights Amendment. In March of 1972, the proposal for a constitutional amendment prohibiting discrimination on account of sex was passed by both Houses of Congress and sent to the states for ratification. In a public speech in 1973, during the early phase of the campaign for ratification, Mary Anne told her audience that she favored the ERA but she felt that public demonstrations in support of the amendment had hurt the cause.[18] Nevertheless, she predicted that the ERA would be successfully ratified, and her prediction at the time was justified. The ERA

---

15. Robbins Interviews, *supra* note 10.

16. Anthony Seed, *Judge Richey, ex-city woman, eyes high court*, THE SHELBYVILLE NEWS, June 23, 1976.

17. Katie Laos, *Judge Advises Girls Staters To Avoid Relying On Gender*, THE ARIZONA DAILY STAR, June 11, 1965.

18. *Judge Richey Expects ERA to be OK'd*, THE ARIZONA DAILY STAR, March 21, 1973.

was ratified by twenty-two states in the first year following its introduction, and Schafly's well-orchestrated attack on the ERA did not take hold until the mid-1970s.

Mary Anne's endorsement of the ERA differentiated her from the vocal far-right segment of the Republican Party. Phyllis Schafly's "StopERA" campaign, which was founded in 1972, ominously portrayed the amendment as a provision that would have abolished all sex differences, forced women into military combat, destroyed men's familial obligations, and left the country vulnerable to Communism.[19] Mary Anne and Schafly, born within a decade of one another, had their Goldwater Republicanism in common. Their ideologies diverged, however, on their interpretations of the meaning of sexual equality.

Other of Mary Anne's activities showed her firm belief that women should take a role equal to that of men in the public sphere. In 1971 she accepted an appointment by Republican Governor Jack Williams to be a member of the Governor's Commission on the Status of Women.[20] The Commission had been established by Democrat Sam Goddard in 1966 during his brief governorship to "eliminate discrimination in all areas of society on account of sex."[21] During Mary Anne's two-year term, the Commission reviewed gender disparities in gubernatorial appointments and made recommendations to revise Arizona's statutes that contained provisions treating men and women differently. Although membership on the Commission did not consume much of Mary Anne's time or energy, she retained mention of it in her official biographies and evidently took pride in her participation.

Mary Anne's position with another organization also evidenced an identification with the concerns of women. Since the early 1960s, Mary Anne had been active with the Tucson chapter of the Young Women's Christian Association. In particular, she had been instrumental in establishing a summer YWCA ranch for girls in the high desert north of Tucson.[22] Her efforts to create a positive outdoors experience for disadvantaged girls reflected the continuing influence in her life of her beloved Vermont camp. In early 1969, she was elected president of the organiza-

---

19. *See* BARBARA EHRENREICH, THE HEARTS OF MEN 152–61 (1983); SHEILA TOBIAS, SEXUAL POLITICS: THE LEGACY (1997).

20. Letter of August 20, 1971, from Judge Mary Anne Richey to Governor Jack Williams, accepting appointment.

21. Executive Order 66–2, Establishing the Governor's Commission on the Status of Women for the State of Arizona, March 1, 1966.

22. *Welcome To Rancho los Cerros*, THE ARIZONA DAILY STAR, June 20, 1962 (photograph with caption).

tion, and in that role she appeared in the press on several occasions smilingly accepting donations for YWCA programs.[23]

Her affiliation with the YWCA was significant for reasons other than a manifestation of her altruistic desire to improve the lives of young women. In 1970, the national YWCA voted at the annual convention to support "the repeal of all laws restricting or prohibiting abortions performed by a duly licensed physician."[24] With its pre-*Roe v. Wade* pronouncement, the YWCA aligned itself unambiguously with the contemporary women's movement. A majority of state laws in 1970, including the laws of Arizona, criminalized abortion except where necessary to save the life of the mother, and the burgeoning women's movement had targeted such prohibitions.[25] Although no record exists of endorsements by Mary Anne of the national YWCA's position on abortion, she must have supported the national vote. In later years in private conversations, she adamantly defended a woman's right to decide whether or not to end a pregnancy. To her, a woman's control over her reproductive functions was an essential part of personal autonomy and gender equality. Mary Anne herself had followed an unconventional path in childbearing, and it had been a path of her own choosing. She believed that women had to decide for themselves whether to continue a pregnancy, and that a governmental prohibition, such as that which existed in Arizona before 1973, would only lead to risky illegal abortions or the births of unwanted children.[26]

Interestingly, Mary Anne's belief in sex equality apparently did not dissuade her from enjoying meals at private clubs that maintained sex-exclusive memberships. The Old Pueblo Club and the Mountain Oyster Club, for example, were the locations of frequent luncheons hosted by her and her husband. For many years, each club generally adhered to a policy of accepting women as members only if they were the wives or widows of male members.[27] "It never bothered her a bit," Bill Richey recalled. "She

23. *YWCA Elects Slate*, THE ARIZONA DAILY STAR, January 21, 1969; *$300,000 Check Accepted*, THE ARIZONA DAILY STAR, February 6, 1970 (photograph with caption).

24. *75 Years—Celebrating the 75th Anniversary of The YWCA of Tucson* (Publication of the Tucson YWCA, describing national organization's history).

25. Arizona criminal statutes on abortion, codified at ARIZ. REV. STAT. Secs. 13-211, 212, 213, were struck down in the wake of Roe v. Wade, 410 U.S. 113 (1973), in Nelson v. Planned Parenthood Center of Tucson, Inc., 19 Ariz. App. 142 (1973)(opinion on rehearing).

26. Author's Conversations with Mary Anne Richey, 1977–78.

27. Old Pueblo Club Bulletin, April 1980 (describing membership categories of "widow who was a Special Honorary Member" and "Ladies Limited Member"); *The Mountain Oyster Club*, ARIZONA HIGHWAYS 10, 13 (September 1971)(explaining that

never, never complained about any of that. She was not one to push on matters like that."[28] Similarly, Mary Anne's classmates from law school did not recall a negative reaction from her regarding the male-only legal fraternities present in the law school. Those fraternities, of course, were a source of potentially valuable contacts for the young law school graduate, more valuable than the fledgling sororities that were open to Mary Anne. Nevertheless, she seemed to exempt private associations from her equality premise. To Mary Anne, perhaps, the important battles to be waged by the women's movement concerned such fundamentals as employment rights, reproductive autonomy, and political participation.

Thus, Mary Anne's response to the women's movement of the 1970s was multi-dimensioned. She disclaimed affiliation with feminist activists and their flamboyant politics, and, as a woman of hard-earned achievement, she was repelled by what she perceived as bids by women for special treatment. To her, equality meant responsibility as well as opportunity. On the other hand, she was a defender not only of formal legal equality for women but also of physical autonomy. Thus, she embraced two core goals of the women's movement: gender equality in employment and public life, and freedom of choice.

Mary Anne responded to the traumatic political events of the 1960s and early 1970s that occurred on the national scene in much the same way that she responded to the cases that came before her. She maintained a dispassionate perspective on the racial violence and political assasinations of the late 1960s and on the later unraveling of the Nixon administration, and she seemed to adhere to certain core values that had evolved over her lifetime. In April of 1968, Mary Anne, Bill, and five-year old Annie watched the grim news of the killing of the Rev. Martin Luther King, Jr., during a visit to Memphis, Tennessee, where he had gone to assist a strike by black sanitation workers. Two months later, the nation, still reeling from King's death, witnessed the murder of Sen. Robert Kennedy in Los Angeles during his campaign for the Democratic presidential nomination. Although neither of the men was Mary Anne's ideological hero, she was shaken by their deaths. Her response to such lawless violence seems to have been a strong commitment to the "rule of law" in her judicial work, becoming to some observers a "law and order judge" in her efforts to strictly enforce the criminal law.[29] At the same time, the political and social unrest on the national arena may have strengthened her commitment to community service in her personal life. Throughout her

apart from four special honorary memberships for women, women's access to the club's dining services was limited to wives and widows of members).

28. William Richey Interviews, *supra* note 3.

29. Interview with S. Thomas Chandler, Tucson, Arizona (Oct. 8, 1992).

state court tenure, for example, she was active in the Salvation Army, serving on the Advisory Board of that charitable organization for more than a decade. She was proud of that involvement and listed it in her biographical summaries for various publications.[30] Indeed, a newspaper photograph from 1970 depicted her ringing a Salvation Army bell outside the Pima County Courthouse, a show of exuberance that led to criticism of her for having engaged in what some considered to be improper charitable solicitation.[31]

As a member of the Republican Party, she endorsed much of the Republican platform in 1968 and again in 1972. She supported Richard Nixon and Spiro Agnew in both elections and agreed with Nixon's proclaimed efforts to bring a decisive end to the war in Vietnam. Because of her own experience in the WASP and the military death of her brother Chuck in World War II, she felt a keen affinity for the United States troops fighting in southeast Asia. Conversely, she had little sympathy for the anti-war protesters, whose numbers escalated as the United States' strategic position in Vietnam became more untenable. In her opinion, their massive parades and disruptive acts of civil disobedience were misdirected and showed disrespect for the brave men and women whose lives were on the line in Vietnam and Cambodia. The student unrest of the late 1960s and early 1970s and the racial tensions of the same era were, in Mary Anne's view, symptoms of a social malaise born of irresponsibility. As a woman who had always been drawn to public service in her adult life, she believed that each citizen had a civic duty to serve his or her country, and that the young men in the United States who were avoiding the draft were shirking that duty.

Mary Anne's commitment to the rule of law was perhaps strengthened in the aftermath of Nixon's downfall. She was a shrewd judge of character, and her perceptiveness had been sharpened by her years on the bench. When reports of the burglary of Democratic headquarters in the Watergate complex surfaced in the national press in 1972, she suspected immediately that Nixon was involved. "He's guilty as sin," she told her husband, and she scoffed as Nixon continued to deny responsibility or knowledge.[32] Her friend Norval Jasper, who would ultimately leave the

---

30. Submission of Mary Anne Richey to Marquis Who's Who Inc., for WHO'S WHO IN THE WORLD, Vol. 6 (June 18, 1982)(listing Salvation Army Advisory Board Membership from 1968 to present).

31. The photograph appeared in The Arizona Daily Star, December 29, 1970. The public criticism that followed the publication angered Mary Anne. Robbins Interview, *supra* note 10. Mary Anne was also criticized in a letter to the editor for her activities on behalf of the local YWCA. *See* Letter from George W. Hulbert, *Letters To The Editor*, TUCSON DAILY CITIZEN, February 14, 1970.

32. William Richey Interviews, *supra* note 3.

Republican Party, had long warned her that Nixon was dishonest and corrupt.[33] Her suspicions were confirmed as the activities of John Mitchell's Committee for the Reelection of the President became known. Together she and Bill watched with increasing chagrin as Nixon's participation in the cover-up became clear. They had applauded when their friend Richard Kleindeinst, whose campaign for governor of Arizona they had vigorously supported in 1964, had been named United States Attorney General in 1972 to replace Mitchell. The honor, however, was short-lived; he resigned a year later, along with presidential aides H.R. Haldeman and John Ehrlichman and presidential counsel John Dean, amidst the growing Watergate scandal.

The demise of another Republican figure—Vice President Spiro Agnew—in late 1973 would have personal significance for Mary Anne. When Agnew resigned in October after pleading no contest to income tax evasion and as a condition of avoiding further prosecution for bribery, Gerald R. Ford, then House minority leader, was designated by Nixon to succeed Agnew. Ford was sworn in as Vice President in December of that year. Nine months later, in August of 1974, Nixon resigned his office in an emotional speech to the nation, following his release of the incriminating tapes he had fought so hard to immunize from scrutiny. As a consequence of Nixon's departure, Ford took the oath of office as the thirty-eighth President. At the time, Mary Anne felt disgust at the corruption that the Watergate prosecution had exposed, and she was ashamed of the behavior of the Republican president. She could not have known that two years later, at the end of President Ford's brief stay in the White House, he would irrevocably touch her life by nominating her for a federal district court judgeship.

Mary Anne's nomination to the federal court bench was in many ways a natural progression for her. Her judicial performance on the superior court bench had met with high praise from various quarters, not only because of her diligence in managing the cases in her courtroom and her readiness to tackle controversial issues, but also because of her willingness to fulfill other functions related to her office. In 1970, for example, the same year she was elected president of the Arizona State Judges' Association, she was also appointed by the Arizona Supreme Court to membership on the Judicial Qualification Commission, a visible and newly-created professional body that evaluated complaints of impropriety against state court judges. Inarguably, her reputation for high integrity contributed to her selection for the commission. From 1971 to 1973, she served as co-chair of the Supreme Court Committee to Revise Civil Jury Instructions, a responsibility that her staff remembered as time-consuming

---

33. Interview with Norval W. Jasper, Tucson, Arizona (Aug. 27, 1992).

and tedious. Mary Anne took the assignment quite seriously, since she viewed instructions as a crucial phase of a civil trial and struggled in her own courtroom to devise clear and accurate instructions. Moreover, in 1973 she was appointed by the Arizona Supreme Court to serve on yet another committee with far-reaching responsibility: the Arizona Criminal Code Revision Commission. Another member of the commission was Sandra Day O'Connor, then a superior court judge in Maricopa County and one of only four female trial court judges statewide.[34] For the three years during which she served on the commission, Mary Anne participated in recommending broadscale changes to the existing criminal laws, including revision of Arizona's abortion laws, changes in procedural rules regarding plea bargaining, and implementation of the precursor to a mandatory sentencing system.[35] Although Mary Anne found sentencings to be her most difficult responsibility as a judge, she was reluctant to relinquish all judicial discretion in the matter and was thus ambivalent about the move to mandatory sentencing. In an interview about the commission's work, Mary Anne seemed to distance herself from the advocates of mandatory sentencing, explaining, "Some feel the authority of setting penalties should be taken away from judges, a wish of the public and of some legislators."[36]

Mary Anne clearly enjoyed the respect of her colleagues, as demonstrated by the polite pressure put on her to accept the position of presiding judge of the Pima County Superior Court in the early 1970s. The presiding judge oversaw case assignments on the burgeoning civil and criminal dockets and also had responsibility over the sensitive area of judicial personnel matters and the potentially controversial area of budgetary allocations. When asked to consider the position of presiding judge, Mary Anne unambiguously refused, to the chagrin of some of her colleagues and the relief of her husband.[37] Although her close friend Robert Roylston had served as presiding judge from 1968 until 1972, Mary Anne did not aspire to the position and did not view it as one of prestige or enviable power. Instead, she saw it as a title that carried administrative burdens and a risk of controversy.[38] She and Bill remembered vividly the fracas with the Pima County Board of Supervisors over furniture styles and were

---

34. Submission of Mary Anne Richey to Marquis Who's Who, *supra* note 30.

35. *Arizona Criminal Code Revision Completion Seen For Late 1975*, ARIZONA WEEKLY GAZETTE, December 10, 1974.

36. *Id.*

37. Telephone Interview with Hon. Robert B. Buchanan, Judge, Pima County Superior Court (Nov. 22, 1992).

38. Interview with Hon. Robert O. Roylston, former Judge, Pima County Superior Court, Tucson, Arizona (Oct. 5, 1992); Buchanan Interview, *supra* note 37.

leery of the potential for further controversy. Thus, she refused the presiding judgeship but was persuaded by her colleagues at the courthouse to accept, albeit reluctantly, the newly-created position of "associate presiding judge" in 1972. Formally appointed by the Arizona Supreme Court, she remained in that position under presiding judge Ben Birdsall, who had joined her on the bench in 1969, until her resignation from the superior court in 1976.[39] According to colleague Alice Truman, Mary Anne was a "good administrator in the sense that she was interested in the whole picture. She cared about other people and about the field we were in. She seemed concerned about the justice system as a whole." Alluding to Mary Anne's apparently boundless energy, Truman added that "Mary Anne always did more than her share and she did it well."[40]

The Arizona State Bar's practice of conducting judicial evaluation polls among lawyers began in the final year of Mary Anne's superior court tenure, and her "scores" placed her at the top of the state court bench. In September 1976, the State Bar conducted its first judicial evaluation survey, asking lawyers to rate trial judges on a variety of criteria: punctuality, attentiveness to testimony of witnesses and arguments of counsel, promptness in rending decisions, fairness to all litigants, courteousness, courtroom discipine, knowledge of substantive and procedural law, consideration of written submissions, and judicial temperament and demeanor. Mary Anne garnered the highest composite scores of any judge in the Pima County Superior Court, and only one judge from Maricopa County received scores equal to or higher than Mary Anne's ratings.[41] Mary Anne was not overly impressed with the poll results and remarked to her staff that such surveys were "popularity contests" rather than real measures of judicial performance.[42] On the other hand, she must have been pleased with the reception she was receiving in the practicing bar.

39. See Annual Report Relating to the Superior Court of the State of Arizona, Pima County 1972; Arizona Supreme Court, The Superior Court in Arizona 1912–1982, at 51–59 (1985).

40. Interview with Hon. Alice Truman, former Judge, Pima County Superior Court, Tucson, Arizona (July 6, 1992).

41. Criteria used in evaluation of judges, The Arizona Republic, September 12, 1976 (accompanying table shows that 99 percent of lawyers polled responded affirmatively to question whether Mary Anne Richey should be retained in office). The poll results made clear that the responding lawyers were capable of voicing disapproval: a majority of respondents recommended that four state court judges not be retained in office. See Lawyers say: Oust 4 judges, Tucson Citizen, September 13, 1976.

42. Robbins Interviews, supra note 10.

Accolades flowed Mary Anne's way with increasing frequency as her judicial career continued, and a shift from state to federal court seemed a logical move to observers. Indeed, during Richard Nixon's presidency, Mary Anne was purportedly under consideration for nomination to the United States Supreme Court, and speculation about such a possibility appeared in the local press. In September of 1971, because of the retirements of Supreme Court Justices John Harlan and Hugo Black, Nixon had the opportunity to nominate two new justices to the Court. According to accounts in the national press, Nixon was considering the naming of "the first woman Justice at a time when the nation's most restless majority group is pressing for recognition."[43] Nixon fueled the speculation by announcing that "no candidates were being struck from his list because they were women."[44] At the same time, Nixon wanted to shore up a conservative majority on the Court and therefore had to find a woman with appropriate political as well as professional credentials. Names mentioned nationally included Cornelia Kennedy, then a federal district court judge in Michigan whom Nixon had appointed; Shirley Hufstedler, a Johnson-appointee on the United States Court of Appeals for the Ninth Circuit and the highest-ranking woman in the federal judiciary; and Constance Baker Motley, a New York federal district court judge also appointed by Johnson. Less than a week after the initial flurry of speculation, the White House passed the word that it was probably not going to select a woman after all. Nixon spokesmen explained that "their search has not turned up a woman who combines the desired judicial philosophy and a sufficiently distinguished legal background."[45] The nominees whom Nixon ultimately put forward were Lewis Powell and Arizonan William Rehnquist.

Before the White House ended the speculation, the Tucson press reported that Mary Anne's name had been submitted to Nixon by local Republican leaders. Mary Anne commented that she "was aware there were a number of telegrams and telephone calls to the President."[46] Her proponents believed that as a former prosecutor, a seasoned trial court judge,

---

43. Fred Graham, *Nixon Problem: Woman Justice?* THE NEW YORK TIMES, September 24, 1971.

44. Fred Graham, *New Justices Awaited,* THE NEW YORK TIMES, September 25, 1971.

45. Fred Graham, *Nixon Reported Unlikely To Pick Woman Justice,* THE NEW YORK TIMES, September 30, 1971.

46. *Judge Richey's Nomination to Court Suggested,* THE ARIZONA DAILY STAR, September 1971; *Judge Richey Backed for Supreme Court,* TUCSON DAILY CITIZEN, September 1971.

and an active supporter of the Republican Party, Mary Anne was a viable candidate. The submission of Mary Anne's name to the Nixon administration and the possibility of her nomination in 1971 seemed sufficiently newsworthy to be mentioned in many biographical descriptions of Mary Anne's life. She apparently did not discourage such reporting.

Mary Anne's actual nomination and appointment to the United States District Court followed a much different route. As others have documented, the appointment of federal judges is a complicated amalgam of formal and informal elements.[47] The formal dimension of the process emanates from Article III, Section 2, of the United States Constitution, which provides that the president "shall nominate, and by and with the Advice and Consent of the Senate, shall appoint...Judges of the Supreme Court and all other Officers of the United States...." Although some ambiguity surrounds the question, it has been assumed for much of the nation's history that federal district court and circuit court judges are "other officers" subject to presidental appointment.[48] The presidential power of appointment, however, has evolved into a practice that frequently gives senators of the president's party the power to select district court judges in their state and the power to veto local candidates to whom they are opposed.[49] Because of the senatorial role, aspirants to the federal trial bench frequently have waged discreet "campaigns" for the office through local political channels, and only rarely do senators recommend a candidate from an opposing party.[50] Former Attorney General Herbert Brownell, who headed the Justice Department when Mary Anne was in the U.S. Attorney's Office, once described the political nature of the appointment process:

> [J]udges are in most instances picked by political leaders.... Even the President still must have his candidate approved by the two senators from the candidate's state. By virtue of "senatorial courtesy," these senators may successfully prevent confirmation of the candidate by the Senate. Senators

---

47. See generally HAROLD W. CHASE, FEDERAL JUDGES—THE APPOINTING PROCESS (1972).

48. In 1948 Congress provided for the first time that all circuit and district court judges would be appointed by the president with the advice and consent of the Senate. 62 Stat. 895 (1948). Current law contains the same directive. See 28 U.S.C. Sec. 133 (1993)("The President shall appoint, by and with the advice and consent of the Senate, district judges for the several judicial districts").

49. See EVAN HAYNES, SELECTION AND TENURE OF JUDGES (1944); JOSEPH HARRIS, THE ADVICE AND CONSENT OF THE SENATE (1953).

50. Chase, supra note 47, at 112–13.

are rightly political animals and do not lightly disregard the desires of the political leaders back home.[51]

Local senators indisputably played a pivotal role in Mary Anne's nomination, but her name surfaced in an unusual manner. As was true of many important transitions in her life, Mary Anne's appointment to the federal bench was facilitated by a mentor and admirer. On February 12, 1976, Judge Walsh, then aged sixty-nine, sent a notice of retirement to President Gerald Ford.[52] Appointed in 1952 to the federal district court by President Harry Truman, Walsh had been for many years the sole federal judge in Tucson. In 1970 he had been joined by William Frey, Mary Anne's outspoken "law-and-order" colleague on the superior court who had been appointed to the federal bench by Richard Nixon. Feeling physically tired and wanting to step down before he lost his mental acuity, Walsh had been thinking of retirement for some time, but he had wanted to ensure that his successor, only the third judge in the federal courthouse, would be a person of quality and integrity. Moreover, he had a particular person in mind.

Walsh was aware that Mary Anne was herself ready for a change. She was finding her state court work less challenging than it once was, and the relentless pressure of the growing case loads in the superior court detracted from the appeal of the judgeship.[53] Moreover, Mary Anne had harbored ambitions to be named to the federal bench ever since her years in the U.S. Attorney's Office, and she remarked once that "most people on the bench aspire to [a federal judgeship],"[54] and that becoming a federal judge had been her "dream."[55] The constitutional guarantee in Article III of lifetime tenure during good behavior and the protection against diminution in judicial salaries for federal judges surely contributed to the allure of a federal judicial appointment, but Mary Anne's "dream" proba-

51. Herbert Brownell, *Too Many Judges Are Political Hacks*, SATURDAY EVENING POST, April 18, 1964, at 10.

52. John Rawlinson, *Fannin To Back Judge Richey*, THE ARIZONA DAILY STAR, February 21, 1976.

53. Mary Anne commented shortly after her confirmation to the federal court that she "needed another challenge. I got so I could do the (Superior Court work) without much improvement. I was getting a little lazy." Anthony Seed, *Judge Richey, ex-city woman, eyes high court*, THE SHELBYVILLE NEWS, June 18, 1976.

54. Ben Cole, *Woman judge is recommended for federal vacancy in Tucson*, THE ARIZONA REPUBLIC, February 21, 1976.

55. Anthony Seed, *Judge Richey, ex-city woman, eyes high court*, THE SHELBYVILLE NEWS, June 18, 1976.

bly sprang more from her simple admiration for Judge Walsh, whom she viewed as the "best federal judge in the United States."[56] According to numerous accounts, Walsh communicated to Mary Anne and to Republican leaders in Arizona that he would retire only if he could be assured that Mary Anne would succeed him.[57] One version was that Walsh prepared a list of three names, with Mary Anne's at the top, and that he let it be known that he would take senior status only if his successor were selected from his list.[58] Walsh's unusual role in the designation of his successor was so well-known that the Los Angeles Times even contained an account of it.[59] Once Walsh's preference became known, various Republican leaders in Tucson got a commitment from Senator Barry Goldwater that he would support Mary Anne's nomination. Goldwater, in turn, communicated with Paul Fannin, then the senior Senator from Arizona. Fannin, of course, had appointed Mary Anne to the superior court in 1964 and was familiar with her judicial performance. On February 19, 1976, Fannin formally recommended to Gerald Ford that he nominate Mary Anne to succeed Walsh, and he made clear that he acted with the concurrence of Goldwater and John Rhodes, Republican Congressman and then House Minority Leader.[60] Mary Anne's contemporaneous comments to the press suggested more uncertainty than she probably felt: "I knew I was under consideration but you never really know that you'll be nominated until it actually happens."[61]

After the senatorial recommendation, the White House referred Mary Anne's name to the Justice Department for investigation and to the Standing Committee on the Federal Judiciary of the American Bar Association for its own evaluation. The governmental background check, carried out as a matter of course by the Federal Bureau of Investigation, dragged on for approximately four months. The seemingly interminable delay be-

---

56. Remarks of Judge Mary Anne Richey, In the Matter of the Installation of Mary Anne Richey, United States District Court, July 9, 1976.

57. William Richey Interviews, *supra* note 3; Robbins Interviews, *supra* note 10; Interview with Hon. Richard M. Bilby, United States District Judge, Tucson, Arizon (Dec. 10, 1992); Chandler Interview, *supra* note 29; Interview with Hon. William D. Browning, United States District Judge, Tucson, Arizona (Sept. 11, 1992).

58. Bilby Interview, *supra* note 57.

59. *Ford Due To Name Arizona Woman To Federal Bench*, Los Angeles Times, May 29, 1976. According to the newspaper story, Walsh "made his retirement from the federal bench conditional on [Mary Anne's] selection as his successor."

60. Ben Cole, *Woman judge is recommended for federal vacancy in Tucson*, The Arizona Republic, Feburary 20, 1976.

61. *Id.*

tween the time of Fannin's recommendation and Ford's formal nomination was frustrating for Mary Anne, and Bill Richey blamed Fannin for not speeding up the process. Finally, in late May, Ford announced his intention to formally nominate Mary Anne for the vacancy created by Walsh's retirement.[62]

Predictably, the nomination attracted attention because of Mary Anne's gender. Mary Anne was Ford's first woman nominee to the federal bench and his only female appointee.[63] At the time, only three women were active federal district court judges out of approximately four hundred district court judgeships, and only one of ninety-seven appellate court seats was occupied by a woman—Judge Shirley Hufstedler of the United States Court of Appeals for the Ninth Circuit.[64] Moreover, because the last appointment of a woman to any federal court had been Richard Nixon's appointment of Cornelia Kennedy to the Michigan federal district court in 1970, Mary Anne became the first woman named to any federal court in the United States in almost six years, a fact remarked upon in the press.[65] Not until Jimmy Carter's presidency would the diver-

---

62. *Ford Due to Name Arizona Woman To Federal Bench*, LOS ANGELES TIMES, May 29, 1976.

63. As reported in the press, Ford nominated Elizabeth Kovachevich to a Florida federal district court in June of 1976 as well, but Kovachevich's nomination never materialized into an appointment. *Hearings Set for Woman Nominee To Federal Bench*, LOS ANGELES DAILY JOURNAL, June 11, 1976. Judge Kovachevich was ultimately nominated by President Ronald Reagan in 1982 and now sits as a judge on the United States District Court for the Middle District of Florida. *See* ALMANAC OF THE FEDERAL JUDICIARY 26 (1994-1).

64. The women federal district court judges in 1976 included June Green of the District of Columbia District Court, a Johnson appointee; Cornelia Kennedy of the Eastern District of Michigan, a Nixon appointee; and Constance Motley of the Southern District of New York, a Johnson appointee. Two other women had taken senior status: Burnita Matthews of the District of Columbia District Court, a Truman appointee; and Sara Hughes of the Northern District of Texas, a Kennedy appointee (who had entered the national limelight in 1963 when she administered the oath of office to Lyndon B. Johnson following Kennedy's assassination). *See* 415 Federal Supplement VII–XXIII (1976)(Judges of the Federal Courts with Date of Permanent Appointment); WINIFRED L. HEPPERLE & LAURA CRITES, WOMEN IN THE COURTS 102 (1978)(National Center for State Courts). The first woman to be appointed to an Article III court in the United States was Florence Ellinwood Allen, appointed in 1934 by Roosevelt to the U.S. Court of Appeals for the Sixth Circuit, where she served until 1959. *See* Ruth Bader Ginsburg & Laura Brill, *Women in the Federal Judiciary: Three Way Pavers and the Exhilarating Change President Carter Wrought*, 64 FORD. L. REV. 281, 281–84 (1995).

65. *Ford Due to Name Arizona Woman To Federal Bench*, LOS ANGELES TIMES, May 29, 1976.

sification of the federal bench in terms of gender, race, and ethnicity become an expressed presidential goal.[66]

The paucity of women in the federal judiciary in the 1970s was a function, in part, of the almost total absence of women from the legal profession in the earlier decades. By 1976, very few women had established sufficiently distinguished careers as lawyers to be considered candidates for the judiciary. According to one study of women judges carried out in 1978, the national proportion of women judges had matched the national proportion of women lawyers on a time lag basis.[67] Thus, in the 1960s when women constituted 1 to 2 percent of the legal profession, women judges filled 1 to 2 percent of the total judgeships in the United States. In the highly charged competition for the elite federal judiciary, however, other cultural barriers also operated to impede women's entry. Some scholars have attributed the underrepresentation of women in the federal judiciary to the discriminatory attitudes of the "gatekeepers," the persons in positions of influence and power.[68] The demanding role of federal trial court judge, for example, which requires the judge to maintain control and an aura of authority *vis a vis* the nation's top trial counsel, had been viewed by many as an office only men could handle. Moreover, the traditional route to appointment required more than a distinguished legal career; nominees had to have the support of political leaders, a privilege few women enjoyed; and they often were expected to come from a traditional "springboard" position, such as the office of U.S. Attorney, or a partnership in a large firm,[69] positions few women

---

66. *See* Elliot E. Slotnick, *Lowering the Bench or Raising it Higher?: Affirmtive Action and Judicial Selection During the Carter Administration*, 1 Yale L. & Policy Rev. 270 (1983). Among other measures, Carter established the use of merit-based nominating commissions for appellate and district court judgeships. These entities successfully searched for and fostered the candidacies of female and minority lawyers. *See* Carl Tobias, *Increasing Balance on the Federal Bench*, 32 Hous. L. Rev. 137, 140 (1995). During Carter's four years in office, 40 of his 258 federal court appointees, or 15.5 percent, were female. See Sheldon Goldman, *Reagan's Judicial Legacy: Completing the Puzzle and Summing Up*, 72 Judicature 318, 322 tbl.2, 325 tbl.4 (1989).

67. Hepperle & Crites, *supra* note 64, at 84.

68. Beverly Blair Cook, *Women Judges in the Opportunity Structure*, in Women, Courts, and Equality 143 (Laura L. Crites & Winifred L. Hepperle, eds. 1987).

69. One study found that the immediately-preceding occupation of 52 percent of federal district judges was partnership in a large law firm. *See* William Kitchin, Federal District Judges 168 (1978)(Table 17). Although none of the judges in the sample had come directly from the United States Attorney's Office, 19 percent had previously served as a government lawyer. *Id.* at 167 n.3. Other studies have found the United States Attorney's Office to constitute a major feeder position. *See* James Eisenstein, *Counsel for the*

had attained.[70] Mary Anne's record was unusual for her gender because her resume did include a stint as the U.S. Attorney, because she had compiled a distinguished record as trial lawyer and trial judge, and because her political connections were strong. As some put it, she was an unabashed member of the "old boys' network," and, through her association with members of the Republican elite, she was able to cross barriers that most women found impenetrable.[71]

Once Ford's formal nomination of Mary Anne went to the United States Senate, the process moved rapidly. Mary Anne, Bill Richey, and Annie flew to Washington, D.C., for a hearing before a subcommittee of the Senate Judiciary Committee on Tuesday morning, June 15, 1976.[72] No controversy existed surrounding Mary Anne's nomination, and the Senate hearing was a necessary but brief formality, lasting only eleven minutes. With Senator Fannin by her side and her husband and daughter in attendance, she answered questions from the only subcommittee member present, Senator Roman Hruska, a Republican senator from Nebraska. Hruska opened the hearing by referring to the unanimous opinion of the American Bar Association Standing Committee on the Federal Judiciary that Mary Anne was "well-qualified" for the appointment.[73] Fannin introduced Mary Anne with accolades and a brief description of her career, and Mary Anne acknowledged that Fannin had been "responsible for [her] judicial career" because of his appointment of her to the superior court in 1964. She responded to a few general questions from Hruska about the work of the Pima County Superior Court and the condition of the docket in federal court in Tucson. Referring to the case load in the Tucson court, she said, "In the event I am confirmed for the position by the Committee, it will be a challenge

---

United States: An Empirical Analysis of the Office of United States Attorney, (unpublished Ph.D. dissertation, Yale University, 1968).

70. Hepperle & Crites, *supra* note 64 at 91–95.

71. Interview with Henry G. Zipf, Tucson, Arizona (Sept. 14, 1995).

72. *See Nomination of Mary Anne Richey to be United States District [sic] For the District of Arizona, Report of Proceedings, Hearing held before Ad Hoc Subcommittee on Nominations of the Committee on the Judiciary, United States Senate*, June 15, 1976.

73. The "well-qualified" rating was the second highest rating then given by the American Bar Association Standing Committee on the Federal Judiciary. Interestingly, the highest rating of "exceptionally well qualified" was not given to any of Ford's judicial appointees but was given to about 5 percent of the judicial appointees under Presidents Nixon and Carter. *See* Sheldon Goldman, *Reagan's judicial legacy: completing the puzzle and summing up*, 72 JUDICATURE 318, 322 (1989) (Table 2). The ABA Standing Committee eliminated the "exceptionally well qualified" rating in 1989. *See* Sheldon Goldman & Matthew Saronson, *Clinton's nontraditional judges: creating a more representative bench*, 78 JUDICATURE 68, 72 n. 22 (1994).

to me and I will do everything I can to fulfill what I feel a federal judge and what I hope you feel a federal judge should do." To Hruska she also confessed that she had felt nervous when she had entered the hearing but that he had made it "very pleasant."[74] At the close of the hearing, Hruska informed Mary Anne that he would forward the recommendation to the Judiciary Committee that same morning. Notably missing from the hearing was any exploration of Mary Anne's ideological views. The following day, June 16, the Senate confirmed Mary Anne's nomination.[75]

Although Mary Anne's nomination proceeded without difficulty, a contemporaneous nomination of a local lawyer did not fare as well. Richard M. Bilby, a prominent Republican and partner in a respected Tucson law firm, was nominated by Senator Fannin in April of 1976 for a seat on the United States Court of Appeals for the Ninth Circuit, to replace retiring Tucsonan Richard Chambers. Although President Ford forwarded the nomination to the Senate Judiciary Committee, the confirmation ultimately failed. Senator Edward M. Kennedy headed the opposition, saying that he had questions about Bilby's "sensitivity" and "judicial philosophy."[76] Clearly, Kennedy and other Democratic senators hoped to preserve the high-level judicial vacancy so that the winner of the 1976 presidential election could fill it. In the words of Senator Dennis DeConcini, "[Bilby's] nomination was denied for purely political reasons."[77] The contrasting lack of controversy surrounding Mary Anne's nomination may have been a function of her gender, her lower visibility in Republican politics, and the Senate's lesser interest in district court appointments.

Three weeks after her confirmation, Mary Anne's installation as United States District Judge took place at the United States Courthouse in Tucson, just two blocks from the Superior Courts Building. At the celebration, seven people made statements on Mary Anne's behalf, some of them very poignant. Jack Hays, then a justice on the Arizona Supreme Court, recalled that he had hired Mary Anne as an Assistant U.S. Attorney and had grown to know and love her over the years. Trying to capture her many dimensions, he added, "Seldom have I seen the qualities of toler-

---

74. Nomination of Mary Anne Richey, *supra* note 72, at 7.

75. Myriad newspapers carried reports of Mary Anne's confirmation. *See Richey Judgeship Confirmed By Senate*, THE SAN DIEGO UNION, June 17, 1976; *Judge Richey confirmed*, TUCSON DAILY CITIZEN, June 17, 1976; *Mrs. Richey Ok'd By Panel*, INDIANAPOLIS STAR, June 16, 1976; *Panel OK's judge for U.S. bench*, THE ARIZONA REPUBLIC, June 16, 1976.

76. Gene Nail, *DeConcini chooses GOP's Bilby as replacement for Judge Frey*, THE ARIZONA DAILY STAR, February 25, 1979.

77. *Id.*

ance, compassion and understanding melted [sic] in a dynamic and active person who is a doer, wife, mother, judge, lawyer, civic leader, horsewoman, sports enthusiast and lover of the out-of-doors, airplane pilot and friend of all who need a friend."[78] Thomas Tang, who was then president-elect of the State Bar of Arizona and would later be appointed to the United States Court of Appeals for the Ninth Circuit, congratulated Mary Anne for her accomplishments as a woman: "As a minority in terms of sex," he remarked, "she is being made a member of the Bench...and so she is entitled to a salute in that regard."[79]

Warren Christopher, then a prominent lawyer in Los Angeles, California, who would later serve as Secretary of State under President Bill Clinton, also spoke at the installation in his capacity as chairman of the ABA Standing Committee on the Federal Judiciary. He assured the audience that Mary Anne had come through the committee's investigation "with flying colors," and he read aloud some of the comments about Mary Anne that lawyers had submitted to the committee. Inevitably, Christopher told the crowd that half a dozen people had paid Mary Anne the "highest compliment" in saying, "Why, that lady tries a case like a real man." He also read several references to Mary Anne's physical attractiveness. To laughter in the crowd, Christopher announced, "One of them said, Judge Richey, that you look much younger than your years, and indeed you do. Another comment is that you have those outdoor good looks."[80] Virginia Trumbull, Mary Anne's close friend from her days in the WASP, also spoke at the event. She regaled the audience with tales of "Ground-Loop Pete's" exploits in the WASP, exploits that, in Trumbull's view, revealed Mary Anne's perseverance, her courage, and her good judgment in an emergency.[81]

In a fitting ceremony, Judge Walsh administered the oath of office to Mary Anne. She then spoke to the group herself. She reflected on the fact that when she started law school, she was "the only girl in a class of one hundred and five," and that she would not have made it through had it not been for the help of Richard and Robert Roylston. She recalled their struggles as fledgling lawyers together, and the bond she felt with the Roylstons was evident in her remarks. She reminded Judge Walsh that he had also once said, "You don't try a case like a woman; you try one like a man." She continued, "I thought I had made it then when he said that. But, as I would sit there, I would really look at him and think: Golly,

---

78. Transcripts of *In the Matter of the Installation of Hon. Mary Anne Richey*, United States District Court for the District of Arizona, July 9, 1976, at 1.

79. *Id.* at 3.

80. *Id.* at 7.

81. *Id.* at 13.

wouldn't that be something to be able to be a Federal Judge; and I never thought I would ever make it." She told the audience that she would try to emulate Walsh, but she felt incapable of "following in his footsteps," since she viewed him as the "best judge in the whole United States."[82] She alluded to the fact that she had not been in a federal court for twenty years and would have to "really almost go back to school" to prepare herself for the judgeship.[83] At some length, she introduced her family and friends in attendance, and thanked, among others, Lorna Lockwood, then Chief Justice of the Arizona Supreme Court, for attending the event. In a rare reference to her own gender and her link with other groundbreakers, Mary Anne commented, somewhat inelegantly, to Lockwood, "I know it is the likes of you that went on ahead of me that makes it possible for me to be sitting here where I am."[84] In sum, Mary Anne's remarks were a combination of characteristic self-directed humor; humility and a glimmer of insecurity in the face of the appointment; affection and gratitude toward her family and many friends; admiration for her mentor Walsh; and simple joy at obtaining what she had "dreamed" about for many years.

Among the many well-wishers who sent congratulatory letters to Mary Anne upon her confirmation were numerous members of the judiciary, including the Chief Justice of the United States, Warren Burger; Sandra Day O'Connor, then a state court appellate judge in Phoenix; and Constance Baker Motley, the Johnson appointee in the Southern District of New York who was one of the four active women federal judges in the country and the first African-American woman appointed to an Article III court. Despite the plethora of letters from prominent political and judicial leaders, one of Mary Anne's most treasured missives came in a handwritten scrawl from the Arizona State Prison. Richard Wassmer, a man she had sentenced in the Pima County Superior Court on a charge of possession of a stolen vehicle and obtaining money by false pretenses, was moved to write her the following words:

> "Your Honor, Congratulations on being appointed a federal judge and I wish you well. All I can say is thank you for the fair treatment I got from you when I appeared before you in A-24263 in the Superior Court. During the next 29 months I will be learning a trade and moving down to Fort Grant for on the job Training. And Anybody who comes before you in the federal courts I am sure will get the same treatment from you. Thank

---

82. *Id.* at 17–18.
83. *Id.* at 19.
84. *Id.*

you for taking your time for reading this letter. And I remain Very truly yours Richard M. Wassmer."[85]

Mary Anne had given Wassmer five years probation, with one year of jail time, in 1974 after a plea of guilty.[86] Despite his having been returned to prison two years later because of a violation of probation, he apparently remained grateful for the leniency she showed in the original sentence. Mary Anne kept the letter in her personal files and sometimes referred to it to remind herself of the very human dimension of her job.

Mary Anne embarked on the final stage of her professional career once again as a pathbreaker. Despite the media attention, however, she preferred to downplay the "gender card." She did write to President Ford in a thank you note, "it is my understanding that I am the first woman you have appointed,"[87] but she did not celebrate the point in public. Moreover, she characteristically rejected any suggestion that her attainments were *because* of her gender. In an interview conducted shortly after her appointment to the federal bench, she stated, "I don't want anything just because I'm a woman. I just want to be equal."[88] Nevertheless, the hapless security guard at the federal courthouse who asked Mary Anne to move her car on her first day at work made it clear to the newly-appointed judge that stereotypes persisted.[89]

---

85. Undated letter from "Richard M. Wassmer to The Hon. Mary-Ann Richey"(sic), Personal Correspondence File of Mary Anne Richey regarding Appointment to Federal Bench.

86. State v. Wassmer, No. A-24263 (Pima County Sup. Ct., sentenced, July 3, 1974, probation revoked, April 26, 1976, due to violation of probation).

87. Letter from Mary Anne Richey to Hon. Gerald R. Ford, July 14, 1976.

88. Anthony Seed, *Judge Richey, Ex-city woman, eyes high court*, THE SHELBYVILLE NEWS, June 25, 1976.

89. The security guard's words and Mary Anne's response are recounted at the beginning of Chapter One.

CHAPTER TWELVE

The Craft of the Federal District Judge

Mary Anne moved to the United State Courthouse in July 1976, at the age of fifty-eight. The transition constituted a mere two blocks in downtown Tucson, from the modern Superior Courts Building, completed in 1975, to the historic United States Courthouse, a four-story cream-colored brick and granite building that had been constructed in 1929.[1] Despite the geographic proximity of the state and federal courts, the significance of Mary Anne's move to the federal bench was profound. As an "Article III" judge, she had achieved a special status: she was entitled under the Constitution to lifetime tenure during "good Behaviour," and her salary was protected against decreases.[2] By insulating federal judges from political pressures, the framers of the Constitution had hoped to foster an independent judiciary, and Mary Anne felt honored to join that privileged group. In particular, she was delighted to be free of the periodic electoral contests she had been required to face in state court.

The elite status of the federal judiciary comes not only from its constitutional stature, but from other factors as well. By 1976, Arizona boasted almost seventy superior court judges, and the Pima County Superior Court had expanded to fifteen judges. In contrast, the District of Arizona had only five active federal trial court judges and one senior judge. In Tucson, Mary Anne was now occupying a courthouse that had only one other active federal trial court judge. Thus, the dramatic difference in numbers alone between the state and federal benches enhanced the prestige of the federal court. Importantly, the move also signified a higher salary for Mary Anne. Her beginning salary on the federal bench was $44,000, a significant increase over her final state court yearly earnings of $33,000.[3] The federal salary, seemingly modest by contemporary standards, rose rapidly under the provisions of the Federal Salary Act of 1967,[4] to a salary of $73,100 by 1983, the year of her death.[5]

---

1. *New Building of U.S. Ample*, THE ARIZONA DAILY STAR, August 25, 1929; *U.S. Courthouse picked for historic register*, THE ARIZONA DAILY STAR, March 5, 1983.

2. U.S. CONST., Art. III, sec. 1.

3. NATIONAL CENTER FOR STATE COURTS, SURVEY OF JUDICIAL SALARIES IN STATE COURT SYSTEMS 3 (1976).

4. *See* Pub. L. No. 90-206, 81 Stat. 642 (1967), codified at 2 U.S.C. 351-361. As of 1975, the Act is adjusted according to the guidelines set out at 28 U.S.C. Sec. 461.

5. *See* 28 U.S.C. Sec. 135 (1993)(Historical and Statutory Notes).

The select group of judges that Mary Anne joined in the summer of 1976 were men who had become accustomed to their Article III stature. In the Tucson division of the federal court, Walsh continued on in senior status. From all appearances, he continued to follow his customary rigorous schedule, rising at four in the morning for his daily walk, arriving at the courthouse before eight, and staying until six in the evening. He had accumulated a wealth of wisdom in his twenty-four years on the bench, which Mary Anne mined regularly. William Frey, the most junior member of the federal judiciary in Arizona, had already served for six years on the district court. Frey was a hot-tempered and outspoken conservative Republican who occasionally let his anger surface in the courtroom and frequently let it be seen in chambers.[6] He believed that the criminal justice system had been distorted by the Warren Court's constitutional rulings, and he was not reticent about expounding his views. As a state court judge, he had accused the United States Supreme Court of "a form of tyranny" under Chief Justice Warren, he had decried the deterioration of "law and order," and he had blamed the Supreme Court for the rising crime rate.[7] Mary Anne was friendly toward Frey but did not perceive him to be a role model. Judge Walsh remained her mentor and her ideal as a federal judge, and she made her way to his fourth-floor chambers several times daily in the early months of her federal tenure.[8]

The three men in the Phoenix division of the federal court, all Democrats, were a seasoned group of jurists. Walter Craig, appointed by John Kennedy in 1963 shortly before Kennedy's assassination, was a Stanford law graduate and a founding partner of Fennemore Craig, one of Arizona's largest firms. Carl Muecke, appointed by Lyndon Johnson in 1964, had graduated from the University of Arizona two years after Mary Anne's graduation. He succeeded Mary Anne as the United States Attorney for the District of Arizona in 1961 under Kennedy and remained in that post until Lyndon Johnson nominated him to the federal bench. Finally, William Copple, also a Johnson appointee who took the bench in 1966, had graduated from Boalt Hall School of Law in 1951, the same year Mary Anne graduated from the University of Arizona.[9]

To Mary Anne's satisfaction, the number of women within the Ninth Circuit increased dramatically in the years following her much-heralded

---

6. Interview with David Burr Udall, Tucson, Arizona (Dec. 13, 1995).

7. Gil Matthews, *Frey Blames High Court For Rising Crime*, Tucson Daily Citizen, January 1, 1968.

8. Interview with Eleanor Robbins, Tucson, Arizona (July 13, 1992).

9. *See* The American Bench 109, 111, 115 (1977).

addition to the federal bench, largely due to appointments during the administration of Jimmy Carter. By executive order, Carter endorsed diversification of the federal bench as a presidential objective, and he established nominating commissions to carry out his goal.[10] Through concerted efforts by the commissions in every circuit, Carter appointed some forty women to the federal judiciary.[11] By the end of his term in office, he had appointed three additional women to the Ninth Circuit Court of Appeals and six to the district courts within the circuit.[12] Throughout her tenure on the federal bench, however, Mary Anne remained the only woman district court judge in Arizona. Moreover, the non-Article III adjudicators in the Arizona federal district court—the magistrates and bankruptcy judges—were all men during Mary Anne's seven years on the bench.[13] Thus, she continued to work in an environment where her professional peers were exclusively male.

Mary Anne brought with her the hardworking and loyal staff that she had assembled in the superior court. Initially, she was assigned to a small temporary courtroom on the second floor, but she later moved to her permanent quarters on the third floor. There she presided over a large and formal courtroom that Judge Walsh had previously occupied. It boasted high arched windows, marble flooring, and a handsome elevated bench. Towards the end of her federal court tenure, when she began to suffer from poor circulation in her legs, she had workers install a wooden leg rest behind the bench so that she could sit in relative comfort for long periods.[14]

A major difference in working environment in the federal court as compared to the superior court was the presence of law clerks to assist the federal district court judges. The Arizona state trial courts lacked funding for law clerks, and Mary Anne, like most state court judges, had grown accustomed to working alone, relying by necessity on counsel for a full exploration of legal issues in a case. In the federal system, in contrast, federal

---

10. *See* Exec. Order No. 12,059, 3 C.F.R. 180 (1979); Exec. Order No. 12,097, 3 C.F.R. 254 (1979).

11. *See* Sheldon Goldman, *Bush's Judicial Legacy: The Final Imprint*, 76 JUDICATURE 282, 287, 293 (1993).

12. At the appellate court level, Carter appointed Mary M. Schroeder, Betty B. Fletcher, and Dorothy Nelson, all in 1979. His district court appointments within the Ninth Circuit were Mariana R. Pfaelzer, Cynthia H. Hall, Marilyn H. Patel, Judith N. Keep, Helen J. Frye, and Barbara J. Rothstein. *See* 575 Fed. Supp. XXII–XXV (Judges of the Federal Courts).

13. *See* STATE BAR OF ARIZONA, MEMBERSHIP DIRECTORY (1976-1983)(United States District Court District of Arizona).

14. Interview with Hon. William D. Browning, United States District Judge, Tucson, Arizona (Sept. 11, 1992).

district court judges were entitled to the services of a full-time law clerk—generally selected from the ranks of recent law school graduates—to assist the judges in legal research and opinion drafting. Moreover, after Francis Copham, her longtime bailiff, retired in 1979, she was able to employ two law clerks, one of whom served as "clerk-bailiff."

Mary Anne's clerks were graduates of various schools, but the majority came from the University of Arizona College of Law.[15] In her hiring decisions, she considered the applicant's traditional paper credentials as well as the person's likely rapport with the judge herself and with other staff members. Mary Anne's interviewing proclivity was to ask straightforward and somewhat enigmatic questions. "Where you a sheltered child?" she unsmilingly asked one clerk in the initial interview. At the time, the clerk's intuition was that the right response was "no."[16] One clerk recalled that during the interviewing process Mary Anne asked him his views on the issue of abortion. "I told her that although I had moral questions about abortion itself, I didn't think it was the government's business. That seemed to satisfy her."[17] Another clerk remembered that during her initial interview, she and Mary Anne spoke for more than an hour about the misery of a failed marriage.[18] Yet another recalled that Mary Anne was "blunt and straightforward during the interview," and that his reputation as a "troublemaker" during law school appealed to her. "I guess she was a maverick, and she saw me as one, too," he added.[19]

Mary Anne's relationship with her staff and law clerks was, for the most part, friendly and informal. She often functioned as confidant and adviser on career decisions as well as family problems. She was nevertheless the undisputed head of the office and she was capable of displays of a steely-eyed anger. Her deputy courtroom clerk quickly learned that Mary

---

15. As Mary Anne's first law clerk, the author was hired hastily in late spring of 1976, once the appointment to the federal court was on track, and remained in that position through 1978. The succeeding clerks were Faith Halter (1978–79), a graduate of the University of Pennsylvania Law School; David White (1979–80), an Arizona law graduate; Nancy Fiora (1979–80), an Arizona law graduate; Maureen DeMaio (1981), a Georgetown law graduate; Joseph Sholder (1980–82), an Arizona law graduate; Mary Ameln (1981–83), an Arizona law graduate; Craig Kaufman (1982–83), a Washburn College of Law graduate; and Ellen Sewell (1983), an Arizona law graduate who was hired less than three months before Mary Anne's death. Personnel File of Judge Mary Anne Richey, United States District Court, Tucson, Arizona.

16. Author's recollection from personal interview in April 1976.

17. Interview with Craig H. Kaufman, Tucson, Arizona (Jan. 12, 1993).

18. Interview with Hon. Nancy Fiora, Magistrate Judge, District of Arizona, Tucson, Arizona (Aug. 20, 1992).

19. Telephone Interview with Joseph M. Sholder (Dec. 20, 1995).

Anne wanted her case files arranged in a particular order. The clerk, who sat immediately in front of the bench when court was in session, recalled her anxiety about performing her job to Mary Anne's satisfaction. "I'd hear the files slam down behind my head," she remembered, "and I'd think, 'oh no, what did I forget to do?'"[20] The judge expected absolute accuracy in research, and she wanted work to be completed by a designated time. One law clerk recalled that at the beginning of her clerkship, Mary Anne always wanted her bench memoranda early so that she could check the research herself. "She wasn't sure she could trust me completely at the start," the clerk explained.[21] Mary Anne would forcefully reprimand her clerks if she perceived that they had produced shoddy work or had failed to follow through on a commitment to her.[22] On occasion, Mary Anne's disapproval went beyond the workplace. One law clerk recalled, for example, that he attended a Democratic Party function early in his clerkship. The function was televised, and his picture was broadcast on the local news. Mary Anne called him to her chambers the following day and said to him, somewhat facetiously, "You are not supposed to be involved in politics, and especially not Democratic politics." According to the clerk, she was "half-joking," but he perceived that she was displeased with his visibility.[23] In other contexts, Mary Anne gave personal advice to her staff, and she similarly communicated her displeasure when the advice was not followed.[24] Thus, Mary Anne's interpersonal style included assertions of clear authority, empathic listening, and sporadic anger.

On the other hand, she was willing to reveal her own self-doubts and to engage in self-deprecating humor, and the occasional revelation of her vulnerability blunted the sting of her anger. Mary Anne entertained her law clerks with tales of her travels in India and her exploits in the WASP, and she sometimes confided in her clerks about her own anxieties. During her federal court years, for example, she was often consumed with worry about her daughter Annie. She spoke frankly to her clerks about her daughter's increasingly uneven adolescence and her flagging interest in school. Professional insecurities also surfaced. At the outset of her federal tenure, for example, she confessed to feeling tentative in her new role, particularly in the writing of opinions.

Because the job of district court judge required more "writing" than did the state court judgeship, she welcomed the services of her law

---

20. Telephone Interview with Kerry Bjorn (Feb. 13, 1996).

21. Telephone Interview with Maureen DeMaio (Dec. 22, 1995).

22. Personal experience of author; Fiora Interview, *supra* note 18; Interview with David R. White, Tucson, Arizona (Dec. 16, 1992).

23. White Interview, *supra* note 22.

24. Robbins Interview, *supra* note 8.

clerks.[25] She did not like to publish opinions and did so only rarely at the request of counsel. In Mary Anne's seven years on the federal bench, she published only seven opinions in the Federal Supplement or other specialized reporter systems.[26] She also found intimidating the prospect of authoring opinions for the Ninth Circuit, a task that periodically fell to her when she sat by designation on the appellate court. When she had to produce a written decree, ranging from a summary judgment to a ruling on an application for attorneys' fees, she typically asked her law clerks to produce a draft. She then would react verbally or with brief written comments and might ask for a redrafting, but she rarely authored opinions herself.

Because Mary Anne had not been present in a federal courtroom for many years, she likewise feared that her substantive knowledge of federal jurisdiction was inadequate. For that reason, she depended heavily on her clerks' legal analyses of issues that came before her, but she maintained the central role of ultimate adjudicator. Her directives to her clerks would often be: "My hunch is that the law on this issue favors this particular disposition, but please make sure I am right." In general, her common sense served her well, and her intuitive assessments of the legal issues were supported in the law. When her intuition or world view seemed to point her in a direction that was against the weight of legal authority, she would hear the clerk out, and, on occasion, change her mind. Her method of adjudication paralleled another federal judge's description of constitutional decision-making:

> I firmly believe that judges, whether conservative, moderate, or liberal, follow basically the same process in deciding cases involving constitu-

---

25. In an interview given six years after her appointment to the federal court, Mary Anne remarked that the least favorite feature of her job was writing. "A federal judge can't just say, 'Motion Denied' and leave it at that. Usually, you've got to write an opinion and writing has always been a chore for me. Fortunately, I have excellent law clerks to help me with the research and writing." Louise Stratton, *Judicial Profile: Judge Mary Anne Richey*, THE WRIT, May 1982 (Official Publication of The Pima County Bar Association).

26. Mary Anne's published opinions, all from the civil docket, were Catalina Cablevision Assoc. v. City of Tucson, 1984-1 Trade Cas. P65,789 (D. Ariz. 1983)(summary judgment in antitrust case); Nolan v. United States, 539 F. Supp. 788 (D. Ariz. 1982)(judicial review of tax assessment); Genson v. Ripley, 544 F. Supp. 251 (D. Ariz. 1981)(summary judgment in Federal Tort Claims Act case); Harbor Mechanical, Inc. v. Arizona Elec. Power Co-op, Inc., 496 F. Supp. 681 (D. Ariz. 1980)(summary judgment in construction case); Fox v. Kennecott Copper Corp., 113 L.R.R.M. 2516 (D. Ariz. 1980)(summary judgment in employment case); United States v. Pima County Community College Dist., 24 Emp. Prac. Dec. P31,225 (D. Ariz. 1979)(award of attorneys' fees and costs against United States); and Fisher v. City of Tucson, 26 Fair Empl. Prac. Cas. 864 (D. Ariz. 1977)(dismissal of complaint under Rehabilitation Act of 1973).

tional issues. First, they individually evaluate any perceived equities in the underlying situation; then, they seek to render judgment in accordance with what they personally comprehend with respect to those equities. It is at this point that judges begin to seriously consider the relevant constitutional law and precedents in order to insure that their personal inclinations do not contravene either.[27]

Mary Anne was pleased with the structure of the federal court work from the start. As compared to the assignment system followed in the Pima County Superior Court, she preferred the "individual calendar" system in the federal court, through which cases were assigned upon filing to a single judge in alternating order and remained with that judge until final disposition. In commenting on the difference between the two benches, she once stated, "[t]he biggest different is the individual calendar. I get to know the case from start to finish. By the time we get to trial, I know almost as much about the case as the lawyers do." She believed that the individual calendar system meant that lawyers were better prepared. "[In federal court] lawyers have to be as well-prepared for pretrial as they would be if they were going to trial." In her view, better preparation by the lawyers and increased familiarity with the case by the judge encouraged settlements, and she had long been a supporter of resolving cases short of trial. "Many settlements are made during pre-trial conferences in my court," she explained.[28]

The case load in the federal court exposed Mary Anne to numerous categories of jurisdiction in both the criminal and civil domains that had not been within her purview as a state court judge and concomitantly eliminated a few categories from her docket. In the criminal domain, the docket of the Arizona district court during Mary Anne's tenure was dominated by cases arising under the federal narcotics laws and immigration laws; it also included a number of prosecutions for firearms violations, bank robbery, mail fraud, racketeering, counterfeiting, and tax evasion, as well as major crimes occurring on Indian reservations and other federal enclaves within the state.[29] In addition, Mary Anne presided over a few

---

27. Hon. William Wayne Justice, *Putting the Judge Back in Judging*, 63 U. COL. L. REV. 441, 442 (1992).

28. Stratton, *supra* note 25.

29. District-wide data show that narcotics and immigration offenses dominated the criminal docket from the beginning of Mary Anne's federal court tenure until her final year on the bench. *See* REPORTS OF THE PROCEEDINGS OF THE JUDICIAL CONFERENCE OF THE UNITED STATES, ANNUAL REPORT OF THE DIRECTOR OF THE ADMINISTRATIVE OFFICE OF THE UNITED STATES COURTS 400-01 (1977)(Table)(hereinafter "ANNUAL REPORT"); ANNUAL REPORT, 370-71 (1983)(Table).

less common federal prosecutions: threats on the life of the President,[30] violations of the strike prohibition for federal employees,[31] and unlawful wire-tapping.[32] In the civil arena, the Arizona district court's docket included diversity of citizenship cases (constituting the largest single category of private civil jurisdiction); cases arising under the Constitution and civil rights and anti-discrimination statutes; actions under the Federal Tort Claims Act; antitrust cases; patent cases; and myriad private and governmental cases arising under miscellaneous federal statutes.[33] Mary Anne found the array of jurisdictional categories interesting, and she was also pleased with what was not on the docket. In particular, she was relieved not to have to hear domestic relations cases. Notwithstanding the seriousness with which she had taken the state-court divorce cases that raised novel issues, she explained that the absence of such cases was one of the joys of being on the federal bench. "Many times," she said, "it's nothing more than people fighting over things like plastic dishes."[34] Her avowed disinterest in domestic relations disputes, it should be noted, was consistent with the views of the federal judiciary in general.[35]

As in district courts across the United States, the workload was intense for Mary Anne and Frey, despite the assistance of federal magistrate Raymond T. Terlizzi. Within the Ninth Circuit, the District of Arizona was second only to California in civil and criminal filings throughout Mary Anne's tenure.[36] Indeed, she may have shared the frustration voiced by a judge from the Northern District of California, who was moved to write in 1978, "The litigation explosion has created an unprecedented crisis in the administration of justice. The burgeoning volume, complexity and

---

30. United States v. Schmidt, CR 76-594 (D. Ariz.), *conviction aff'd*, 572 F.2d 206 (9th Cir. 1978).

31. United States v. Florence, CR 81-00186 (D. Ariz.), and United States v. Taylor, CR 81-00185 (D. Ariz.), *convictions aff'd*, 693 F.2d 919 (9th Cir. 1982).

32. United States v. McIntyre, CR 77-00303 (D. Ariz.), *conviction aff'd*, 582 F.2d 1221 (9th Cir. 1978).

33. District wide data show that federal governmental actions dominated the civil docket in 1977, but that by 1983, private civil actions had surpassed the federal governments' filings. *See* 1977 ANNUAL REPORT, *supra* note 29, at 324–25 (Table C-3); 1983 ANNUAL REPORT, *supra* note 29, at 252–53 (Table C-3).

34. Stratton, *supra* note 25.

35. *See* Judith Resnik, *"Naturally" Without Gender: Women, Jurisdiction, and the Federal Courts*, 66 N.Y.U.L. REV. 1682, 1685–89 (1991)(describing the federal courts' entrenched resistance to consideration of domestic relations or family law matters).

36. *See* 1983 ANNUAL REPORT, *supra* note 29, at 252, 328 (Tables C-3, D-3)(showing civil and criminal cases commenced); 1977 ANNUAL REPORT, *supra* note 29, at 324, 363 (Tables C-3, D1AD)(showing civil cases commenced and criminal defendants commenced).

cost of civil litigation threatens to exhaust the resources of courts and litigants."[37] By 1977, Mary Anne's first full year on the federal bench, civil case filings in the federal courts across the United States had reached a record number of 328 per judge.[38] In her last year on the bench, the filings per judge had climbed to 470.[39]

Although Mary Anne's years on the federal bench predated the civil justice reforms of the late 1980s and early 1990s, she favored many of the goals of such reforms, including the greater use of alternative dispute resolution methods and greater judicial control over abusive practices by counsel.[40] The intense workload in the district court surely colored her attitude toward efficient methods of dispute resolution. She did not aggressively "manage" cases in her courtroom in the sense that has provoked scholarly critique,[41] but she did encourage parties to settle when she perceived that the case was nearing an agreement point. One lawyer remembered her asking, "How far apart are you from settling? I don't want to know the numbers, but I want to know if you're close."[42] According to a law clerk, "The judge would let down on formality in chambers, and she was good at encouraging lawyers to resolve their differences in that relaxed atmosphere. She used her common sense."[43] In her court, as in the courts of all the district judges, most cases did settle—even difficult, hard-

---

37. Hon. William W. Schwarzer, *Managing civil litigation: the trial judge's role*, 61 JUDICATURE 400, 401 (April 1978).

38. *See* 1977 ANNUAL REPORT, *supra* note 29, at 186.

39. *See* 1983 ANNUAL REPORT, *supra* note 29, at 119.

40. In 1983, Rule 16 of the Federal Rules of Civil Procedure was amended to enhance the federal district judge's authority in encouraging settlement, *see* FED. R. CIV. P. 16(a)(5),(c)(7). In the same year, Rule 11 was amended to increase the judge's authority to sanction abusive litigation practices. FED. R. CIV. P. 11 and Advisory Committee Notes to 1983 Revisions. Five years later, Congress enacted the Judicial Improvements and Access to Justice Act, Pub. L. 100-702, 102 Stat. 4663, authorizing, among other changes, the use of court-annexed arbitration. Pursuant to that Act, the District Court of Arizona established a program of court-annexed, voluntary, non-binding arbitration in 1992. *See* Rule 2.11, RULES OF PRACTICE OF THE U.S. DIST. CT. FOR THE DIST. OF ARIZ. Moreover, the Civil Justice Reform Act of 1990, 28 U.S.C. Secs. 471–482 (Supp. IV. 1992), requires each United States district court to implement a "civil justice expense and delay reduction plan...to facilitate deliberate adjudication of civil cases on the merits, monitor discovery, improve litigation management, and ensure just, speedy and inexpensive resolutions of civil disputes."

41. *See, e.g.*, Judith Resnik, *Managerial Judges*, 96 HARV. L. REV. 374 (1982); Leroy J. Tornquist, *The Active Judge in Pretrial Settlement: Inherent Authority Gone Awry*, 25 WILLIAMETTE L. REV. 743 (1989).

42. Interview with David Burr Udall, Tucson, Arizona (Dec. 13, 1995).

43. Interview with Mary O. Ameln, Tucson, Arizona (April 29, 1993).

fought cases. Some of the more rancorous disputes in which she may have played a subtle role in achieving settlement included a well-publicized tort action brought by three Mexican nationals who were robbed and tortured by a ranching family from southern Arizona,[44] a trade-secrets case between competing corporations involving the production of digital watches,[45] and an antitrust action brought by several individual dentists against various local and national dental associations.[46] In these and other cases on her docket, Mary Anne created an atmosphere conducive to settlement through such measures as status conferences, pretrial conferences, and the resolution of pivotal preliminary motions.[47]

The move to the federal bench surely had a psychological impact on Mary Anne. On the one hand, she held on to a style of relaxed informality when off the bench, and she found great pleasure in human relationships. She befriended the staff in the clerk's office as well as the custodians of the courthouse and took a genuine interest in their lives. She remained unpretentious, and her conversations were often peppered with colloquial phrases and whimsical anecdotes drawn from her Indiana girlhood. "There's no gettin' the cow back in the barn door," she would say, commenting on a lawyer's futile efforts to remedy the effect of a witness's damaging testimony. Frequently, on a Friday afternoon, she would come walking down the long tiled hallway from her chambers and in a loud voice would call out, "Let's all blow this joint!" Her personal staff would eagerly oblige her with a prompt exit from the courthouse. She was known to greet lawyers with a cheerful "Howdy!", and she often engaged in good-natured ribbing about their performances in court.[48] She maintained social friendships with several lawyers in Arizona, many of whom

---

44. Order of Dismissal, Mata v. Hanigan, CIV 77-244, Loya v. Hanigan, CIV 77-245, Zavala v. Hanigan, CIV 77-246, (D. Ariz. May 26, 1983). All three actions were dismissed with prejudice after an out-of-court settlement. The Hanigan brothers had been earlier acquitted by a state court on assault charges, and one had been acquitted but the other convicted in federal court for criminal civil rights violations. *See Arizona*, UNITED PRESS INTERNATIONAL RELEASE, May 27, 1983.

45. Order of Dismissal, American Atomics Corp. v. Coherent, Inc., CIV 77-210 (D. Ariz. Oct. 10, 1979).

46. Dismissal upon settlement and permanent injunction order, Vinall v. Southern Arizona Dental Society, CIV 77-009 (D. Ariz. Sept. 21, 1977).

47. In *Harbor Mechanical, Inc. v. Arizona Electric Power Coop., Inc.*, 496 F. Supp. 681 (D. Ariz. 1980), for example, Mary Anne resolved two hotly-contested motions to dismiss in a dispute arising out of the construction of a power plant. Her interpretation of Arizona law in the diversity case resulted in a dismissal of one of plaintiffs' primary claims. The case settled four months after her ruling. *See* Dismissal, Harbor Mechanical, Inc. v. Ariz. Elec. Power Coop., Inc., CIV 80-27 (D. Ariz. Dec. 11, 1980).

48. Interview with William Kimble, Tucson, Arizona (Sept. 29, 1995).

frequently visited her in chambers. There, amidst much laughter, they often discussed the latest news in the world of sports, and she was known to wager a few dollars with some of them on her favorite football teams.[49]

On the other hand, some observers concluded that Mary Anne's demeanor changed once she moved to the federal system and that she became more "testy" or impatient with counsel. Her critical eye, some believed, focused more intently on female lawyers than on male lawyers; she seemed to demand that the few women lawyers who appeared in her court perform flawlessly.[50] One female Assistant U.S. Attorney remembered Mary Anne's brusque reprimand in open court during a civil forfeiture proceeding, only to be followed by a friendly telephone call from the judge after the lawyer returned to her office. "Judge Richey seemed to be saying, implicitly, that I shouldn't take it personally. I appreciated the message."[51]

Some attorneys were under the impression that Mary Anne's anger surfaced more quickly as a federal judge and that she was less tolerant of overly-zealous lawyering.[52] William Browning, who was appointed to the federal bench upon Mary Anne's death, suggested that once a person becomes a judge, one's attitudes toward lawyering change. "It is a different view from this perch than when you're trying cases," he explained. "She was impatient with lawyers who 'over-try' their cases." Browning recalled a case he litigated before Mary Anne under the Federal Tort Claims Act where she exhibited that impatience. The case, in which Browning represented one of the plaintiffs, went to a four-day court trial in Mary Anne's court after a protracted period of pretrial discovery. Mary Anne's law clerk who worked on the case recalled that the case was highly technical with many factual disputes, and that it was fatiguing for the judge and for counsel. According to the clerk, once the case got to trial, Browning seemed displeased with the way the trial was progressing.[53] His apparent displeasure was well-founded: Mary Anne reluctantly rendered a defense verdict at the close of trial.[54]

49. Robbins Interview, *supra* note 8.

50. Fiora Interview, *supra* note 18; DeMaio Interview, *supra* note 21.

51. Conversation with Virginia A. Mathis, Assistant United States Attorney, Phoenix, Arizona (May 7, 1993).

52. Kimble Interview, *supra* note 48; Browning Interview, *supra* note 14; Telephone Interview with Howard A. Kashman (July 11, 1995).

53. DeMaio Interview, *supra* note 21.

54. Doak v. United States, CIV 79-0170 (D. Ariz. Jan. 27, 1982), *aff'd*, 714 F.2d 152 (9th Cir. 1983). Mary Anne's law clerk at the time of *Doak* recalled that "the judge wanted there to be compensation, but she felt that it wasn't available under the law. The case distressed her." Ameln Interview, *supra* note 43.

The displeasure itself, however, may have angered Mary Anne. On one of the trial days, during a long afternoon of evidentiary contests, Browning objected to the introduction of certain defense evidence as hearsay. "After I objected, the other lawyer said, 'Well, Judge, we think there is an exception to the hearsay rule that makes this admissible,' and he went off on his speech. I was tired and it was late in the day, and I said, 'Oh, let him answer.' At that point, she said, 'I'll decide who answers questions in this courtroom of mine.' And I thought, 'Oh shit, I think she will.'" In spite of her reprimand, Browning viewed Mary Anne's posture in the case not as overbearing but rather as evincing frustration with the contentiousness of the litigation. "We were all at the end of our tether, and I would bet that Mary Anne was sorry she said that."[55]

At another point in the same trial, Mary Anne again showed anger, but in that instance she came to regret her rebukes of counsel quite quickly. During an afternoon recess, she let it be known that she was "sick and tired of the case dragging on." Browning recalled her saying to the lawyers, "This case ought to come to a close and we are going to bite the bullet. We will go until six o'clock tonight, we will go until six o'clock tomorrow night, and we will try it on the weekends if we have to, but this case will be over by Tuesday." After a short break, Mary Anne returned to the courtroom and was "transformed." According to Browning, "She looked angelic, and she said, 'Counsel, I have a problem. I would like to ask your indulgence.' We nodded, and she explained that during recess she had spoken with her husband and learned that he had acquired tickets to a big prize fight for that evening. She said to us, 'I would really like to go but I'll have to leave at about four o'clock.' We said, 'Well, we think you can be excused, your honor.'" In Browning's view, she was somewhat sheepish and seemed to have a good-humored embarrassment about her earlier remarks.[56]

Another incident that occurred early in Mary Anne's federal court tenure also illuminates her "Article III" demeanor. The incident involved a dispute between Stephen Dichter, then an Assistant U.S. Attorney, and David Hoffman, the same criminal defense attorney who had successfully defended Yvonne Edwards in Mary Anne's court in 1974. The lawyers were heatedly disputing a motion to suppress in Mary Anne's small temporary courtroom in the federal courthouse. When Hoffman sensed that the judge was going to rule against him, he rolled his eyes in a gesture of exaggerated frustration. According to both Hoffman and Dichter, she

---

55. Browning Interview, *supra* note 14.
56. Id.

slammed down her gavel and summoned counsel into her chambers. There she turned to Hoffman and said, without a trace of humor, "Mr. Hoffman, you know I don't think I was sprinkled with holy water when I put these black robes on. But, goddamit, if you ever roll your eyes at me again in court, I'll hold you in contempt." At that point, Hoffman's recollection was that he retorted, "If you want to hold me in contempt, go ahead. But you used to be the gutsiest judge around, and now, I don't know what happened since you came over here to the federal courthouse." Dichter's memory was slightly different. After her threat of contempt, Dichter recalled that he attempted to capitalize on her anger toward Hoffman. "Your Honor," he began, "as long as you're at it, there are some other things Hoffman has been doing...." Mary Anne turned abruptly to Dichter and said, "You, shut up." Despite the outbursts, both lawyers perceived that Mary Anne respected their candor, at least in chambers, and each remained on good terms with her.[57]

The raw anger that Mary Anne revealed to Hoffman and Dichter stemmed, in part, from her insistence that counsel observe ordinary rules of courtroom decorum. The informality that Hoffman thought was appropriate, based on his prior appearances before her in state court, was perceived by Mary Anne as an affront, a sign of disrespect. Perhaps her anger was a signal that she expected the deference owing to a federal judge and that she would not tolerate misplaced familiarity. In addition, her sharp rebuke to Hoffman clearly told him that he could not engage in assumptions about her behavior based on her rulings in prior cases.

The move to the federal bench did not seem to alter Mary Anne's view of criminal sentencings, which remained to her the "most difficult" of her judicial tasks. Some lawyers, however, believed she was more impatient with the criminal docket, and more stringent in criminal sentencings. Her husband's impression was to the contrary: while Bill perceived that criminal sentencings became an even more draining task for Mary Anne, he speculated that she leaned toward more leniency in sentencings once she had joined the federal judiciary.[58] Anecdotal evidence suggests that she would sometimes blink at the law in order to award a lenient sentence or to avoid

---

57. Conversation with Stephen M. Dichter, Phoenix, Arizona (May 7, 1993); Telephone Interview with David S. Hoffman (May 13, 1993). The dispute arose in the context of Hoffman's representation of Robert Mackay and Joyce Anne Moore in a criminal prosecution charging multiple defendants with conspiracy to import and sell marijuana. *See* Denial of Motion to Suppress, United States v. Spanhook, CR 76-460 (D. Ariz. Nov. 17, 1976).

58. Interview with William K. Richey, Nutrioso, Arizona (July 16–17, 1992); Telephone Interviews with Richey (Sept. 20, 27, 1992, Sept. 21, 1994).

giving the defendant prison time when she found the defendant personally sympathetic.[59] In any event, the available data indicate that her sentencing practices, which predated mandatory sentencing in the federal system, were consistent with those of her colleagues on the federal district court bench in Arizona and more lenient than the national sentencing averages.[60]

Mary Anne's intense interest in the candidacies of individuals who were nominated to join her as federal district judges in Tucson may reveal an additional psychological impact resulting from her appointment. The Omnibus Judgeship Act of 1978 gave Arizona three new federal district court judgeships, including one in Tucson.[61] In the fall of 1978, Senator Dennis DeConcini floated several names of local lawyers for the nomination, including Superior Court Judge John Collins, a Democrat whose judicial career had been fraught with controversy, and Richard Bilby, a Republican and friend of Mary Anne's who had already experienced one unsuccessful federal-court nomination. In early February of 1979, DeConcini named Collins as his choice for the new judgeship. Predictably, the nomination sparked a wave of protests by critics of Collins's conduct as a superior court judge and, in particular, as juvenile court judge. His leniency with juvenile offenders and his enthusiasm for controversial rehabilitation programs ultimately had led the superior court judges to vote to remove him from the juvenile bench in September of 1978.[62] Mary Anne, who recalled Collins from the days when they were colleagues on the same court, weighed in strongly on the side of the critics, and she candidly communicated her misgivings about Collins to federal investigators. Friends recalled that she thought "Collins just wasn't the kind of person who ought to be on the federal bench."[63]

---

59. Conversation with with Suzanne Rabe, Tucson, Arizona (Dec. 12, 1995) (recounting Rabe's representation of a defendant at a sentencing hearing before Mary Anne).

60. The criminal docket sheets from Mary Anne's court from 1976 through 1983 show that the average sentence of imprisonment imposed by her was 42.7 months, and the average period of probation she imposed was 37 months. The average prison sentence imposed in the district of Arizona from 1978 through 1983 was 41 months, and the average probationary sentence was 38.7 months. In contrast, the average term of imprisonment imposed nationwide over the same time period was 51 months. *See* 1978 ANNUAL REPORT, *supra* note 29, at 429 (Table D-7); 1979 ANNUAL REPORT, *supra* note 29, at 489 (Table D-7); 1980 ANNUAL REPORT, *supra* note 29, at 491 (Table D-7); 1981 ANNUAL REPORT, *supra* note 29, at 487 (Table D-7); 1982 ANNUAL REPORT, *supra* note 29, at 325 (Table D-7); 1983 ANNUAL REPORT, *supra* note 29, at 355 (Table D-7).

61. *See* The Omnibus Judgeship Act of 1978, Pub. L. 95-486, 92 Stat. 1629.

62. John Rawlinson & Cheryle Rodriguez, *Collins stepping down as judge*, TUCSON CITIZEN, May 29, 1980.

63. Browning Interview, *supra* note 14; Interview with Hon. Lawrence Ollason, United States Bankruptcy Judge, Tucson, Arizona (Feb. 27, 1996).

Ultimately, DeConcini withdrew the nomination of Collins after Attorney General Benjamin Civiletti refused to submit the name to the White House. Alfredo Marquez, a Democrat whom Mary Anne had known since they were classmates in law school, received DeConcini's second nomination in February of 1980.[64] "I never felt bad that I was second choice," Marquez remarked. He said that once his name went to the Senate, he visited the federal court and spoke with Mary Anne. "She was very helpful, gave me handbooks, explained certain procedures to me. I had known her very well and we liked each other."[65] Thus, Mary Anne supported the Marquez nomination and took an active role in orienting Marquez to his likely new position. Interestingly, two other members of Mary Anne's law school class—Valdemar Cordova and Earl Carroll—were appointed to fill the newly-created judgeships for the Phoenix division of Arizona's federal court.[66]

Mary Anne's negative response to Collins' nomination was significant. She took it upon herself to evaluate his candidacy and to let it be known that she did not hold him in high regard. In so doing, she showed that she had a definite vision of the kind of individual who would be qualified to fill the office. Her reaction revealed a sense of pride in the federal judiciary, a personal identification with it, and perhaps an elitism. Speaking years after his own appointment to the federal court, William Browning explained, "When you get this job, you tend to get a little possessive about it and it tends to swell your ego. You want someone of the same temperament as you and the rest of the judges."[67] Thus, by 1979, the aura of Article III seemed to have had an effect even on Mary Anne.

Nevertheless, Mary Anne's core humanity remained intact when she moved to the federal courthouse. She treated litigants with respect, even when their claims were devoid of merit, and she took particular care not to embarrass *pro se* litigants. Aware of the import of her office *vis a vis* the lay public, she seemed to want to humanize her courtroom to do what Judge Henry Friendly once described as the "job" of federal district judges—to demonstrate "the qualitiy of federal justice to ordinary citizens—parties, witnesses and jurors."[68] In one unusual case, *Genson v.*

---

64. Tom Beal, *Local lawyer new nominee to U.S. bench*, THE ARIZONA DAILY STAR, February 28, 1980.

65. Interview with Hon. Alfredo C. Marquez, United States District Judge, Tucson, Arizona (Jan. 26, 1993).

66. Valdemar A. Cordova was appointed June 21, 1979, and Earl H. Carroll was appointed June 30, 1980. *See* 506 F. Supp. XXII (1981)(Judges of the Federal Courts).

67. Browning Interview, *supra* note 14.

68. Henry J. Friendly, *The "Law of the Circuit" and All That*, 46 ST. JOHN'S L. REV. 406, 407 (1972)(giving a "job description" of federal district judges).

Ripley, her demeanor revealed such inclinations. Genson, a *pro se* plaintiff, filed suit against the Smithsonian Institution for negligence and fraud.[69] Genson claimed that he had found a Gaelic coin of great historical significance and had given it to the Institution. The Institution, however, had determined the coin to be of little value and returned it. Genson alleged that the museum had failed to serve its educational purpose toward the American people by misrepresenting his discovery. At the hearing on cross motions for summary judgment, Mary Anne listened to the emotional testimony of Genson as he described the symbolic meaning of the Smithsonian in his life and the momentous importance of his discovery of the coin. At points in his presentation, he was reduced to tears.[70]

Unfortunately for Genson, the Smithsonian was a federal agency under the law, and Genson, as a claimant, had failed to comply with the strict requirements of the Federal Tort Claims Act. Although the resolution of the summary judgment motions was clear to Mary Anne and her law clerk at the time of the hearing, Mary Anne did not give any indication from the bench of her ruling. After the hearing, the law clerk asked Mary Anne in chambers why she hadn't been more forthcoming, since the outcome was obvious. According to the clerk, she replied, "You know, there was no reason to humiliate that man. If I had ruled from the bench, he would have known how meritless his case was. That would have hurt."[71] A week and a half later, she issued a detailed written ruling, explaining why she had no jurisdiction to proceed with the case. In her decision, she commented, "The court recognizes the difficulties of the plaintiff who must represent himself. No special exceptions can be made, however, for those appearing before the court pro se."[72] She thus handed Genson his inevitable defeat but did so in a manner that respected his human dignity.

For the same quality of humanity, Mary Anne especially enjoyed another judicial function that she had not known in the state system—her role in presiding over naturalization proceedings to admit new citizens. She liked looking out over the crowd of excited faces, representing numerous countries of origin, and she carefully planned her remarks for such occasions. "Usually when I sit up here I am involved in a trial or sentence," she often said to the groups, "in which one side wins and one loses. Someone ends up unhappy. It is such a pleasure to be a part of a

---

69. *See* Complaint, Genson v. Ripley, CIV 81-0090 (D. Ariz. March 26, 1981).

70. Sholder Interview, *supra* note 19.

71. *Id.*

72. Genson v. Ripley, 544 F. Supp. 251, 253 (D. Ariz. 1981). Genson, whose determination was admirable, took an unsuccessful appeal to the Ninth Circuit and was ultimately denied certiorari by the United States Supreme Court. *See* Genson v. Ripley, 681 F.2d 1240 (1982), *cert. den.*, 459 U.S. 937 (1983).

proceeding in which everyone is happy and everyone is the winner."[73] Her life-long passion for travel, dating from her early excursion to India, informed her approach to the task, and she often mentioned that the United States was also a "winner" because of the diverse cultures, ideas, and abilities that the new citizens would bring.

* * *

Mary Anne's impact as a federal trial judge came predominantly from the myriad rulings that never led to appellate review. Only a small percentage of a federal district court's rulings are appealed; most civil cases either settle after the initial filing, after pretrial litigation, or after a pivotal pretrial ruling.[74] Of those that do not settle and are finally resolved on the merits by judge or jury, most go no further.[75] In the criminal arena, final disposition of most cases similarly occurs through the entry of guilty pleas by defendants, and relatively few criminal cases actually go to jury trial.[76]

---

73. Working File on Naturalization Ceremonies, Judge Mary Anne Richey's Federal Court Papers, United States District Court, Tucson, Arizona.

74. *See* RICHARD POSNER, THE FEDERAL COURTS—CRISIS AND REFORM 81–90 (1985)(suggesting that average appeal rates from district courts are low but may be increasing, reported in 1960 to have been 10.3 percent of selected district court civil and criminal terminations and an increase in 1983 to 20.9 percent).

75. During the last full year of Mary Anne's service on the federal bench, about two-thirds of the civil cases on the docket of the Arizona district court terminated without court action. Of the third that terminated after some form of court action, about 90 percent were resolved before pretrial, and only 1.8 percent of the cases reached trial. *See* 1983 ANNUAL REPORT, *supra* note 29, at 277. Statistics for federal district courts across the United States show a larger percentage of cases terminated through court action and a larger percentage reaching trial but still reveal that the vast majority of cases are resolved short of trial. *Id.* at 276 (46 percent of all civil cases terminated without court action, and 5.4 percent of all civil cases reached trial). A study by the RAND Corporation's Institute for Civil Justice revealed that from 1980 to 1993, only 3.9 percent of federal civil cases went to trial, and only about a third of all such dispositions were through judgments; all other cases terminated without adjudication. The same study showed that two-thirds of all civil cases were closed within one year of filing. *See* Terence Dunworth & James Kakalik, *Preliminary Observations on Implementation of the Pilot Program of the Civil Justice Reform Act of 1990*, 46 STAN. L. REV. 1303, 1310–12 (1994). *See also* Herbert M. Kritzer, *Adjudication to Settlement: Shading in the Gray*, 70 JUDICATURE 161 (1986)(concluding, based on study of federal and state courts, that only 7 percent of cases went to trial and reached a jury verdict or court decision, another 15 percent terminated through some other form of adjudication, such as arbitration or dismissal, and another 9 percent settled following a ruling on a significant motion).

76. National statistics for the last full year of Mary Anne's service on the federal bench show that about 82 percent of all criminal defendants in the federal court were convicted and that of those convicted, 84 percent pled guilty and only 11 percent were convicted by

Thus, Mary Anne's judicial identity on the federal bench was established in large part through actions that were never scrutinized by a higher court. As one commentator has put it, "Not only are district judges important as an initial stage in the federal judicial process, but they are also important as *final* deciders of a very high percentage of cases."[77] Or, as another judge remarked, "Justice stops in the district. They either get it here or they can't get it at all."[78] Therefore, the remainder of this Chapter focuses primarily on Mary Anne's rulings that did not lead to appellate review, while Chapter Thirteen describes her appellate record in the Ninth Circuit and her own contributions to the Ninth Circuit's jurisprudence.

As was seen in Mary Anne's state court rulings, her life experiences informed the style and substance of her adjudication on the federal bench. Politically moderate, she adhered to a philosophy of judicial restraint, but she did not back away from controversial rulings when the law seemed to require it. In the civil liberties area, her willingness to find that "the law required" a particular ruling sometimes reflected a special sensitivity to the nature of the claims before her. One civil case that was filed early in Mary Anne's federal court tenure is particularly illuminating. In 1977, a female sergeant in the United States Army filed a class action sex discrimination case against her superiors, including the Secretary of Defense, the Secretary of the Army, and lesser military officials. The plaintiff, Virginia Todd, asserted a claim for damages directly under the fifth amendment to the United States Constitution.[79] Todd, who was assigned to the United States Army Intelligence Center and School in Fort Huachuca, Arizona, alleged that she and other women working in military intelligence at Fort Huachuca had been regularly subjected to discriminatory work assignments, biased evaluations, sexual harassment, and abusive treatment by her male colleagues and commanding officers. She alleged that the pattern of harassment included not only verbal taunts but also the hanging of life-size nude dolls in the women's restrooms and the writing of sexually explicit graffiti on the walls of her sleeping quarters.

At the time, the complaint raised a serious constitutional question of first impression in the Ninth Circuit—whether a "*Bivens*" action for damages could be brought directly under the equal protection component of the fifth amendment's due process clause—and the governmental defen-

---

a jury. Moreover, the average time to disposition from date of filing was only 4.3 months. *See* 1983 Annual Report, *supra* note 29, at 170, 172.

77. WILLIAM KITCHIN, FEDERAL DISTRICT JUDGES—AN ANALYSIS OF JUDICIAL PERCEPTIONS 13 (1978)(emphasis in original).

78. Quoted by R. Carp and R. Wheeler, *Sink or Swim: The Socialization of a Federal District Judge*, 21 J. OF POLITICS 359, 361 (1972).

79. Complaint, Todd v. Brown, CIV 77-00185 (D. Ariz. Aug. 24, 1977).

dants promptly moved to dismiss the complaint, arguing that the *Bivens* doctrine could not be extended to Todd's claim of sex discrimination and urging that the military context of the complaint precluded any judicial remedy.[80] Six years earlier, in *Bivens v. Six Unknown Named Agents*,[81] the Supreme Court had recognized that a damages action could be brought for violations of the fourth amendment. The reach of the *Bivens* doctrine remains unclear today, but in 1977, when Mary Anne was faced with the issue, it was even less clear because the Supreme Court had not yet had occasion to consider its application to other constitutional violations.

In late 1977 and early 1978, when the parties in *Todd v. Brown* were disputing the legal sufficiency of Todd's complaint in multiple memoranda and oral argument before Mary Anne, the case of *Davis v. Passman* was working its way through the federal court system on the other side of the country.[82] In *Davis*, a female legislative assistant who had been fired from her job with Louisiana Congressman Otto Passman brought a sex discrimination claim directly under the fifth amendment against Passman. In January of 1977, the Fifth Circuit Court of Appeals ruled that the equal protection component of the fifth amendment afforded Davis a damages remedy.[83] Thus, when Todd filed her complaint in the federal court in Tucson, the Fifth Circuit's ruling in *Davis* was an important but nonbinding precedent favoring the plaintiff. A year and a half later, the Fifth Circuit sitting *en banc* reversed the earlier decision and held that a private damages action could *not* be inferred from the fifth amendment's due process clause.[84] Less than two months after that *en banc* decision was handed down, Mary Anne heard oral arguments on the government's motion to dismiss in *Todd*.

Thus, at the time of oral argument the law was in a state of active uncertainty on the reach of the *Bivens* doctrine. Plaintiff's counsel, Eric O'-Dowd, perceived that the weight of the case law was against his client, but he recalled that the government lawyers at the argument "dumped a load of cases on the judge, all in the government's favor, and the judge began to scowl." When O'Dowd stood up to respond to the defendants' contentions, he began somewhat apologetically: "I realize the precedents are against us, your Honor." With that statement, a look of impatience crossed Mary Anne's face, a facial expression that seemed to communicate to O'Dowd that he should be more vigorous in his representation of the

---

80. Defendants' Motion to Dismiss, *Todd* (D. Ariz. Dec. 1, 1977).

81. 403 U.S. 388 (1971).

82. *See* Davis v. Passman, 544 F.2d 865 (5th Cir. 1977), *rev'd en banc*, 571 F.2d 793 (1978), *rev'd*, 442 U.S. 228 (1979).

83. 544 F.2d 865 (5th Cir. 1977).

84. 571 F.2d 793 (5th Cir. 1978)(*en banc*)(decided April 18, 1978).

plaintiff. By the end of the argument, O'Dowd was convinced that Mary Anne was going to rule in the plaintiff's favor.[85]

Mary Anne's preference for judicial restraint, as well as her affinity for the governmental viewpoint, ordinarily would have persuaded her to rule in favor of the defendants and to grant the motion to dismiss on the authority of the *en banc* Fifth Circuit decision. Indeed, in another case some eights months earlier Mary Anne had refused to recognize a private right of action under a federal statute mandating affirmative action in employment for qualified "handicapped" individuals. In that case, *Fisher v. City of Tucson*,[86] Mary Anne had dismissed the plaintiff's complaint for failure to state a claim upon which relief could be granted, despite the powerful policy arguments advanced by plaintiff's counsel and the absence of clear binding precedent requiring dismissal.[87] Thus, Mary Anne could have been expected to rule against Todd on the face of her pleading. Nevertheless, as O'Dowd had predicted, after painstaking consideration of the constitutional issue, she denied the defendants' motion on all counts.[88] In her order, she rejected the Fifth Circuit's *en banc* analysis, noted that the *Bivens* issue was unresolved in the Ninth Circuit, and reasoned that Todd had "stated a claim sufficient to withstand a motion to dismiss on the pleadings."[89] At the same time, however, Mary Anne remained sensitive to the military's asserted need to be free of judicial intrusion. Although she rejected the government's position that the military context precluded relief altogether, she did order that all proceedings in the action would be stayed pending Todd's exhaustion of administrative remedies before the appropriate military tribunal.[90]

---

85. Telephone Interview with Eric O'Dowd (Dec. 6, 1995).

86. *See* Fisher v. City of Tucson, 26 Fair Empl. Prac. Cas. 864 (D. Ariz. 1977), *aff'd*, 663 F.2d 861 (9th Cir. 1981), *cert. denied*, 459 U.S. 881 (1982)[holding that plaintiff did not have a private right of action under section 503 of the Rehabilitation Act of 1973, 29 U.S.C. Sec. 793(a)].

87. Plaintiff William Fisher was represented by William E. Morris, a Legal Aid lawyer who successfully litigated several landmark cases in Arizona on behalf of indigent clients. In *Fisher*, Morris argued that his client had been unlawfully denied employment with the City of Tucson, a federal contractor, in violation of the affirmative action mandate of section 503 of the Rehabilitation Act of 1973. On the precise legal question, only one federal district court had addressed the issue and had ruled against the recognition of a private cause of action. That case, in turn, was affirmed by the Fifth Circuit, but over one dissenting vote. *See* Rogers v. Frito-Lay, Inc., 433 F. Supp. 200 (N.D. Tex. 1977), *aff'd*, 611 F.2d 1074 (5th Cir.), *cert. denied*, 101 S.Ct. 246 (1980).

88. Order of June 14, 1978, *Todd*.

89. *Id.* at 3.

90. *Id.* at 5–6.

For a period of about five years, Todd's case lay dormant on the federal docket while Todd pursued her military remedies, but the constitutional damages claim recognized by Mary Anne remained intact, albeit delayed. For a while, the law seemed to be moving in a direction that favored Todd. In 1979, the Supreme Court, in its own decision in *Davis v. Passman*,[91] reversed the Fifth Circuit's *en banc* opinion and reinstated the panel's holding that a damages action for sex discrimination could be brought directly under the fifth amendment. Thus, *Davis* was a vindication of Mary Anne's reasoning: the judiciary remained the primary means through which remedies for constitutional injuries might be pursued. Nevertheless, Todd's case was ultimately to fail. The failure resulted not from any weakness in the *Bivens* claim but from the military context of her complaint. In *Chappell v. Wallace*, decided in June of 1983, the United States Supreme Court flatly held that, due to the special nature of the military regime, military personnel could not assert damages claims against their superiors for constitutional violations.[92] Faced with the ineluctable command of *Chappell*, Mary Anne dismissed Todd's action one month later.[93]

Despite Todd's ultimate defeat, Mary Anne's initial response to the case is revealing. She had kept Todd's lawsuit alive in a crucial preliminary order, an order that contradicted the most recent federal appellate precedent on the issue. Her uncharacteristic resolve to render a ground-breaking constitutional ruling may have resulted from a core theme of her judicial philosophy. Todd's allegations of rampant sex discrimination offended Mary Anne's basic sense of fairness as well as her belief in equality of opportunity. Moreover, Todd's case triggered memories from Mary Anne's own past. Surely, her response to the legal issue in *Todd* was informed by her service in the WASP some thirty years earlier. As a WASP, she had witnessed the blatant resistance among military men to the presence of women pilots—a resistance that took the form of discrimination in working conditions, sexual harassment, and verbal taunts. Those memories must have engendered in Mary Anne a unique emotional response to Virginia Todd's allegations and a willingness to push the contours of the law further than she would have otherwise. Arguably, none of the other federal district judges in Arizona could have had a comparable empathy for the plaintiff.[94]

91. 442 U.S. 228 (1979).

92. 462 U.S. 296 (1983).

93. Order of Dismissal, July 19, 1983, *Todd*.

94. The lack of sensitivity of some male judges to sex discrimination claims was illustrated by Judge Frey's ruling in a case decided a year before Mary Anne's appointment to the federal bench. In *Corne v. Bausch and Lomb, Inc.*, 390 F. Supp. 161 (D. Ariz. 1975),

Another civil rights case that consumed much of Mary Anne's judicial time came to her docket through an unexpected and sad turn of events. In February of 1979, William Frey, her sole colleague on active status in the Tucson federal court, died of a heart attack at the age of fifty-nine while scuba diving off the coast of Honduras.[95] After news of the incident reached the courthouse on the afternoon of February 16, Mary Anne immediately joined in efforts to assist in having Frey's body flown back to Arizona. While Senator Dennis DeConcini worked through the U.S. State Department, Mary Anne called her old friend Raul Castro, then the United States ambassador to Argentina. She telephoned Castro that afternoon and explained the problem to him in her matter-of-fact style: "Raul, this is Mary Anne. Bill Frey has drowned in Honduras and we can't get his body back. Can you help?"[96] Through the combined efforts of Castro, DeConcini, and the American Embassy in Honduras, Frey's body was flown back three days later.[97]

Frey's untimely death was a personal loss for Mary Anne, since over their long acquaintance each had achieved parallel milestones in their professional lives. They had served together on the state court bench in Pima County, and, as the only Republicans on the Arizona federal court, they also had shared a political perspective. Mary Anne was shocked by news of the heart attack, and she knew she would miss her outspoken colleague for years to come. Ironically, Richard Bilby, whom Senator DeConcini had passed over a few months earlier in favor of John Collins for Tucson's newly-created federal judgeship, was himself appointed in September of 1979 to fill the vacancy created by Frey's death.[98]

Frey's death had direct professional consequences for Mary Anne. One week after the death, Chief Judge Walter Craig announced that Mary Anne was assigned to handle *Fisher v. Lohr*, a consolidated desegregation

---

vacated, 562 F.2d 55 (9th Cir. 1977), he held that sexual harassment of a female employee by a supervisor was not actionable under Title VII of the Civil Rights Act of 1964, a decision that was summarily vacated without opinion by the Ninth Circuit.

95. David Teibel, *Frey dies of heart attack*, THE ARIZONA DAILY STAR, February 17, 1979.

96. Telephone Interview with Hon. Raul H. Castro, former Judge, Pima County Superior Court, former Governor of Arizona, former Ambassador (July 28, 1993).

97. *Frey funeral tomorrow in Tucson*, THE ARIZONA DAILY STAR, February 20, 1979.

98. *Bilby confirmed to spot on U.S. bench*, THE ARIZONA DAILY STAR, September 26, 1979. In contrast to his earlier nomination for a position on the Ninth Circuit Court of Appeals, Bilby's nomination and confirmation for the federal district court were free of controversy. *See Senate panel backs Bilby for judgeship*, THE ARIZONA DAILY STAR, September 12, 1979.

class action involving Arizona's largest public school district.[99] Toward the end of his life, Frey had remarked that the desegregation lawsuit was the most significant case he had presided over in federal court.[100] Plaintiffs' lawyers as well as defense counsel ultimately praised Frey's management and firm control of the case,[101] but the acrimony and inevitable public controversy surrounding the litigation had taken its toll on the judge. When the desegregation case then shifted to Mary Anne's docket, she initially felt overwhelmed. She had not followed the five-year-old litigation in detail and had to immerse herself in Frey's voluminous files for weeks. "She had to work hard to come up to speed," Ruben Salter, a lead counsel for plaintiffs, recalled. "The exhibits, depositions, and legal documents in the case filled a large room at the courthouse—a room we all called 'the war room.'"[102] Bill Richey likewise recalled that once Mary Anne got the case, she seemed to always carry the issues with her mentally, even on vacations. "I remember when we were in Russia in the late 70s on the coast of the Black Sea. She was out on a raft in the sun, and she came paddling up to me and said, out of the blue, 'Bill, I just solved that matter in the desegregation case.'"[103]

Fisher actually involved two consolidated actions. In May of 1974, a school desegregation complaint had been filed against Tucson School District No. One (later renamed the "Tucson Unified School District") by Black elementary and junior high school students.[104] Two of the named plaintiffs were Roy and Josie Fisher, a Black couple represented by Salter. Several months later, a separate action was filed on behalf of the District's Mexican-American elementary, junior high, and high school students, under the lead of named-plaintiff Maria Mendoza.[105] Michael Zavala, a young and aggressive civil rights lawyer, represented the Mendoza plaintiffs. In their separate complaints, the plaintiffs alleged that the District operated a racially and ethnically segregated school system, as revealed by comparative minority populations at the district's schools. The complaints

---

99. *Judge Richey assigned to desegregation lawsuit*, THE ARIZONA DAILY STAR, February 24, 1979. The original case was captioned Fisher v. Lohr, CIV 74-90 (D. Ariz.).

100. David L. Teibel, *Frey dies of heart attack*, THE ARIZONA DAILY STAR, February 17, 1979.

101. Interview with William J. Brammer, Jr., Counsel for the District, Tucson, Arizona (July 5, 1993); Interview with Ruben Salter, Jr., Counsel for *Fisher* plaintiffs, Tucson, Arizona (May 18, 1993).

102. Salter Interview, *supra* note 101.

103. Richey Interviews, *supra* note 58.

104. Fisher v. Lohr, CIV 74-90 (D. Ariz. filed May 24, 1974).

105. Mendoza v. Tucson School District No. 1, CIV 74-204 (D. Ariz. filed Oct. 1974).

also alleged other indicia of discrimination such as disparate tracking of minority students, inferior curricula and facilities for minorities, discrimination in the hot lunch program and special education programs, inadequate accommodation of linguistic differences, and lack of bilingual notices.[106] In late 1975, Frey certified the Fisher and Mendoza plaintiffs as class representatives for the Black and Mexican-American classes, and he consolidated the two actions for hearing and disposition. After extensive discovery and an arduous period of pretrial maneuvering, including the intervention of a group of white parents opposed to busing[107] and the intervention of the United States as a party,[108] a consolidated trial was held in January 1977. Over the next year and a half, during which Frey and his law clerk worked virtually nonstop on the case, Frey formulated his findings and conclusions.

Finally, on June 5, 1978, Frey ruled.[109] In a 495-page decision, he found that the District had "to a limited extent" failed to dismantle its former dual school system and had continued since 1951—the year Arizona repealed its laws mandating racial segregation in education—to discriminate against minority students at nine schools within the District.[110] While he determined that the District had failed to eradicate "root and branch" the remnants of state-imposed segregation in the nine targeted schools, he concluded that there was no evidence of a continuing system-wide intentional practice of discrimination. A product of the very school system he was examining, Frey concluded that the existence of disparate minority enrollment in the District's schools stemmed largely from voluntary geographic population clusters within the city, and he was openly critical of the plaintiffs' attempts to prove otherwise.[111] Clearly ambivalent in his own mind, Frey wrote, "It appears to the Court, after carefully considering all the evidence and applicable law, that the defendants are

---

106. The Ninth Circuit's consideration of one of the appeals from Judge Frey's approval of a settlement plan in *Fisher* provides a comprehensive factual background to the litigation. *See* Mendoza v. United States, 623 F.2d 1338 (9th Cir. 1980).

107. *See* Order Granting Application of Sidney L. Sutton to Intervene, *Fisher* (March 1975). Sutton ultimately lost in his bid to overturn Judge Frey's approval of the settlement plan. *See* Fisher v. Tucson School Dist. No. One, 625 F.2d 834 (9th Cir. 1980).

108. *See* Order Granting Application of United States to Intervene, in *Fisher* and *Mendoza* (filed December 1976).

109. *See* Order of June 5, 1978, in *Fisher* and *Mendoza*.

110. *Id.* at 213.

111. In his order, Frey stated, "The plaintiffs' 25-year-old, backward view of the District and its decision involved in this case is indeed a narrow one....Some of the evidence and argument amounts to carping criticism, ill-formed speculation, conjecture and opinions of questionable validity." *See id.* at 196 ("Comment").

not as faultless as they contend and certainly not as much at fault or as bad as plaintiffs contend."[112] The opinion was widely viewed as a partial victory and a partial defeat for both sides.[113]

As to the several schools suffering the current effects of past intentional segregation, Judge Frey ordered the District to prepare a plan "to remove the vestiges of segregation." Although counsel for plaintiffs considered appealing the ruling since Frey had only partially upheld their allegations, the parties began settlement discussions relatively soon after Frey's decision. After public hearings and extended negotiations with plaintiffs, the District, through its counsel William Brammer, proposed a desegregation plan that included mandatory busing of students and the closing of three of the targeted schools. The proposal immediately triggered objections. The white intervenors, for example, categorically opposed student assignment remedies, and a member of the *Mendoza* class unsuccessfully sought to represent a subclass of parents affected by the school closures.[114] Nevertheless, Frey approved the desegregation plan proposed by the District in early August. Three weeks later, on August 31, 1978, he approved of the parties' stipulation of settlement. Under the terms of that settlement, the District was to remedy the racial and ethnic imbalance in identified District schools and to achieve equity in educational programs. In particular, the order required the closing of three inner-city schools and the reassignment of about 1,000 students to desegregate other target schools. The settlement order also mandated the creation or expansion of reading programs for Mexican-American elementary school students and programs to assist Black students through career counseling, Black awareness courses, and initial instruction in Black dialects as alternatives to standard English. Aware that the desegregation process was long-term, the parties provided in the settlement that the District could move to dissolve the order on or after July 1,1983.[115]

When Mary Anne entered the case only six months later, the core issue of constitutional violation had thus been resolved by Frey, but the daunting phase of implementation of remedies lay ahead. Over the four years during which Mary Anne had the case, the parties frequently applied to

112. *Id.* at 205.

113. Edith S. Auslander, *Judge Frey—Decision favors plaintiffs but treats district gently*, THE ARIZONA DAILY STAR, June 6, 1978.

114. Sutton's objection to the settlement plan was rejected by the Ninth Circuit in Fisher v. Tucson School Dist. No. One, 625 F.2d 834 (1980). The Ninth Circuit likewise rejected the efforts of a member of the *Mendoza* class to intervene for the purpose of forming a subclass of affected parents. *See* Mendoza v. United States, 623 F.2d 1338 (9th Cir. 1980).

115. Order Approving Settlement, *Fisher* and *Mendoza* (filed August 31, 1978).

the court for resolution of conflicting interpretations of the settlement agreement and for guidance on issues unresolved by the agreement. The questions that came before Mary Anne primarily concerned the adequacy of the District's compliance with the terms of the agreement, although she also had to periodically resolve objections by intervenors who remained hostile to the settlement.

Mary Anne's resolution of two issues in the desegregation suit are revealing of her judicial philosophy. One of the questions concerned the District's compliance with the settlement order in the revamping of educational programs, and the other concerned proposed boundary changes for student enrollment in the target schools. According to Ruben Salter, Mary Anne emphatically urged the lawyers to reach an agreement outside of the court, and in each instance she ultimately "cut the baby in half."[116] The lawyers sensed that she was not totally in favor of the District, but also that she required convincing proof from the plaintiffs.

Of the two kinds of legal issues, Mary Anne subjectively preferred to address boundary changes and student enrollment questions rather than to select among competing proposals for educational programs. As to the latter, she felt that she lacked the necessary expertise to evaluate the parties' plans. In the summer of 1979, however, Mary Anne entertained arguments on "Phase II" of the proposed desegregation plan and was squarely faced with such disfavored programmatic issues. At that point in the litigation, the *Fisher* plaintiffs had filed objections to various proposals for educational programs submitted by the District on the ground that the settlement order required the District to serve more directly the needs of the Black student population.[117] In particular, the *Fisher* plaintiffs wanted the District to implement more educational programs designed to enhance cultural awareness among Black students, as required by Judge Frey's original settlement order, and to train more teachers in the use of "S.E.S.D./B.A.S.E." (Standard English as a Second Dialect/Black Alternative: Standard English)—a general name for programs designed to help children who use a Black dialect to learn the use of standard English. The plaintiffs also requested that Mary Anne extend her jurisdiction over the settlement for an additional year to ensure that all students who needed the special language instruction would receive it. Mary Anne held a full-day's hearing on August 1, 1979, during which Salter on behalf of the *Fisher* plaintiffs put on a parade of educational consultants as witnesses.

---

116. Salter Interview, *supra* note 101.

117. Fisher Plaintiffs' Objections to Defendants' Report Pursuant to Paragraph 17 of Stipulation of Settlement and Request for Hearing re Same, *Fisher* (May 16, 1979).

Mary Anne gave both issues her close, albeit reluctant, attention. In her view, the objections regarding the District's efforts at enhancing cultural awareness among Black students stemmed from "personality conflicts" between the District's representatives and the plaintiffs' representatives. Through discussions in court, apparent misunderstandings about the District's plans were resolved.[118]

The thrust of the plaintiffs' objections as to the District's language program was that the reading and performance level of Black students would improve by greater use of S.E.S.D./B.A.S.E, and much testimony was devoted to that question. During an afternoon recess, Mary Anne talked about the case with her law clerk, Nancy Fiora. When Fiora, a former school teacher, expressed some skepticism about the virtues of S.E.S.D./B.A.S.E., Mary Anne replied, "I see you brought all your big city prejudices with you." Fiora was stung by the remark and suggested to the judge that she have one of the expert witnesses demonstrate the use of Black dialect on the stand.[119] The following morning, Mary Anne requested that the plaintiffs put on some "demonstrative evidence" in court. Salter obligingly called a witness to the stand who proceeded to decline a verb in Black dialect. Fiora recalled that Mary Anne looked at her, at the witness, at Salter, and then sternly asked, "How does that differ from poor grammar?" With that clear signal from the bench, Salter realized his chances of fully succeeding on his objections were slim.[120] In fact, in her ruling on plaintiffs' objections, Mary Anne found that the District was in compliance with its duties regarding S.E.S.D./B.A.S.E. under the settlement order. She also expressed reservations about the value and practicability of the language programs, noting that "educators are still uncertain about the relationship between use of [B]lack dialect and ability to perform well in school," and that no standardized means existed for identifying students whose use of Black dialect interfered with their learning.[121] Moreover, she rejected the plaintiffs' request for an extension of the court's jurisdiction, reasoning that such a request was "premature." "It is far too early," she wrote, "for the Court to consider whether it will be

---

118. Order Regarding Fisher Plaintiffs' Objections to Defendant District's Report Pursuant to Paragraph 17 of the Settlement Agreement, *Fisher* (August 8, 1979).

119. Fiora Interview, *supra* note 18.

120. *Id.*

121. Order Re: Fisher Plaintiffs' Objections to Defendant District's Report Pursuant to Paragraph 17 of the Settlement Agreement, *Fisher* (August 8, 1979) at 3. Years later, a similar proposal in California for the recognition of Black dialect as a second language would provoke a national furor. *See, e.g., Oakland Schools Sanction Ebonics,* CHICAGO TRIBUNE, December 19, 1996.

necessary to extend its jurisdiction beyond the time currently contemplated by the Settlement Agreement."[122] Thus, Mary Anne gave a lukewarm reception to the *Fisher* plaintiffs' arguments and was frankly skeptical of the benefits of the educational use of Black dialect.

During the hearing on the *Fisher* plaintiffs' objections, Mary Anne expressed her frustration with counsel when the proceedings seemed to degenerate into unnecessary squabbling. Brammer, who represented the District throughout the litigation, recalled sensing Mary Anne's impatience. "She was fed up with our fighting, and I think she said, in so many words, 'Gee, why can't you folks figure this out and quit wasting my time and your time and everybody's money and get on with it?'"[123] Indeed, her final order sent a frank message to the lawyers. In denying the plaintiffs' application for attorneys' fees, Mary Anne reasoned that plaintiffs had dropped most of their objections and that the remaining difficulties "arose from misunderstandings, rather than from the District's failure to comply with its obligations." She concluded her order with the following pointed advice:

> As this Court and its predecessor, the late Judge Frey have stated many times, the role of the Court is to protect the constitutional rights of the parties and to enforce the obligations of the Settlement Agreement. The role of the Court does *not* include usurping the responsibilities of the District, or judging the wisdom of decisions made by the elected officials of the school board. The Court can only determine whether decisions of the District are rational and reasonably calculated to fulfill its obligations, given the information available.[124]

In the same document, Mary Anne urged the parties to "make every effort to work out disagreements among themselves before they ask the Court to intervene." She reasoned that "[i]f the students...are to obtain the maximum benefit from the terms of the Settlement Agreement, the parties must cooperate with each other as much as possible."[125] Finally, she expressed reservations about her own competence to evaluate educational programs: "It is very difficult for the Court to render a decision on technical educational matters when the parties only provide general information. The parties should also be mindful of the fact that the Settlement

---

122. *See* Order, *supra* note 121 at 4.
123. Brammer Interview, *supra* note 101.
124. Order of August 8, 1979, *Fisher* and *Mendoza* at 6.
125. *Id.*

contains some innovative programs, and that it will often be difficult or impossible to judge their effectiveness before they have been put into operation. Therefore, we must necessarily allow for some trial and error."[126]

Mary Anne's resolution of the *Fisher* plaintiffs' objections was characteristically pragmatic. Although she herself had been educated in a segregated public school district in Indiana, a district at one point presided over by her father, she seemed committed to remedying the constitutional violations that Judge Frey had found to exist in Tucson's public school system. On the other hand, she did not wish to micro-manage the District. She was acutely conscious of her own limitations in designing educational programs and clearly admonished the parties to make full use of their own resources. In addition, her loyalty to the terms of Judge Frey's original order was tempered by a recognition that the goals expressed in the order were to some extent aspirational. As the "implementation" judge, she had to concern herself with the practical realities of experimental educational programs. Finally, she perceived that difficult interpersonal dynamics between the District and the plaintiffs' representatives were impeding the process, and she bluntly pointed out those problems to counsel.

Student assignment issues arose regularly in the desegregation case, and Mary Anne handled a problematic assignment question in 1983 as her last significant action in the case. Under the terms of the original settlement order, Judge Frey had ordered the District to bus students from Brichta Elementary School, a predominantly Anglo school on Tucson's northwest side, to Manzo Elementary School, a predominantly minority school in the central city, in order to achieve a better racial balance at Manzo. Five years later, the parents of the Anglo children who were subject to the mandatory busing objected that their children were being taken out of their neighborhood school and placed into a distant school that was already overcrowded. Moreover, they argued, the presence of the Anglo children at Manzo had not significantly improved the school's racial composition. According to William Brammer, the District's counsel, Mary Anne was sympathetic to the position of the objecting parents and prevailed on the District to come up with an alternative plan. "Judge Richey probably felt that taking the children from Brichta out of their neighborhood and putting them on a bus for a long ride across town to an overcrowded school, where their presence didn't improve things, was not a good idea. She figured that it would relieve some of the overcrowding at Manzo if the kids were sent back to their home school, and it would make the lives of this particular little group of kids much better. A pretty

---

126. *Id.* at 7.

common sense approach and not very legalistic."[127] After the plaintiffs agreed, Mary Anne granted the District's petition to modify the original settlement order to eliminate the Brichta-to-Manzo busing.[128]

In that final action in the desegregation case, rendered close to the end of Mary Anne's life, she again revealed her pragmatism. Although the terms of the original order had prospectively required the mandatory busing of the Brichta children, Mary Anne had the advantage of reviewing the mandate after it had been in effect for five years. Her review convinced her that a group of children were being displaced for no discernible good. To her, the minimal change in racial composition of the overwhelmingly minority Manzo school might have been an abstract improvement in the constitutional sense but simply did not justify the remedy. She consequently expressed her concerns about the original order in a candid communication to Brammer and asked the District to come up with an alternative. Her practical assessment of the merits of the busing remedy and her straightforward approach with counsel were characteristic of her judicial style. There, as elsewhere in her handling of the desegregation lawsuit, she took very seriously the litigants' legal and factual contentions, but her dispute-resolution forte was in encouraging the parties to settle their difference outside of the courtroom.

An extra-judicial factor that may have influenced Mary Anne's consideration of the desegregation case sprang from her identity as a mother. When Mary Anne first acquired the case, her daughter Annie, then in the midst of a turbulent adolescence, was a fifteen-year-old student at Catalina High School. Catalina was a public school within the Tucson Unified School District, the very district that was subject to the federal court's oversight in the desegregation suit. At that time, Mary Anne frequently worried about her daughter's grades, her flagging interest in academics, and her friendship with similarly disaffected teenagers. The only vociferous arguments Annie ever remembered between her parents occurred during her adolescence and were typically disputes about their contrasting approaches to parenting.[129] Bill Richey was tolerant of Annie's academic performance and believed in an approach of gentle encouragement. Mary Anne, on the other hand, was a perfectionist; she expected her daughter to bring home "A" report cards and was angry when she did not do so.[130] She discussed her intense concerns about Annie with friends

---

127. Brammer Interview, *supra* note 101.

128. Order Granting Defendants' Petition to Modify Order of August 8, 1978, *Fisher* (Sept. 1, 1983).

129. Interview with Annie Richey, Tucson, Arizona (Aug. 22, 1992).

130. *Id.*

and colleagues and sought advice from numerous quarters.[131] In some of those conversations she acknowledged the tension she felt between the demands of her career and the demands of her role as a mother, and she expressed doubts about whether she had given Annie sufficient attention through the formative years.[132]

The anxiety Mary Anne experienced over her maturing daughter and her increasing sense of powerlessness to control Annie's activities may have influenced her judicial response to the desegregation lawsuit. Because of her concern with Annie's schooling, she was acutely conscious of the quality of education provided within the very district that was subject to her judicial supervision. She was sensitive to the personal impact of student assignment remedies on children and parents, and she may have looked longingly to the past, a time of traditional neighborhood schools and compliant children. In that sense, the complaints of the Brichta parents would have been received with particular sympathy. Further, she was skeptical of programs that seemed to circumvent the teaching of basics. She may have felt ill-equipped to choose among competing educational plans since, in her view, she was not able to successfully direct even her own daughter's education. Her refusal to sustain Salter's position regarding the use of Black dialect in classrooms reflected her obvious reluctance to second-guess the District. Thus, Mary Anne's identity as a mother may have influenced her approach to the case as profoundly as her judicial conservatism and her characteristic pragmatism.

Mary Anne was assigned another revealing case involving constitutional liberties in 1978. In her approach to it and similar cases on her docket involving politically unpopular claimants, she showed her trademark independence. In *Erickson v. Dupnik*,[133] a group of pretrial detainees at the Pima County Jail brought suit against Pima County officials alleging that the conditions of confinement at the jail, including the jail's physical facilities and the medical services for inmates, were so inadequate as to be violative of the cruel and unusual punishment clause of the eighth amendment to the United States Constitution. The plaintiffs sought declaratory and injunctive relief as well as damages. The jail suit bore certain similarities to *Sexton v. Board of Supervisors*, the lawsuit on behalf of indigent alcoholics that Mary Anne had heard in state court in 1973: it

---

131. William Richey Interviews, *supra* note 57; Telephone Interview with Hon. Gordon Thompson, United States District Judge (May 12, 1993); Interview with Hon. Richard M. Bilby, United States District Judge, Tucson, Arizona (Dec. 10, 1992).

132. Interview with Hon. Richard M. Bilby, United States District Judge, Tucson, Arizona (Dec. 10, 1992); Telephone Interview with Virginia Pothoff Trumbull (Aug. 29, 1992).

133. Complaint, Erickson v. Dupnik, CIV 78-008 (D. Ariz. Jan. 5, 1978).

involved some of the same governmental defendants, it raised questions of civil liberties asserted by a politically unpopular group, and it was filed as a class action. In the jail suit, as in *Sexton*, Mary Anne approached the legal arguments neutrally, if cautiously, and ultimately found in favor of the plaintiffs.

In the jail lawsuit, the class certification motion was predictably the first pivotal battle of the litigation. In any representative action, if plaintiffs succeed in proceeding on behalf of a class, the pressures to achieve settlement dramatically increase for the defendants. Conversely, if plaintiffs fail on the question of class certification, the stakes considerably diminish from the defendants' perspective. In a later case brought by the same Legal Aid office, for example, the named plaintiffs alleged racial and ethnic "red-lining" against various home insurance companies. Mary Anne denied the hotly-contested class certification motion and, in the view of plaintiffs' counsel, did so in a "baffling" order that was an unexpected setback in the litigation.[134] In *Erickson*, on the other hand, the class certification motion succeeded. The plaintiffs filed their motion for class certification in January of 1978, only five days after the complaint was filed. Two weeks later, Mary Anne presided over what she viewed as a "pre-hearing" on the motion for class certification.[135] At the hearing, she told all counsel that she wanted specific information about the nature of the class and the adequacy of the named plaintiffs as representatives. Her hands-on approach to the certification question communicated to the lawyers that she would not rubber-stamp a loosely-defined class and that she wanted assurance that the named plaintiffs would take their role seriously. At the same time, her posture at the "pre-hearing" made clear to the defendants that she was sympathetic to the need for class-wide relief. A flurry of discovery and pretrial maneuvering ensued during which the defendants deposed each of the named plaintiffs and several intervenors, plaintiffs in turn deposed several county officials, and both sides filed lengthy memoranda disputing whether the circumstances satisfied the standards of Rule 23 of the Federal Rules of Civil Procedure.

---

134. *See* Order Denying Plaintiffs' Motion for Class Certification, Yslava v. Farmers Insurance Co., CIV 81-0345 (D. Ariz. April 19, 1982). Mary Anne and her law clerk at the time debated the issue of class certification. In Mary Anne's view, the plaintiffs had failed to show that sufficient common questions of law or fact justified class action treatment. Ameln Interview *supra* note 43. Plaintiff's counsel saw Mary Anne's denial of class certification as "baffling and troubling," but the individual plaintiffs nevertheless prevailed after the case was reassigned to Judge Bilby. *See* Judgment, *Yslava* (November 28, 1984). Telephone Interview with William E. Morris, Plaintiff's Counsel (Jan. 5, 1996).

135. Minute Entry from Prehearing on Motion for Class Certification, Erickson v. Boykin, CIV 78-008 (D. Ariz. Jan. 26, 1978).

The defendants challenged the adequacy of the named plaintiffs as class representatives, arguing that they were unlikely to responsibly represent the class and that the conditions of detention of various named plaintiffs at the Pima County Jail were not typical of the purported class.[136] Plaintiffs' counsel, on the other hand, contended that the claims of the named plaintiffs were typical of those of the class and that, given the nature of the population of jail inmates, the designated plaintiffs were as likely as any to adequately represent the class.

The actual hearing on the motion occurred June 16, 1978, at which the lawyers for Southern Arizona Legal Aid, John Balentine and William Morris, pressed their contentions that at least one named plaintiff and an intervenor were fully capable of representing the class through the assistance of counsel.[137] Importantly, Balentine and Morris headed up the Legal Aid Office's reform litigation unit and had experience in class-action litigation. Their obvious competence impressed Mary Anne and colored her consideration of the "adequacy of representation" issue. On the other hand, Balentine and Morris conceded at the hearing that their efforts to locate a willing female detainee to proceed as named plaintiff had not been successful.

Two weeks later, on June 29, 1978, Mary Anne issued her ruling. In the order, she designated Erickson and Jackson as class representatives for a class, certified under Rule 23(b)(2), for purposes of injunctive and declaratory relief only. The class, as defined by Mary Anne, consisted of "all males who are or will be incarcerated in the Pima County Jail solely because they are awaiting disposition of criminal charges against them or because they are subject to federal immigration detainers."[138] Knowing that the lawyers for the plaintiffs wanted to include female detainees if possible, Mary Anne explicitly provided in the order that plaintiffs might move to intervene additional representative parties for the purpose of expanding the class definition to include female detainees in the future. Finally, the order acknowledged that the inclusion of federal detainees might be altered later if the evidence revealed that the group was subject to materially different conditions or procedures within the jail. Mary Anne's ruling was an important early victory for the plaintiffs. While she eliminated the unwieldy issue of class-wide damages and excluded women from the class at least temporarily, in all other respects her order upheld the plaintiffs' motion for class certification.

---

136. Defendants' Supplemental Memorandum in Opposition to Class Certification, *Erickson* (March 15, 1978).

137. Minute Entry, *Erickson* (June 16, 1978).

138. Court's Findings of Facts and Conclusions of Law, *Erickson* (June 29, 1978).

The order and Mary Anne's evident sympathy for plaintiffs' legal position preceding the order significantly strengthened the plaintiffs' leverage
in bringing defendants to the negotiation table. Not surprisingly, shortly
after Mary Anne announced the certification order, the parties began a
long, sometimes acrimonious process of settlement. Almost immediately,
counsel joined in a stipulation settling the portion of the suit that addressed medical and dental care for inmates.[139] The case was transferred
from Mary Anne's docket to that of Gordon Thompson, a visiting district
court judge from San Diego, in early April of 1979, after Mary Anne in-
herited the desegregation lawsuit from Judge Frey's court. Under Thompson's oversight, the remaining issues in the litigation relating to such matters as overcrowding, contact visitation, and costs and fees were
eventually resolved by counsel, and the case terminated in January of
1981 under the terms of a consent decree.

Mary Anne, however, had permanently influenced the course of the
lawsuit by upholding plaintiffs' class action request. She knew the case
would attract media attention, which she disliked, and she knew that the
relief requested by plaintiffs would come about only by significant expense to the county and ultimately the taxpayer—a fiscal consequence she
likewise disliked. Nevertheless, she concluded that the class action device
was the appropriate means of resolving the litigation, and she ruled accordingly. Her judicial approach, perhaps overly-cautious from the perspective of plaintiffs' counsel, was in her mind an objective attempt to follow the terms of the procedural rules.

A category of cases that shared certain themes with the jail case and as
to which Mary Anne likewise exhibited caution were prisoner civil rights
claims. During her years on the federal court, the filing of such claims dramatically increased: in her first year on the bench, 110 prisoner civil rights
claims were commenced in the District Court of Arizona,[140] and by her
last year on the bench, the number had risen to 479.[141] Since most of such
petitions were *pro se*, the judges and their law clerks had the responsibility of reviewing the complaints on the merits; most were promptly dismissed as frivolous. Similarly, Mary Anne rejected numerous habeas corpus petitions during her tenure.[142] Occasionally, however, a serious claim

---

139. Order Approving of Stipulation of Counsel on Proposed Inmate Medical Care
Program, *Erickson* (July 7, 1978).

140. 1977 ANNUAL REPORT, *supra* note 29, at 325 (providing data for twelve-month
period ending June 30, 1977).

141. 1983 ANNUAL REPORT, *supra* note 29, at 253 (providing data for twelve-month
period ending June 30, 1983).

142. *See, e.g.,* Berg v. U.S. Parole Comm'n, 735 F.2d 378 (9th Cir. 1984)(affirming
Mary Anne's denial of federal prisoner's habeas corpus petition); Douglas v. Long, 661

would emerge, and Mary Anne gave her attention to one such case in 1976. In *Boag v. Araza*, a state prisoner brought suit against the Arizona Board of Pardons and Parole under the due process clause of the fourteenth amendment, alleging that the board had denied his application for parole without providing him an adequate statement of reasons for the denial.[143] His claim was based on the developing theory that the state's denial of an expectancy interest in liberty had to be accompanied by more than a *pro forma* explanation. Through some obviously astute jail-house lawyering, Boag had appropriately framed the constitutional claim in his complaint. As a result, when the defendants confidently moved to dismiss the action on the ground of abstention, Mary Anne denied the motion. Finding that the doctrine of abstention was inapplicable to the case, Mary Anne ruled that she would entertain the plaintiff's constitutional claim on the merits, much to the surprise of the defendants.[144] From that pivotal ruling by Mary Anne until the case terminated in 1979, Boag and the Parole Board traded numerous discovery requests and separate motions for summary judgment.

Mary Anne took the case seriously, but she had mixed reactions to the legal issues and the requested relief. On the one hand, Boag's claim appealed to her sense of fairness, and she was aware of her duty not to prejudge the *pro se* petitioner's legal arguments. On the other hand, as a former prosecutor and state court judge, she was reluctant to issue a ruling that would mandate changes in the administration of the state parole system. The Parole Board was itself apparently reluctant to press Mary Anne on the ultimate question: the Board paroled Boag and mooted the case temporarily. When Boag found himself back in prison after having his parole revoked, the Board denied him parole and voluntarily provided him with a statement of reasons.[145] Boag himself withdrew his complaint in March of 1979.

As in *Erickson*, Mary Anne's approach to *Boag* was initially skeptical. Nevertheless, in both cases she was able to achieve balance and objectivity in her rulings, an objectivity that led her to render important preliminary victories for the plaintiffs. In both cases her rulings were not politically popular, but the strength of the plaintiffs' respective legal arguments persuaded her to take the position she did.

One additional example of her ability to disregard the public's reaction to her rulings came in a very different context. In *Nolan v. United*

F.2d 747 (9th Cir. 1981)(affirming Mary Anne's denial of state prisoner's habeas corpus petition).

143. Complaint, Boag v. Araza, CIV 76-203 (D. Ariz. Oct. 26, 1976).

144. Order of December 21, 1976, *Boag*.

145. *See* Defendants' Motion to Dismiss, *Boag* (Nov. 29, 1978).

States,[146] the former leader of a motorcycle gang ("Big Jim Nolan") sought judicial review of an Internal Revenue Service tax assessment against him for unreported income. The IRS became involved after the Tucson police informed the agency that cash and jewelry exceeding a value of $220,000 were in Nolan's possession when he was arrested for murder. The evidence before Mary Anne revealed that Nolan had profited from illegal drug sales as well as prostitution.

The relatively deferential standard of review applicable to Nolan's action required Mary Anne to determine whether the assessment by the IRS was reasonable under the circumstances and whether the amount was appropriate.[147] Mary Anne readily found that an assessment was warranted, but she concluded that factual uncertainty existed as to the assessed amounts. Despite a presumption of propriety in favor of the IRS, Mary Anne ruled that "substantial doubt" as to the amounts assessed was raised by conflicting reports about the income that Nolan earned from prostitution. According to her law clerk at the time, she was "outraged at the scope of authority asserted by the IRS."[148] In her opinion, one of the few that she agreed to publish, she wrote, "These 'substantial doubts' allow this Court to find that the amount of income on which the assessments are based should be redetermined by the Secretary...."[149] Numerous other federal courts later relied on her reasoning in *Nolan*.[150]

Mary Anne thus handed Nolan, a man of notorious lawlessness who had been recently paroled from a Florida prison, a modest victory against the federal government. Her experience with tax cases as a federal prosecutor surely influenced her review of the IRS's evidence. In scrutinizing the facts and directing the IRS to refigure its determination, Mary Anne forced the government to be more exacting in its proof. Thus, her willingness to question administrative agencies, demonstrated in her state court tenure, surfaced in federal court as well. At the same time, she showed a willingness to set aside public opinion and rule in favor of a uniquely unsavory litigant.

One prominent theme that surfaced in Mary Anne's work as a trial judge was her respect for, and deference to, the role of the state as sovereign. As a former state court judge, she strongly believed in the authority

---

146. Complaint, Nolan v. United States, CIV 81-0508 (D. Ariz. Oct. 26, 1981).

147. *See* Nolan v. United States, 539 F. Supp. 788, 789 (D. Ariz. 1982).

148. Ameln Interview, *supra* note 43.

149. *Nolan*, 539 F. Supp. at 791.

150. *See, e.g.*, Kenney v. United States, 622 F. Supp. 219 (D. Me. 1985); Hirschhorn v. United States, 662 F. Supp. 887 (S.D.N.Y. 1987); Balaguer v. United States, 656 F. Supp. 383 (D.P.R. 1987).

and competence of the state judiciary, and she was accustomed to deferring to the state's legislative prerogative as well. Because of her background, she strongly identified with the need for the state to operate independently, free of unnecessary federal intrusion. Pursuant to her brand of political conservativism, moreover, she favored resolution of social problems at the local rather than national level.

In Mary Anne's court, her regard for the competence of state sovereign authority emerged in a variety of circumstances. In tort and contract cases based on diversity of citizenship jurisdiction, for example, Mary Anne's reading of state substantive law was cautious and restrained.[151] Her approach in such cases revealed that she perceived her role under the *Erie* doctrine[152] to be solely that of an interpreter, even if she viewed the state law as unwise. Her respect for state authority, however, emerged most starkly in her willingness to abstain in deference to state courts. In *Henson v. Hoy*,[153] for example, she abstained in a constitutional challenge to Ariz. Rev. Stat. Sec. 32-2625, a law denying security guard licensing to anyone convicted of a felony. Ralph Henson had been summarily denied a security guard license by the State of Arizona on the basis of his felony record, without being afforded the opportunity to put on evidence of mitigating circumstances. Mary Anne was quite sympathetic to the plaintiff's due process challenge, although the case law in support of his claim was not overwhelming.[154] Rather than invalidate the statute herself, she opted for a resolution that would allow the state courts to construe the statute so as to eliminate the constitutional issue. She issued an order staying proceedings in her court and directing the plaintiffs to obtain a definitive construction of the statute from the state courts.[155] Importantly, her written decision expressly pointed out the constitutional vulnerabilities of the statute, and she cautioned, "If plaintiff's interpretation of state law is correct, the validity of the statutory scheme is subject to serious question."[156]

---

151. *See* Stay Order, Campillo-Vega v. Alvarez, CIV 81-0066 (D. Ariz. June 22, 1981)(interpreting *Erie* to require medical malpractice plaintiff to pursue state-created procedure for panel review, despite conflict of authority on application of *Erie*); Harbor Mechanical, Inc. v. Arizona Elec. Power Coop., Inc., 496 F. Supp. 681 (D. Ariz. 1980)(applying somewhat dated state decisional law to bar negligence action by contractor against engineering firm on basis of privity of contract).

152. *See* Erie Railroad Co. v. Tompkins, 304 U.S. 64 (1938).

153. Henson v. Hoy, CIV 78-043 (D. Ariz. 1978).

154. Plaintiff's primary favorable authority was a memorandum decision of the United States Supreme Court affirming by an equally divided vote a holding in the Seventh Circuit. *See* Miller v. Carter, 547 F.2d 1314 (7th Cir. 1977), *aff'd* 98 S.Ct. 786 (1978).

155. Abstention Order, *Henson*,(July 5, 1978).

156. *Id.* at 5.

Less than a year after Mary Anne's abstention order, the parties reached a settlement giving plaintiff complete relief.[157]

Mary Anne's actions in *Henson* was characteristic of her judicial posture. She hesitated to wield the authority of the federal court to strike down state law if a less intrusive resolution was available. Her decision to abstain reflected her faith that the state judges would cure the constitutional defects if given the chance. Clearly, her determination in *Henson* to avoid the risk of federal-state friction was successful. Indeed, Legal Aid's William Morris, who represented Henson, viewed Mary Anne's decision as her "most far-reaching judicial act" on the federal court because it led to significant reforms in state law.[158] That she accomplished such a result through a carefully worded abstention order is a testament to her perception of the primary role of state courts in construing state law and their competence to adjudicate constitutional claims.

Other rulings from Mary Anne's court likewise demonstrated her deferential posture. For example, she was faced with a complaint by the White Mountain Apache Tribe asserting an exclusive right to determine the custody of Indian children who were the subject of a parental-rights termination action in state court. Rather than intervene in the ongoing state proceedings, Mary Anne stayed the federal case pending final disposition of the severance petitions in the state court.[159] Similarly, in resolving one of her last civil matters, she refused a well-publicized application by the Roman Catholic Diocese of Tucson to enjoin discovery of its personnel records in a pending state court libel action.[160] The Diocese had applied to federal court for relief on first amendment grounds only after pursuing its objection through the state court system without success.[161] "The judge seemed to struggle with the case," her law clerk recalled, "and we went through many

---

157. Consent Judgment, Henson v. Arizona Dept. of Public Safety, No. 177414 (Pima County Sup. Ct. March 9, 1979).

158. Morris Interview, *supra* note 134.

159. *See* Stay Order, White Mountain Apache Tribe v. The House of Samuel, CIV 77-145 (D. Ariz. Oct. 26, 1977). Interestingly, Judge John Collins had earlier ruled that the tribe had exclusive jurisdiction over the status of the children, but the Arizona Supreme Court had reversed. In In the Matter of the Severance of Valerie Duryea, 115 Ariz. 86, 563 P.2d 885 (1977), the court ruled that the Arizona state courts had subject-matter jurisdiction over the petitions. It was in the wake of that decision that Mary Anne characteristically opted for a stay. The federal action was dismissed pursuant to stipulation in August of 1978.

160. Edmund Lawler, *Diocese asks federal judge to quash state court subpoena*, THE ARIZONA DAILY STAR, Sept. 3, 1983.

161. *See* Complaint, Roman Catholic Church v. Superior Court, CIV 83-00578 (D. Ariz. Sept. 2, 1983).

revisions of the proposed ruling."[162] Ultimately opting for a deferential posture, Mary Anne ruled against the Diocese. She noted in her order that the Diocese had received a fair hearing on its first amendment objections in state court, and she emphasized the pivotal importance of the subpoenaed records in the state court action.[163] In those cases, as well as others,[164] Mary Anne's reluctance to intrude on the state's authority reflected her abiding respect for state court decision-making, her conviction that the state forum was competent, and her sense that federal intrusion was unwise.

In sum, Mary Anne's many trial court activities in her years on the federal bench helped define her contribution as a judge. Her interaction with lawyers on and off the bench showed her humanity as well as her sense of authority. The attorneys who appeared before her appreciated the warmth of her interpersonal style but recognized that she expected absolute professionalism in her courtroom.[165] Her substantive rulings reflected a pragmatism—a willingness to look at problems concretely with full awareness of the limitations of human reason.[166] She exhibited a preference for judicial restraint tempered by a readiness to take the unpopular stand if she perceived the law to require it. In cases such as *Todd* and the desegregation suit, moreover, Mary Anne's personal values and gendered life experiences seemed to inform her interpretation of what the law required.

Judge Mary Schroeder of the Ninth Circuit Court of Appeals has remarked that "justice with compassion is a legitimate, even necessary end for judges to strive to achieve, if the law is to serve human needs," but she cautions that judicial compassion is always constrained by relevant precedent and codified law.[167] In a related vein, Judge Frank Johnson once observed that "the essential attribute of judicial integrity is a *passion* for justice in-

---

162. Telephone Interview with Ellen M. Sewell (Dec. 20, 1995).

163. *See* Order of Dismissal, *Roman Catholic Church* (Nov. 28, 1983).

164. Tucson Law Enforcement Assoc. v. City of Tucson, CIV 90-0036 (D. Ariz. order filed April 16, 1981), *aff'd*, 676 F.2d 713 (9th Cir. 1982)(Table)(in civil rights action brought by Tucson Law Enforcement Association seeking to compel city to recognize association as bargaining unit for city police officers, court stayed the action "until such time as the parties obtain a determination in the Arizona state courts as to whether the City can deal with [a competing union] as an exclusive bargaining agent.").

165. According to Judge Stephen McNamee, who appeared numerous times in Mary Anne's court as an Assistant United States Attorney, "She had a real warmth, almost a magic, on an interpersonal level. In the courtroom, though, you knew where you stood. She did not suffer fools gladly." Conversation with Hon. Stephen M. McNamee, United States District Judge, Tucson, Arizona (March 8, 1996).

166. *See* RICHARD A. POSNER, THE PROBLEMS OF JURISPRUDENCE 464–66 (1990)(defining judicial pragmatism).

167. Hon. Mary M. Schroeder, *Compassion on Appeal*, 22 ARIZ. ST. L.J. 45, 46 (1990).

formed by a deep and abiding morality, a *compassion* that propels the judge to a just conclusion even when the party or the issue before the bar is unpopular."[168] In cases such as *Genson*, Mary Anne's compassion was apparent to her law clerks, if not to counsel, as she tried to soften the impact of an unavoidable adverse ruling. In *Nolan* and other rulings involving people at the margins of society, where the legal issues were momentous only to the parties involved, she established a reputation for true integrity.

---

168. Hon. Frank M. Johnson, Jr., *Civilization, Integrity, and Justice: Some Observations on the Function of the Judiciary*, 43 Sw. L. J. 645, 650–51 (1989)(emphasis in original).

CHAPTER THIRTEEN

The Federal Appellate Record

Mary Anne's "appellate record" on the federal bench, as used here, refers to those judicial acts that were reviewed by the Ninth Circuit Court of Appeals or the United States Supreme Court and also to her participation by designation in the work of the Ninth Circuit. In each sense, her adjudications contributed to legal precedent and formed a more public (albeit incomplete) record of her judgeship than her many unreviewed and unreported judicial actions. On the whole, her trial court rulings as a federal judge fared better in the higher courts than did her state trial court decrees. Her affirmance/reversal record in the Ninth Circuit showed a higher percentage of affirmances, in both the criminal and civil arenas, than she had accumulated in the state court. Including published and unpublished dispositions, fifty-nine criminal appeals were taken from Mary Anne's rulings to the Ninth Circuit during her seven years on the federal bench, and one was granted full review by the United States Supreme Court. Of that total, fifty-five, or 93 percent, were affirmed, and four were reversed.[1] On the civil side, twenty cases were appealed to the Ninth Circuit, and Mary Anne's rulings were affirmed in seventeen, or 85 percent, of the total, again including published and unpublished dispositions.[2] Those rates were consistent with general data for the federal district courts across the United States.[3] Mary Anne's colleagues on the

---

1. The cases in which Mary Anne's rulings were reversed in whole or in part by the Ninth Circuit Court of Appeals were United States v. Provencio, 554 F.2d 361 (1977); Moroyoqui v. United States, 570 F.2d 862 (9th Cir. 1977); United States v. MacKay, 606 F.2d 264 (9th Cir. 1979); United States v. Gallegos-Curiel, 681 F.2d 1164 (9th Cir. 1982). The Ninth Circuit reversed Mary Anne in another case, but it was reversed, in turn, by the United States Supreme Court. See United States v. Gagnon, 721 F.2d 672 (9th Cir. 1983), rev'd, 470 U.S. 522 (1985). Another reported case, United States v. Cortez, 595 F.2d 505 (9th Cir. 1979), rev'd, 449 U.S. 411 (1981), gives Mary Anne's name as the trial judge, but the sole evidentiary question in that case arose from Judge Thomas Murphy's denial of defendants' motion to suppress before trial, not from a ruling by Mary Anne.

2. The civil cases in which Mary Anne's rulings were reversed in whole or in part by the Ninth Circuit were Scott and Fetzer Co. v. Dile, 643 F.2d 670 (9th Cir. 1981); Hardy v. Bureau of Alcohol and Firearms, 631 F.2d 653 (9th Cir. 1980); and Catalina Cablevision v. City of Tucson, 745 F.2d 1266 (9th Cir. 1984).

3. Data from the Director of the Administrative Office of the United States Courts, for example, reveal that about 85 percent of district court rulings (civil and criminal) were affirmed on appeal. See William Kitchin, Federal District Judges 13 (1977)(quoting 1974

federal district court bench in Arizona had comparable affirmance rates in the civil cases, and somewhat lower affirmance rates in criminal cases.[4]

The contrast between Mary Anne's affirmance/reversal record as a state court judge and as a federal judge suggests that she may have been more attuned to prevailing legal doctrine in her federal trial court rulings than in the state court, or that she had more of an ideological fit with the Ninth Circuit than she had enjoyed with the state appellate courts. The difference may also be attributable to the greater deliberative opportunity and greater resources available to judges in the federal court. The assistance of law clerks, the lighter docket, and the availability of more time to generate a decision in the federal court as compared to the state court may have produced a less hurried, more cautious judicial approach. Moreover,

---

ANNUAL REPORT OF THE DIRECTOR OF THE ADMINISTRATIVE OFFICE OF THE UNITED STATES COURTS at 1X-12).

4. Because of the difficulty in retrieving unpublished decisions by judge, the comparative data for other judges is based only on reported opinions. The affirmance rate is lower for published opinions because a reversal of the trial court is more likely to be in the form of a published opinion than memorandum opinion. The following statistics were based on published opinions from the time periods indicated. For the sake of comparison, Mary Anne's record based only on published opinions is given.

Mary Anne Richey (Based on published opinions from 1977 through 1985):

    22 total criminal appeals
    18 (82%) affirmances
    8 total civil appeals
    5 (63%) affirmances

James A. Walsh (Based on published opinions from 1973 through 1980):

    46 total criminal appeals
    34 (74%) affirmances
    22 total civil appeals
    15 (68%) affirmances

Carl A. Muecke (Based on published opinions from 1978 through 1985):

    64 total civil appeals
    43 (67%) affirmances
    26 total criminal appeals
    16 (62%) affirmances

Earl Carroll (Based on published opinions from 1981 through 1989):

    44 total civil appeals
    31 (70%) affirmances
    28 total criminal appeals
    17 (61%) affirmances

Source: WEST'S FEDERAL REPORTER SECOND SERIES (1973-1989).

in light of the higher prestige of the federal judiciary, Mary Anne may have felt more disheartened when she was overturned in the federal system than in the state court and may have endeavored harder to avoid reversal. "She cared a great deal about getting affirmed," one law clerk commented, "and she was gleeful when a tough decision that she struggled over got a higher court's approval."[5] Another clerk remembered hearing her utter, "Those idiots," when a reversal came down.[6] Whether or not Mary Anne saw merit in the reasoning of an appellate opinion reversing one of her rulings, she often found such decisions troubling. The words of another jurist may aptly describe the views of many trial judges, including Mary Anne: "Do I wince when a decision of mine is reversed by an appeals court? You bet I do. Sometimes I am embarrassed by my stupidity being glaringly revealed; sometimes I am angry at the stupidity of the appellate judges; and sometimes I am resigned to the vagaries of appellate review that all trial judges must suffer. But always a bit of my pride is bruised."[7]

Mary Anne found reversals to be sobering messages from the higher courts, but she was particularly dismayed when she was wrongly reported to have been reversed. Once, in West's preliminary advance sheets, she was mistakenly identified as the trial judge in a case in which Judge Thomas Murphy was reversed for "multiple errors" that, in the view of the Ninth Circuit, had denied the defendant a fair trial.[8] According to an assistant federal public defender at the time, Mary Anne was "furious" that her name had been used in connection with such poor judicial performance.[9] She saw to it that the error was corrected for the reported version of the case. She was again identified as the trial judge in a later case that provoked a reversal from the Ninth Circuit where the appellate court's disapproval rested solely on Murphy's pretrial denial of the defendants' motion to suppress.[10] To Mary Anne's chagrin, she was associated with Murphy in a third reversal, this time in the civil docket, when the Ninth Circuit overturned a preliminary injunction that Murphy had erroneously issued and she had merely enforced.[11]

---

5. Telephone Interview with Joseph M. Sholder (Dec. 20, 1995).

6. Interview with David R. White, Tucson, Arizona (Dec. 16, 1992).

7. JUDGE ROBERT SATTER, DOING JUSTICE 227 (1990).

8. *See* United States v. Allsup, 566 F.2d 68 (1977).

9. Interview with Hon. Bernardo P. Velasco, Judge, Pima County Superior Court, Tucson, Arizona (Dec. 20, 1992).

10. *See* United States v. Cortez, 595 F.2d 505 (9th Cir. 1979), *rev'd,*449 U.S. 411 (1981).

11. *See* Scott and Fetzer Co. v. Dile, 643 F.2d 670, 673–674 (9th Cir. 1981).

Mary Anne's decision-making in the criminal arena generally reflected her affinity for the government's position,[12] her confidence in her subjective assessments of factual disputes, her desire to resolve cases efficiently, and her low tolerance for legal argumentation that seemed to her to lack substance. She strongly believed in the vigorous enforcement of the criminal law, especially drug laws, and she actively protected the authority of the grand jury.[13] In several rulings, she demonstrated her sense that severity of penalty should follow culpability.[14] At the same time, she was alert to guard against prosecutorial excesses.[15] Although some lawyers viewed

---

12. In United States v. Murrieta-Bejarano, 552 F.2d 1323 (9th Cir. 1977), for example, Mary Anne gave a jury instruction in a drug smuggling case that, at least in the view of then-Judge Kennedy, was too favorable to the prosecution in that it would allow juries to convict under a standard "analogous to negligence." See 595 F.2d at 1326 (Kennedy, J., concurring in part and dissenting in part).

13. For example, Mary Anne held a witness in civil contempt who refused to testify before a grand jury under a grant of immunity. She rejected his argument that neither the immunity nor the secrecy of the grand jury could shield him from prosecution in Mexico. See In re Federal Grand Jury Witness, 597 F.2d 1166 (9th Cir. 1979).

14. That perspective was manifest in the explanation Mary Anne gave to a defendant at the time of sentencing as to why he was not entitled to probation: "As you know, I have handled quite a few cases out of this case and I have heard testimony in two different trials, and I can only say that in listening to those, at least your ranch was used and used and used over and over again, Mr. Serapo, as a place where marijuana was stashed, and a place where it was brought into your ranch. If you lived there, it would have to be, with the activity that went on, completely within your knowledge. To me, you are more involved than the people who were just lookouts, and such, that this court has handled prior to this time, and I just cannot see straight probation in this matter." Serapo v. United States, 595 F.2d 3, 3 n.1 (9th Cir. 1979). On two other occasions, Mary Anne's jury instructions were scrutinized but affirmed by the court of appeals where they permitted the jury to infer guilty knowledge on the part of the defendants. See United States v. Rocha, 553 F.2d 615 (9th Cir. 1977); United States v. Murrieta-Bejarano, 552 F.2d 1323 (9th Cir. 1977).

15. See, e.g., United States v. Mikka, 586 F.2d 152 (9th Cir. 1978). Mikka involved a prosecution for possession of a firearm by a felon. In closing argument, the prosecutor urged the jury to consider the risk that the defendant might "do something dangerous" or engage in "illegal conduct" with the firearms. Without objection from defense counsel, Mary Anne interjected the following: "I don't think there is anything before this court as to anything that was going to happen as far as the guns. The charge is only that somebody who has been convicted of a felony is in possession of firearms. That is all that is required, and proof of it, and to argue beynd that without any evidence is improper." 586 F.2d at 154 n.5. On appeal, the Ninth Circuit held that, in light of Mary Anne's prompt warning, no prejudicial error occurred. Mary Anne showed a similar intolerance for governmental excess when she ruled that a prosecutor had improperly used information obtained during plea negotiations to obtain a search warrant. See United States v. Kandik, 633 F.2d 1334, 1335 (9th Cir. 1980).

her as too willing to accept the veracity of federal agents where credibility was at issue,[16] she was not reluctant to rule against the government if she sensed that dishonesty or vindictiveness played a role in the government's preparation of its case. Her rulings revealed not only a skepticism towards many arguments from the defense table but also a readiness to condemn prosecutorial misconduct. A law clerk recalled watching a criminal trial in Mary Anne's courtroom during which defense counsel seemed to be unduly badgering an FBI agent. At recess, the clerk went into Mary Anne's chambers and asked, "Judge, how can you just sit there and let the defense lawyer get away with such nonsense?" According to the clerk, Mary Anne responded, "That's how the game is played. And you have to remember that sometimes the FBI agents are lying."[17]

The criminal cases in which Mary Anne's rulings garnered a reversal from the Ninth Circuit provide a window into her judicial philosophy on the federal trial bench. The legal issues raised by the cases ranged from fourth amendment evidentiary challenges and fifth amendment double jeopardy claims to a claim of prosecutorial vindictiveness, but the first reversal Mary Anne experienced and the most troubling for her personally turned on a question of basic courtroom fairness. In *United States v. Provencio*,[18] a case assigned to Mary Anne only two weeks after her appointment to the bench, the sixth amendment's right of confrontation took centerstage, and Mary Anne's error paralleled some of her rulings in state court in giving insufficient attention to the confrontation right. In *Provencio*, the defendants were convicted of transporting aliens. Before trial, depositions of the aliens as material witnesses were taken in anticipation of the aliens' release, but in fact the aliens were not released and were still available at the time of the trial. The aliens' availability as witnesses, however, was not known to defense counsel or to Mary Anne, and their depositions were admitted at trial without objection.[19]

To Mary Anne's consternation, the Ninth Circuit reversed, and the tone of its *per curiam* opinion was condemning. The panel in *Provencio* con-

---

16. One Tucson attorney, for example, believed that Mary Anne may have disregarded misconduct by agents of the FBI leading to the criminal prosecution of William McCollum for union embezzlement and racketeering. Interview with Thomas S. Chandler, Tucson, Arizona (Oct. 8, 1992). McCollum ultimately pled to a misdemeanor and received probation from Mary Anne. Minute Entry of Sentence, United States v. McCollum, CR 78-00200 (D. Ariz. July 11, 1978).

17. Interview with Craig H. Kaufman, Tucson, Arizona (Jan. 12, 1993).

18. CR 76-384 (D. Ariz. filed July 21, 1976).

19. At trial, government counsel suggested that the depositions were to be used according to statutory procedures, and the implication was that the witnesses had been deported to Mexico. United States v. Provencio, 554 F.2d 361, 363 (9th Cir. 1977).

sisted of Judges Shirley Hufstedler (the only other woman federal judge within the Ninth Circuit at the time), Joseph Sneed, and Anthony Kennedy, all persons whom Mary Anne admired. "[I]t is unnecessary for us to decide whether the error in admitting the evidence without objection was plain error," the court wrote, "because it is crystal clear that the introduction of the evidence was in violation of appellants' constitutional rights to confrontation."[20] The court went on to elucidate the "fundamental," "old," and "well-settled" principles underlying the confrontation clause, and it concluded that the failure of defense counsel to object was not a waiver of such basic rights. It thus handed Mary Anne her first reversal on the federal bench, holding that she had committed "constitutional error in admitting the depositions of the aliens."[21]

The didactic tone of the opinion embarrassed Mary Anne and increased her resolve to avoid reversals in the future. As an experienced trial judge, she was chagrined by the appellate court's focus on her oversight, but she was also irritated that the government had fostered a misimpression about the location of the aliens at the time of trial. The decision was a very public reminder of her obligation to monitor every phase of the trial, whether prompted by a defense objection or not. *Provencio* also may have contributed to her impression that Judge Hufstedler, a woman of very different ideological perspective, had viewed Mary Anne's appointment to the bench with ambivalence.[22]

In the one criminal case that was ultimately reviewed by the United States Supreme Court, Mary Anne's conduct of the trial was called into question. In *United States v. Gagnon*,[23] four defendants were tried and convicted in Mary Anne's court of conspiracy to possess cocaine with intent to distribute and related felony drug offenses. On the first day of trial, one of the jurors noticed defendant Gagnon sketching portraits of jury members. The juror became alarmed and informed the clerk-bailiff, who in turn informed Mary Anne. In open court but out of the presence of the jury, Mary Anne admonished the defendant that it was "very improper for a defendant to draw pictures of a jury while they are sitting in the box." She confiscated the sketches and ordered Gagnon to refrain from further drawing.

---

20. *Provencio*, 554 F.2d at 362.

21. *Provencio*, 554 F.2d at 363.

22. The description of Mary Anne's reactions to *Provencio* are based on the author's observations as her law clerk at the time of the decision. Judge Hufstedler wrote a pointed concurrence in another case criticizing Mary Anne's enforcement of a grand jury subpoena. *See* In re Federal Grand Jury Witness, 597 F.2d 1166, 1168–69 (9th Cir. 1979).

23. 721 F.2d 672 (9th Cir. 1983), *rev'd*, 470 U.S. 522 (1985).

Counsel for Gagnon then asked Mary Anne to question the juror to determine if the incident had produced a bias. Mary Anne responded, still in open court in the presence of each defendant, "I will talk to the juror in my chambers and make a determination. We'll stand at recess." None of the defendants objected or requested to be present at the questioning. Mary Anne then went into her chambers and asked that the clerk bailiff bring the juror and Gagnon's counsel. The following exchange then took place:

> THE COURT: Mr. Gagnon is an artist. It was just one of those things that happened. The Court has stopped it. It won't continue. However, if because of this you feel like you couldn't be—you know—that that would affect you in any way, then I want you to tell us about it.
>
> THE JUROR: As far as any judgment on what's going on, it doesn't affect me. I just thought that perhaps because of the seriousness of the trial, and because of—whichever way the deliberations go, it kind of—it upset me, because—of what could happen afterwards.
>
> THE COURT: Well, do you feel that it upset you to the extent that you couldn't judge Mr. Gagnon fairly—
>
> THE JUROR: No.
>
> THE COURT: You could be fair to everyone concerned; you're sure of that?
>
> THE JUROR: Yes.[24]

The questioning continued in the same vein, with Mary Anne pressing the juror to consider whether the incident had prejudiced him in any way against Gagnon. Mary Anne also invited Gagnon's lawyer to raise any additional concerns, and at the conclusion of the questioning, the lawyer indicated that the issue had been resolved to his satisfaction. With the juror's assurances that he could continue to serve without bias, Mary Anne assumed that the incident was closed. No defendant objected to the proceeding during the remainder of the trial. On appeal, however, all four defendants contended that the in camera proceeding violated their right to be present at all stages of their trial, codified for federal criminal trials in Rule 43 of the Federal Rules of Criminal Procedure.[25]

---

24. The transcript is reprinted in Petition for a Writ of Certiorari to the United States Court of Appeals for the Ninth Circuit, United States v. Gagnon, No. 84-690 (U.S.), at Appendix C.

25. Rule 43(a) provided: "Presence Required. The defendant shall be present at the arraignment, at the time of the plea, at every stage of the trial including the impaneling of the jury and the return of the verdict, and at the imposition of sentence, except as otherwise prvoided by this rule." The other subdivisions of the Rule excluded situations of waiver, where the defendant has voluntarily absented himself from trial or has been barred because of disruptive conduct; conferences or arguments on questions of law; and other circumstances not relevant to the *Gagnon* case. *See* R.43, FED. R. CRIM. PRO.

The Ninth Circuit, over a dissent, reversed the convictions, emphasizing that the defendants' statutory right to be present at all stages of the criminal trial rested on important constitutional principles under the fifth and sixth amendments. Finding that Mary Anne had violated the defendants' due process rights by conducting the in camera proceeding without determining whether their absence was voluntary, the majority applied the "fundamental error" doctrine. It reasoned that the right at stake was "so fundamental that, in certain circumstances, its violation must be noticed by a reviewing court regardless of a failure to raise the issue below."[26] The court concluded that the error was not harmless beyond a reasonable doubt, since "the presence of the defendants was necessary in order to safeguard another constitutional right—the right to an impartial jury."[27] The decision was announced December 8, 1983, two weeks after Mary Anne's death.

Mary Anne would have been troubled by the Ninth Circuit's reversal in *Gagnon* and the implication that she had disregarded her obligation to accord basic fairness to the defendants. Appellate review of *Gagnon*, however, was not over yet. In a *per curiam* decision rendered without full briefing, the United States Supreme Court soundly reversed the Ninth Circuit two years later and reinstated the defendants' convictions. In a matter-of-fact tone, the Court declared that "respondents' rights under the Fifth Amendment Due Process Clause were not violated by the in camera discussion with the juror."[28] Treating the in camera proceeding as a minor incident in a complex conspiracy trial, the Supreme Court reasoned that "the conference was not the sort of event which every defendant had a right personally to attend under the Fifth Amendment."[29] The Court concluded, moreover, that even if Rule 43 guaranteed to the defendants the right to attend the conference in Mary Anne's chambers, the defendants' failure to object to the proceeding or to request to attend constituted a "waiver" of the right. On the whole, the high Court was dismissive of the Ninth Circuit's reasoning: "Unlike the Court of Appeals, we find nothing in Rule 43 which requires that latter-day protests of the District Court's action with respect to a relatively minor incident be sustained, and the case tried anew."[30] Thus, Mary Anne's initial response to the juror question was vindicated.

---

26. 721 F.2d at 677.

27. 721 F.2d at 678. Judge Skopil dissented on the ground that Mary Anne's error in examining the juror without all defendants present was harmless beyond a reasonable doubt.

28. 470 U.S. 522, 526 (1985).

29. 470 U.S. at 527.

30. 470 U.S. at 529.

Mary Anne's handling of the juror issue in *Gagnon* was in keeping with her style as a trial judge. When she was alerted to the problem by her clerk-bailiff, she took the matter seriously and addressed it immediately. Although defense counsel did not ask to attend the in camera session, Mary Anne nevertheless invited the lawyer for the affected defendant to participate in the interrogation of the juror. Her persistent questioning of the juror showed her concern for the risk of prejudice. Although defendants argued on appeal that Mary Anne's questioning was inadequate,[31] she did ask the juror multiple times about the potential for bias, and the juror repeatedly avowed that he could be fair. Thus, Mary Anne satisfied herself that the juror's neutrality was intact. On the other hand, the transcript of the in camera proceeding does reveal that the juror was worried about the defendant's intended use of the drawings. A more cautious judge might have made clear to the juror that he could withdraw or might have disqualified the juror as a prophylactic measure and substituted an alternate. Mary Anne would not have favored such a strategy, however, because of the potential for delaying the trial. Her desire to have the complex prosecution go forward expeditiously and her subjective impression that the juror was free of bias dictated her response to the incident.

Mary Anne heard and resolved motions to suppress in almost every criminal case that came before her, and her record was similar to that established in state court. "Unlike some of the judges over there, she would actually suppress evidence when a search was really bad," one defense lawyer said,[32] and her docket sheets show that she periodically granted suppression motions throughout her seven years on the federal bench.[33] She strongly condemned governmental misconduct, and a law clerk recalled that she was impatient with after-the-fact justifications for searches. "In one alien smuggling case, the agent got on the stand and said the stop was justified because the car was riding low and was obviously loaded with Mexicans. Then it turned out that there was only one Mexican na-

---

31. *See* Appellant Glenn Edward Martin's Opening Brief, United States v. Martin, No. 82-1350 (9th Cir.), filed Nov. 8, 1982, at 46–47.

32. Velasco Interview, *supra* note 9.

33. In the realm of immigration offenses, for example, she granted motions to suppress in United States v. Hernandez-Robles, CR 76-532 (D. Ariz. December 15, 1976); United States v. Valenzuela-Alegria, CR 80-00047 (D. Ariz. April 4, 1980); and United States v. Salcido, CR 81-00133 (D. Ariz. July 20, 1981). In the only counterfeiting prosecution she heard, she suppressed an aluminum printing plate because of a defective warrant. United States v. Kandik, CR 79-00165 (D. Ariz. Nov. 2, 1979), *conviction aff'd*, 633 F.2d 1334 (9th Cir. 1980).

tional in the trunk and he was a little ninety-pound guy. The judge threw the evidence out and showed her anger in court."[34]

On the other hand, Mary Anne found the vast majority of suppression motions in her court to be meritless, and defense lawyers were sometimes put off by her attitude. One anecdote in this regard is telling. An assistant federal public defender recalled that he represented a man in her court who was charged with the transportation of 1,500 pounds of marijuana. Pursuant to a plea agreement, the defendant entered a plea of guilty to a reduced charge. When Mary Anne asked the prosecutor why the government had agreed to such a plea, the prosecutor replied that there was a "good motion to suppress in the case." Obviously displeased, Mary Anne retorted, "There is no such thing as a good motion to suppress for 1,500 pounds of marijuana."[35] That off-hand remark, as recollected by the public defender, suggested that she harbored a profound skepticism about the jurisprudence of the fourth amendment. Her remark indicated that if the evidence were sufficiently compelling, no illegality by law enforcement would justify suppression. Not surprisingly, one of the few reversals she experienced in the criminal docket was based on her mistaken denial of a suppression motion.[36]

In resolving suppression motions, Mary Anne was characteristically reluctant to block the introduction of reliable evidence, and at times she may have been willing to subordinate fourth amendment principles to the vindication of the public rights protected by the criminal law. One case in which Mary Anne's ruling on a motion to suppress met with mixed reactions from the Ninth Circuit is particularly illuminating. In *United States v. Burnette*,[37] a bank robbery prosecution involving multiple defendants, Mary Anne ruled on various pretrial motions for each defendant. One defendant, Lynette Burnette, contended that a warrantless search of her purse shortly after the robbery was unlawful and that the $5,000 in cash found in the purse was therefore inadmissible. At the time of the search, Burnette had initially disclaimed ownership but had acted ambivalently when the arresting officer began to examine the contents of the purse. Mary Anne's law clerk produced a memorandum prior to the suppression hearing that indicated that the warrantless search of the purse could be upheld as incident to arrest.[38] After the hearing

---

34. Sholder Interview, *supra* note 5.

35. Velasco Interview, *supra* note 9.

36. *See, e.g.*, United States v. MacKay, 606 F.2d 264 (9th Cir. 1979)(holding that trial court should have suppressed evidence found in defendant's suitcase because of failure of government to obtain warrant).

37. CR 80-00248 (D. Ariz. filed Nov. 25, 1980), *convictions aff'd*, 698 F.2d 1038 (9th Cir. 1983).

38. Memorandum from Joe Sholder, United States v. Burnette, January 13, 1981, Judge Mary Anne Richey's Papers, United States District Court.

and presumably in partial reliance on the clerk's memorandum, Mary Anne verbally denied the motion to suppress.[39]

One week later, however, the law clerk submitted a supplemental memorandum to Mary Anne, this one explaining that although the warrantless search of the purse appeared on reconsideration to have been illegal, the defendant lacked standing to challenge it. The tone of the memorandum suggests that the clerk's task was to articulate a justification that would allow Mary Anne to adhere to her original ruling: "Although the law is unsettled," the clerk wrote, "I think the majority and better reasoned view is that [the officer's] warrantless search of the purse was illegal. It appears that the court will not have to change its ruling, however, because it is fairly clear that Lynette Burnette cannot object to the search of the purse because she had no reasonable expectation of privacy in the purse."[40] Four days after receiving the clerk's supplemental memorandum, Mary Anne issued her final ruling, denying the motion to suppress on the ground that the defendant lacked a reasonable expectation of privacy in the purse.[41] Following the clerk's recommended analysis, Mary Anne held that Burnette's disclaimer of ownership in the purse at the time of arrest constituted an abandonment.

On appeal, the Ninth Circuit affirmed the denial of Burnette's motion to suppress but it disapproved of the theory Mary Anne had invoked. The court of appeals held that Mary Anne's finding of abandonment was "clear error." Viewing the defendant's actions at the time of arrest as indicating a desire to prevent an examination of the contents of the purse, the court held that the defendant "intended to retain a 'reasonable expectation of privacy' in the purse."[42] Thus, Mary Anne's conclusion of abandonment was flatly rejected by the appellate court. Nevertheless, the court of appeals concluded, over a dissent, that the evidence seized from the purse was properly admitted at trial as a search incident to a lawful arrest.[43]

Mary Anne's participation in *Burnette* revealed a prosecutorial predisposition and also a characteristic of her working relationship with her law clerks. At the suppression hearing, Mary Anne developed an immediate response to the evidence and to counsel's legal arguments and ruled accordingly. She remained determined to deny the suppression motion even when her clerk later had second thoughts about the legality of the search. In so doing, she relied on a theory that triggered a rare finding of clear error from the court of appeals. On the other hand, her instinct that the search

---

39. United States v. Burnette, CR 80-00248 (D. Ariz. Order of Jan. 16, 1981).

40. Sholder Memorandum, *supra* note 38.

41. United States v. Burnette, CR-80-00248 (D. Ariz. Order of Jan. 26, 1981).

42. *Burnette*, 698 F.2d at 1048.

43. *Id.*

should be upheld was ultimately vindicated. She did not perceive that law enforcement had abused its authority in investigating the robbery, and two of the three members of the appellate panel agreed with her.

In contrast, when Mary Anne perceived governmental dishonesty or animosity in the investigation or prosecution of crimes, she was often quick to react. In one instance, her anger over perceived government misconduct led her to dismiss an indictment, only to be reversed by the Ninth Circuit. In *United States v. Gallegos-Curiel*,[44] the defendant, a Mexican national, had been charged with a misdemeanor illegal entry by the Immigration and Naturalization Service and had entered a plea of not guilty at his initial appearance. A few days later, however, an Assistant U.S. Attorney reviewed the defendant's file and obtained an indictment from a grand jury for felony illegal entry. The defendant through his appointed counsel later moved to dismiss the indictment on the ground of vindictive prosecution, arguing that the not-guilty plea had prompted the felony charge. At the hearing before Mary Anne, the Assistant U.S. Attorney testified that he sought the felony indictment because of the defendant's prior immigration record and his record of non-immigration violations. The immigration agent testified, moreover, that had he known of the non-immigration violations, he would have requested a felony prosecution in the first place. Despite such testimony, Mary Anne dismissed the indictment, reasoning that the INS agent through diligent effort could have discovered the non-immigration record, and that the U.S. Attorney's Office would never have reviewed the defendant's file had he pled guilty. Importantly, she rested her decision on "presumed" rather than actual vindictiveness and thus did not find bad motive on the part of the prosecutor. Rather, she determined that the sequence of events raised a presumption of vindictiveness, and she found that the government had failed to satisfactorily rebut the presumption.[45]

The Ninth Circuit thoroughly disapproved of Mary Anne's dismissal, holding that she abused her discretion in presuming vindictiveness. Taking the opportunity to clarify its own jurisprudence of vindictive prosecution claims, the appellate court explained that "the appearance of vindictiveness results only where, as a practical matter, there is a realistic or reasonable likelihood of prosecutorial conduct that would not have occurred but for hostility or a punitive animus towards the defendant because he has exercised his specific legal rights."[46] On the facts before it, the court

---

44. CR 81-00048-01 (D. Ariz. filed March 10, 1981). The appellate court opinion is reported at 681 F.2d 1164 (9th Cir. 1982).

45. Dismissal of Indictment, United States v. Gallegos-Curiel, CR 81-00048-01 (D. Ariz. March 23, 1981).

46. 681 F.2d at 1169.

concluded that the circumstances surrounding the felony indictment did not raise "a threshold appearance of vindictiveness sufficient to trigger an inquiry into the prosecutor's actual motives."[47] Thus, the court determined that Mary Anne should never have questioned the motives underlying the felony charge. The reversal carried with it some words of admonition for Mary Anne: "The appearance of vindictiveness does not embody the post hoc ergo propter hoc fallacy,"[48] the court instructed, and it emphasized that "[t]he severe presumption [of vindictive prosecution] should not be invoked lightly."[49]

The tone of the reversal in *Gallegos-Curiel* bothered Mary Anne. She had struggled to follow the uneven law on vindictive prosecution and had admitted to her own uncertainty at the hearing.[50] Trying to interpret the case law accurately, she concluded that the facts called for a presumption of vindictiveness and had ruled accordingly, but she had not done so "lightly." The reversal, as an emphatic disapproval of her reading of the case law, implied that she had not given the question sufficient attention. Her error in *Gallegos-Curiel* may have been a function of the ambiguity in the case law, but it also may have been informed by her characteristic anger when she perceived governmental misconduct. As a former U.S. Attorney, she expected law enforcement agents and federal prosecutors to be scrupulously fair in their processing of cases.

One reversal she experienced in her criminal docket in federal court concerned a double-jeopardy claim, and her error occurred in an ironic context because of the vagaries of appellate review. In *United States v. Moroyoqui*,[51] the defendant was charged with a cocaine-distribution conspiracy. At Moroyoqui's first trial, Mary Anne granted a mistrial when a government agent improperly testified about other narcotics investigations of the defendant. Mary Anne set the case for a new trial, but before the trial date Moroyoqui moved for a dismisal of the indictment on the ground of double jeopardy. In an effort to expedite the defendant's second trial, the judge not only denied the motion, but she also refused to permit the defendant to take an immediate appeal from her order. During his second trial, the defendant entered a guilty plea pursuant to a plea bargain and was sentenced by Mary Anne to three years. The defendant then appealed in an attempt to set aside his plea and conviction, arguing that the double jeopardy clause had barred the second trial.

---

47. 681 F.2d at 1171.

48. 681 F.2d at 1168.

49. 681 F.2d at 1171.

50. *See* Brief of Appellant, United States v. Gallegos-Curiel, CA 81-1258 (9th Cir.), filed May 28, 1981, at 9, 20.

51. United States v. Moroyoqui, CR 76-479 (D. Ariz. filed Sept. 29, 1976).

At the time of Moroyoqui's double jeopardy argument before Mary Anne, the Ninth Circuit's position was that a denial of a motion to dimiss an indictment on double jeopardy grounds was not immediately appealable. Mary Anne was well aware of that procedural doctrine because she had authored the controlling Ninth Circuit opinion when she sat on the court of appeals by designation shortly after her appointment to the district court. In *United States v. Young*,[52] she had written for the court that a denial of a motion to dismiss an indictment lacked the finality that is a prerequisite for appellate review. In the opinion, announced in October of 1976, she reasoned that the double jeopardy claim could be fully reviewed on appeal from a conviction, and with a trial judge's perspective she explained that "the delays and disruptions caused by intermediate appeals are especially detrimental to the effective administration of the criminal law."[53] Two weeks after her opinion in *Young* was issued, Moroyoqui was arguing in district court before Mary Anne that he should be allowed to take up on interlocutory appeal her denial of his double jeopardy motion. Thus, her rejection of his argument was compelled by the Ninth Circuit's decisional law at the time.

The United States Supreme Court, however, was itself considering the same issue, and in *Abney v. United States*,[54] decided in June of 1977, the Court ruled that an order denying a motion to dismiss on double jeopardy grounds was a final decision and therefore immediately appealable under 28 U.S.C. Sec. 1291. The Supreme Court's decision in *Abney* contrasted markedly with Mary Anne's opinion in *Young* because of the high Court's focus on the meaning of the double-jeopardy guarantee: "It is a guarantee against being twice put to *trial* for the same offense.... [It] assures an individual that...he will not be forced...to endure the personal strain, public embarrassment, and expense of a criminal trial more than once for the same offense."[55] The Court in *Abney*, writing from the highest tier in the judicial system, gave little weight to the government's contention that its ruling would lead to dilatory appeals.

Because *Abney* was decided while Moroyoqui's appeal was still pending, the Ninth Circuit had to apply the newly-announced doctrine. Thus, in *Moroyoqui v. United States*,[56] the Ninth Circuit held that under *Abney* Mary Anne had lacked power to proceed with the defendant's second trial once he had lodged his appeal from her denial of his double jeopardy claim. The court therefore set aside the conviction. Nevertheless, on the

---

52. 544 F.2d 415 (9th Cir. 1976), *cert. den.*, 429 U.S. 1024 (1977).
53. 544 F.2d at 419.
54. 431 U.S. 651 (1977).
55. 431 U.S. at 661 (emphasis in original).
56. 570 F.2d 862 (9th Cir. 1977).

merits of the double jeopardy claim, the Ninth Circuit agreed with Mary Anne's disposition and held that reprosecution of the defendant on remand was not barred.

The *Moroyoqui* reversal therefore contained great irony. Mary Anne was caught between the conflicting views of the Ninth Circuit and the United States Supreme Court. The Ninth Circuit's decisional law she herself had authored, and it reflected the concerns of a trial judge on the question of interlocutory appeal. She believed that interlocutory appeals from adverse double jeopardy rulings would lead to delay and to the proliferation of attacks on indictments based on meritless claims of double jeopardy. In *Moroyoqui* she saw the scenario play itself out. Although the appellate court ultimately rejected the defendant's double jeopardy claim on the merits, the retrial of the defendant was significantly delayed until his appeal was resolved.[57] Mary Anne's desire for efficiency in criminal prosecution and her skepticism about the merits of most double jeopardy claims informed her opinion in *Young*, and her experience with *Moroyoqui* cemented her belief that the Supreme Court's opinion in *Abney* was bad policy.

The criminal case in Mary Anne's court which attracted perhaps the most public attention during her federal tenure involved the prosecution of two air traffic controllers for illegally striking against the federal government. In the consolidated cases of *United States v. Taylor* and *United States v. Florence*,[58] two officers of a local chapter of the Professional Air Traffic Controllers Organization (PATCO) went on strike as part of a nationwide walkout by union members in early August of 1981. As federal employees, the controllers were prohibited from striking by federal statute,[59] and each had signed a no-strike affidavit as a condition of employment. The strike followed a seven-month period of failed negotiations between PATCO and the Department of Transportation about various complaints from the air traffic controllers, including wages, benefits, and many facets of the controllers' working conditions. Sensing the impasse, the Reagan Administration had warned PATCO shortly before the walkout that a strike would lead to job terminations and criminal prosecutions. The defiant union, however, went forward with the work-stoppage,

---

57. The reprosecution of Moroyoqui never went forward. On remand from the court of appeals, defendant filed yet another motion to dismiss the indictment on the ground of former jeopardy. Defendant failed to appear at the hearing on the motion, however, and has been a fugitive since that time. *See* Docket Sheet, United States v. Moroyoqui, CR 76-479 (D. Ariz.).

58. United States v. Taylor, CR 81-00185, and United States v. Florence, CR 81-00186 (D. Ariz.), *aff'd*, 693 F.2d 919 (9th Cir. 1982).

59. *See* 18 U.S.C. Sec. 1918(3).

and more than 12,000 controllers walked off the job on August 3, 1981. Shortly after the walk-out, President Reagan called on the controllers nationwide to return to work and gave them a forty-eight-hour grace-period in which to do so. A few hundred returned, but about 11,400 controllers remained on strike and were promptly fired by the Federal Aviation Authority.[60] PATCO, which was later decertified as the controllers' union, filed for bankruptcy after the strike.[61]

The panoply of events unfolding on the national scene was viewed as an important symbolic victory for Reagan early in his presidency, and he received broad public support for his actions. The strike, which had been portrayed largely as a money dispute rather than a controversy about safety, had failed to generate much public sympathy. Although PATCO ironically had been the only labor union to endorse Reagan in the presidential election in 1980, the strike and its aftermath led to the demise of the union and to personal hardship for the thousands of PATCO members who lost their jobs. For a few dozen union members, however, the strike also led to criminal prosecution.

Although forty-one union members participated in the strike in Tucson, only William Taylor and Billy Florence were charged with the statutory violation, and the defendants launched a comprehensive attack on the prosecution. Arguing that President Reagan had made ambiguous public remarks during the strike relevant to questions of amnesty, the defendants moved to take the President's deposition by videotape. Surely reluctant to compel Reagan to provide testimony in the case, Mary Anne denied the motion, finding that the defendants had failed to show that the testimony would be material. Both defendants later moved to dismiss the indictments, contending that they had been the victims of impermissible selective prosecution. Taylor and Florence contended that they were being punished for having exercised their first amendment rights as union leaders. At the hearing on the motion to dismiss, the government admitted that it had been selective in prosecuting the defendants, but it explained that it had chosen the two defendants for prosecution because "they, by virtue of their offices, were presumed to be leading illegal activity," and

---

60. *See* Fed. Reg. 2235 (1983).

61. The PATCO story is revealed in the many reported court decisions that addressed the myriad legal issues relating to the controversy. *See, e.g.*, PATCO v. Federal Labor Relations Agency, 685 F.2d 547 (D.C. Cir. 1982)(affirming PATCO's decertification); *In re* PATCO, 724 F.2d 205 (D.C. Cir. 1984)(addressing disputes in PATCO's bankruptcy petition); United States v. Haggerty, 528 F. Supp. 1291 (D. Col. 1981)(dismissing indictments against PATCO officers); United States v. Amato, 534 F. Supp. 1190 (E.D.N.Y. 1982)(upholding indictment of PATCO leader for illegal striking).

because their prosecution would deter others from illegally striking.[62] Three days after the hearing, Mary Anne denied the motion to dismiss. "The uncontroverted evidence," she wrote, "is that the defendants organized and led the strike activity."[63]

When the joint prosecution went forward in late October of 1981, the press reported that Taylor and Florence were the first defendants in the United States to be brought to trial in connection with the strike.[64] The jury trial lasted two days, and the jury deliberated for less than thirty minutes in arriving at a guilty verdict for both defendants.[65] Before sending the jury to deliberations, Mary Anne said to the jurors in jest that if they did not reach a verdict by five p.m. that day, she would order them to recess until the next day so that she could watch the World Series. Defense counsel later seized on that remark as a sign of the judge's insensitivity to the defendants' plight.[66] According to a law clerk, Mary Anne was angry that the press had picked up her comment to the jury since she had meant it as joke.[67]

Two weeks after the convictions in Mary Anne's court, the defendants had a temporary surge of hope. In the Phoenix division of the Arizona district court, Judge Charles L. Hardy, a Jimmy Carter appointee who had joined the bench in 1980, dismissed indictments against two PATCO officers arising from the same strike on the ground of selective prosecution. In *United States v. Paisley*, Judge Hardy ruled that the United States had "shown neither evidence that [the defendant] organized or led the local strike activity nor any reasonable basis for selecting for prosecution only [defendant], the local Union President [and, in a separate prosecution... the local union Vice-President]." Hardy went on to conclude that the decision to prosecute the defendants was based on impermissible grounds, namely the "exercise by [the defendants] of the constitutional right to belong to a Union and to hold office in that Union."[68] Taylor and Florence hoped to capitalize on the ruling, and the day after Hardy announced his

---

62. Brief of Appellee, United States v. Taylor, C.A. 81-1753 (9th Cir.), filed March 15, 1982, at 17.

63. United States v. Taylor, CR 81-00185, and United States v. Florence, CR 81-00186 (D. Ariz. Order of Oct. 19, 1981).

64. *Two major trials are scheduled to open in U.S. District Court Tuesday*, U.P.I RELEASE, Arizona Region, October 26, 1981.

65. Docket Sheet, United States v. Taylor, CR 81-00185, and United States v. Florence, CR 81-00186 (D. Ariz. Oct. 28, 1981).

66. Shawn Hubler, *PATCO officers given probation*, TUCSON CITIZEN, November 30, 1981.

67. Interview with Mary O. Ameln, Tucson, Arizona (April 29, 1993).

68. CR 81-196 (D. Ariz. Order of November 12, 1981).

decision, they moved to reopen their motion to dismiss in Mary Anne's court on the basis of selective prosecution. Mary Anne again held a hearing on the question, and for the second time she denied the motion. In her view, the government's explanation of its decision to prosecute Taylor and Florence adequately distinguished the case from the *Paisley* case in Phoenix.[69] She believed the government had selected the two for prosecution because of their leadership role in the strike and not because of their positions as union officers.

Immediately after denying the defense motions, Mary Anne pronounced sentence. She imposed the minimum sentence of one year probation with limited supervision on both defendants and imposed no fines on the men at all. At the time of sentencing, she reportedly remarked that she believed the legal proceedings had left the two defendants financially strapped.[70] Interestingly, the defendants' reaction to the sentence was irate. Press reports quoted Taylor as being "outraged" by Mary Anne's remark that she would not impose a fine, despite the apparent success of a PATCO fundraising effort. "It seems to be a sign of the government's weakness that after all this time and money and prosecution all we get is a year's probation," Taylor commented to news reporters.[71]

On appeal, Florence and Taylor asserted numerous points of error, but the most serious contention again was that of selective prosecution. The government's prosecutorial strategies had come under fire in numerous prosecutions of PATCO officers, and at least two federal district court judges, in addition to Judge Hardy in Arizona, ultimately sustained claims of selective prosecution involving PATCO leaders.[72] Nevertheless, the Ninth Circuit affirmed the convictions in all respects. In rejecting the claim of selective prosecution, the Ninth Circuit relied on Mary Anne's findings that the defendants were prosecuted because they were strike leaders and because their prosecution might deter others from striking.[73]

Mary Anne's response to the PATCO prosecutions was informed by her political conservatism, her own experience as a prosecutor and as a pilot, and her human sympathy for the defendants. As a Republican and fiscal conservative, she would ordinarily side with management rather

---

69. Order denying motion to dismiss and to set aside guilty verdict, United States v. Taylor, CR 81-00185, and United States v. Florence, CR 81-00186 (D. Ariz. Dec. 1, 1981).

70. Shawn Hubler, *PATCO officers given probation*, Tucson Citizen, November 30, 1981.

71. *Id.*

72. *See* United States v. Haggerty, 528 F. Supp. 1291 (D. Col. 1981); United States v. MacDonald, 553 F. Supp. 1003 (S.D. Tex. 1983).

73. United States v. Taylor, 693 F.2d 919, 922–23 (9th Cir. 1982).

than labor. In addition, her view would surely have been that the ban against strikes by government employees was wise policy. Just as she had enjoined the Tucson city police from striking when she was on the state court bench, she sided with the Reagan administration in standing firm against the PATCO walk-out. Moreover, as a former prosecutor, she would have been predisposed to defer to prosecutorial discretion; indeed, she seemed to agree clearly with the government's strategy of targeting the strike leaders. On the other hand, as a former pilot, she also would have understood the job strain experienced by air traffic controllers and the need for improved working conditions. Although the public might not have perceived the strike to concern issues of safety, Mary Anne would have appreciated the safety implications of the controllers' demands. Moreover, despite the accusations from defendants and defense counsel, Mary Anne was sympathetic to the defendants. In contrast to other reported prosecutions of PATCO leaders,[74] she was notably lenient in sentencing. Overall, she disliked the media's focus on proceedings in her court and was content when the case terminated.

In the civil arena, Mary Anne's interpretations of the law tended to be faithful to textual authorities, cautious, and pragmatic. Her deference to the state as sovereign manifested itself in several cases, and the Ninth Circuit concluded on one occasion that she had expanded the scope of a state's eleventh amendment immunity from suit in federal court beyond permissible limits.[75] Predictably, her rulings in cases involving governmental parties tended to favor the government,[76] but not always. When the decisional or statutory law seemed to her to compel an order favoring the private litigant, she would rule accordingly. Just three out of twenty civil appeals resulted in reversal in the Ninth Circuit, and one of the reversals was due to another district judge's error.[77]

Interestingly, the two civil cases in which Mary Anne's decrees were squarely overturned involved instances in which she ruled against govern-

---

74. *See* United States v. Hoover, 727 F.2d 387 (5th Cir. 1984)(defendants sentenced to 90 days in custody and 18 months probation); United States v. Greene, 697 F.2d 1229 (5th Cir. 1983), *cert. den.*, 103 S. Ct. 3542 (1983)(defendants sentenced to $750 fine, 90 days in custody and 18 months probation).

75. Ronwin v. Shapiro, 657 F.2d 1071 (9th Cir. 1981).

76. *See, e.g.,* Fisher v. City of Tucson, CIV 77-037 (D. Ariz. Order of Nov. 23, 1977), published at 26 Fair Empl. Prac. Cas. 864, *aff'd*, 663 F.2d 861 (9th Cir. 1981); Mena v. Weeks, CIV 77-070 (D. Ariz. Order of Dec. 6, 1977), *aff'd*, 626 F.2d 866 (9th Cir. 1978); Ronwin v. Shapiro, CIV 79-0084 (D. Ariz. Order of Jan. 25, 1980), *aff'd on different grounds*, 657 F.2d 1071 (9th Cir. 1981); Perri v. Department of the Treasury, CIV 79-0080 (D. Ariz. Order of Dec. 11, 1979), *aff'd*, 637 F.2d 1332 (9th Cir. 1981).

77. *See* Scott and Fetzer Co. v. Dile, 643 F.2d 670 (9th Cir. 1981).

mental litigants. In 1978, a Freedom of Information Act case was assigned to Mary Anne's docket in which she had to grapple with an unresolved question under the Act. In *Hardy v. Bureau of Alcohol, Tobacco, and Firearms*, the *pro se* plaintiff, a lawyer and outspoken champion of the right to bear arms, had requested the "Raids and Searches" Manual of the BATF.[78] Hardy wanted the Manual for purposes of "an extensive study of allegations of illegal and unconstitutional abuses on the part of the BATF."[79] The BATF had sent Hardy a copy of the Manual with about half of the text deleted, maintaining that the deleted portion was exempt from disclosure under the Freedom of Information Act, and Hardy had sought relief in federal court to obtain the withheld portions of the Manual.

Following an in camera inspection of the Manual, Mary Anne granted partial summary judgment in favor of each party. She found that, as a matter of law, the exemption claimed by the BATF (a statutory exemption for matters "related solely to the internal personnel rules and practices of an agency") applied only to "materials concerning employer-employee relationships" and hence did not protect law enforcement manuals. Mary Anne's somewhat surprising interpretation of the exemption was based on a reading of ambiguous legislative history. Despite this holding, however, she found that "disclosure of some of the deleted portions might have a harmful effect on the agency's performance of its enforcement function and the safety of its agents." This threat, she concluded, "constitutes an exceptional circumstance that justifies the exercise of the court's equitable powers to prevent disclosure of potentially dangerous materials."[80] She thus asserted an equitable authority, outside the dictates of the Act, to protect against high-risk disclosures. Nevertheless, Mary Anne did order significant disclosures, despite the government's insistence that such disclosures would severely impede the law enforcement activities of the BATF. The ordered disclosures included material containing guidelines to agents for initiating and conducting surprise raids, locating incriminating evidence, preventing escapes, and other similar conduct. Mary Anne granted a stay of the disclosure order, however, so that the government could obtain a definitive ruling from the Ninth Circuit.

On appeal, the Ninth Circuit noted that the precise issue before it was one of first impression and that relevant decisions from other circuits did not point in a single direction. In a carefully worded opinion, the court con-

---

78. Hardy v. Bureau of Alcohol, Tobacco, and Firearms, CIV 78-0189 (D. Ariz. filed Aug. 10, 1978).

79. *Id.* (Order of January 17, 1979). *See also* Brief for the Appellee, Hardy v. Bureau of Alcohol, Tobacco and Firearms, No. 79-3202 (9th Cir.), filed October 1, 1979, at 1.

80. Brief for the Appellant, Hardy v. Bureau of Alcohol, Tobacco, and Firearms, No. 79-3202 (9th Cir.), filed August 27, 1979, at 3.

cluded that "law enforcement materials, disclosure of which may risk circumvention of agency regulation, are exempt from disclosure" under the FOIA.[81] The court directed Mary Anne on remand to consider the government's explanation of how disclosure would risk circumvention of agency regulation. If the explanation were reasonable as a matter of law, the Ninth Circuit admonished, the materials should be deemed exempt. On remand, Mary Anne resolutely followed the appellate court's directive and ordered that the contested portions of the Manual need not be disclosed.[82]

Mary Anne's position in *Hardy* was illuminating. Her initial ruling demonstrated that she would not automatically accept the government's legal contentions, even where the authorities seemed evenly divided as between the BATF and Hardy. Although her history as a federal prosecutor surely would have engendered sympathy for the law enforcement arguments advanced by the BATF, she thought her disclosure order was required by the FOIA and she ruled accordingly. Moreover, her own discomfort with governmental secrecy, dating from her open-file policy in the U.S. Attorney's Office, might have weighed against the government's position. Ironically, Mary Anne's assertion of "equitable authority" was a concession to the government's interest but not one that the government particularly desired. Finally, her ruling revealed a concerted effort to remain objective; the *pro se* plaintiff whose fiercely-held political agenda obviously fueled his lawsuit might have received a colder reception in other courtrooms.[83]

The other civil case in which a ruling by Mary Anne against a governmental litigant triggered a reversal from the Ninth Circuit was *Catalina Cablevision Associates v. City of Tucson*.[84] The case involved a battle between two competing cable television companies within the Tucson metropolitan area. Pursuant to state law authorizing cities to regulate and license cable television systems, the City in 1981 held a public bidding process and granted a fifteen-year license to Cox Cable, a competitor of plaintiff Catalina. Several months later, Catalina filed a lawsuit in federal

---

81. Hardy v. Bureau of Alcohol, Tobacco, and Firearms, 631 F.2d 653, 657 (9th Cir. 1980).

82. Hardy v. Bureau of Alcohol, Tobacco, and Firearms, CIV 78-0189 (D. Ariz. Order of Dec. 10, 1980).

83. The same lawyer who represented himself in *Hardy* appeared on behalf of the plaintiff in Perri v. Department of the Treasury, CIV 79-080 (D. Ariz.), challenging the BATF's revocation of a license to sell firearms. In that action, Mary Anne handed Hardy a quick defeat, ruling against his client without an evidentiary hearing. Her disposition was affirmed at 637 F.2d 1332 (9th Cir. 1981).

84. Catalina Cablevision Assoc. v. City of Tucson, CIV 82-459 (D. Ariz. Order of July 21, 1983), *rev'd*, 745 F.2d 1266 (9th Cir. 1984).

court under the Sherman Act, alleging that the City had created an unlawful monopoly in the arrangement with Cox. In its answer, the City asserted a "state action" immunity from suit under *Parker v. Brown.*[85]

Pretrial proceedings in Mary Anne's court quickly focused on the availability of the immunity defense to the City. After hearing arguments from counsel, Mary Anne issued her written opinion granting to Catalina partial summary judgment. In her last published decision, she reasoned that the "state action" immunity was unavailable because the City's award of an exclusive license to Cox had not been authorized, explicitly or implicitly, by statute. "Because the statutes nowhere address or imply that it was the state's policy to displace competition with a monopoly," she wrote, "City cannot take advantage of Parker immunity."[86] Apparently far from certain that her ruling would be sustained on apppeal, Mary Anne certified her order as involving a controlling question of law open to difference of opinion, and the Ninth Circuit accepted the City's interlocutory appeal.

The Ninth Circuit, in an opinion announced after Mary Anne's death, disagreed with her reading of Arizona statutory law. In contrast to Mary Anne's narrow view of Arizona's statutory scheme, the appeals court declared that "[t]he State of Arizona has provided a clear and affirmative state policy to displace competition in Arizona cable television service with regulation."[87] The court further held that Tucson's grant of a single non-exclusive license was contemplated by the state. According to the court, the Arizona legislature "necessarily contemplated that cities would limit the number of cable providers despite the anticompetitive effects that such action might have."[88] The appellate court accordingly reversed Mary Anne's ruling, and on remand the case was dismissed.

In her ruling in *Catalina Cablevision,* Mary Anne exercised caution to the detriment of the City. The attorney for Catalina believed Mary Anne accurately interpreted the law as it stood at the time of the summary judgment, but he recalled that intervening decisions had expanded considerably the availability of governmental immunity.[89] Moreover, in that nascent era of cable television, Mary Anne may have been skeptical of the City's need to engage in anticompetitive licensing. A believer in the free-market system, she probably thought that consumers would be better

---

85. 317 U.S. 341 (1943).

86. Catalina Cablevision Assoc. v. City of Tucson, CIV 82-459 (D. Ariz. Order of July 21, 1983), published at 1984-1 Trade Cas. p65,789.

87. Catalina Cablevision Assoc. v. City of Tucson, 745 F.2d 1266, 1270 (9th Cir. 1984).

88. 745 F.2d at 1270.

89. Conversation with John A. Baade, Tucson, Arizona (Dec. 31, 1995).

served through competition among companies rather than through the City's bidding process. Indeed, Catalina maintained publicly that it could provider superior and less expensive service to city residents than Cox.[90] Unwilling to construe the relevant state statutes as authorizing the City's licensing arrangement, Mary Anne took the route of denying the antitrust immunity. Nevertheless, she was characteristically circumspect about the fate of her ruling on appeal and took steps to ensure a quick review.

As a district judge, Mary Anne was subject to designation by the chief judge of the Ninth Circuit to periodically sit on the appellate court.[91] During her tenure on the federal bench, she participated in adjudicating appeals before the Ninth Circuit in almost thirty cases and authored opinions in nine of them.[92] In keeping with the subdued voice of most district judges sitting by designation on appellate panels, she wrote only one concurrence and no dissenting opinions.[93] Her approach to the appellate court assignments was to ask her law clerks for bench memoranda summarizing the cases and the parties' legal contentions and recommending a

---

90. *Arizona Briefs*, U.P.I. RELEASE, July 23, 1983.

91. The designation process is authorized by 28 U.S.C. Sec. 292 (1993).

92. The reported Ninth Circuit opinions which Mary Anne authored covered a wide range of subjects: Young v. United States, 544 F.2d 415 (9th Cir. 1976)(holding that a district court's denial of a motion to dismiss an indictment on the ground of double jeopardy was not a final and appealable order); Shakesteers Coffee Shops v. United States, 546 F.2d 821 (9th Cir. 1976)(holding that a bankrupt's trust fund was a general asset of the bankrupt's estate); United States v. Hunt, 548 F.2d 268 (9th Cir. 1977)(holding that any error in admitting evidence discovered during a search of defendant's car was harmless); Maugnie v. Compagnie Nationale Air France, 549 F.2d 1256 (9th Cir. 1977)(holding that an injury incurred by an airline passenger was outside the scope of the Warsaw Convention); United States v. Erwin, 625 F.2d 838 (9th Cir. 1980)(holding that a body cavity search of the defendant was lawful and that the evidence discovered in the course of that search was therefore properly admitted into evidence); Hirunpidok v. Immigration and Naturalization Service, 641 F.2d 778 (9th Cir. 1980)(reversing a decision by the Board of Immigration Appeals that denied petitioners' application for permanent resident status); United States v. California State Board of Equalization, 650 F.2d 1127 (9th Cir. 1981)(affirming a district court's ruling that a California sales tax was unconstitutional as applied to leases of property to the United States); Crawford v. Ranger Insurance Co., 653 F.2d 1248 (9th Cir. 1981)(affirming a district court's declaratory judgment of noncoverage of insurance). She also wrote a separate concurrence in a case that reversed a district court's dismissal of a plaintiff's civil rights complaint. *See* Bouse v. Bussey, 573 F.2d 548, 551–552 (9th Cir. 1977)(Richey, J.,concurring).

93. Mary Anne's reluctance to file seperate opinions parallels the practice of most designated judges. Such judges, as outsiders, rarely file solitary opinions. *See* Justin J. Green & Burton M. Atkins, *Designated judges: how well do they perform?* 61 JUDICATURE 358, 368–69 (1978).

disposition. Armed with that preparation, she would attend oral arguments (generally held in San Francisco) and participate in the post-argument conferences with the other members of the panel. In conference, she and the other judges usually arrived at a consensus as to result. When she was assigned responsibility for authoring the court's opinion, she would return to Tucson and give her law clerk the task of drafting the opinion.

Mary Anne took the Ninth Circuit assignments seriously and worked hard perfecting the opinion drafts her clerks would give to her. She wanted the text to accurately reflect the reasoning and result in plain English, without linquistic flourishes, and she would sometimes eliminate unnecessary legalisms. Wanting to avoid any appearance of presumptuousness, she objected to the use of the first-person plural pronoun when describing past holdings of the Ninth Circuit. "I don't want to say 'we have held in prior decisions' because I wasn't there," she instructed her clerks.[94] Above all, she wanted her opinions to withstand appellate review in the Supreme Court.

Mary Anne's contribution to the Ninth Circuit's substantive law through her authored opinions reflected familiar aspects of her judicial outlook. She demonstrated great deference to lower court findings,[95] a reluctance to find reversible error in criminal proceedings,[96] a fidelity to the text of codified law and a concern for fair notice,[97] and a characteristic judicial restraint on constitutional matters.[98] Nevertheless, some of her as-

---

94. By 1981, Mary Anne was able to use the first-person plural pronoun in a manner that satisfied even her sense of accuracy. In Hirunpidok v. Immigration and Naturalization Service, 641 F.2d 778, 780 (9th Cir. 1981), in referring to a prior opinion issued by a panel in which she had participated, she was comfortable writing, "we concluded" and "[w]e further noted."

95. In Crawford v. Ranger Ins. Co., 653 F.2d 1248 (9th Cir. 1981), for example, she authored the court's opinion upholding a declaration of non-coverage in an insurance case and finding that the district court did not abuse its discretion in refusing to give collateral estoppel to an earlier ruling from another court.

96. See United States v. Erwin, 625 F.2d 838 (9th Cir. 1980); United States v. Hunt, 548 F.2d 268 (9th Cir. 1977). In Hunt, it should be noted, Judge Sneed dissented, decrying the majority's "use of the harmless error doctrine to avoid confronting the legality of the search of appellant's car." 548 F.2d at 271.

97. See Hirunpidok v. Immigration and Naturalization Service, 641 F.2d 778 (9th Cir. 1981)(holding that the INS improperly applied governing regulations to petitioners' application for permanent status and failed to give petitioners fair notice of new regulatory interpretation).

98. In Bouse v. Bussey, 573 F.2d 548, 551–52 (9th Cir. 1977), for example, she wrote a separate concurring opinion criticizing the majority for deciding a constitutional question regarding a warrant requirement on the merits without the benefit of a factual record.

signed opinions rejected the government's asserted position. In one, for example, she enforced the policy underlying the federal Bankruptcy Act to preserve assets for bankruptcy administration and in so doing rejected a claim by federal and state taxing authorities.[99] In another, she reversed the Immigration and Naturalization Service for wrongly denying permanent resident status to the petitioners.[100] While most of Mary Anne's assigned opinions involved merely the application of settled law to difficult facts and thus had little precedential value, at least two decisions that she authored announced potentially far-reaching interpretations of law.

In *United States v. California State Board of Equalization*,[101] the Ninth Circuit affirmed a district court's holding that a California sales tax could not be constitutionally applied to leases of personal property to the United States. In an attempt to overcome the barrier of the United States' constitutional immunity from state taxation, California had revised its tax laws. Under the scheme that was before the court, the tax laws purported to leave the decision of who would pay the state sales tax to the transacting parties. Mary Anne's opinion, however, described in detail how the operation of the taxing scheme belied its seeming neutrality. After a cautionary explanation that the governmental immunity is narrow and does not operate to shield federal contractors, she pointed out how the scheme at issue directly imposed the sales tax on the United States as lessee. "Despite the facial neutrality of [the tax laws]," she wrote, "the strong economic incentive created by [the levying methods] all but compels the lessor to collect the tax from the lessee." She concluded that California's revised tax laws placed "the legal incidence of the tax on the United States and, therefore, violates the United States' constitutional immunity from state taxation."[102] The Supreme Court affirmed the ruling without opinion.[103]

Mary Anne was nervous in working on the opinion, and required her law clerk to produce several drafts before she was satisfied. "At first the panel couldn't agree, and one judge threatened to dissent. Judge Richey wanted to write an opinion that would satisfy everyone, and that's what we ended up doing. But it was a struggle, and she poured over it. Then, when the Supreme Court summarily affirmed, she was absolutely gleeful."[104] Overall, Mary Anne's approach in *California State Board of Equalization* was consistent with basic facets of her judicial philosophy.

99. Shakesteers Coffee Shops v. United States, 546 F.2d 821 (9th Cir. 1976), *cert. den.*, 431 U.S. 974 (1977).

100. Hirunpidok v. Immigration and Naturalization Service, 641 F.2d 778 (9th Cir. 1981).

101. 650 F.2d 1127 (9th Cir. 1981), *aff'd*, 456 U.S. 901 (1982).

102. 650 F.2d at 1132.

103. 456 U.S. 901 (1982).

104. Sholder Interview, *supra* note 5.

She did not want to decide the case in a more expansive manner than necessary; indeed, her opinion vacated certain portions of the district court's order that were unsupported by the record. Moreover, she was not taken in by the "illusory" neutrality of the tax scheme; instead, she applied common sense and economic realism in assessing the operation of the scheme. Her reasoning appealed to logic and has been relied on in later cases, especially for the proposition that economic incentives can cause the legal incidence of a facially neutral tax to fall on the purchaser.[105] Her cautionary dictum, moreover, which evidenced a characteristic restraint, has also been cited by later courts in distinguishing certain valid taxing schemes.[106]

Another opinion by Mary Anne interjected her into the law of international aviation and the Warsaw Convention, the international agreement that imposes strict liability on air carriers for injuries incurred by passengers on board aircraft or "in the course of...embarking and disembarking."[107] In *Maugnie v. Compagnie Nationale Air France*,[108] the court had to determine whether plaintiff's injuries, incurred within a common-use area of the Orly Airport terminal in Paris, France, were suffered in the course of "disembarking" within the meaning of the Convention, thereby allowing plaintiff to recover against Air France. In her opinion for the majority, Mary Anne characterized the purpose of the Convention as one of cost allocation. She explained, "Today the Convention functions to protect passengers from the hazards of air travel and also spreads the accident cost of air transportation among all passengers."[109] In deciding whether the Convention applied, she reviewed the various tests announced by other circuits for determining when a passenger's injuries are within the scope of the Convention, tests that included, on the one hand, strict attention to geographical location of the passenger and, on the other, a competing, more flexible view. Uncomfortable with a single categorical standard, Mary Anne opted for a more fluid approach. She wrote, "[S]ince the Convention drafters did not draw a clear line, this Court is

---

105. *See, e.g.,* United States v. State of Michigan, 851 F.2d 803, 809 (6th Cir. 1988)(invalidating imposition of state sales tax on federal credit unions).

106. *See, e.g.,* Howell v. State Board of Equalization, 731 F.2d 624, 627–28 (9th Cir. 1984).

107. Article 17 of the CONVENTION FOR THE UNIFICATION OF CERTAIN RULES RELATING TO INTERNATIONAL CARRIAGE BY AIR, 49 Stat. 3000 et seq. (1934), *reprinted* at 49 U.S.C. sec. 1502 Note. Under the Convention, the trade-off for the imposition of strict liability on air carriers is a limitation on damages.

108. 549 F.2d 1256 (9th Cir.), *cert. den.,* 431 U.S. 974 (1977).

109. 549 F.2d at 1259, *citing* Day v. Trans World Airlines, Inc., 528 F.2d 31 (2d Cir. 1975).

also reluctant to formulate an inflexible rule. Rather we prefer an approach which requires an assessment of the total circumstances surrounding a passenger's injuries, viewed against the background of the intended meaning of Article 17. Location of the passenger is but one of several factors to be considered."[110] Even under her more flexibile interpetation of the Convention, however, Mary Anne concluded that the plaintiff, who was in a common passenger corridor at the time of injury and no longer under the control of the airline, could not claim under the Convention.

Significantly, Judge Clifford Wallace, a member of the panel, made clear that he disagreed with Mary Anne's approach. Concurring in result, he criticized her for unnecessarily resolving an important question concerning an international treaty. "We ought not to be reaching out to do so," he pointedly wrote.[111] Moreover, if forced to choose, Wallace preferred the simpler geographical test over Mary Anne's open-ended interpretation which, he feared, was borne of sympathy for injured plaintiffs.

Mary Anne's opinion in *Maugnie* was, at least according to Wallace, an exercise of judicial activism unwarranted by the facts. Her opinion, however, revealed an unwillingness to adopt a rigid test that might be unduly excluding. As a frequent international traveler herself and as a former pilot, she wanted to formulate a standard that would evolve with "modern air transportation technology" and would accommodate such innovations as the mobile boarding unit.[112] The *Maugnie* opinion has been squarely relied on in other cases involving similar facts,[113] and it has been approvingly cited for its "broad cost allocation theory of liability under the Convention."[114]

Strands of Mary Anne's judicial philosophy clearly surfaced in her work on appeal, but she was a trial judge at heart and was at her best in the dynamic give-and-take of the courtroom. Sitting as an appellate judge, her opinions were inevitably shaped by her trial judge's perspective, as in her ill-fated opinion on the appealability of a district court's rejection of a double-jeopardy claim. Through her work as an appellate judge, she came to view intra-panel dynamics as battles often driven by ego, frequently turning on irrelevant abstractions, and she was always pleased to return to her own courtroom in Tucson. It was in that courtroom, where real people came before her daily in their sometimes anguished quests for justice, that she established her identity.

---

110. 549 F.2d at 1262.

111. *Id.* (Wallace, J., concurring).

112. *Id.* at 1261–62.

113. *See, e.g.,* McCarthy v. Northwest Airlines, Inc., 56 F.3d 313 (1st Cir. 1995); Schmidkunz v. Scandinavian Airlines System, 628 F.2d 1205 (9th Cir. 1980).

114. Saks v. Air France, 724 F.2d 1383 (9th Cir. 1984).

CHAPTER FOURTEEN

Taking Leave

Mary Anne's years on the federal bench were cut short by her early death, but not before she had accumulated a record of success. In 1978, the judicial evaluation polls conducted by the Arizona State Bar ranked her higher than any other federal district judge in Arizona.[1] Although her rankings dropped gradually through 1982, she still received the endorsement of the vast majority of lawyers who had appeared before her.[2] She gained the respect and affection of her colleagues within the federal judiciary and served on both the Executive Committee and the Judicial Tenure Committee of the Ninth Circuit and on the Executive Committee of the National Conference of Federal Trial Judges.[3] Finally, in August of 1982, Chief Justice Warren Burger tapped Mary Anne to chair the newly-created Federal-State Relations Subcommittee of the United States Judicial Conference Committee on Court Administration.[4] Because she was a veteran of the state judiciary and by that point a seasoned federal judge, Mary Anne's selection by Burger was not surprising. She looked forward to heading up the committee and immediately asked her law clerks to gather case law and academic writing on questions of federalism.

A recognition of a different sort had come Mary Anne's way in 1981. In June of that year, Justice Potter Stewart publicly announced his resignation from the United States Supreme Court, and there was immediate speculation that President Ronald Reagan might appoint a woman. The speculation stemmed from Reagan's campaign pledge to name a woman to one of the first vacancies on the nation's highest court. In fact, the Reagan administration had known of Stewart's resignation for several months and had quietly been searching for a woman to replace the retiring Justice.[5] Amidst that speculation, the names of two women judges in Arizona

---

1. *Federal judge in Tucson given top rating*, PHOENIX REPUBLIC, October 12, 1978.

2. *Judicial Evaluation Poll Results*, ARIZONA BAR BRIEFS 3 (October 1982)(reporting approval ratings for Mary Anne of 98 percent in 1978, 97 percent in 1980, and 94 percent in 1982).

3. Biographical File, Federal Court Papers of Judge Mary Anne Richey, United States District Court, Tucson, Arizona.

4. Letter of August 5, 1982, from Chief Justice Warren E. Burger to Hon. Mary Anne Richey.

5. Lou Cannon, *Reagan Nominates Woman to Supreme Court*, WASHINGTON POST, July 8, 1981.

surfaced: Sandra Day O'Connor, then a state court appellate judge, and Mary Anne Richey. According to local news reports, although Senator Dennis DeConcini immediately began campaigning for O'Connor after Stewart's announcement, Mary Anne's name was also submitted to Reagan.[6] Mary Anne's candidacy was serious enough to be reported in newspapers outside of Arizona, including The Baltimore Sun and the local newspaper of Mary Anne's hometown, Shelbyville, Indiana.[7]

As experienced female judges and longtime Republicans, Mary Anne and O'Connor were both logical candidates for the vacancy on the Supreme Court. Each had distinguished careers in public service: O'Connor's professional life had spanned all three branches of state government, and Mary Anne had worked as a federal prosecutor, a state court judge, and was now an Article III judge. Each woman had a judicial philosophy comporting with the President's announced goals—a belief in the principle of judicial restraint *vis a vis* the other two branches of the national government, and a respect for the fundamental role of the states as sovereigns in the federal system. Interestingly, O'Connor herself viewed Mary Anne as a "kindred spirit." "We both had families and careers, and we were both at home in the West," she explained. "When I was on the Arizona state court, she was someone I instinctively liked because we had more in common than some of the other judges."[8]

Despite the press coverage of Mary Anne's candidacy, she downplayed the matter in private conversations. In an interview with a law clerk during the time when her name was being considered, Mary Anne minimized the news. "When I went to the interview," the clerk recalled, "her name had been in the papers just the day before as a possible Supreme Court candidate. When I mentioned it at the interview, she pooh-poohed it and said that she wouldn't want to go to Washington, anyway."[9] She confided in her old friend Alice Truman, still a superior court judge, that her views on abortion would keep her off the Supreme Court in any event,[10] and she told her secretary Robbins that, at sixty-three, she was "too old for the

6. 'Mrs. Justice' from Arizona?, TUCSON CITIZEN, June 22, 1981.

7. Former local woman considered for high court, THE SHELBYVILLE NEWS, June 19, 1981; Curt Matthews, Woman justice may replace retiring Stewart, THE BALTIMORE SUN, June 19, 1981 (reporting that two Arizona women jurists, Sandra Day O'Connor and Mary Anne Richey, were among those "who might be under consideration").

8. Telephone Interview with Hon. Sandra Day O'Connor, Associate Justice of United States Supreme Court (Jan. 23, 1993).

9. Interview with Craig H. Kaufman, Tucson, Arizona (Jan. 1, 1993).

10. Interview with Hon. Alice Truman, former Judge, Pima County Superior Court, Tucson, Arizona (July 6, 1992).

appointment."[11] O'Connor was unaware that Mary Anne's name had been mentioned in connection with the vacancy, and recalled that it was not on the short list that Attorney General William French Smith had shown her.[12] Less than three weeks after Stewart's announcement, Reagan nominated O'Connor for the position and ended the flurry of speculation

Mary Anne was gratified by the brief mention of her name as a potential nominee to the high Court, just as she had been pleased a decade earlier when she had been under consideration during Nixon's presidency. On the other hand, she and those who knew her well realized that appellate court judging would not have suited her. The isolation of the Supreme Court, the nature of its workload, and the focus of the public eye all would have been incompatible with her personality. Moreover, she was profoundly tied to the West, not only because of her husband's Tucson-based law practice but also because of her affinity for the joys of western life—the riding and hunting trails, the expanses of desert, the towering mountains, and the unique sunsets that she watched almost daily from her patio.

The speculation about a Supreme Court appointment prompted Mary Anne to reflect on her life and her future. She did not relish the thought of a new and daunting professional challenge. She had tried to maintain balance in her life during her years on the federal bench and thus had continued her habit of vacationing in the out-of-doors, taking overnight trail rides with her husband and friends, and spending an occasional week on a rented houseboat at Lake Powell in northern Arizona.[13] To escape the growing congestion of Tucson, whose population had increased to 330,000 people by 1980, she and her husband Bill had purchased acreage in the White Mountains in eastern Arizona and were engaged in renovating an old farm house on the land.[14] Rather than a transition to a demanding new position in the national spotlight, she longed for more opportunity to spend time with Bill and to be free of the pressing responsibilities at the courthouse. Under the existing statutory guidelines governing the retirement of federal judges, she could retire with full salary by the age of seventy,[15] an age she would have attained in 1987, and she

---

11. Interview with Eleanor Robbins, Tucson, Arizona (July 13, 1992).

12. O'Connor Interview, *supra* note 8.

13. Interview with William K. Richey, Nutrioso, Arizona (July 16–17, 1992), Telephone Interviews with Richey (Sept. 20, 27, 1992, Sept. 21, 1994); Interview with Hon. Richard M. Bilby, United States District Judge, Tucson, Arizona (Dec. 10, 1992); Interview with Hon. William D. Browning, United States District Judge, Tucson, Arizona (Sept. 11, 1992).

14. Richey Interviews, *supra* note 13.

15. *See* 28 U.S.C. Sec. 371 (1993).

was counting the days until her retirement would fully vest. She looked forward with palpable anticipation to the date when she and Bill could move permanently to their tranquil country home.[16] Indeed, she remained uncertain as to whether to retire early and take the cut in her federal annuity, or to stay on the bench until the age of seventy to receive the full benefit of the federal retirement plan. The choice was difficult for her and one that she reevaluated on an ongoing basis.[17]

In addition, when Mary Anne's schedule allowed time for introspection, her thoughts invariably turned to her daughter. Annie continued to provoke anxiety in Mary Anne because of her seeming lack of ambition, and her disinterest in academics. In 1981, when Annie was eighteen years of age, she won a $10,000 jackpot in the state lottery and, to Mary Anne's anger and dismay, applied the money to finance an apartment away from home. Although Annie remained close to her father Bill, her relationship with her mother seemed laden with tension. They spoke frequently on the telephone, but Mary Anne could not hide the disappointment she felt that Annie was not following a track to traditional success.[18] Mary Anne seemed unable to implement the advice of friends that she accept her daughter for who she was and not impose her values on the young woman. Some confidants surmised that Annie's very independence and stubborn determination to make her own choices in life were qualities that Mary Anne herself possessed and had passed on to her daughter.[19] Although Mary Anne did not live to see her daughter's future successes, the strong-willed drive that Annie inherited from her mother did ultimately enable her to secure a college degree, a promising career as a federal probation officer, and a stable home-life—the very things Mary Anne had feared Annie would never achieve. Ironically, Annie's place of work became the United States Courthouse in Tucson.[20]

In March of 1983, Mary Anne discovered a small lump on her side that was of more concern to her doctors than to her. When the doctors recommended a biopsy, she informed her staff and other judges at the courthouse in a manner that indicated she was not worried. "She called us into her chambers," Judge Alfredo Marquez recalled, "and said, 'I've developed a little cyst. I'll be out for about a week, so we need to divide

---

16. William Richey Interviews, *supra* note 13.

17. Telephone Interview with Maureen DeMaio (Dec. 22, 1995).

18. Interview with Annie Richey, Tucson, Arizona (Aug. 22, 1992); Interview with Eleanor Robbins, Tucson, Arizona (July 13, 1992); Telephone Interview with Virginia Trumbull (Aug. 29, 1992).

19. Trumbull Interview, *supra* note 18; DeMaio Interview, *supra* note 17.

20. Annie Richey Interview, *supra* note 18.

my calendar.'"[21] She also had to cancel her attendance at a long-scheduled meeting in Florida of the Federal-State Relations Subcommittee, for which she had diligently prepared.[22] As it happened, she was never able to assume the responsibility of chairing the group. Her secretary Robbins hugged her and wished her "godspeed" as she left for the biopsy. A few days later Robbins received a call from Bill Richey, and she could sense the devastation in his voice. "Ellie," he said, "it's malignant, and they have had to remove several inches of her rib cage."[23]

Shortly after the surgery, Mary Anne told her colleague Richard Bilby that she felt "pretty hopeful." Bilby advised her to force the doctors to reveal to her the absolute truth about her condition and her prognosis, and Mary Anne followed his suggestion. She called him a few days later. "I took your advice, and I'm sort of sorry now that I did," she said without humor. "They told me that I have cancer of the kidney and that it's metasticized. They don't think that I'll live another year, but they've mentioned some new treatments, and I'm going to try them all."[24]

Mary Anne thus seemed to accept the grim news of her cancer with equanimity, and she set out on a course of aggressive treatment over the ensuing months. Characteristically, she was not willing to admit defeat. At the University of Arizona Cancer Center, she received chemotherapy and radiation therapy on an outpatient basis, including treatment with interferon. Her mood at the beginning was optimistic, and news reports reflected that optimism. Judges Marquez and Bilby released a joint statement for the press: "Upon her successful completion of this [interferon] treatment, [Judge Richey] will be returning to the bench."[25] Open to nontraditional therapy as well as medical approaches, she played self-healing tapes at night.[26] Although she remained at home during the three-month period of chemotherapy, she continued to work on matters under advisement and would send in rulings on pending motions. In July, Mary Anne returned to the bench part-time and presided over a few criminal and civil matters, but her stamina had been drained by the debilitating treatments. When the cancer spread to her bone structure, the pain was excruciating, and her staff would see fleeting grimaces on her face as she walked or sat for long periods.[27] In late fall, she became too ill to work.

21. Interview with Hon. Alfredo C. Marquez, United States District Judge, Tucson, Arizona (Jan. 26, 1993).

22. Kaufman Interview, *supra* note 9.

23. Robbins Interview, *supra* note 11.

24. Bilby Interview, *supra* note 13.

25. *Richey*, REGIONAL NEWS FOR ARIZONA-NEVADA, U.P.I. RELEASE, April 6, 1983.

26. Annie Richey Interview, *supra* note 18.

27. Robbins Interview, *supra* note 11; Kaufman Interview, *supra* note 9.

Mary Anne's demeanor was enigmatic to many of her staff and friends. "So be it," Robbins recalled Mary Anne saying after the discovery of the cancer, as if she were yielding to the inevitable. Others perceived that she was angry that her life was being cut short. She grieved her loss of energy and the loss of her future. "I have so much more to do," she said to one clerk, but she remained "upbeat" to most eyes.[28] By late summer, however, when it was clear that she was losing the battle, she wept openly in front of one former law clerk. According to Nancy Fiora, who at the time was an Assistant U.S. Attorney, "I was in her chambers on a legal matter, and she said to me that she had just been told by her doctors that she had only three months to live. When I asked the judge if she were scared, she began to cry. I felt that I had invaded her privacy, and I knew she did not let many people see that vulnerable side of her."[29] Mary Anne's friends perceived that ultimately her major anguish was for Bill and for Annie and that she struggled emotionally with the reality of leaving her husband and daughter.[30]

Bill Richey, who had lost other family members to cancer, was devoted to Mary Anne in her illness. He toted her court files home to her in a saddle bag when she was too sick to go to the office. He sat with her under a ramada that he had built for her to shade her from the brutal summer sun, and together they would watch the quail and rabbits near their home. He arranged to have her flown by helicopter to their beloved property in eastern Arizona so that she could enjoy once more the chill evenings and the vanilla scent of Ponderosa pine.[31]

During her final months, Mary Anne attended church regularly. Over the years, she had periodically taken Annie to one of the several Presbyterian churches in Tucson, but when she was faced with her own mortality, religion loomed as a larger force in her life. Mary Anne attended the Northminster Presbyterian Church, a building with a white steeple that is reminiscent of the Presbyterian church she attended as a child in Shelbyville. She seemed to draw strength from hearing the familiar services and hymns, and she liked sitting anonymously among the congregants where her status as a federal judge went unnoticed. As she began to be aware of the true extent of her cancer, she sought out the minister of the church. In a series of private conversations with Dr. Richard Rowley, she

---

28. Robbins Interview, *supra* note 11; DeMaio Interview, *supra* note 17; Interview with Mary O. Ameln, Tucson, Arizona (April 29, 1993); Kaufman Interview, *supra* note 9.

29. Interview with Hon. Nancy Fiora, United States Magistrate Judge, Tucson, Arizona (Aug. 20, 1992).

30. Interview with Johanna Stephens, Tucson, Arizona (Oct. 27, 1992).

31. Interview with Henry G. Zipf, Tucson, Arizona (Sept. 14, 1995).

explored the questions she was confronting on a daily basis. "She had questions about why God would do such a thing," Rowley recalled. "She did not want to die at this point, but her faith was strong."[32] Prayer seemed to calm her, according to Rowley, and over the course of their sessions he gradually saw a greater sense of acceptance in her. "I felt she had come to the realization that she was going to do everything she could, but now it was in God's hands, and there was a point where she could do no more. It was an inspiration to be with her and to see this inner strength. She was not afraid to die."[33]

In the last few weeks before her death, Mary Anne sensed that each interaction with friends and coworkers might be her last, and she tried to enjoy the time that was left to her. She took her secretary to see the movie version of the opera "La Traviata," and Robbins felt that the afternoon they spent listening to the soaring music was a peak in their long association.[34] Mary Anne spent a few days in California with her close friend from the WASP, Ginny Trumbull, enjoying the sea air and the sound of the ocean. She reflected on her life and wondered aloud whether she had made the right choices as a parent and whether she had given Annie enough of herself.[35] Mary Anne took drives with another close friend and neighbor, Johanna Stephens, and conversed openly with her about her great sadness.[36] She spoke with friend Judge Gordon Thompson, who flew to Tucson to see her. "I sat at the foot of her bed and we spent the time reminiscing about our joint experiences. I remember that before I left, we said goodbye. We knew it was for the last time."[37] Mary Anne's colleague Richard Bilby also visited her in her final days. "I sat there in her bedroom holding her hand—the only time I can remember ever doing that—and we spoke of personal matters." In that conversation, Bilby recalled, Mary Anne also seemed to wish for a role in the selection of her successor, but she realized such matters were beyond her control. Her parting words to Bilby were, "'Be sure and take care of Bill.'"[38]

Toward the end of November, Mary Anne was scheduled for surgery to relieve the severe pain she was suffering in her sciatic nerve, but her system was unable to withstand more assaults. Hospitalized in preparation for the surgery, she died on November 25, at the age of sixty-six,

---

32. Interview with Dr. Richard Rowley, Tucson, Arizona (Sept. 8, 1992).

33. *Id.*

34. Robbins Interview, *supra* note 11.

35. Trumbull Interview, *supra* note 18.

36. Stephens Interview, *supra* note 30.

37. Telephone Interview with Hon. Gordon Thompson, Jr., United States District Judge (May 12, 1993).

38. Bilby Interview, *supra* note 13.

with her husband at her side.[39] Neither Mary Anne nor Bill had revealed to Annie the precariousness of Mary Anne's physical condition, and she had not known her mother was so near death. Grief-stricken, father and daughter leaned on one another in the aftermath of Mary Anne's death, and Annie, then just twenty years old, moved immediately back into the Richey home.[40]

Four days after Mary Anne died, a memorial service was held at the Northminster Presbyterian Church, with services conducted by Mary Anne's advisor and confidant, Dr. Rowley. Among the several hundred people in attendance at the service were a half-dozen proud members of the WASP, for whom a pew was specially reserved. The printed program at the service contained a favorite poem, "High Flight," by John Gillespie Magee. The World War II verse about plane flight, which describes the exhilaration of challenging the unknown ("Oh, I have slipped the surly bonds of earth, And danced the skies on laughter-silvered wings....") could have been a metaphor for Mary Anne's life.

In accordance with Mary Anne's wishes, her body was cremated, and Bill scattered part of her ashes on the treasured White Mountain property where she had looked forward to spending her retirement. Bill carried the remaining ashes high above the cliffs of southern Arizona's Pusch Ridge in an airplane and there released them into the cold air. As Mary Anne directed, no gravestone marks her death.[41] Mary Anne thus died as she had lived—bravely and compassionately. Although she ultimately lost in her battle against cancer, she fought tenaciously for nine grueling months. At the end, she faced death with a powerful dignity, but it was a dignity tinged with a grieving concern for those she was leaving behind.

From her rugged tomboy youth in Indiana to her days on the federal trial court bench in Tucson, Mary Anne was a woman who actively shaped her own destiny. Her life itself manifested a courage, independence of spirit, and irrepressible capacity for joy that drew others to her. A pathbreaker from the beginning, she fiercely believed in, and lived, a model of female equality. That core value surfaced throughout her life—in her androgynous self-image during childhood when she was the athletic "Pete," in her early exploration of the colonial world of India, in her determination in the WASP to show that women could fly as well as men, and in her singular success in the male-dominated legal profession.

---

39. The local newspapers carried news of Mary Anne's death in laudatory obituaries. *See* Jeff Spivak, *Judge Richey dies at 66, is praised as legal scholar*, THE ARIZONA DAILY STAR, November 26, 1983; *In Memoriam—Hon. Mary Anne Richey*, THE WRIT, December 1983.

40. Annie Richey Interview, *supra* note 18.

41. William Richey Interviews, *supra* note 13.

As a trial judge in the state and federal courts, Mary Anne's judicial philosophy, demeanor, and rulings manifested her indomitable spirit. Her refusal to be defined by gendered stereotype in her personal life informed her view from the bench. She demonstrated that she was quite willing to issue the controversial ruling and to sustain the claims of individuals as against governmental action, especially where she perceived that the claimant had been denied fair treatment. Ensuring equality of opportunity was a theme of several of her rulings. In her own life, she had fought to open up opportunity, and she used her judicial authority to advance that goal for others. At the same time, she strongly believed in respecting institutional constraints, and she maintained a deep respect for her former colleagues in the state courts.

Mary Anne's earnest devotion to the task of judging was apparent to attorneys and litigants, even when her rulings seemed to misinterpret the governing law. Her habit of seeking counsel from other judges, and of occasionally changing her mind after issuing an interim decree, were indications of her ongoing effort to "get it right." Although she had an abiding self-confidence throughout her life, it was tempered by an awareness of her own limitations in the face of the judicial tasks before her, an awareness that was especially apparent in criminal sentencings—the most difficult of her judicial tasks. To the extent that humility is essential to wise judging,[42] Mary Anne's sense of her own fallibility surely enriched the quality of her individualized, day-to-day decision making.

Justice Frankfurter once described the judge's task in the following way:

> [A]mid tangled words, amid tangled insights... the judge must find the path through precedent, through policy, through history... to the best judgment that poor fallible creatures can arrive at in that most difficult of all tasks, the adjudication between man and man, between man and the state, through reason called law.

He added that the judge must do all this with "allegiance to nothing except the effort."[43] In her judicial work, Mary Anne's allegiance to the effort to achieve justice was constant, even if she sometimes faltered along the way.

---

42. As Justice Felix Frankfurter once commented, the ingredient essential to judging is "first and foremost, humility and an understanding of the range of the problems and [one's] own inadequacy in dealing with them..." Quoted by Justice Tom C. Clark in his address, *Some Thoughts on Supreme Court Practice*, at the University of Minnesota Law School Alumni Association, 11–12 (April 13, 1959), reported in Views From The Bench 27 (Mark W. Cannon & David M. O'Brien, eds. 1985).

43. Justice Felix Frankfurter, *Chief Justices I Have Known*, 39 Va. L. Rev. 883, 905 (1953).

Outside the courthouse, Mary Anne was anchored in a family unit of great importance to her, and at the end of her life, her thoughts were dominated by concerns not for her legacy on the bench but for the welfare of her husband and daughter. As many women judges have reported, she felt an ongoing tension between her parental role and the demands of her professional position.[44] Inevitably, her identity as wife and mother pervaded her identity on the bench.

In a well-known collection of lectures, Virginia Woolf speculated that without "a room of her own," a woman could not fully realize her creative potential, but with such a room—a quiet place where she is master—a woman might produce artistic or scholarly works of great genius.[45] In Woolf's view, the scarcity of female artists and leaders throughout history was because women lacked the time, money, and space necessary for serious work. Clearly, formal and informal barriers to entry operated in the legal profession, such that few women achieved positions of prominence until the second half of the twentieth century. Significant contributions by women to the development of the law until that time were sporadic.

Entering the legal profession at the mid-century mark, Mary Anne was among the pioneers who proved by example that women could succeed where only men had succeeded before. Mary Anne, the trial lawyer, was at home in the courtroom, but the courtroom was not her "own" until she became a judge. As Woolf might have predicted, it was there that Mary Anne's humanity, her well-honed sense of fairness, and her intellectual honesty flourished. In a courtroom of her own, she aspired to be a great judge. On occasion, the circumstances of a case and Mary Anne's unique attributes combined to allow her to succeed, and at other times, they detoured her from the wiser course. Her multi-faceted judicial identity, however, reminds us that women bring their individuality to the work of judging. Mary Anne's story suggests, finally, that as women judges increase in number, their impact on American law will be profound, pervasive, and richly colored by the themes of their lives.

---

44. Elaine Martin, *Men and women on the bench: vive la difference?* 73 JUDICATURE 204, 208 (Dec–Jan 1990)(women federal judges continue to experience more conflict between their parental and career roles than their male colleagues).

45. *See* Virginia Woolf, A ROOM OF ONE'S OWN (1929).

Index